Inside the TV Newsroom

Inside the TV Newsroom
Profession Under Pressure
A Newsroom Ethnography of Public Service
TV Journalism in the UK and Denmark

Line Hassall Thomsen

intellect Bristol, UK / Chicago, USA

First published in the UK in 2018 by
Intellect, The Mill, Parnall Road, Fishponds, Bristol, BS16 3JG, UK

First published in the USA in 2018 by
Intellect, The University of Chicago Press, 1427 E. 60th Street,
Chicago, IL 60637, USA

A catalogue record for this book is available from the
British Library.

Cover designer: Holly Rose
Copy-editor: MPS Technologies
Production manager: Mareike Wehner
Typesetting: Contentra Technologies

Print ISBN: 978-1-78320-883-8
ePDF ISBN: 978-1-78320-885-2
ePUB ISBN: 978-1-78320-884-5

Printed and bound by Hobbs, UK

This book is in part based on the Ph.D. thesis *New Struggles, Old Ideals:
The Everyday Struggle Towards Being a 'Good Journalist' Inside Public
Service TV Newsrooms in the UK and Denmark* submitted for the
degree of Doctor of Philosophy to the Department of Aesthetics and
Communication at Aarhus University, Denmark.

Drawing in chapter 8.2 courtesy of graphic illustrator at TV Avisen, DR.
All other photos and illustrations courtesy of the author

This is a peer reviewed publication.

Contents

Acknowledgements

I could not possibly name *all* the people who have helped make this book a reality. Here I attempt to acknowledge just some of the key people to whom I am indebted.

First, and most importantly, I am indebted to all the TV news workers who have shared so openly their everyday working lives with me. From 2007 until 2017, the openness and frankness with which they have shared their everyday work with me has meant everything to this project. Thanks to all the staff at *BBC News*, at *ITV News*, at DR's *TV Avisen* and at *TV2 Nyhederne* without whom this project would have been impossible. Also thanks to the management staff and News Editors of each of these four broadcasters who have granted access. Without the access and the openness with which I was met, this book could have never been. The whole idea of this study relies on years of working as a journalist inside both print and TV newsrooms in the UK. I am grateful to all the people who helped me get on and learn about news work during my time working as a journalist in Britain – particularly the journalists at the Home and Arts Desk of *The Independent*, my fellow colleagues at *ITV News Channel*, the newsroom at *ITV News*, *More 4 News* and everyone at *Channel 4 News*.

In taking the step from the practice of journalism to the theories of it, numerous academics have been a great help and inspiration. Henrik Bødker has been an invaluable guide throughout the process of writing the Ph.D. which inspired this book. I am very grateful to Nils Bubandt for his sharp eyes on content reading. Unni From, Charlotte Wien and Karin Wahl-Jorgensen have given constructive comments on an early version of this book. Nigel Rapport, Georgina Born, Brian Winston and Robin Nelson have each commented on earlier drafts of several of the chapters. Thanks to Annette Markham, Inka Salovaara and Anja Bechmann for detailed comments and engaged discussions of parts of the book. I am grateful to so many other academic colleagues, both at the Department of Media and Journalism Studies at Aarhus University and at universities abroad.

I am much obliged to Jørgen Bang for enabling funding from the three sponsors: *Update* at the Danish School of Media and Journalism, the *Department of Information and Media Studies* at Aarhus University and the national doctoral school, *Forskerskolen i Medier, Kommunikation og Journalistik*. I am of course thankful to each of these sponsors. As I realised during the initial stages of application, funding a cross-disciplinary and inter-disciplinary project such as this, particularly with an applicant who has been out of academia for a few years, does not happen often. I am very grateful that my three sponsors had enough trust in the project to deviate from this norm.

This project was initially part of the project *Dansk public service på journalistikkens betingelser: Udviklinger, dilemmaer, visioner*, funded by the Danish Radio- og TV-Nævnet fund for research into Public Service Broadcasting. Being a part of this project, a collaboration between researchers from Aarhus University and the Danish School of Journalism, has been fruitful for the early stages of this book.

Thanks is also due to my aunt Anette and uncle Lars who let me stay with them during fieldwork at DR in Copenhagen, and to Lisbet and family for letting me stay with them in Odense during my fieldwork at TV2. It meant a great deal that I could feel so at home while being in the near vicinity of the newsrooms I studied.

The book in hand would have not existed without the enthusiasm, encouragement and sharp eyes of the excellent staff at Intellect Books. In particular, I would like to extend thanks to production editor Mareike Wehner.

Lastly, and crucially, I am indebted to my family. I am grateful to my mum Susanne Højlund, for supervision and baby-sitting services, to my dad Kurt Thomsen for sailing and lobster-fishing when needed. Thanks to Emil, Marie, Sigurd, Ivan and to Sofie, Leo and Gala. Finally, I am grateful beyond words to my husband John, our son Viktor James and daughter Matilda Aila. Thanks for the music and for keeping alive the sense of wonder.

Line Hassall Thomsen

Prologue

Crossing the Gap

'We need more bodies!', yells a Programme Editor. '… and make sure you can't make out their faces … just bodies! I don't want disfigured body parts, just bodies and body bags!' I stay on target, working alongside my colleagues. We all look stern, staring into the screen. We have been covering the tsunami for almost a week now. Today, video feeds of corpses are coming in. The bodies have been laying in tropical climate waiting to be identified. By now I should be used to the sight. But tears are welling up. I cut the last images for the next news bulletin, which goes on in a few minutes, then I hurry to the bathroom. You do not cry in the newsroom.

To my surprise, hiding inside the toilet cubicles I find both a reporter and a producer with mascara running down their cheeks. We laugh. Then we cry and talk about the tragic pictures. Dry our eyes and walk hurriedly, professionally, into the newsroom. And we keep on working, without mentioning our emotions.

– January 2005, inside the ITV Newsroom, Kings Cross, London

The morning meeting has just begun and we are discussing the stories to run today. There is an excited mood in the newsroom. Journalists, Programme Editors and producers are all sat in a semi-circle, relaxed, leaning back on their chairs, coffee in hand. Some reporters share a joke about yesterday's news programme. Our News Editor has had a cake designed with the Olympic rings on it, and it has just arrived for us to enjoy during the meeting. Yesterday, London was chosen to be the host city for the Olympic Games in 2012. Today we are celebrating.

Suddenly, the bright neon light in the room flickers. The computer screens go black for a moment. Our constant newswire on the computer goes still. One editor starts swearing, tells us to check out the system and get the newswire up again. There's a top line flashing on the wire when it starts again. The London underground, just below us, has had a power failure, it says.

Moments after, we realise the scale of what is happening. Bombs have exploded in the underground. And then the whole room starts moving at a much quicker speed. There

is yelling across the room, orders are given fast. But most people don't need orders, they know where to go, what to do. As if on autopilot, all staff start their routines around the room, and out of it. We are a beehive of action. We are running around all of us together, to find out and tell in simple terms exactly what has happened. We work like that for the next 24 hours. Constantly with the competitors' news on, so we can keep track of who gets the right news out first.

7 July 2005, inside the ITV Newsroom, Kings Cross, London

The two above experiences were crucial in making me want to explore the shared values of journalists at play in everyday work inside the TV newsroom. Many other experiences inside this and other newsrooms came before, but these two particularly made me stop, look and think about the way journalists work. It was in the middle of this day, in July 2005, while being immersed in the job of cutting a disaster video, that I remember first feeling conscious of being part of a tribe. I felt that all of us instinctively worked as one unit, always knowing what to do and how to work together.

At that moment in the toilets of ITN, I was surprised and relieved when I found that I was not the only journalist in the newsroom to be suppressing my emotions in order to act as I thought it most professional. The day of the London bombings was the most busy news day I have ever worked on; it was also the working day where I felt the most worried about the events I covered, as bombs exploded so near me. As the attacks happened in my neighbourhood, there was an entirely new sense of reality behind the stories of tragedy we covered that day. On the 7 July 2005, inside the newsroom I sensed a feeling among us all, stronger than usual, that our work was necessary and important and that, together, we were working towards making a positive change to what took place outside our windows.

From the day of the London bombings, I began to look at the news division I had worked in for years as an object of study. As my first degree was in anthropology, I began to consider how a newsroom and our everyday practices could be of interest to an anthropologist. I began to consider that what we shape as news might turn into other people's truths. And therefore, I thought, how we come about creating such 'truths' needed to be explored. I started wondering why we do as we do, and how we have all come to know exactly what to do and not do inside the newsroom.

Though I continued working as a journalist and producer at ITN, from this day on I felt like an anthropologist in the newsroom. I started thinking about our everyday practices, and talking to colleagues about how we work in ways I had not done before. This mind-change happened involuntarily and seemed to be a process that I could not stop. After having begun to reflect on the way we journalists work, it seemed as if I could not stop reflecting. Getting the idea to do this project was thus the first step I took in crossing what I later felt to be a gap between the practice of journalism and theories about journalism (Thomsen 2008).

In time, I decided to make a proposal to study the practice of TV news journalism from a cultural anthropological perspective. Two years later I received a Ph.D. stipend and embarked on a study of newsrooms, doing fieldwork in the TV newsrooms of the largest national news broadcasters in the UK (BBC and ITV) and in Denmark (DR and TV2) (see Thomsen 2013). This book is largely based on that Ph.D., with updates and amendments from a 2017 perspective.

Part I

Journalists and Newsrooms as Objects of Research

Introduction

An introduction to the project and to the guiding research questions

Today, the free, instantly available news accessible through your mobile phone is challenging traditional media like never before. In 2007, as this study began, traditional TV news journalists were sensing this threat more and more.

Recently, values of the journalism profession have been under public scrutiny. With a number of high-profile controversies in Denmark and the UK, particularly the Public Service Broadcasters DR and BBC have been in the public eye. After Brexit in the UK, the partisanship of British public service media has been questioned (see for instance Preston 2016). In Denmark, most of the press reported that PM Lars Løkke would stay in his position, while in fact he stepped down – causing a huge public debate about the press partisanship and bias (see for instance Ringgaard 2014). While in the US, biased media coverage of the Trump vs Clinton election caused both journalists and readers to suggest that 'the American journalism is collapsing before our eyes' (Goodwin 2016).

In the wake of the News International phone hacking scandal, the Leveson inquiry into the culture, practices and ethics of the British press made professional values of journalism front-page material.[1] In the UK, in the autumn of 2012, incidents involving flagship news programme *BBC Newsnight*'s reporting (and lack thereof) of high-profile child abuse cases were the centre of public discussions surrounding BBC's editorial values.[2] Following these controversies, BBC Director General George Entwistle resigned, the director of news and her deputy stepped aside and an enquiry into the chain of command inside the BBC news division was initiated.[3] Commenting on the controversy, Culture Secretary Maria Miller wrote to the BBC Trust Chairman Lord Patten urging him to become more personally involved because 'very real concerns are being raised about public trust and confidence in the BBC' (according to Holton and Holden 2012).

Similarly, in January 2013, when a film crew employed by Danish public broadcaster DR were found to have constructed a demonstration in front of a local bank in Denmark in order to use footage of the demonstration in a news story, trust and confidence were highlighted as being at risk. The broadcast of a staged demonstration created public discussion of the ethical values not only of DR staff but the journalism profession as a whole.

Now that journalists are more outspoken than ever on social media, both news staff and news viewers often give their personal and uncensored reflections on the values of their profession. Thus, this study has been conducted at a time where journalists and the public are engaging in heated debates over values of the journalism profession.

While culture secretary Maria Miller's quote above appears concerned with trust in BBC as an institution, these and other similar cases have not only impacted on the different journalistic institutions but on the profession of journalism as a whole. As Freidson writes of professionalism, one of the key defining elements is 'an ideology serving some transcendent value and asserting greater devotion to doing good work than to economic reward' (2001: 180). The recent controversies involving BBC and DR have questioned the very core of expectations of journalism's professional values. From this perspective, the recent high-profile controversies at BBC, DR and other media institutions concern not only the institutions but the notion of journalistic professionalism as a whole.

In this book, I investigate the values of journalism professionalism today. I observe how ideal-typical values matter to the daily work, and through fieldwork I analyse how journalists strive towards shared goals.

Key questions: Differences *and* similarities

This book is the result of intensive fieldwork and constant contact with four newsrooms. The study began with 18 months of fieldwork inside the TV newsrooms of the four largest broadcasters in the UK and in Denmark, commencing in early 2007 and ending in 2008. After this, I have kept in constant touch with each of the newsrooms until 2017.[4] Of the four broadcasters two are licence funded – the BBC and DR – and two are funded commercially but still have public service obligations – ITV and TV2. The specific interest fuelling my research was to study the everyday work of TV journalists and news workers at national newscasters.[5]

As research began, I expected to meet differences rather than similarities between the newsrooms that I visited. This expectation was founded on both experience of being a journalist and research of organisations. First, the private experience of being a journalist in a given newsroom where the newsrooms of other organisations were talked about as being different made me arguably socialised (cf. Harrison 2000) into believing that these differences do indeed exist. As I had a practice experience working within a newsroom, which defined itself by being different, I strongly believed in the ideology of this practice community. This arguably practice-stubborn approach can act as an example of how journalists define their values by those shared within the practice community (I return to the value of practice communities in Chapter 6). As it will be illustrated, journalists at the different broadcasters talk of their own way of working as very different compared to the ways of working at competing broadcasters.

Secondly, from an institutional perspective, I found it interesting to explore how differences in funding affected news production routines. As Helland (1995: 53–54) has pointed out, economic and political factors of the two different models of broadcasting can be assumed to reflect on the way of working and presenting reality. Particularly at a time where traditional broadcasters are challenged by an ever-increasing media market, I was keen to study how the two different models of broadcasting, public service and commercial, approached the challenge in their everyday work.

Within each broadcaster, I met journalists who told me that their way of working was different and better than the way they worked at competing broadcasters. Exploring how staff defined themselves and their way of working as different to competing broadcasters therefore became one of my first interests. From the articulated differences, my interest turned to what I found to be fundamental similarities between the newsrooms.

During fieldwork at the four different newsrooms, I was struck by how similar the working routines and ideals of news workers were. Moreover, fieldwork showed a remarkable cultural similarity between the newsrooms, a similarity which seemed to encompass what news workers described as 'a family-relation' across the four different newsrooms. I therefore decided to abandon the focus on differences between broadcasters in favour of an exploration of the myriads of ways in which I found the newsrooms and news divisions to be connected and similar. Thus, the project turned from a study of many institutions to the study of one profession. In moving from studying differences to similarities between newsrooms, I thus moved from what Soloski (1989: 218) terms the *intraorganisational* policies to the *transorganisational* ideology and professional norms of journalists (see Chapter 1.2.).

When I left the newsrooms, the overall sense I returned with was that the news journalists I had studied perceived themselves to be constantly struggling to reach an ideal of being a 'good journalist'. The two primary similarities between journalists in one broadcast newsroom and others I have found to be: the sense of struggle and tension between ideals and everyday working condition, and the definition of ideal values of the profession. This ideal-typical value carried with it key concepts, such as objectivity, individualism and the idea of 'doing good', which I found central to the everyday work of all the journalists I worked alongside. The notion of all journalists across broadcasters working towards a shared ideal suggested that I should view journalists as distinguished by shared professional values rather than institutional or organisational ones. Thus, I came to agree with researchers of journalism who contend that it is possible to talk of a 'shared culture' of journalists (Harrison 2000), in a sense that journalists can even be talked about as sharing 'family resemblance' (Ryfe 2017), making it possible to give a 'portrait of a European Journalist' (O'Sullivan and Heinonen 2008). In order to accommodate the findings I made during fieldwork, I posed the following different research question:

> TV news journalists at both licence-funded and commercial broadcasters understand their work to be a constant struggle towards being a 'good journalist'. How are these struggles played out in everyday life inside the newsrooms?

To answer this question, I rely on my own experience as a participant observer as well as many other collected sources of data, such as interviews and materials collected in the field. In analysing the observations I made during fieldwork, I employ theories from within studies of professions and studies of work (Brante 2010; Evetts 1999; with emphasis on Freidson 2001) as well as journalism research focusing on professionalism (such as Deuze 2005; Alridge and Evetts 2003; Singer 2003, 2004; Witschge and Nygren 2009; Witschge 2013) and communities of practice (see Wenger 1998a, 1998b).

Inspired by Freidson (2001), I have found ideal typical values during the study such as definitions of the good news story and ideals of public service to be important for understanding journalists' notion of professionalism. However, as emphasised by Larson (1977: xii) discussing the *professional project*: 'ideal-typical constructions do not tell us what a profession is, only what it pretends to be'. Rather, Larson argues, researchers should ask 'what professions actually do in their everyday life to negotiate this special position' (1977: xii). Inspired by this approach, it is the aim of this study to both consider the way professions talk about their work and the way they are observed to work. During participant observation, I kept a particular interest in the social and the cultural. Culture here is best seen as a series of processes, actions, beliefs, rituals and rhetoric of a group. Inspired by Frederik Barth (1989), this study treats culture not as a bounded entity, but as the interface between groups and the inter-relatedness of news workers in a newsroom.

Why study the news media?

An important point of departure for this study has been the idea that news are crucial in shaping the world and public debate – a view much heralded by various strands within social sciences and humanities, such as cultural studies and media communication studies (see for instance Giddens 1991; Gauntlett and Hill 1999: 54; Lewis 1991; Schudson 1982). Thus, I believe the Danish minister of Culture, Bertel Haarder, had a point when he lamented in a reader's letter in a national Danish newspaper that 'DR has much more influence than a political party does' (Haarder 2011, my translation from Danish).[6] As Knut Helland has expressed it: '[…] the television as a medium is both shaped by, part of shaping and passes on a kind of ideological foundation for how the world should be understood' (2001: 231, my translation from Norwegian).

Today, news media has made it possible for anyone with an Internet connection to make news stories, thus enabling both amateurs and professionals to compete in the constant flow of information and news. The possibility for anyone to be a journalist has been expressed by journalists and researchers alike as a threat to the profession. In this vein, Deuze warned that 'a profession of journalism without journalists cannot bode well for the necessary checks and balances on a future global capitalist democracy' (Deuze 2009: 317). At a time where it is possible for people, whether trained in journalism or not, to be journalists, I find it worthwhile to explore the values and ideals of journalists employed at traditional public service media broadcasters. According to Witschge, there is a 'need to be creative and think of how we can inject new life into public-service journalism, acknowledging the value this has for democracy' (2013: 171). In order to think up ways of injecting new life into public service journalism, it may be useful to explore the core values of public-service journalism today. With this study I hope to begin such exploration.

Through an increasing amount of platforms, news are a primary information source for what takes place in the world around us. In this sense, the media has what Danish media researcher Anker Brink Lund (2002) calls *editorial power* over the information that the public receives and how this is defined and presented. Thus, news frames the reality and constructs debate. National news plays a crucial role in creating the nation's shared memory, history, knowledge and identity. Further, I agree with the idea that through televising 'media events', such as a terror attack, the death of a cultural icon, an election, reporting from sports events such as the Olympics, the media creates a 'We-feeling' among viewers (Curran and Gurevitch 1996: 27; Lund 2000). This rhythmic ordering of news can be seen as a continual reaffirmation process, a part of what Giddens (1990) terms the project of 'ontological security', strengthening the national idea of 'Us' and 'Them' (Bonde 1998). Particularly at a time when the audiences are 'ever-fragmenting' (Broersma and Peters 2013: 1), there is a need to reconsider the role of the journalist at work today.

Why study the TV profession today?

Newsrooms and news workers have been studied by interdisciplinary scholars since the mid-1950s and the dominating literature stems from the late 1970s (see e.g. Epstein 1973; Tuchman 1973, 1978; Schlesinger 1978; Gans 1979; Fishman 1980). This first wave of newsroom studies agreed to a remarkable extent that news is the outcome of routine, largely implicit, organisational rules that all news workers follow. From this perspective, news workers and the entire news industry in general work and function rather mechanically by doing what Tuchman calls 'routinizing the unexpected' (Tuchman 1973). Since then, newsrooms have changed considerably, and thus there is a need to re-enter the newsroom if we want to include the lived experience and perception of the journalists at work in debates of news, journalism and media practices today.

The working situation inside TV newsrooms today is very different from how it was only a couple of years ago. As I have seen during the last decade of studying newsrooms, the everyday working routines are changing rapidly. As Cottle (2000) has argued in his article 'New(s) times: Towards a "second wave" of news ethnography', the change in media ecology means that it is now crucial to bring audiences up-to-date and revise the first wave's earlier findings and theory by using empirical observations as the main foundation for conducting research.

Being in touch with the same four newsrooms over a period of 10 years has given me in-depth insights, a shared history with my informants and a near-experience of the struggles faced by news workers over a longer period. One of the crucial struggles that the newsrooms have all battled with over the last 10 years is economic: how to make money from TV news bulletins in an ever more competitive market? In early 2007, as I begun this study, market logic was beginning to matter more and more in the everyday work. Today, 10 years later, the need to generate money is even more talked about at all levels of the newsrooms. Various different business plans, paywalls and selling of video feeds have been set up by newscasters, but today as viewer figures on TV are dwindling, all four newsrooms studied are still struggling to find ways of making money. As Head of News at TV2 Nyhederne Jacob Kwon told me in 2016: 'The biggest challenge for us today is figuring out what we shall live from in five years. This is a nut that we have yet to crack. I do not know of any newscaster who has found a solution to this problem – yet' (interviewed 27 October 2016).

Since the first wave of newsroom studies, the reality of newsrooms and news has changed dramatically. The newsrooms of today have much more competition than 30 years ago: both from an increasing amount of possible news outlets, nationally, globally and digitally, and from ever-increasing platforms of alternative news media (Atton 2002, 2009; Atton and Hamilton 2008), bringing news not at the same hourly bulletin but as-it-happens. This competition puts new demands on news workers and on each news outlet to be flexible and innovative in keeping the audiences, which has been said to leave some of the basic rules of journalism today in a state of profound flux (see for instance Preston 2009: 1; Steensen 2011). With this increased amount of new news providers, a new criticism of the national TV news in general and Public Service Broadcasting in particular has emerged, arguing that the national news is no longer as useful or as necessary as it used to be. A critique against which defenders such as the Chairman of the BBC Trust, Lord Patten, has argued that 'the case for Public Service Broadcasting is stronger than ever in the digital age, given the plethora of distribution channels available today' (Patten in BBC Trust 2011). At a time when news and journalism are challenged like never before by economic and commercial needs, and an audience that is less and less dependent on the broadcaster, the traditional public service newsrooms face a new reality, which makes for a renewed need to enter the newsroom.

From its very beginning, this project has been interdisciplinary. Not only in the sense that I am both a journalist and a researcher of journalism, but also in that this study has relied on theories and practices of *both* journalism studies and anthropology. While working in the interpretive tradition of anthropology I aim to add to and engage with the field of journalism studies.

The methodological approach is anthropological enquiry based on participant observation fieldwork. In order to analyse and explore the findings of fieldwork this study makes use of different theories of journalism studies, practice theory, theories of organisation and theories of professions. Using such differently founded theories is risky of course; but it is my firm conviction that research should not be governed by theory; rather, it should be the other way around. As Goffman has put it: 'a multitude of myopias limit the glimpse we get of our subject matter. To define one source of blindness and bias is engagingly optimistic' (1983: 2). From this perspective, framing a study before the study is commenced may limit results. With the same argument, however, I have no doubt, knowingly or unknowingly, limited my field in the very way I have chosen to present it (see Chapter 2).

Why study the newsroom?

With this study I hope to introduce a new way of exploring newsrooms. I have chosen to focus on studying the national TV newsmakers, as I believe these to be particularly relevant for the shaping of public debate today, even despite the increase in competing distribution channels. Thus, my aim is to contribute to the current discussions of the journalistic profession through ethnographic accounts of the inside workings of a TV news organisation, the room and the mechanism by which it functions. Through this ethnographic approach, I hope to create new knowledge on current journalistic practices and cultures of practice in national TV newsrooms.

Media Studies consists of much research and analysis of the content of news and its reception and effects on audiences and users. The aim of this study, however, is to explore media differently, namely through venturing into the content-creating newsroom. Recently, a wave of researchers has taken an interest in studying news production. As I will highlight in the following chapter, I see this study as both a part of this wave but also different from it. The reason why I set out to do this project is that I wanted to study the everyday working life of TV news journalists at national news broadcasters and provide space for reflection on the factors that are important for the everyday work of TV news workers. I thought it important to not only study one newsroom as I wanted to explore how news work differs inside the newsroom of a national licence-funded broadcast news division compared to the inside of a national commercial broadcaster.

Commencing this study, I particularly wanted to study the production of news, as my time as a journalist inside one of these newsrooms showed that there is very little time to reflect on the ways that news journalists work. A saying was often shared among the journalists studied, which reinforced a constant pacing towards the future, and a constant closing up for evaluation of the past. I heard this saying expressed in all four of the newsrooms, phrased almost exactly the same: 'You are only as good as your next news story!'. As one of the journalists I met during fieldwork expressed bluntly: 'Of course we don't have the time to reflect much about what we do'.[7] The lack of reflection over everyday work among colleagues I see as a lack of open discussion of professional values and ideals. With this study, I hope to engage in such discussions by applying theories of the profession to studies of journalism practice. In doing so, my aim is explicitly to view the newsroom from *within* rather than from without. In focusing on practice, this study deliberately does not include content analysis. I see the inside approach, enabled through a unique access to the newsrooms, as the primary force of this study. Thus, my argument for studying the culture of news making is simple, however crucial. With this project, I would like to provide space and time for reflection on how TV journalists work today, thereby highlighting some of the cultural factors, which arguably affect what we see on the TV news every day.

New challenges for the old media

When the Grenfell Tower in Kensington, London, burned down in June 2017, the news hit Twitter and Facebook with live commentating and pictures long before national TV had arrived to the scene. That evening, BBC reported there to be only 17 people dead after the sudden blaze burnt down an entire building block housing approximately 600 inhabitants. 'The BBC are not reporting the truth! There's bound to be hundreds dead – look, how can anyone survive this?!', an angry young woman living nearby said while holding her mobile phone camera to show the burnt down building. She posted this video on her Instagram account @DjIsla_, and within hours her post had over 100,000 views. The day after, the young angry woman was invited to report her side of the story live on Sky News. Weeks after the fire, the fire services have revealed that the number of casualties are likely to be much more than a hundred. This is just one of many examples of how mobile phones have made it possible for anyone to be a journalist and to broadcast news instantly – at times with figures and facts that are more true than those reported by national media.

First, there was a clear monopoly of news broadcasting, later there was duopoly. Today, news is available from a multitude of platforms at all times. Recent international reports suggest that 54% of people with online access use social media as a news source (see Reuters Institute 2017). This trend and the rising use of mobile phones to access news are undermining traditional business models and challenging old news media such as the daily TV news bulletins. This study began at a time where editors, management and all news staff where still finding ways to make use of the Internet as a news platform. As fieldwork began in 2007, editors were keen to encourage journalist and reporters to post blogs on the Internet as a teaser to upcoming news items. Now, 10 years later, journalists are still finding new ways of using the Internet to highlight news pieces on the evening news bulletin. Selected reporters and correspondents now have the so-called Social Media Field Producers with them, who make sure that behind the scenes clips are out on Snapchat, Instagram, Twitter or Facebook before the TV bulletin (see for instance Claus Borg Reinholdt in Bruun-Hansen 2016). So before viewers turn on the TV, they may have already seen the making of a TV clip on Snapchat, or they have seen the reporter 'go live' on Facebook or do a '360-degree video' with a behind the scene shot.

But the Internet is now seen as more than a way to promote the TV bulletin. Rather, broadcasters today use social media as a way of presenting news – often breaking a news story online before they do so on TV. Indeed, as the media manager at ITV News, Lincoln Hooper, describes it today, the newsrooms are primarily chasing changing media use:

> The main challenge for our newsroom is keeping up with the changing ways our audience consumes their news. Social media is gradually taking the lion's share of consumers. We are constantly expanding that team and looking for new and innovative ways of attracting new viewers on mobile devices.
> (Lincoln Hooper, ITV News Media Manager, Interview, 5 September 2016)

First, Public Service Broadcasting was broadcast on one media platform only; today, the BBC is responsible for eight different TV services, ten national and dozens of local radio stations, not forgetting BBC news sites, Twitter feeds and Facebook pages. At the time of press, the

BBC News Facebook page has over 45 million followers. In the early days of BBC's online presence, the corporation was responsible for one of the most watched websites worldwide; today the BBC is still dominating UK digital news by generating a 30% market share (according to Similarweb 2016 in *The Guardian* 2016). However, the news site bbc.co.uk is placed lower than 100th on the ranking of most visited websites worldwide, surpassed by sites such as Facebook, YouTube, Wikipedia, Twitter and Google.[8]

In Denmark, though the audience is news-interested, the Public Service Broadcasters are facing a very similar challenge. Recent research has found that the Danes watch more news programmes today than at the turn of the Millennium. According to the figures, 40.3% of overall TV-viewing in the year 2011 was shared between the categories 'news actuality and debate' and 'education, information and culture'.[9] While more keen on watching news programming, today's audiences receive their news updates from many more platforms than before. Statistics point to the news bulletins at DR and TV2 being among the most watched news programmes, though still accounting for only 12% and 7% of all TV news viewing (see TNS Gallup TV-Meter 2016). Critics of the news media have argued that the first casualty of the Internet will be old media (see Barnhurst 2013: 214):

> Providing a service to publics in a multimedia and multicultural environment is not the same safe value to hide behind like it used to be in the days of print and broadcast mass media. After all this is the age of individualization, audience fragmentation and attention spans ranging from minutes while watching to seconds while surfing.
>
> (Deuze 2005: 455)

As Deuze describes above, public expectations to the news media is very different today as compared to the days when Public Service Broadcasters and a handful of print news had a near-monopoly of providing the news. This change in expectation and attention among the public has led newscasters to change both the presentation of news and structural routines within the newsroom. Thus, the journalists I have studied are asked to work differently. It is the aim of this project to discover what these challenges to professional values and ideals of journalists mean to their everyday work.

At the time of my fieldwork, the news workers I spent time with all appeared aware of an added pressure, both economically and from an ever fragmented audience. There was a notion that this pressure was shared among all Public Service Broadcasters. Staff at DR TV Avisen and TV2 Nyhederne in Denmark expressed the idea that they were under a shared pressure, just as staff at BBC News expressed themselves to be under a pressure similar to ITV News in Britain. At DR, this was expressed in an email sent to all news staff as early as 2006 by the internal media research unit, warning that now the 'big channels in Britain are being pressured' (Hedegaard 2006). The email submitted a warning that 'other channels than the "big five" are continuing to take a greater and greater share of the British people's TV viewing. A crucial part of the explanation is that more and more households in Britain get access to Freeview and thereby a host of new channels. The same picture is emerging in Denmark [...]' (Hedegaard 2006).[10] While Freeview may have been one of the first challenges to the national Public Service Broadcasters, today's competition to the traditional media comes through the new and ever-expanding media platforms such as blogs and social media news feeds or news sites suited to specific interests on the Internet. I find it crucial for understanding the media landscape today to explore the impact on journalistic ideals and professional values that the current challenges may have on journalists in their everyday work at traditional broadcasters.

Why study these specific four news divisions?

I initially aimed to stay in different newsrooms so as to study the culture of TV news workers in different organisations, and I was interested in whether there was a difference between news workers at licence-funded institutions and those of commercial broadcasters. I thought it important to commence the study with the founder of public service, the BBC News, before returning to ITV News.

As a previous staff member of ITV News, I was aware of a connection and competition with BBC News. While working at ITV, news workers always kept a constant glance at the screens showing the output of the BBC News, and among ITV news workers there was constant comparison to the BBC: We wondered what kind of equipment they had, how they would cover a certain story, whether they already had a certain story and if they did, who would get it first on air – us or 'them'? So, although I found the notion of returning to a newsroom in which I had previously worked as a researcher challenging, it was crucial to include both the BBC and ITV in my study if I was to follow TV news workers and move beyond the stigmatising of how different TV news workers view each other towards a comparison of public service news divisions.

In order to compare these two different groups of news workers, I wanted to include two similarly positioned groups of news workers in Denmark, namely, those at Denmark's licence-funded broadcaster DR, and at DR's closest rival in broadcast news, the commercially funded TV2. This choice was made due to two primary factors: firstly, the funding for my research was sought from the Danish Public Service fund; secondly, because of the ease of understanding I felt I had being Danish and already having an understanding of the Danish language, culture and the history of DR and TV2.

The journalism that the newsrooms in these two different countries produce is by definition different, not only because news stories and the interests of the people in the different countries differ, but also because the journalists themselves present the news in a way, shape and form that best suit their respective national audiences. Indeed, as Park observed already in 1940, 'journalism is a craft of place; it works by the light of local knowledge' (Park quoted in Carey 2007: 4).

Choosing these specific news divisions, it has not been my aim to study journalism content but journalism working structure, ideals and values inside licence-funded versus commercially funded newsrooms. To do so, I have found it crucial to include the founder of public service, BBC, as well as its first direct competitor, ITV. In order to compare the relationship between these two news divisions, I have included the two Danish news divisions positioned historically and competitively in a similar relationship, DR and TV2.

The everyday struggle towards being a good journalist

A defining method behind of this study has been to move in a circular fashion from theories of the field to observations in the field and then back to re-considerations of theories of the field and so forth (see Chapter 2). This method meant that the study began with one focus, and ended up with another one as I found that the first research focus did not adequately suit what I found most important during my participant observations in the newsrooms.

The title of my research as I set out on fieldwork was *Editorial Culture in Journalistic TV News Production, with Focus on Public Service*. But in order to match focus with what was found in the newsrooms, this research question was changed a few times during fieldwork. As I found the similarities between the newsrooms more curious than the differences among them, I began to consider what makes the newsrooms I visited appear so similar: What do the newsrooms and the journalists have in common? What do the journalists and fellow news workers themselves perceive to have in common? And what did I, as a participant observer in the different newsrooms, perceive to constitute similarities? One subject that appeared to be on all news workers' mind, in all newsrooms I visited, was the idea of a 'good news story'. During the morning meeting, a news story would be introduced with the words: 'THIS is a *good* news story!' while other stories would be dropped because they were deemed 'not a good news story'. The notion of the 'good news story' was thus mentioned many times a day, and appears as a guideline for what to cover and what not to cover.[11] In practice, when the notion of a 'good news story' was not verbally used to argue for the covering of an event, it appeared that two central aims would steer a journalist to work in a certain way: firstly, the notion of what other colleagues from within a similar practice community would deem 'good work' was important; secondly, the idea of doing good work in the sense that one's work would help 'better the world' was also of great importance. Thus, I have come to see the ideal of making 'good news stories' as closely linked to a moral, democratic ideal. This ideal is illustrated as important to licence-funded news staff but equally important to commercial broadcast news staff. In exploring the everyday ideals of journalists, I identify Eight Key Factors, which were expressed as key to making a 'good news story'. Throughout this book, the focus therefore is on conveying, theorising and exploring this constant ideal and the challenges it faces in the everyday work. As will be shown, the ideal of being 'good' is not one that the journalists consider to be a new one; what is new today, however, is the challenges that the journalists face in reaching this ideal.

Chapter outline

During the initial 18 months of conducting fieldwork, and the following years of being in constant touch with the newsrooms, I have come to view the institutions studied as different but above all connected by the journalistic profession and by everyday practices striving towards ideals of their profession. I have encountered a number of clashes between what can be viewed as a shared professional ideal and a new structure of news work. Throughout this book, a number of these clashes and negotiations between ideal and reality are outlined. The juxtaposition of ideal values and structures of work are particularly interesting as it portrays a clash between the ideal and the real within which journalists work in the everyday. While the word 'clash' alludes to a violent conflict, I have found staff primarily able to negotiate the struggle to the point where a mismatch of ideal and reality is talked about as 'a struggle' or as 'problematic' rather than a violent confrontation.

In studying journalists at work, I have found newsroom staff across different newsrooms a part of a strong bonded practice community, which has at its core one shared ideal, namely that of making what they term as 'good work' and 'good news stories'. The more staff work together, the stronger this shared ideal becomes. I have aimed to structure the book as a journey towards finding out what this shared ideal consists of and what challenges the ideal brings to the everyday work of news journalists today. In Chapter 1, as the first step of the research journey, I describe what I brought with me into the newsroom: the historical framework and theoretical approaches with which the study commenced and which have developed during fieldwork analysis. One key approach introduced is that of theories of the profession. In Chapter 2, the methodological approach is explored. Placing the study in the recently emerged subfield of anthropology, Media Anthropology, I describe and define what I see as the strong points of studying journalists through participant observation. Moreover, methodological issues and challenges of doing fieldwork among TV news journalists are introduced.

In Chapter 3, I introduce briefly the history of the four news divisions studied, and proceed to characterise the relationship between the broadcasters as one of constant competition. In introducing the four news divisions, I focus on how staff members at different news divisions define each other. In this introduction of how members of staff define their news division, it becomes apparent that staff members at each one of them think the way they work entirely different from how the staff works at the competitor's news division, with staff at each broadcaster talking of their organisation as 'being best'. I end this chapter by discussing the current economic challenge facing all four newsrooms and begin exploring how organisations work to combat this challenge in similar ways at all four public service broadcast news divisions.

In Chapters 4 and 5, I further explore the similar organisation of news work at the four different news divisions from two different perspectives. Inspired by Wenger (1998a: 241), I analyse the news division as seen from two perspectives: the designed organisation and the practice within the organisation. In Chapter 4, the newsroom is introduced with a focus on how the organisation is designed, structured and organised.[12] I describe the scene, the newsroom, the structure of work and meetings in the everyday inside the room. During my analysis of the newsroom, it is illustrated how the newsroom can be seen as a stage, already set with expected behaviour set up by the very structure of the design of the newsroom area. One of the consequences of the new, circular-shaped newsroom is that staff members feel more observed and can observe other colleagues more easily than in the square, divided newsroom. This, I argue, makes for increasing potential for collaboration between members of staff, but it also makes staff feel that they are always 'on', with little personal space and possibility to act differently to how the structure prescribes. Through interviews and my personal experiences from the newsrooms, analysis throughout Chapter 5 focuses on how design affects the practice of work within the four news divisions studied. One of the primary critiques of the new structure of working expressed by journalists is that the idea of multi-skilling is challenging to making a 'good' journalistic product. The perception among journalists that management demand something different to what journalists view as a professional ideal is explored as a mismatch between professional and market logic.

Exploring the connections between each news division further, in Chapter 6 I illustrate how the journalism profession can be viewed as a practice community with bonds that are perceived as stronger than the divisions of competition between the broadcasters. As I discuss throughout this chapter, the feeling of camaraderie and strong practice bonds functions to instigate bonds with other journalists and as a way of creating distance between journalists and the Others. Thus, I venture behind the apparent 'fronts' of differences and into what I see as a very similar shared ideology of journalism. Finally, in Chapter 7 I discuss what I have found to be a shared ideal among all news workers from all four news divisions. The idea for this chapter came at the end of fieldwork, when I began to notice how all news workers have very similar arguments for working as a journalist. One of the key shared ideals among staff that I noticed is whether something is 'good'. Being a good journalist, making 'good news stories' and doing 'good work' are some of the most explicit ideals referred to in the everyday work. The tension between the ideal of doing 'good work' and the everyday reality for each individual news worker is what forces journalists, as I have observed it, to engage in a seemingly constant struggle. Each tension, I argue, leads to a negotiating struggle between professional and personal identity. Returning to the example of feeling emotional towards events one has to cover as a journalist, one of the ideals of a good journalist is to be objective at all times, while one of the realities of journalists is that at times they become emotionally affected by the news stories they cover. In order to suit the ideal of being a good journalist, emotions are therefore hidden in a place situated outside of the newsroom, for instance, by crying in the toilets. In Chapter 8, the main points are briefly summarised and implications for research findings are discussed.

Notes

1 Recommendations of the eight-month long Leveson Inquiry, presented 28 November 2012, were that the British press should be regulated by an independent law-backed regulation-model.

2 In October 2012, it became clear that *Newsnight* shelved a documentary that investigated BBC presenter Jimmy Savile's involvement in sexual abuse. In another controversy in November 2012, BBC's *Newsnight* was found to have wrongly reported that Lord McAlpine had been involved in underage child abuse.

3 The *Newsnight Enquiry* began in November 2012.

4 After fieldwork, I have kept in touch with informants through additional visits to the newsrooms, face-to-face interviews, meetings with journalists outside the newsroom, emails and phone conversations.

5 I use the term 'news workers' to describe all the different positions of members of staff who work to produce news. The long list of workers that fit into this description covers but is not limited to journalists, producers, cameramen, News Editors, Programme Editors, heads of news, stringers, graphic designers, guest bookers and planners. All can be employed as either freelance, permanent or contract position.

6 Pitts puts this point more boldly when he says: 'In a world where media set the public agenda and drive the dialogue those things media ignore may as well not exist' (quoted in Gravengaard 2010: 11).

7 All interviews in Danish have been translated into English by the author.

8 Figures according to the list of most visited websites, 4 September 2016 (Alexa Internet).

9 This figure is an increase from 2010 when the figure was 37%, according to analysis of figures by Danmarks Statistik in Børsen (23 March 2012).

10 Freeview is the name for the collection of free-to-air services on the Digital Terrestrial Television platform in the UK. The service is jointly run by its five equal shareholders: BBC, ITV, Channel 4, Sky and transmitter operator Arqiva. Britain's 'Big Five' are BBC1, BBC2, ITV, Channel 4 and Channel 5.

11 The word 'good' is in this sense not used to denote positive or happy connotations, but quality (see Chapter 10.1).

12 My focus on the shape of the room is inspired by theorists such as Creswell (2004), who states that '[p]lace provides a template for practice – an unstable stage for performance [...] Place provides the conditions of possibility for creative social practice' (2004: 39). With this definition of the meaning of place in mind, I find it relevant to the study of actions within a room to include a discussion of the layout of the physical place for these actions, the newsroom.

Chapter 1

Studying Journalists at Work

On theoretical framework and a professions approach to journalism studies

How do TV journalists work today? What values guide the choices, selections, judgement and work of TV journalists in the everyday? These are some of the questions fuelling my research. I have approached the reflection on professional values from various angles: observations, participation and interviews with journalists at work. When analysing fieldwork, I have focused on journalism as a profession, as this approach suits the shared ideals encountered during fieldwork. It has been my experience that news workers themselves rarely get the time or space for such reflection while at work.[1]

Beginning fieldwork, my interest in TV news work was driven by a sense of curiosity. I was particularly curious about how journalists can cover unpredictable, complex world events everyday while seemingly being united in mind without discussing openly what to do. I wondered, how do TV news journalists know exactly what events to cover, and how? And as I visited four different national TV newsrooms in Britain and Denmark and found that journalists across the each newsroom had a similar, united way of working, this curiosity grew. Thus, I came to realise that although the four newsrooms visited had different organisational values of how to present news, professional ideals appeared very similar. Other journalism researchers have had a similar focus. Through this chapter, related ideas and theories from within the framework of journalism studies and studies of professions are introduced.

1.1 Review of News Production Studies

Since the mid-1950s, scholars from various disciplines have studied the production of news. News workers have been the subject of various and different enquiries, ranging from qualitative to quantitative production studies, to discussions of the journalistic profession and how news workers suit the larger framework of the institutions and corporations they work for.

The first wave of newsroom studies

In early journalism research, the individual qualities of the journalist were regarded as the primary explanatory factor for media content. This notion is most directly expressed in the idea of the journalist as a 'gatekeeper' (White 1950; McNelly 1959), responsible for regulating the flow of information. However, as the idea that journalists within a newsroom can be seen as responsible for keeping some stories out and others in the news was criticized as being too focused on the individual, demands came for a more structural approach to the study of news making.[2]

During the 1970s, at a time where researchers arguably had ideological reasons for wanting to demonstrate that media institutions were 'part of society's ideological machinery of power' (Syvertsen and Moe 2007: 150), there was a wave of studies with a more structural approach to news making. From the initial stage, this group of researchers had an interest in mapping the larger structure of the newsroom in terms of strategic and definitional power. Though informed by anthropological approaches such as fieldwork and participant observation, these highly influential studies of journalism were conducted by sociologists, psychologists, media studies scholars and journalism scholars but not by anthropologists.

With the first group of researchers entering the newsrooms, an entirely new insight into the everyday work of journalists came to light, and the former 'black box' of news production, the cultural milieu and professional domains of news making, was opened up like never before. Coined 'the first wave of newsroom studies', these ethnographic studies are still regarded as classics in the field of news production research (see Epstein 1973; Sigal 1973; Tuchman 1973, 1978; Altheide 1976; Burns 1977; Schlesinger 1978; Gans 1979; Golding and Elliot 1979; Fishman 1980). These studies centred on newsroom observations spanning from a few months to years in duration. The newsrooms observed were primarily set in the West (mainly in the US) and primarily in large, established newsrooms (as pointed out by Bird 2010a and Wahl-Jorgensen 2010). All of these researchers rejected White's idea of the individual journalist as the primary gatekeeper responsible for selecting the news; rather, they considered organisational factors in affecting a routinized production.

'Craft-related habits of mind' and collective gatekeeping

Of the first wave of newsroom researchers, particularly the sociologist Gaye Tuchman's study (1973) of two newsrooms, based on participant observation and interviews conducted during a period of two years in one American city, remains influential to journalism studies today. Focusing her analysis on how news workers routinize unexpected events in order to create news, Tuchman's study took ideas from the sociology of work to the newsroom. Tuchman argues that what aids journalists in covering such complex and unpredictable events is their ability to 'routinize the unexpected', that is by classifying events in already known typifications, which suit the organisational structure in which they work. News, she stressed, is a result of strategic working routines, which the journalists have in order to fulfil expectations from the organisation. In this sense, events are not already news, but the way that news workers are trained to categorize events make them able to quickly define some events as 'events-as-news' (1973: 112) – potentially newsworthy material – thus speeding up the process of selecting news stories and creating an overall agreement between staff. Using news workers' own terminology, she entitles these 'typifications' of news stories: 'Hard', 'Soft', 'Continuing', 'Spot', 'Developing' and 'What a Story!' – news, which the news worker routinely recognises as they happen (1973: 114). According to Tuchman, this 'routinized knowledge' has been embedded in practical tasks in the everyday life of the news worker by the organisation. As Tuchman puts it:

> News organizations can process seemingly unexpected events, including emergencies and disasters, because they typify events-as-news by the manner in which they happen and in terms of the ramifications 'this manner of happening' holds for the organization of work. Each of the typifications is anchored in a basic organizational issue concerning the control of work.
>
> (Tuchman 1973: 129)

Using the theories of Tuchman, it is possible to explain my experience of the ITV Newsroom, working in perfect unison covering the complex story of the London Bombings in July 2005 (see Prologue), as a case of where all members of staff know how to typify the event and therefore all know exactly how to work. With my approach to journalists at work, however, I view the fact that staff worked in such unity as not only a case of staff knowing how to typify an event but also an instance of all staff working towards the same shared ideals of journalism. I shall return to the notion of shared professional ideals shortly.

I find Tuchman's description of how journalists typify everyday happenings in order to perceive them as events-as-news interesting, as I too have thought it important to investigate how journalists decide whether an event is newsworthy or not. I too have sought to make enquiries into how journalists can spot a news story with such speed and certainty. And though I would add other typifications to the everyday work of the news workers included in my study, I too have experienced that journalists view events as different types of potential news in their everyday work. However, what I find most interesting is not the actual typification and systematising of events as stories, but the way that this typification and agreement is imbued in each worker in the newsroom, and the way that working under such shared consensus creates tensions between the reality of each individual journalist and the shared ideal.

Tuchman has described the ability to judge an event as news as 'sacred knowledge' (Tuchman 1972). Further, Tuchman finds the journalism practice to be centred on a 'strategic ritual' of constantly positioning oneself among fellow journalists, thus pleasing editors and peers. To me, the agreement among staff of what constitutes a 'good news story' cannot stem from organisational power alone, nor do I believe that the strong silent consensus, which I experienced in the newsrooms, can be reached by top-down leadership and an organisation of controlled routines alone. Rather, I view the actions of individual journalists as also driven by individual and personal values – values that are shared with fellow journalists. When Tuchman does enter into explaining the individual, she suggests an agreement with a fellow newsroom researcher of the time, Barbara Phillips (1976: 92), who has argued that the nature of news work creates 'craft-related habits of mind'. The notion that journalists' habits are created by the everyday practice of work appears similar to the key argument behind theories of 'communities of practice', a theory set out by Etienne Wenger (1998a; see also Lave and Wenger [1991] 2001).[3] Discussing practice communities in general, rather than journalists specifically, Wenger holds that the community of a group of people doing the same practice is constantly strengthened by the everyday repetition of that practice. In time, such strong bonds between practitioners can be much stronger than the bond an individual worker may feel obliged to have towards his supervisor, his editor or the broadcaster for whom he is working. I find both Phillips' notion of craft-related habits and the theories of communities of practice put forward by Wenger (1998a) and Lave and Wenger (2001) fruitful for understanding the strong bonds that I have found between staff within and across the four newsrooms studied. My study suggests that journalists share ideals of the profession, which are reinforced by the everyday sharing of practice (see Chapter 6).

The shared value of 'good'

Common to research within this first wave of studies inside the newsroom was the notion that news are shaped by the organisation that makes the news, and that the news we get therefore is a product of a type of organised, collective gatekeeping or more poignantly, a 'creation' of world events. As Schlesinger put it in his book on the BBC, *Putting Reality Together*: 'The doings of the world are tamed to meet the needs of a production system in many respects bureaucratically organised' (1978: 47).

Following Schlesinger, the notion that news is the product of bureaucratic organisations was repeated by researchers such as Ericson et al.: 'It is the organisation of news, not events in the world, that creates news' (1987: 345).[4] As researchers saw the organisation of news as the main instigator for creating news, their research became mainly interested with the systematic organisation of news workers as a whole, arguably resembling 'organisation functionalism' in their thinking (Cottle 2007: 13).

But who and what was considered responsible for this 'taming' or 'creating of the news'? According to researchers of the first wave of newsroom studies working within a sociological paradigm, the individual journalist could not be held responsible. Rather, news becomes a construction, a self-referential interaction between reporters and their sources (Ericson et al. 1991: 49). From this perspective, the organisation of news workers as a whole is responsible for the news output and the selections that this organisation makes in, for instance, sources that the individual journalist uses and the way in which this source is being formed so that peers will judge the news story as 'good' (Tuchman 1973). To Tuchman, then, the idea of what fellow colleagues will consider good determines the work that a journalist does.

According to Freidson, members of a profession are 'more dedicated to doing *good work* for their own satisfaction and for the benefit of others than to maximising their income'

(Freidson 2001: 2 , original emphasis). From this perspective, I see the notion of 'good work' as a professional ideal, which strengthens the bonds between journalists and enforces a distance to management ideals of profit making. Similarly to Tuchman, I have found the shared value of what is 'good' to be important for the everyday work. But the definition I have found important is the one that each news worker has *as well as* the imagined idea of what fellow colleagues see as good. This notion of constantly being concerned about what colleagues deem 'good', I describe as a 'constant peer review'. As I will illustrate (in Chapter 6), I found that the practice communities within a news division often loudly review other colleagues' work. Such ongoing evaluation of work contributes to the impression that members of staff have an agreement about what constitutes good work. Furthermore, the ongoing reference by peers to what is good and what is not good work functions towards socialising new staff into adopting the same definitions of good work (Harrison 2000: 137). Adding to Tuchman's definitions of what journalists deem 'good', I have come to view journalists as working simultaneously towards two different interpretations, both of which journalism colleagues from the same practice community define as the best working practice *and* as work that does good for society, informs, educates and helps better the world (see Chapter 7).

The newsroom as a factory floor

In her newsroom study, Tuchman concludes that the pattern of newsgathering leads to support for the status quo, a 'reconstituting of the everyday world' (1973: 127). Thus, along with other researchers of the time (see for instance Sigal 1973), she paints a picture of journalists being mere parts in machinery, which in turn is part of manufacturing consent (Herman and Chomsky 1988) to the elite's view of the world. During the early 1980s, researchers appeared to agree that the newsroom resembles a factory in which news workers do nothing but act according to already determined roles (see also Krumsvik 2009).[5] However, some researchers found this factory organisation to be problematic for the journalists at work. As Bantz et al. concluded in their sociological study of a TV newsroom, aptly titled *The News Factory*:

> To illustrate a routinized news organization, we propose a factory model [...]. The model reflects an assembly line approach to news that limits news workers' involvement in the organization and its product. The specialization, routinization and mechanization of television newswork has four observable consequences: flexibility, lack of personal investment in the product, and evaluation of news work in productivity terms, and a mismatch between news workers' expectations and the reality of the news factory.
>
> (Bantz et al. 1980: 1)

The model proposed by Bantz et al. concludes that there is a mismatch between news workers' expectations and the reality of what he terms 'the news factory'. I find the idea of a mismatch interesting as it raises the point that news workers do not aspire to be cogs in a news machine only, but have ideals of their own, which may not suit that of the machinery in which they work. Though I have worded my findings differently and have a different approach to the study of news workers, I too have found a mismatch between news workers' ideals and those of the organisation for which the news workers are employed. The finding that news workers find themselves to be struggling in their everyday work, due to ideals that do not fit the working structure of their employer, I see as an interesting move away from what many of the first wave of newsroom researchers appear to regard as a completely unaware and uncaring news worker, who does not care about the fact that s/he is reduced to a cog in a wider machinery in which s/he plays no unique role.

Also common to research of news production during the 1970s and 1980s was the belief that different factors outside of the newsroom and outside of the culture of the news workers – such as authorities, legal regulations, media ownership, organisational structure, professional roles and routines – control and constrain what is produced. While effective and illustrative of some of the larger organised aspects of news-making, this focus risks losing sight of the individual at work; reducing the individual news workers to what Peterson has called 'mere agents and vehicles of the institutional structure, acting out predetermined roles' (Peterson 2003: 163).

Another critique of early newsroom studies has been the focus on outside agents being more powerful in terms of controlling the news than editors and peers inside the newsroom. As Schudson (1997) has pointed out, the first wave of research gave more attention to reporter-official relations than on reporter-editor relations, no doubt a critical aspect of the social organisation of news work. It should be noted that Tuchman's (1973) study discribes the importance of impressing peers in her research, noting that working along certain groups of people may mean that the individual news worker wants to fit into the given group and thus writes news stories that fit the opinions of the peers on that group. For instance, as most of the news workers in Tuchman's study are male, stories on the Women's Movement are turned into light-hearted rather than serious news stories. In this sense, Tuchman considers cultural issues of gender that are rarely included in the sociological approach. However, her interest in cultural values appears limited to those that she deems to have impact on the wider organised system inside the newsroom. This approach risks not seeing the smaller cultural determinants, which do not become visible when looking at the newsroom through an overarching organisational prism.

As highlighted by Cottle, what the first wave of newsroom studies tends to lack is a sense of the culturally mediating nature of news. With this in mind, Cottle has called for the news to be approached by researchers as not just having social interests and political power, but in terms of its very constitution as a 'cultural medium of communication' (2001: 429). Indeed, as has been shown, the idea of the cultural impact on the news-making process is not very prominent in the first wave of newsroom studies and is often underplayed with not much thought of how culture may condition the larger system of organisation.

At the beginning of the Millennium there were a few calls for a new wave of newsroom studies within the field of journalism research (see for instance Cook 1998; Cottle 2000; Lund 2001). In his article 'Invitation til Mediesociologi' (2001), Lund lamented the lack of empirical observations from inside the newsrooms since the 1970s. The fact that Danish researchers since the 1970s prioritised *content* over *production* of news meant that the media research field lacked an 'analytical understanding of key ideas [among news workers] such as education, organisation and authority' (Lund 2001: 5, my translation). As I aim to map out ideal typical values within the journalism profession and study how these professional values matter to journalists today, what Lund terms 'key ideas' are of primary concern to my study. In the following, I explore how understanding 'key ideals' among journalists relate to a professions approach to journalism studies.

1.2 Journalism as a Profession

There has been much debate over whether to define journalism as a craft or a profession. Some argue that journalism cannot fully be regarded as a profession, but maybe a 'semi-profession', primarily due to the inability to keep those seen as 'untrained' and 'non-professionals' out of the field of journalism (see Tunstall 1971: 68; Witschge and Nygren 2009: 39–40).[6] Some point out the fact that the lack of one exclusive educational route into journalism problematises professionalisation (see for instance Shoemaker and Reese 1996). Others argue that journalism acquired the status as a profession little more than a century ago with university degrees devoted to journalism, shared codes of ethics and agreed rules of legal protections on confidentiality (see Conboy 2011 and McNair 2013: 77).

Through analysis of fieldwork, I have come to view journalism as *both* a craft and a profession. I view journalists at work as part of a craft related practice community (cf. Wenger 1998a) *and* part of a group, which shares professional values. This view of craftsmanship and specialized knowledge coupled with shared values is closely connected to Freidson's (1999, 2001) definition of professionalism.[7] According to Freidson (2001), professionalism is an ideal type among workers which is characterised by elements such as:

1. **Specialised knowledge.** The specialised knowledge of workers allows them to provide especially important services and gives power to control and organise their own work. This knowledge gives public prestige and official privileges. Specialised knowledge is founded on practical, everyday work based on 'skill' and 'working knowledge'.
2. **Working knowledge.** Can be tacit, embedded in experience, without being verbalised, codified or systematically taught. Segmented into:
   a. Practical knowledge. Learned by experience, both conscious and tacit, and shared only by those who do the same work.
   b. Formal knowledge. Information and ideas organised by theories and abstract concepts.

3. **Skill.** The capacity to *use* either or all of these forms of knowledge in accomplishing a task.
4. **Self-control.** Only other workers from within their profession may supervise and correct the work of colleagues.
5. **Dedication to doing good work.** Workers are more dedicated to doing good work for the benefit of others and for their own satisfaction than in order to maximise income.

(2001: 1–2, 31, 33–34)

Freidson describes professionalism as a 'third logic', which can be contrasted with two other central logics in society, namely 'the market' and 'bureaucracy'.[8] Although definitions of professionalism have differed over time (see for instance Parsons 1954; Allison 1986; Barber 1965; Larson 1977; Brante 2010), there is substantial agreement about many of the key principles defining professionalism and professions (as discussed in Singer 2003: 141). Many of the above definitions, with a few moderations, form a basis for most of sociology's definitions of professionalism.

I find Freidson's (2001) definition particularly relevant to journalism for at least three different reasons. Firstly, his model delves on professions as containing inherent 'tacit knowledge', which may be 'unverbalized or unverbalizable' (Freidson 2001: 25).[9] To Freidson, tacit knowledge is created by the repetition of tacit skills, which 'cannot be codified or described systematically; they must be learned by practice' (2001: 26). I find the focus on tacit knowledge particularly relevant for the profession of journalism, as journalists themselves refer to their work as a 'learning by doing', 'a gut-feeling' or a practice, which is as natural and unexplainable 'like riding a bike' (see Chapter 7).

Secondly, I find the idea of 'self-control', as discussed by Freidson, apt for describing how journalists expect editors and audiences alike to trust their work. As highlighted by Krogt (2007), Freidson's model defines the relationship between the professional and others as a trust-based relationship. Regarding ideal typical professions, the 'client' in the relationship trusts that the professional uses his/her knowledge and skill in the best way and that s/he is 'morally involved' (Freidson 2001: 26–35; see also Krogt 2007: 2). This protected status of trust towards the profession cannot be bought or forced but is gained by a 'project of successful persuasion' (Freidson 2001: 214). The recent controversies involving the news divisions of DR and BBC have arguably made audiences question the protected status of journalists, thus potentially lessening the trust between the audiences and the profession of journalism at large.

Thirdly, as I have found journalists to describe Freidson's fifth element above, the ideal of doing 'good work' and 'public service' as crucial to everyday work (see Chapter 3 and Chapter 7.2), I find the category useful for understanding the values, which matter to journalists. To Freidson, the idea of moral value is seen as a duty for the profession (collectively) to serve both their clients and society as a whole. This definition of professional values appear similar in descriptions on how journalists talk of their role in society as 'scouts' who have a part in 'dressing people up to understand the world we live in, being a part of telling what is happening. Be a part of putting critical questions so that the ones in power can explain themselves' (interview with DR reporter, 28 July 2007; see Chapter 7 for more on the notion of journalists as scouts).

I thus rely on the definitions of Freidson (2001; 1986, 1999) when approaching an analysis of empirical findings from a professionalism perspective. As I show throughout this book, viewing journalists as *both* craftsmen and professionals relates closely to the way journalists talk about their own work. As pointed out by Aldridge and Evetts, many journalists do not merely refer to themselves as 'being professional' but as 'member[s] of a profession' (2003: 560). The theories of Freidson (along with those of Parsons 1968; Larson 1990; Evetts 1999) have been criticised by Brante (2010) as requiring members of a profession to have a higher education. I agree with Brante's critique. As Aldridge and Evetts have pointed out, 'university-based, degree level training' is not necessarily an essential characteristic of the traditional profession (Aldridge and Evetts 2003: 554). However, when it comes to the journalism profession, my empirical study has found most journalists today to have a higher education – with the exception of a couple of elder journalists I encountered, who had had vocational training only before being employed.

Why ideal typical values?

> It is by studying how journalists from all walks of their professional life negotiate the core values that one can see the occupational ideology of journalism at work.
>
> (Deuze 2005: 458)

Researching the professional identity and ideology of journalism, Deuze (2005) has shown that it is useful to revisit what he terms 'old' concepts in journalism in order to theorise about what journalism is or could be today. Introducing journalistic concepts such as 'public service', 'objectivity', 'autonomy', 'immediacy' and 'ethics', Deuze analyses what he calls the 'operationalization of the values that journalism's ideology consists of' (2005: 458). As I have found that journalists in contemporary newsrooms talk about and work towards these 'old' professional values (much alike those discussed by Deuze), I find Deuze's approach to be inspirational to my work. In the analysis of my fieldwork, it has therefore been my aim to map out the everyday operationalization of journalism values with attention to those that I have found to be shared. It is important to point out here that, while journalists may share values, they can still produce a different journalistic product, a factor I see as a result of intra-organisational values (Soloski 1989).

According to Schudson and Anderson (2009), it is fruitful for research to focus on journalism practices and processes with which journalists express their status as professionals: 'Rather than outlining the traits that best characterize professionals and then assessing the degree to which journalists attain them, we can analyse the social process through which journalists struggle to claim professional status' (Schudson and Anderson

2009: 90). Inspired by this notion, in my analysis of journalists at work I explore what I have found to be the key values, which journalists define as central to their profession. It is important to note that my study of ideal type values here is primarily centred on the values that I have observed journalists to use and talk about in their everyday work. In this way, I have allowed the practice of the informants to guide my categories of ideal types rather than the other way around.

The 'good news story' and objectivity

The matter of how traditional media are affected by new challenges, such as competition from new media, has been central to recent studies of journalists at work. In discussions of the value of public service media, arguably the promise of trustworthiness and objectivity is one of traditional media's most important selling points. In the definitions proposed by Freidson (2001: 26–35), professionalism brings with it a trust relationship based on the belief that the professional uses his/her knowledge and skill in the best way and that s/he is 'morally involved' (Freidson 2001: 26–35). For such trust to be upheld, it is essential for journalists to strive towards pragmatic objectivity (see Ward 2004).

As has been highlighted, 'policies for broadcasting in many countries impose, by various means, a requirement of objectivity, on their public broadcasting systems, sometimes as a condition of their independence' (McQuail 2000: 173). Political broadcasts are a good example. Parties are allowed to go on air but each has equal airtime in the attempt to control that a broadcaster does not show bias towards one political group and objectivity is thus achieved. With more and more presenters and journalists being active on social media such as Twitter, the objective and non-biased position is often hard to keep. However, whenever asked for an opinion, objectivity is claimed. During the summer of Brexit in the UK for instance, ITV presenter Alastair Stewart commented a question on his personal opinion on Twitter with the words: 'Fortunately that is a private matter in a democracy, and anyway, publicly, I am fiercely impartial' (Alastair Stewart via his Twitter account @alstewitn, 3 June 2016).

In journalism studies, the notion of objectivity has often been described as the cornerstone of journalistic integrity and the single most important professional value (Preston 2009: 36; Curran and Gurevitch 1996: 238). Representing this approach, Lichtenberg describes objectivity as 'embraced as one of the fundamental norms of a journalists profession [...] intertwined with truth, fairness, balance, neutrality, the absence of value judgements, objectivity is a cornerstone of the professional ideology of journalists in liberal democracies' (Lichtenberg in Curran and Gurevitch 1996: 238). This core value is the underlying ideal behind other professional values such as being 'balanced' and 'fair' in reporting events. Studying how cultural values of news producers matter in the changing everyday work of terrestrial TV news, Harrison (2000) refers to objectivity as a key element, which 'underpins journalistic conceptions of newsworthiness and newsroom culture and practice' (2000: 137).

With my study I show how the shared ideal of the 'good news story' and that of the 'good journalist' can be seen as an overarching element, which also encompasses ideals such as objectivity within the professional norms and values of journalism. As illustrated in Chapter 7, the shared definitions of the 'good news story' and the 'good journalist' carry key concepts and values of journalistic professionalism such as objectivity, public service and the idea of 'doing good'. As I discuss (see Chapter 7.4), the notion of being a 'scout' can be seen as a primary drive for public service journalists today. I find journalists to be driven by this ideal both in their work hours and out of work. Indeed, the notion of journalists being driven by work ideals to an extent where they consider their personal lives as well as their working lives as always connected to being a journalist, suits historical uses of the word profession. The word 'profession' derives from the Latin *professiō*, which together with the verb *profitēri* was used in the thirteenth century to mean 'public declaration'. These words were used in a religious context to describe the taking of vows upon entering a religious order. From this perspective members of a profession can be expected to find work a calling or they should have a certain 'commitment' towards their work (see Staugård 2011: 163).

Social control and norms of professionalism

One of the early newsroom researchers, Warren Breed (1955), introduced a notion that I have found particularly intriguing throughout my own research, namely that of social control in the newsroom. Breed sets out to analyse why staffers within a newspaper newsroom appeared to conform to their publisher's policy, and he concluded that at the time he did not find the press to enjoy much freedom in their work and their way of working. One important factor, which he found to challenge imposed control from a publisher, was 'the existence of ethical journalistic norms' (1955: 326).

Inspired by Breed's study of social control, another US newsroom researcher, John Soloski, entered a newspaper newsroom as a participant observer a few decades later, in order to find out what controls the way journalists work in the everyday. Focusing specifically on what Breed had termed 'journalistic norms', Soloski found that what governs the way journalists work is their shared values and norms of professionalism. The development of professional journalism, Soloski found, 'establishes norms of conduct for journalists' that 'reduce the need for news organisations to put in place elaborate rules and regulations for staff' (Soloski 1989: 213). These shared professional norms of journalism can, however, be challenging for management. According to Soloski, the shared professional norms may be so powerful that they give journalists an autonomy, or power base, which can resist heavy-handed interference by management. News organisations may then respond by developing new procedures to further limit the professional autonomy of their journalists (Soloski 1989: 213; Preston 2009: 10). In the light of my fieldwork experiences of very dominating, shared values across newsrooms, I find Soloski's study of professionalism particularly interesting.

In his study of professionalism, Soloski, like Warren Breed, finds institutional policies important to the everyday work. However, Soloski deviates from Breed's notion of top-down control of staff in that he classifies a set of equally important values guiding journalists' work to be their professional norms, which are shared across organisations. Policies will be different from newsroom to newsroom, argues Soloski, but what stays the same are the shared professional norms. From this perspective, Soloski defines the shared professional norms as *trans-organisational* ideologies, while the individual newsroom's policies can be defined as *intra-organisational*:

> Just as news professionalism can be seen as a transorganization control mechanism, the idiosyncratic news policies of individual news organizations can be seen as an intra-organizational control mechanism. [...] Since the norms of news professionalism are shared by all journalists, the news organization needs only to concentrate on teaching journalists its own news policies, and needs only to develop techniques for ensuring that its journalists adhere to the policies.

> (Soloski 1989: 218)

Soloski's notion of the trans-organisational versus the intra-transorganisational resounds with what I have found during fieldwork; though newsrooms have very different policies and mission statements, above all they have a set of shared values determining the way journalists work. My studies, however, have found the shared values of journalists to receive more importance among news staff than the policies and mission statements of each individual broadcaster.

Other journalism researchers have focused on the notion of ideology in relation to the news staff. Tuchman (1973) has portrayed journalists as driven by a 'strategic ritual' to position themselves among peers. Schlesinger (1978) views journalism as a collective practice of gatekeeping, which 'tames' the doings of the world (1978: 47). In the past, researchers of the journalism profession have pointed towards journalists as sharing values across nationalities and media platforms, termed invariably 'occupational ideology' (Schlesinger 1978; Golding and Elliott 1979) or 'ideology of professionalism' (Soloski 1989; Zelizer 2004).[10] The notion of a shared ideology has been much discussed among journalism researchers, and as Deuze points out: 'even though scholars are comfortable to refer to journalism as an occupational ideology, *the distinct building blocks of such an ideology are sometimes left to the imagination of the reader*' (2011: 20, emphasis added). During my study I have been keen to explore and introduce what Deuze views as the 'distinct building blocks' of the ideology of journalism. Viewing journalists as members of a group with shared ideological values has long been the interest of professions studies. For the purpose of my research I draw particularly on the notion of ideal type values as put forward by Freidson (2001) among others.

Similarly to Soloski (1989), Harrison has found in her study of the culture of production of terrestrial TV news in Britain what she describes as 'a shared culture' (Harrison 2000:

108–38) across newsrooms. Harrison describes the similarities as 'grounded in the sharing by journalists of a set of extant formulas, practices, normative values and journalistic mythology' (Harrison 2000: 108). This definition of shared journalistic culture is not far from Freidson's (2001) definition of elements characterising professionalism. Harrison defines journalistic culture as a culture to which all journalists see themselves as belonging, like a 'closed club' within which the understanding of newsworthiness is of 'intrinsic value' (Harrison 2000: 108). During my fieldwork, I have reached conclusions similar to those of Harrison, in that I have found that journalists regard themselves as working within a closed tribe (see Chapter 2.1). I have found this idea of being part of a community of shared practice as more important to journalists than the organisation within which they are employed. Harrison sees the journalistic culture to be governed on a daily basis by editors and management. To Harrison, editorial control comes across through at least five observable factors:

1) Editors giving orders with no time for dissent
2) Journalists expressing that they feel watched over[11]
3) Editors conducting numerous meetings
4) Power residing in very few hands
5) Journalists second-guessing what the editor wants

(2000: 131–34)

Harrison describes the controlling elements of journalists at work as both helpful towards conformity of work but also problematic for journalists as they believe themselves always 'working to the Programme Editor's vision' (2000: 134). I have found journalists to express a similar critique of being watched over by editors. While journalists experience editorial control, similar to what is outlined by Harrison above, I have found the journalists to express the controlling factors as something that needs to be fought against and battled daily.

A study of practice: The second wave of newsroom studies

Recently, a new wave of newsroom studies has begun rolling through international journalism research, with the idea of journalistic practices, rather than routines, at its core. Arguably borrowed from Foucault, the conceptualisation of practice seeks to accommodate both a sense of the 'discursive' and the 'administrative' in social processes. When taken to the newsroom, the idea of a practice study over routine study arguably leaves behind the notion of power, control and regulation as imposed from outside or from above, and gives increasing possibility for individual agency and action – thus leaving room for viewing news work practices and discourses as potentially 'productive and facilitative *as well as* repressive or imposed' (Cottle 2000: 22, emphasis added).

The effects of new demands on journalists have been studied by researchers within a practice tradition with special attention to the social and technical dimensions of the Internet (see for instance Boczkowski 2004; Deuze and Paulusen 2002; Domingo 2006; Paterson and Domingo 2008, 2011; Heinonen 1999; Quinn and Trench 2002; Weaver 1998). Recent research has been done in the field of cross-media and convergence (see for instance Cottle 1999; Duhe et al. 2004; Erdal 2008; Bechmann 2009; Hartley 2011; Volkmer and Firdaus 2013).

Anja Bechmann (2009) has explored the new practice of cross media production by traditional media, which likewise focuses on everyday practices rather than routines inside the newsroom. Bechmann's approach to fieldwork has been similar to the one with which I have conducted my research in that we both aim to work towards what Wadel (1991: 129) describes as a round-dance between design focus, gathering of analysis and theory development (see Bechmann 2009: 49). However, as Bechmann is primarily interested in conceptualising cross-media within traditional media organisations (2009: 20), the research question at the beginning of her methodological round dance is different to the one initiating the project in hand. The aim of my study is not to focus specifically on technical changes but rather on how changes within the newsroom affect professional ideals of journalists in the everyday.

In Denmark, recent studies of the news making processes have taken on the task of looking at journalism from a practice perspective to task. Schultz (2006) and Gravengaard (2010), both of whom follow traditions within the sociological approach, represent two Danish contributions to a second wave of newsroom studies. Both Gravengaard and Schultz research journalistic practices and journalists' self-defined values and ideals. Akin to the ideas of Tuchman (1973), Schultz and Gravengaard view news as the outcome of routine, largely implicit, organisational rules that news workers follow. As these rules are unwritten, they are constantly being negotiated both verbally and through working practices. I too have found journalism work to be defined by a constant negotiation process reinforcing a shared journalistic ideology (see Chapter 7.1). However, my study differs from that of Gravengaard and Schultz in its methodological approaches.

The research question of Schultz has much in common with the research question with which I began my study. As discussed elsewhere (see Schultz and Thomsen 2008), we both began research with a concern for how journalists define public service in the everyday work. As Schultz studies newsrooms with an analytical framework borrowed from Pierre Bourdieu, journalists at work are seen through categories such as doxa and habitus while news judgement is discussed as orthodox or heterodox (see also Schultz 2007: 196). Following Bourdieu, Schultz views the newsrooms as parts of a journalistic field, a 'semi-autonomous microcosm which has both own logics and practices and at the same time mirrors the logics and practices of society' (Schultz 2006: 19, my translation from Danish). Schultz's approach has yielded valuable reflections of journalism work and introduced new ways from within the sociology of Bourdieu with which to study journalism. As my methodological approach is founded on methods borrowed from anthropology, my approach to fieldwork is different. Moreover, the research of Schultz differs in the sense that the study in hand covers participant observation within both English and Danish public service newsrooms, while Schultz research relies on non-participant observations at DR and TV2. When it comes to an analysis of news values used by broadcast journalists, my study has come to a conclusion similar to that of Schultz (2006): That the values of the good news story are crucial to everyday negotiations among journalists (see Chapter 7.3). Furthermore, both our research projects point towards the definitions of Public Service as contested both in government, among critics and media researchers, but also as an institutional logic guiding everyday journalistic practice. As shown (see Schultz and Thomsen 2008), this logic has increased drastically in value and appears particularly outspoken during recent years when it has been under threat. Research from both Schultz and I indicate that while economic and governmental pressure has been put on Public Service Broadcasters, the very foundation on which public service is based is discussed and worn as a badge of honour among broadcast journalists (see also Chapter 7.2).

Gravengaard's (2010) study engages in a discussion of a central ideal typical value of the journalism profession, the good news story and what reasons journalists use for negotiating the selection of events as news. With this focus, Gravengaard's research can be placed among journalism researchers, who examine 'institutional structures or shared professional values' within which news journalists operate (see e.g. Deuze 2005; Harrison 2000; Tuchman 1978; Schlesinger 1978; Witschge and Nygren 2009; Witschge 2013). This approach involves examining professional codes employed by journalists in order to make decisions about the news value of events and about the routines used to construct news reports. As I have found ideal typical professional values such as 'the good news story' to be important factors in the everyday negotiations by journalists, I too centre my research on shared professional values with and by which journalists operate. My study differs from Gravengaard's (2010) in that I did not set out to study the professional values of journalists but was interested in what structures the everyday work of journalists. With this interest as a catalyst, I began fieldwork and found the prevailing structure among all the journalists to be that of ideal typical values, a discovery that led me to study professional values of journalists.

While many of the current studies into journalism values (such as Gravengaard 2010; Hartley 2011; Harrison 2000; Schultz 2006) study professional values of journalists through a study of everyday practice and discussions about practice, with my study, I include a spatial and temporal level of analysis (see Chapters 4 and 5). In her study of the regional BBC newsroom in Nottingham, Emma Hemmingway (2004, 2008) has a similar interest in the spatial and temporal as an exploration of 'the geographical and the professional "real" space' within which 'news fictions are created' (Hemmingway 2004: 410).[12] While I agree with Hemmingway in that the newsroom is an important symbolic space to include in studies of journalism, my focus and method of spatial analysis is different to Hemmingway's approach. Furthermore, the newsrooms that I have studied have different spatial and organisational layouts compared to the bimedial newsroom she presents.

Adapting Bakhtin's (1981) chronotopic analysis of literature to a textual analysis of news, Hemmingway describes how the news programme is a result of a 'complex mutation process' involving three states of news, which she terms: the 'world itself', the 'world in news' and the 'world of the news'. Hemmingway finds the regional BBC newsroom in Nottingham to be divided by two separate working 'zones': newsgathering and news output. The space between these two zones is referred to in Hemmingway's study as 'the silent heart of news' (2004). While both zones share the common purpose of producing what she describes as 'the world of the news', Hemmingway finds each of the two zones to have strategically separate aims. When a news story moves from the newsgathering zone to the output zone of the newsroom, it begins a mutation from 'the world in news' to 'the world of the news' (2004: 417).

Bakhtin's theories are useful tools for analysing the newsroom space as a battle between input and output providers, and they offer an original way of studying structures within the newsroom. The newsrooms Hemmingway studies are different in layout and organisational structure to the ones I have studied. Moreover, I have found the new circular layout of the British newsrooms to have decreased the competition and division between working zones. In the Danish national newsrooms of DR and TV2, the distinction between newsgathering and news output does not exist. However, the DR news division has just initiated a change of working structure largely inspired by the British model of dividing the newsroom into out and input zones.[13]

Hemmingway uses the Actor-Network Theory as a tool for studying the adoption of new technologies in newsroom work. Anderson (2009, 2010, 2011a, 2011b) is similarly inspired by the Actor-Network Theory in analysis of news work.[14] However, Anderson connects the Actor-Network Theories with those of Social Network Analysis and thus widens research to not only cover the newsroom but the larger '"journalistic ecosystem" that is emerging and coalescing outside the newsroom walls' (Anderson 2011a: 152). This study of connections shows how human actors, technological devices, sources, hyperlinks, documents and journalists can be seen as 'networked' together to create both the journalistic product and news organisations. Anderson's study illustrates how journalistic ideals of the good news story are constantly competing with market logics such as getting clicks and views online (see Anderson 2011b). Through my study, I find broadcast journalists facing a similar pressure between market logics and professional ideals. But as I use a different methodology, my fieldwork has been less occupied with connections between human and non-human actors.

Recent research of the online arm of public service broadcast media (see for instance Martin 2007; Brevini 2012; Brügger 2012) points towards traditional public service news broadcasters as making use of their Internet websites to slowly re-invent themselves and 'adapt to the new political and economic conditions' (Martin 2007: 27). My study points towards broadcast journalists as being less willing to adapt their ways of working.

Focusing specifically on online news and online news production, Jannie Møller Hartley (2011) has conducted a study of Danish online news desk practices. In the tradition of Schultz (2006), Hartley employs Bourdieu's field theory in her study of Danish online newsrooms. One of the primary elements connecting my study and Hartley's research is the interest in the encounter of new and old journalism as a contact point between old ideals and new demands. With reference to online journalists, Hartley has shown how journalists position themselves in opposition to 'old' forms of journalism while at the same time accepting the 'old' as 'better' journalism (Hartley 2013). During my fieldwork, I too have found tensions between what journalists describe as 'old' values and new demands (see Chapter 7). Hartley finds online journalists to be 'stalled by a field doxa, which tells them that "proper" journalism is deep, investigative, informative (as a public service), time consuming and polished' (Hartley 2013: 11). The broadcast journalists I have studied find themselves stalled by similar perceptions of what constitutes good journalism. However, while the online journalists may perceive an existential struggle towards being recognised by other journalists, my study shows that public service broadcast journalists perceive it as less of a struggle to be recognised among peers. Furthermore, I suggest that broadcast journalists in particular can use the current media changes as an opportunity to create journalism, which fulfils these professional ideals (see Chapter 8).

Investigating the social context surrounding the production of letters to the editor section in US newspapers, Wahl-Jorgensen (2007) has found journalistic ideals of public participation and democracy to be keeping strong amidst growing constraints of new media.[15] However, the study also shows how journalistic ideals exist in what Wahl-Jorgensen describes as a 'tension with a set of antidemocratic and often elitist tendencies within the culture of commercial media operation' (2007: 5). According to Wahl-Jorgensen, journalists 'vividly' experience 'tensions' (2007) in their everyday work. During my research, I have also found journalists to experience tensions, most often between journalistic ideals and institutional reality. I have found journalists to talk about such tensions as 'journalistic' versus 'management' ideals.

In his ethnographic study of a mid-range daily paper in the US, Ryfe (2012) has studied journalists put under new demands in order to increase sales. According to Ryfe, the new demands, such as new editorial routines and the idea that content should be created for more media platforms, were met with hostility by most journalists. The journalists he met were critical of the new demands primarily because of what they described as 'bad journalism'. This finding supports the 2001 survey commissioned by the World Association of Newspapers conducted among media executives worldwide, which 'cited as the biggest obstacle to media convergence the "individualistic nature of journalists"' (according to Deuze 2005: 452). During my research, I too have found journalists to be overwhelmingly critical of new demands to their everyday work (see Chapter 5.3).

Critique of the profession

In a time where anyone with access to social media can act as live reporters, values of the journalism profession are arguably more important than ever. As highlighted in the

Introduction, the journalism profession has recently been under public scrutiny as a number of high-profile controversies at the public broadcaster in both Denmark and the UK led to core journalism values being questioned by both the public and the press (as discussed in the Introduction). Adding to the critique, a number of journalists and editors have criticised the state of journalism today (see for instance Hansen 2016; Rusbridger 2001; Bell 2003; Krause-Kjær 2003; Snow 2004; Marr 2004).[16] The current state of journalism has been charged with a decline of public values, with former journalists arguing that the news journalist today has 'no time to think' (Rosenberg and Feldman 2008; Davies 2009), and investigative reporter Carl Bernstein holds the journalism climate accountable for creating what he terms an 'idiot culture' (Bernstein 1992).

Recent research of journalism has been critical of the profession, as many deem contemporary journalism to be 'continuously refractured' (Broersma 2013), simply 'ending' (Charles 2014) and in a 'state of crisis' (Schlesinger 2006; McNair 2013), which results in a journalistic product that forgets that 'it is the role of journalists to challenge people, not merely amuse them' (Bernstein 1992: 24–25). Others, talk of journalism simply needing a crucial 'rethinking' (Zelizer 2017) or 'reconsidering' (Alexander et al. 2016). When criticising journalism of today, researchers particularly talk of a decline in what Lund (2001) has termed 'key ideas'. Economic pressure to the traditional news media has been charged with forcing journalists to strive to depart from the ideal of informing the public in favour of ideals of entertainment, which has been described as 'churnalism' (Davies 2009), 'infotainment' and 'Newszak' (Franklin 1997). The many new media platforms have arguably proven to be a particular challenge for Public Service Broadcasters, as basic rules of news production and presentation have changed radically, thus creating 'new challenges for old media' (Lund et al. 2009).

Nick Davies' book *Flat Earth News* (2009), based largely on research conducted by Cardiff University (Lewis et al. 2008c), exemplifies many of the key critiques of working conditions of the journalism profession today. According to this research, journalists today produce three times more in less time than they did twenty years ago (2008c: 3). This pressure on fast production is crucial for making journalists choose press releases as sources rather than go out and find original stories themselves. The researchers found that '41% of press articles and 52% of broadcast news items contain PR materials which play an agenda setting role or where PR material makes up the bulk of the story' (2008c: 21). The extensive copying of press releases and news agency stories by the British media is particularly surprising, as the news media appear to want to 'give the impression that they depend on their own journalists rather than agencies or other outside sources' (Lewis et al. 2008a: 5).

The journalists who Lewis et al. interview say that they felt that the pressure to produce a high number of stories on a daily basis had intensified and to a greater extent this made them rely on recycling stories despite their ideals of investigating independently (Lewis et al. 2008a: 4).[17] The journalists that I spoke to during research expressed similar concerns. I have found journalists to be particularly frustrated with new production demands, as they appear to go against journalists' professional values and ideals.

To many researchers, the current working conditions of journalists make for a decline in product and a challenge to ideal type values such as newsworthiness and objectivity. According to Franklin,

[e]ntertainment has superseded the provision of information: human interest has supplanted the public interest; measured judgement has succumbed to sensationalism; the trivial has triumphed over the weighty; the intimate relationships of celebrities from soap operas, the world of sport or the royal family are judged more 'newsworthy' than the reporting of significant issues and events of international consequence. Traditional news values have been undermined by new values; infotainment is rampant.

(Franklin 1997: 4)

For Franklin, just as for many other media researchers, the transformation in the news product has crucial implications for public information and democracy (see for instance Silverstone 2007: 128–29; Harrison 2000; Witschge 2013).[18] Today, journalism as it once was, has undoubtedly come to an end (Deuze 2008: 4). But with the change in working conditions, are the professional values and ideals of journalists changing, too? As the product of journalism has changed, has the profession changed, too? I have chosen to focus on professional values, which are central to the everyday work of journalists today. While I have found public service journalists to be worried by much the same issues as Franklin above, I have found journalists to hold onto traditional values, and struggle to uphold these in the face of current challenges. As Witschge and Nygren have concluded in a study of journalists at work in Sweden and Britain:

The defence of the profession from within seems to indicate that journalists are at least not ready to let go of the professional standards. They try to guard the boundaries of the profession and ensure its perceived distinctiveness.

(Witschge and Nygren 2009: 57)[19]

While I base research on different newsrooms and at a different time, I have come to similar conclusions – which suggests that the ideals of the journalism profession appear far from forgotten. Schudson writes of the current challenges for journalists: '[...] with all this, a commitment of serious journalists to independent truth seeking, to verification, and to holding government accountable – the central value-orientations of the professional project in journalism – are upheld' (Schudson 2013: 195). Arguably, the current challenges have made journalists more aware of the strength in traditional ideals. As Usher (2010) shows, journalists who are leaving their job reference clearly to traditional journalism ideals and importance to sustaining information and democracy. In studying goodbye-letters from journalists to their former colleagues, Usher finds the discourse to be nostalgic and 'insistent upon the values and practices of established journalism' (Usher 2010: 916).[20] As Witschge and Nygren point out: 'When people's identities are threatened, they may try to reinforce it' (2013: 57).

The 'cultural' approach to journalism studies

Following the first wave of newsroom studies, a new interest within media research emerged, which focused on the importance of the cultural in media production. Following the example of researchers in the US and Britain, the mid-1980 and 1990s brought several contributions to the study of news production in Scandinavia (see Siverts 1984; Klausen 1986; Pittelkow 1986; Puijk 1990; Helland 1995). With this beginning of a second wave of newsroom research, researchers began a new combined research, which was inspired by Schlesinger (1978) and aimed to explore how news production 'contexts' and news 'texts' are connected and interlinked in the everyday work inside the newsroom, rather than viewing them as separate analytical entities. Following this second wave, newsrooms and the process of news making were productively approached as mutually interpenetrating and not as analytically separate elements (see Helland 1995; Cottle 1999; Clausen 2001).

In media research, what I see as a 'cultural approach' is dominated by the notion that media producers are social actors each with special competences in manipulating cultural artefacts and symbols – what Peterson (2003: 162–68) has called a 'sociocentric analysis' of the media. Researchers of this school have offered another view of media producers as less dominated by institutions and authorities, and more *of* their society and people than the general view put forward by researchers within the sociological tradition. Rather, the culturalist paradigm within journalism studies means that researchers view an event as what anthropologist Marshall Sahlins has termed 'not just a happening in the world; it is a relation between a certain happening and a given symbolic system' (1985: 135).

Future challenges for news production studies

The first wave of newsroom studies has put crucial and much-needed spotlight on the practices and everyday routines of journalists at selected newsrooms at a time when the newsrooms were a dark spot on journalism and cultural studies. But the newsrooms have more insights they can offer researchers of journalism today. Ethnographies from newsrooms inside less elitist institutions, such as local and regional news organisations and newsrooms in different places than the West, are still only scarcely included in journalism research (for examples see Franklin 2006; see also Bird 2010b for the first collection of global perspectives of news making). Also lacking within newsroom studies is the comparable element.

Since the first wave of newsroom studies (with the notable exception of Golding and Elliot's study in 1979) focused on the practices of one institution, one newsroom and thus one specific group of newsroom workers, few researchers have explored and compared many different newsrooms. Thus, we still know little about the interrelation, connection and comparisons between different newsrooms across different organisations, cities and countries. Apart from this geographical framing of news making, the fact that the first wave of newsroom studies is still very dominant in research of news production today may lead to a framing of news making in a certain time. As insightful, revealing and necessary as this first wave of studies was, there is an urgent need to refresh the research and provide an updated account of how newsrooms work today, including contemporary trends of convergence, privatisation, conglomeratisation and corporatisation, to name a few.

Overall, the first wave of newsroom studies brought attention to the structural organisation of news workers, focusing on the logic of text production and the streamlining of news output. My aim is to focus less on the news output produced and more on other social effects of the way news workers are organised. In this sense, I approach the newsroom with the culture of the newsroom as my primary interest, notwithstanding that this culture affects the output of news, as well as many other factors in the life of news workers, newsrooms and news broadcasters. In this bridging of paradigms from within the sociology of news-making and cultural studies, I aim to recognise both the agency of each news worker within a cultural system *and* the part this news worker may play in the wider structures of power (Peterson 2003: 164). This mode of research represents a rather late entry to the field of media studies, termed invariably 'media anthropology' or 'anthropology of news and journalism'. Researchers from within this field focus on the nature of media as a form of cultural meaning making: be it in the production, content or reception of the news, thus moving the onus from theories of control, organisation and routines. In the following, I briefly map out this subfield of anthropology.

1.3 Media Anthropology with a Focus on Production

What characterises previous studies of newsrooms and of news making is an interest in putting words on what some have called a 'silent knowledge' of the practice of making news. In many ways, my interest is much the same. As many researchers have found before me, media practitioners find it virtually impossible to describe the knowledge they have of how they work as they do: 'I just do it', 'it's a gut feeling!', they say (Schultz 2007). In order to word this knowledge, anthropologists bring a new method to the study of the journalists at work. The term 'media anthropology' covers a new territory in which the disciplines of anthropology and media studies meet, representing what Rothenbuhler has called the use of 'anthropological concepts and methods within media studies and the study of the media by anthropologists. [...] best described as a territory of contact between two fields, giving rise to a moment of inter-disciplinary discussion' (Rothenbuhler 2008: 2).

Anthropology is not a science of a specific object, but of the social and the cultural. As Hansen (1995) writes, the object in anthropology can contain: '[A]ll sides of the human life, both biological, societal and cultural sides' (1995: 117–18, my translation from Danish). Thus, the 'media anthropology' approach often includes research into various different aspects of media use and media culture. Viewing media as part of a larger ecology, many media anthropology studies focus on audiences and uses rather than media production (see e.g. Rao 2010; Pedelty 2010; Peterson 2010 and the many contributions in Postill and

Bräuchler 2010). Though my study primarily concerns the production practices of media, the methodological approach has much in common with the ideals of media anthropology. That is to say, I view the news product as part of an ecology in which not only the way that journalist work matters, but what matters is also the way that staff *say* that they work and the way in which they talk about their own work in relation to the work of colleagues. Furthermore, I consider factors such as the structure of space and time within the newsroom important parts of the wider ecology within which journalists produce news. In the following I briefly introduce the discipline of anthropology and some of its main practices.

A situated knowledge

Anthropological knowledge is largely *situated* knowledge, as the basis of anthropological work is ethnography. In this instance ethnography is defined as a 'description based on intimate, long-term reflexive encounters between scholars and the peoples they are studying' (Peterson 2003: 8). In the anthropological tradition, ethnography involves a thickly contextual mode of detailed description, as introduced by Clifford Geertz (1973). Much like other schools of thought using the ethnographic approach, the aim of an anthropologist situating him/herself within a group of people s/he wants to study is to 'make direct contact with social agents in the normal courses and routine situations of their lives to try understand something of *how* and *why* these regularities take place' (Willis 2000: xiii, original emphasis). This situated praxis makes media anthropologists differ to some extent from how researchers of the first wave of newsroom studies worked.

Until recently, media has been widely neglected by the discipline of anthropology. Anthropology's first engagement with mass media is generally traced back to the culture-at-a-distance approach, which was in fact not aimed at studying media production but media content. Inaugurated in the US during the Second World War, the aim of this approach was to study cultures, particularly those posing a threat to national defence that could not be visited directly. Relying on cultural expressions such as music, films, novels and newspapers as sources, the anthropologists of the culture-at-a-distance approach would examine media for 'variables of dynamic psychology' (Dickey 1997: 414; Wolfenstein 1953: 267).

Though later forgotten and overlooked for almost 50 years, half a century ago one anthropologist, Hortense Powdermaker (1900–70), professor in anthropology and student of Malinowski, ventured into the anthropology of media production. Her fascination with media took her to Hollywood where she went on a year-long fieldwork among writers, producers, actors, set designers and lighting crews, which culminated in the book *Hollywood the Dream Factory: An Anthropologist Looks at the Movie-Makers* (1950). Throughout her career, Powdermaker kept her use of mass media as a source and key in cultural analysis, including radio and film; for instance, in her later ethnography of a Zambian copper mining town (see Powdermaker 1953, 1962).

Apart from Powdermaker, anthropology's engagement with the media has been a rarity at the time, and until the 1990s only few anthropologists have looked directly at the creation, consumption or content of media (Dickey 1997: 414). The field of anthropology's recent interest in media has been largely inspired by cultural studies. Thus, the anthropology of media inherited an interest in reception processes, focusing on how media is used and manipulated by different (sub)cultures to their own cultural, economic and ideological ends (Askew and Wilk 2002). Initially then, anthropology's interest in media focused on how different cultures engage with media, rather than on how media is produced. This question led anthropologists to study the differences in interpretations in different cultures of the same media, such as soap operas (see Abu-Ludghod 1995; Das 1995) or cinematic films (see Dickey 1993, 2001; Hahn 1994), and how the media can work as a powerful means of self-expression and resistance to outside cultural domination for minority groups and indigenous people (see Ginsburg 1991, 1996; Turner 1991, 1992).

'Media anthropology' has so far served as an umbrella for describing a plethora of studies into people, phenomena and ideas affected by or affecting the media. As previously mentioned, while I see this study as methodologically connected to media anthropology, media anthropologists have primarily focused on media audiences within a wide media ecology. But what binds all these studies together? Media anthropology can be grouped as research into human interaction and experience in at least three different categories: The production processes, the distribution process and the experiences of the users/receivers/readers/audience. One fact that necessarily complicates this neat categorization, however, is that many of these areas frequently overlap, since a user of media can also be a producer of media content, and a producer of media content can also be distributor of media.

But what is so special about studying the media with an 'anthropological' method? As the field called 'media anthropology' is still in its infancy, researchers from all kinds of backgrounds and schools of thought continue to debate the exact meaning of the term. This can be seen in the vibrant debates on online groups, such as the Media Anthropology Network, and in recent discussions of the field, such as the published debate between John Postill and Mark Allen Peterson titled *What Is the Point of Media Anthropology?* (2009).

A booming subfield of anthropology

While studies of the media have proliferated throughout this last half-century, anthropologists have only recently turned attention to the field. But anthropology is making up for lost time. Within the last few years, the bookshelves, conferences and networks devoted to the field of media anthropology have begun to blossom to the extent that there is now talk of a 'boom' in the discipline (Postill and Peterson 2009).

It was a surprisingly long time in the making and the acquaintance is still fresh, but today the friendship and mutual collaborations between the field of anthropology and media studies seem stronger than ever. Within this last decade of mutual interest in each other's fields, a number of interdisciplinary and indeed multi-disciplinary journals have come about as an affirmation of the shared relationship. No less than three peer-reviewed journals have sprung up on the international arena since 2000, each devoted to interdisciplinary study, including ethnographies of media practices in general or journalism in particular: The *Journal of Media Practice* was launched in 2000, *Journalism Studies* in 2001 and, more recently in 2007, *Journalism Practice* was founded. Furthermore, 2013 saw the launch of the journal *Digital Journalism*, giving space for research on the new digital sides to journalism research. In Denmark, the journal *Journalistica*, with a less ethnographic focus but still interdisciplinary in its approach to research into journalism practice today, was founded in 2006.

Never before has the anthropological study of media been booming as it has been within the last few years. In the years 2002–05 alone, no less than four overviews of this emerging subfield were published (Askew and Wilk 2002; Ginsburg et al. 2002; Peterson 2003; Rothenbuhler and Coman 2005). In this first decade of the millennium, a new wave of interdisciplinary journalism research has emerged, and a large group of these researchers are anthropologists (see for instance Askew and Wilk 2002; Hannerz 2004; Born 2004; Rothenbuhler and Coman 2005; Paterson and Domingo 2008; Bird 2010b; Postil and Brauchner 2010; Domingo and Paterson 2011).

In 2005, the EASA Media Anthropology Network was founded, which by 2011 boasted over 1000 participants in the lively debates. As the network's first co-ordinator, anthropologist John Postill, writes: 'These are very exciting times indeed for the anthropology of Media' (Postil and Peterson 2009: 334). Focusing particularly on the ethnographic study of media, the two books *Making Online News, Vol. 1* and *Vol. 2* (Paterson and Domingo 2008, 2011) constitute the first gatherings of recent research into the newsrooms of online journalism made using purely the ethnographic method.

More recently, in 2009, another reader with a distinct focus on the anthropology of news and Journalism was published (see Bird 2010b), and Berghahn Books has initiated a book series devoted solely to the anthropology of media. So far, the series has published four books, each in part aiming to address 'the need for works that describe and theorize multiple, emerging, and sometimes interconnected, media practices in the contemporary world' (Berghahn Books online 2011). Still, however, the skewed interest in the field holds true, just as it does in journalism studies. Publications on this emerging subfield of anthropology have so far been geographically limited to derive from either the US or the UK.

1.4 Conclusions

Throughout this chapter, a number of relevant studies and research approaches have been highlighted. As this book proceeds, I return to selected themes and topics within news production research and the discussions of journalism as a profession. Researchers within the first wave of newsroom studies appeared to approach the newsroom with an organisational functionalist way of thinking. This approach has been criticised as losing sight of the agency of the individual journalist. To counter this trend, researchers such as Cottle (2007: 13) have called for a conceptional shift from considering 'routine' to considering 'practice' within newsrooms. Rather than routine, I have found the notion of practice to be fruitful for revisiting Breed and Soloski's discussions of what controls the way that news workers work together. In order to study such practice driven factors, I have found anthropology to be the most useful method. For inspiration, I have turned to Tuchman's study of news journalists. I found her focus on how journalists typify everyday happenings in order to perceive them as events-as-news particularly interesting. However, to me the focus is not on the actual typification and systemising of events as stories, but on the way that this typification and agreement is transferred to each worker in the newsroom and the way that working under such shared consensus may create tensions between the reality of each individual journalist and the shared ideals.

Breed's (1955) study of social control in the newsroom differs from my research in that it has a functional approach and is focused on print news production in the US. However, I have found his central research question and spirit of inquiry into how 'newsmen' are socially organised to have much in common with my own curiosity during fieldwork: Which factors are at play in the everyday organisation of news workers? And how do broadcaster and management policies matter to journalism and news production processes? While Breed found the organisational policy to play a dominant part in the everyday work of the news journalists he studied, my study points towards another more dominant factor playing the key part in the journalistic work, namely a shared professional community of practice. This community of practice and the shared values within this practice, I argue, matter more to the production process than does broadcaster policy.

As I have introduced, researchers working within the first wave of newsroom studies pointed towards there being a unity in the newsroom, which they related to the organisation and the system of editorial and source control of the news workers. My research takes a different approach to researching the newsroom, so although I share the attention to unity with the first wave of newsroom researchers, my conclusions are different. Though I did find that the newsroom at first appeared organised in a mechanical fashion, it soon became apparent to me that the news workers themselves *choose* to work as they do, not in order to obey their editor or the authorities, but in order to follow what they, and colleagues within their practice-related communities, deem as the ideal of being a 'good' journalist. As the bond of professional values shared among practice communities appears stronger than the bonds existing towards a manager or a broadcaster, as Bantz et al. (1980) argue, I have at times found there to be a mismatch between news workers' ideals and those of the management and corporation for which the journalists work. Before returning to discussions of what I see as the ideal typical values among journalists, I will introduce some of the methodological foundations on which I place my research.

Notes

1 The lack of reflexivity may not concern journalists at work only. Researching staff who leave the profession, Nikki Usher (2010: 913) finds journalists to fail to 'self-reflexively examine' their role in the occupational culture.

2 However, the tradition of considering the journalist a gatekeeper, or indeed viewing the newsroom as consisting of a string of gatekeepers, still exists today. Shoemaker (1991, 2009), for instance, has developed the gate-keeping model to comprise the social and the ideological and cultural context within the news making process.

3 According to Lave and Wenger, learners in any community of practice will 'inevitably participate in communities of practitioners' and 'the mastery of knowledge and skill requires newcomers to move toward full participation in the sociocultural practices of a community' ([1991] 2001: 29).

4 Research was conducted at two major news organizations in Toronto.

5 As Wahl-Jorgensen (2010) points out, the sociological paradigm in newsroom studies creates an emphasis in the field of journalism studies on control and routine, rather than on 'the spontaneous and unpredictable elements favoured by the professional myth of journalists' (2010: 25).

6 The concept of 'semi-professions' was developed by the sociologist T. Caplow in 1954 (according to Dahle 2008: 218) and has since become used to describe professions in which staff need shorter education, have less control over their own work and are less able to legitimise a special status compared to the classic professions (see also Staugård 2011: 165).

7 Freidson finds that the ideal type of 'professionalism' is applied to 'organized occupations', which control their own work. His definition of 'organized occupation' is similar to the English definition of 'profession', however, as he finds the word to have 'pretentious, sometimes sanctimonious overtones' (Freidson 2001: 13) he 'uses the word "occupations" instead of "professions"' (2001: 13). In my analysis, however, I primarily use the word 'profession', as I have found that journalists primarily use this word to describe their job.

8 In narrowing his definitions of logic to only those three, Freidson no doubt narrows his optic and may become blind to other logics such as the scientific and political (see Dahl 2005).

9 According to Freidson (2001: 25–26), the notion of 'tacit knowledge' within professions is inspired by Polanyi (1964).

10 Akin to Soloski (1989), Zelizer (2004) talks of 'journalists' professional ideology'. In a similar vein, Weaver (1998: 468) talks of 'occupational standards' in journalism – standards with characteristics that he finds very similar but finds it impossible to make a universal definition of due to 'too much disagreement on professional norms and values' (1998: 468).

11 Harrison points towards the news medium as important for the terrestrial journalists feeling constantly watched over, as they appeared aware that a 'top-brass' might tune in and watch the news at any time (Harrison 2000: 133).

12 Hemmingway's fieldwork in the Nottingham based regional BBC newsroom took place in the summer of 2003.

13 According to a conversation with current consultant for the DR news restructure project (10 December 2012).

14 Anderson's study is based on fieldwork in newsrooms of *Philadelphia Daily News*, *Philadelphia Enquirer* and Philly.com. Thus, the study covers both traditional and non-traditional news production sites in Philadelphia, PA, and Newark, NJ. Primary observations were conducted in May–August 2008.

15 Wahl-Jorgensen's study is based on both interviews; editorials and observations inside the daily *Bay Herald* (see Wahl-Jorgensen 2007).

16 Though these journalists have different perspectives, they share a critique of the current state of the news media and all express concerns that the current working conditions for journalists are worsening the news product considerably.

17 See also Lewis et al. (2008b) and Paterson (2007) on the extensive use of copy provided by public relations sources and news agencies by the British press. A recent Australian study conducted by Forde and Johnston (2013) tracks both news agency copy, press releases and online news articles in Australia and comes to strikingly similar conclusions.

18 As Joseph Pullitzer has put it: 'A cynical, mercenary, demagogic, corrupt press will produce in time a people as base as itself' (Pullitzer in Davies 2009: 397).

19 The Swedish study was based on observations in eight different newsrooms producing regional and national print, radio and broadcast news. The British study likewise involved newsroom studies in a local media newsroom (MEN-group), the BBC and *The Guardian* newsroom (according to Witschge and Nygren 2009: 42).

20 Usher makes use of Jameson's (1988, 1993) work on nostalgia for her analysis. According to Jameson, a turn towards nostalgia as a 'relationship with a past that never existed' is one of the hallmarks of postmodernity (Usher 2010: 914).

Part II

An Anthropologist Among Journalists

Chapter 2

Anthropology as a Method of Studying Journalists at Work

On being an anthropologist among journalists and thinking up methodological strategies during fieldwork

This book is the result of 18 months of intense participant observation, followed by years of revisits and constant contacts with the four TV newsrooms at BBC News, ITV News, DR's TV Avisen and TV2 Nyhederne. The study has spanned 10 years, between 2007 and 2017. I commenced fieldwork in the DR newsroom in May 2007, and my last fieldwork visit took place in the TV2 newsroom in December 2017. It has been my aim to research and capture the everyday working life of TV news journalists at national news broadcasters in Denmark and Britain today. Being in touch with the same four newsrooms over a period of 10 years has given an in-depth insight into the state of TV newsrooms today, which I could have never imagined when fieldwork began. Due to the long period of contact, I have a shared history with the field and my informants and a repertoire of events, challenges and experiences that I can refer to when reflecting on TV news today.

During fieldwork, the primary research methods have been participant observation using ethnographic methods derived from anthropology. Throughout this chapter, I introduce my methodological strategies and explore how anthropological methods can be useful for studying the everyday lives of a group of TV news journalists at work. The word 'ethnography' is central to both my method and observations; I see my fieldwork as ethnographic, and the account that I give of journalists at work constitutes ethnography. Before I commence this chapter, it is therefore necessary to clarify how I understand the term. One of the most succinct descriptions of the word *ethnography* comes from anthropologist and ethnographer Harry F. Wolcott, who argues that one of the problems with the term is that it.

> refers both to the *processes* for accomplishing it – ordinarily involving original fieldwork and always requiring the reorganization and editing of material for presentation – and to the presentation itself, the *product* of that research, which ordinarily takes its form in prose.
> (Wolcott 1995: 82–83, original emphases)

My understanding of what ethnography means is contained in exactly these two different areas that Wolcott highlights: the process and the product. Indeed, I view the process of research as so connected to the product of the same that I find it crucial to provide a thorough and detailed description of the 'complex specificness' (Geertz 1973: 23) of the processes of my fieldwork in order to validate the ethnographic product. Talking of 'ethnographic validity', Sanjek (1990) has argued that it is founded on explicit choices (such as how to participate, who to talk to, how to talk to people and what questions to ask) and the range of the field (i.e.

where to go and which limits to draw in fieldwork), as well as direct evidence from field notes. It is with this in mind that I, throughout this chapter, will strive to give a thorough account of and reflection on the practical process of my fieldwork. Indeed, as Murphy writes: '[I]f ethnography is in fact both "process" and "product", then how can we, as readers, fully appreciate the latter without a clear sense of the former?' (2011: 387).

Due to the unpredictable nature of news events, the space and place that comprised my fieldwork at times seemed unlimited, and the daily working time was impossible to foresee in advance. Following the journalists at work, I realised that I could not confine my field to the newsroom only; rather, I found my fieldwork space to be travelling alongside the journalists at hours that were long, unpredictable and at many different times of the day. The methods I used for observing and presenting what I experienced while doing fieldwork will be explored throughout this chapter.

Firstly, I will attempt to map out the field, which constitutes my fieldwork, and introduce the people that the study focuses on. Observing a group of people that I had previously considered myself a part of made for certain challenges during the study. In introducing my strategy of fieldwork and participant observation, I explore my way of working as a constant balancing act on a thin edge between participation and observation.

Crucial to doing participant observations among news journalists has been the ability to gain full access to what is arguably the sanctuary stronghold in news journalism, namely the newsroom. In this chapter, I include a detailed account of the challenges I encountered in gaining access, as I believe it serves as an introduction to the value put on distancing to The Others among the community of journalists and news broadcasters.

Lastly, this chapter explores the challenges of interviewing a group of people who themselves are interviewers, and the ethical considerations of observing and rendering anonymously a group of people who themselves work in observing events, and who pride themselves in naming and revealing sources and facts.

As I embarked on this research project, my hope was to capture the everyday working life of TV news journalists in Denmark and Britain. Why did I choose the method of participant observation fieldwork to do so? I could have attempted to capture the everyday working life of TV news journalists in other ways: I could have based research on interviews only or on surveys or questionnaires of the news workers; guessed at the everyday working life of the same journalists through quantitative analysis of facts and information. Arguably, doing participant observation and choosing to stay for a lengthy period of time among the people I wanted to study is a natural way of working for me, as I have a background in anthropology, not political science or philosophy. Others may have different methodological approaches, but to me spending time with the people I want to study in their everyday work environment is the closest I can get to a depiction of the everyday life and culture of that people. Participant observation gives a lived feeling, which could not be achieved through merely observing news bulletins or talking to journalists about how they perceive their work.

The method of participant observation is particularly useful for learning about a realm that is closed to the public, such as that of news workers and journalists inside a newsroom. As research into newsrooms otherwise relies on insider accounts or interviews, participant observation can help 'go beyond the taken-for-granted assumptions or established professional norms of news producers' (Cottle 2007: 8). During fieldwork, I came to realise that the journalists who were most active in the everyday work were also the ones who did not feel able to find time to reply to my emails, to schedule interviews at a set time or to take part in focus groups. As I was in the midst of this type of news staff on an everyday basis and therefore able to interview them whenever they found the time, I believe I have managed to include voices and opinions in my research that are often neglected by other forms of research of media workers.

A research of culture

Media anthropology is an offspring of the *cultural anthropology* branch of anthropology. Thus, in research, media anthropologists use the notion of 'culture' as an analytical tool for the unwrapping, understanding and representation of people. So what, to media anthropologists, is culture?

When discussing anthropology and ethnography, a vague but often used abstraction is that culture is to cultural anthropologists what life is to biologists, what force is to physicists and what God is to theologians. Even under pressure, researchers of culture are reluctant to offer a clear definition of the word 'culture' and would rather use a variation of other words such as 'knowledge, practice, tradition, technology, discourse, ideology or habitus' (Van Maanen 2001: 239). In his book on *Culture* (2000), anthropologist Adam Kuper treats the notion with scepticism, arguing that there is so much confusion about the term that 'the more one considers the best modern work on culture by anthropologists, the more advisable it must appear to avoid the hyper-referential word altogether [...]' (Kuper 2000: 2). Similarly, Clifford and Marcus have lamented that everything that the anthropologist refers to as culture should be contested because that which is described as culture cannot be represented as a 'unified corpus of symbols and meanings that can be definitely interpreted' (Clifford and Marcus 1986: 19 in Barth 1989: 122). Yet, towards the end of his book, Kuper reflects that the idea of culture is simply the only descriptive tool of which anthropologists are aware, which can explain differences among people:

> The concept of culture provides us with the only way we know to speak about the differences between the peoples of the world, differences that persist in defiance of the processes of homogenization.
>
> (Kuper 2000: 212)

One of anthropology's common definitions of organisational culture derives from a metaphor Geertz borrowed from Weber, namely that 'man is an animal suspended in webs of significance he himself has spun [...] I take culture to be those webs, and the analysis of it to be therefore not an experimental science in search of a law but an interpretive one in search of meaning' (Geertz 1973: 5). To Geertz, culture is not something locked inside people's heads but is rather visible in actions and in symbols through which members of a society 'communicate their worldview, value orientations, ethos, and all the rest to one another, to future generations and to anthropologists' (Ortner 1984: 129).

The idea of culture as a web has been furthered by Frederik Barth (1989), as an analytic way of exploring relations. Writing about the complexities of culture in what he calls 'complex societies', Barth's motive is to 'suggest that we can most usefully work substantively, by exploring the extent and kinds of connections which obtain in the domain of culture under various conditions of society' (Barth 1989: 121). To Barth, one set 'culture' of a specific society does not exist; rather, what we may call culture consists of many different relations. As culture is a relational phenomenon according to him, the term culture itself offers the analysing key element in a transactional interpretation of others.

Following the ideas put forward by Clifford and Marcus, all notions within the term culture are in need of contest as the term cannot be represented as a 'unified corpus of symbols and meanings that can be definitely interpreted' (Barth 1989: 122). Thus, Barth sets out to consider the various local templates of culture, and rather than aiming to create one single interpretation, he makes use of culture's indeterminate role to analyse locals from a transactionalist perspective.

This transactionalist method of offering an analytic value to the term culture is put into practice in Barth's description of marriage in Bali (1993). In his ethnographic representation of the marriage, Barth aims to give the most truthful account possible by including as many 'cultural accounts' as possible. In this sense, Barth aims to make culture the tool for an unwrapping of the relations of many 'streams' (Barth 1989: 132–40) of culture that together form an ethnographic experience. To Barth, each stream has its own dynamics and identity, and it is only by identifying and characterising each stream that one makes the most thorough representation of society. Interestingly, however, Barth regrets that a scientifically valid and truthful depiction of any given culture can never be given (Barth 1993: 271). Perhaps by admitting to never being able to depict a universal truth, Barth succeeds in making a very valid attempt at analysing cultures through the very term itself. Adding to debates from within journalism research, I believe a new understanding of the way national news broadcasters work can be gained from actually *being there*, by letting the practitioners and their lived experience of everyday production practices form the centre stage for investigation.

2.1 Entering the Newsroom

The most significant challenge of this research project was an unexpected one. After years of working for established British news organisations, I had become accustomed to getting instant access to people, information and places that made the stories of the day. So, though I was aware that journalists were less than fond of being looked over the shoulder, I was very surprised and unprepared for the difficulties I faced in getting access to study the four newsrooms I had planned to include in my project. In time, I realised that the process of working out, negotiating and gaining access was an illustrative introduction to the way news businesses function today. To illustrate, I will give an account of the obstacles I had to negotiate in order to enter each of the four newsrooms.

'I am one of you!' – Gaining access by being similar

My first negotiation of access was surprisingly simple and with no indication of the battles of access to come. I mustered my arguments and walked into the office of my editor at what was then the ITV News Channel. I explained to my editor that I was considering leaving my job in order to study how we journalists work, that I was applying for a grant to do a Ph.D. I then asked whether he thought I could include the ITV Newsroom in my study. The talk took less than a minute and ended with him promising full access, and at the end of that day the same editor had written a letter of recommendation for the Ph.D. project. Later, as I wanted to confirm the exact time of my fieldwork, the first editor I had agreed permission with had left the ITV (to work for the BBC), so I re-arranged the access permission with the managing editor of ITV News. This too took only minutes.

I first began making contact with the BBC at the end of 2006. I sent emails to various departments introducing my study and asking for permission to work as a participant observer in their newsroom. But as I did not have the same internal knowledge of the 'gatekeepers' and the hierarchy of staff at BBC as I had at ITV, it was hard for me to discern who I should rely on to open the gate.[1] And as none of the emails I sent or phone calls I made to different secretaries within the BBC News Centre led to any openings, after a year of waiting for phone calls and emails to be returned, I realised I had to take alternative measures if I was to enter the BBC as a researcher. In the year I spent attempting to get access to the BBC, a handful of my former colleagues from the ITV News Channel went to work for the BBC. Some gave me advice on who to call, but as they were new in the job at BBC, they too did not have enough internal knowledge, and perhaps not enough trust from the corporation, to help grant me access. Curiously, it seemed easier to get a journalistic job inside the BBC for me than to enter the place as a researcher. There were vacancies at the BBC News Centre that I was encouraged to apply for, but there was no interest in having me work as a participant observing researcher.

My breakthrough with access to study the BBC happened when I finally got to meet one of the 'gatekeepers' of the BBC News Centre face to face, while at the same time proving that I was a journalist *as well as* a researcher. At the end of 2006, I had begun to think it was entirely impossible to get access to the BBC newsroom as a researcher. At the same time, I had begun to make contact with editors at DR in Denmark to enquire whether they would grant me access to at least a one-month period of fieldwork. DR seemed very interested in whether the BBC would be included in the study, and it seemed that if BBC would be included, they would no doubt be interested too. After learning how one broadcaster warmed to granting me access if I already had access to another newsroom, I thought it best to wait with contacting TV2 in Denmark until I had been granted access to the DR newsroom. In this sense, getting access to the BBC newsroom had now become vital to me gaining any access at all to other broadcasters than ITV. So when a few of my former colleagues had arranged an event to which some of the most prestigious and influential news workers in the business in Britain were invited, and I was asked to work on the night as a volunteer producer, I jumped at the chance.

Thus, my big break into the BBC came in the guise of *The Ultimate News Quiz 2007*, a charity event where all the top names in British TV news gathered to test their knowledge on current events. Held at the Bloomberg news headquarters in the City of London, and hosted by one of Britain's most well-known TV news presenters from BBC, the event really was a bringing together of all the most famous on screen and radio news workers and their less visible employers, the chairmen, managers and heads of news. I was given the task of being the BBC quizmaster's producer, making sure that he kept time and asked the right questions in the correct manner. On the night, however, it became clear that the BBC presenter did not consider himself in the need of a producer, and he did not seem willing to take the directions that the editor of the news quiz gave him through his earpiece. This frustrated the editor so much that he began to yell through the presenter's earpiece, at which the presenter took off his earpiece and continued off-script and off-schedule. So, as the presenter was to stay on his podium for another hour and the editing team now had no contact with him, it was handed to me to act as the physical earpiece, being a messenger for the editor of the quiz and the famous BBC presenter. I spent a great part of the evening walking backwards and forwards, on the podium in front of the news industry and the team editing the news quiz show, with little written notes with instructions to the presenter from his editor.

Towards the end of the night, I had indeed been seen by the news industry workers in the room, at which point it dawned on me that now would be the time to introduce myself if only I could spot the right gatekeeper from the BBC. I asked around to find the most influential person from the BBC, and an editor I knew from ITN pointed him out. Peter Horrocks, the Head of Television News, was standing up from his table, appearing to be about to leave. 'I'll go talk to him!' I said. 'No, no!' exclaimed the ITN editor, 'You don't just talk to Peter Horrocks, he's someone you have to be introduced to!' However, the ITN editor said he would not be able to make an introduction, as he did not really know Horrocks enough. Seizing the moment, I walked over to Horrocks and introduced myself. We talked about how I had been working as the BBC presenter's producer for the night, then about me being Danish and about the Mohammed Cartoon story, which I had been covering as a reporter for *More 4 News*. In this way, I aimed to show that I had a certain cultural capital and a practical experience within the journalism profession.[2] Then I explained my Ph.D. study, and how I was hoping that BBC would like to be included in the fieldwork. He seemed interested and said he was sure he could arrange for me to stay inside the BBC newsroom for a period of time, and he gave me the number of one of his Personal Assistants who would arrange the details of my stay. The next day, I had officially been granted permission to do a month of fieldwork at the BBC newsroom.

I have included all these details in the story of how I got access to the BBC as I believe it illustrates a crucial point in the relationship between the academic world and the media, researchers and practitioners. The media practitioners are very open to each other. Although they compete, they often meet socially; they are very keen to show each other around their newsroom. Similarly, different broadcasters share information and even equipment when out covering stories and in need of a lead, a microphone or a satellite dish.[3] However, the openness and sharing of information does not extend to academics interested in researching the news workers. Rather, as shall be highlighted further in the following chapters, journalists appear guarded towards researchers from outside their profession. Thus, the profession and practical experience works as a boundary gate keeping some in and others out.

When I presented myself physically as 'one of them' – a news worker about to do academic research, rather than primarily an academic with an interest in news – I was let through the boundary gate, accepted, listened to and granted access. Before that, I was forwarded to different secretaries and voicemails. After *The Ultimate News Quiz*, my emails to the BBC always received replies. The story of how I met one of the key people at the BBC News serves to illustrate how chance and luck often play a big part in fieldwork, as Buchanan et al. (1988: 56) have explained: '[N]egotiating access for the purpose of research is a game of chance, not of skill'.

Another point illustrated here, important to accessing media organisations as with accessing organisations in general (Mascarenhas-Keyes 2001: 214), is the necessity of finding the key person and the right gatekeeper to talk to. Once access has been discussed with the key person, the constant contact and actual arrangements are made with the key person's equally powerful Personal Assistant. Of course there is also something to be said for meeting in person and talking directly to a key gatekeeper. But I believe it was crucial to my initial conversation with the BBC Head of News that I could talk his language, and that I had shown myself to be a part of the team of news workers behind an event as close-knit as an evening with news workers, held only for news workers, talking about news stories.

The challenge of being a part of my field

Much as my previous career has helped this study, it has also been a challenge, both to the project and to me personally. Arguably, already being familiar with the field makes me blind to certain facts and biased towards others.[4] During my journalistic career, I became socialised into the world of journalism. Having worked as a news journalist, I began to share routines, norms, values and traditions with news workers that I neither noticed nor questioned. I did not initially consider it interesting that news workers did not show much emotion in the newsroom, as I was used to this fact and had always personally taken it for granted that one goes outside of the newsroom to cry, argue or show other emotions that are not suitable for the role of a journalist. It was only when I began realising that I did not feel able to write in my notebook at certain times inside the newsroom and began going inside the toilet cubicle, the corridors and the empty edit suites to write, that I began considering how being in the newsroom affects behaviour. This made me take an interest in how people behaved outside the newsroom in the more private places, compared to how they acted inside it, and I was surprised to find how differently people behaved. My surprise at this made me wonder why people acted differently and consider the type of behaviour that was acceptable in the newsroom and the forms of behaviour that were never displayed. Perhaps a researcher who had not already been a part of the newsroom would have begun to wonder at an earlier point why there were not more diverse emotions displayed.

As can be seen throughout this study, in many ways, the fact that I have been one of the people studied has had a great influence on my project. These influences are manifold, ranging from the initial idea stage to the access, the fieldwork and the final book in hand. Firstly, the idea of this project came about inside a newsroom, rather than outside it. Rather idealistically, my initial aim was for this project to make a difference to news workers in particular, rather than to academics in general. In a sense, I wanted to do what Aristotle terms a Practical Science (*phronēsis*), concerned with making knowledge in order to better the Productive Science of journalism.

Secondly, having worked as a TV journalist before made my participation less challenging than if I had been new to the profession. I also believe that the fact that I had worked in TV journalism before made staff more open to me than if I had been thought of as primarily an academic.

Thirdly, and crucially, the fact that I had already worked for an established news organisation greatly facilitated the process of getting access to study another newsroom. Had I not already worked as a journalist, I could not have been granted the access I got to do this study, both in terms of access to the broadcasters and their newsrooms, but also to their various editorial meetings and daily work. The issue of access is crucial to newsroom studies and cannot be emphasised enough. Academia's struggle with getting access to study news workers seems particularly poignant, as news workers themselves expect access to all areas of authority (Cottle 2001).

'The others are in too!' – Gaining access by having some already

Soon after having negotiated access to the BBC newsroom, I sent an email to the Head of News at DR, telling him that the BBC had agreed to be a part of my study and that, if interested, they could be a part of it too. The News Editor agreed to have a meeting with me at the offices that DR had just moved into at Ørestaden in Copenhagen.

At the arranged time and day I turned up to the broadcaster's newly opened headquarters, DR-byen, which still had scaffolding and was surrounded by cranes, tractors and plenty of builders at work. I went to the entrance information desk and was asked to wait in the lobby, as the Head of News was busy. For half an hour I sat waiting behind the glass wall in the busy new lobby at the bottom of a rolling staircase going up towards the newsroom. Feeling forgotten, I then again went up to the information desk. I was told that the Head of News was now no longer answering his phone. Suddenly, I saw a face I knew, Arne Notkin, the then head of DR2 was walking down the rolling stairs. I had met Notkin a year earlier at the former DR News building while I was sent to Denmark working on the Mohammed Cartoon story as a reporter for British TV. I walked up to him and was glad to see he remembered me, and we chatted about the stories I had been working on when we last met. Then, finally, the Head of News arrived to pick me up and I parted with Notkin, at which the Head of News appeared tense and slightly confused. The initial interest from the Head of News appeared to be how I had come to know Arne Notkin (the Head of DR2).

When I explained that I had a working relationship with Notkin, as I had been a reporter for British TV, the Head of News appeared less tense, exclaiming, as he opened the door to the newsroom, 'Ah, so you are a journalist too, then of course you must have seen newsrooms before!?' He explained that there are many academics interested in visiting their newsroom, but have never seen a newsroom before.

To commence the meeting, I began explaining the details of my study. But after I had confirmed that both the BBC and ITV had agreed to be part of my study, we did not talk much more about the project. Instead, we chatted about news stories of the day and what news stories I had been covering in Britain, until the Head of News suddenly interrupted me by asking when it would suit me to begin fieldwork with them. 'Because', he said, 'of course we would like to be *a part* of the study'.

I believe having already gained access to the two largest and most elite TV newsrooms in Britain was a defining factor for me gaining access to the Danish Public Service Broadcaster, DR. It should be noted that the access that I was granted to all four newsrooms was unlimited. I stressed to every broadcaster the necessity that I would be allowed to enter *all* meetings and be allowed to work along *any* staff inside the newsroom at *all* times in order to make the most fair, unbiased and true account of news work. This, it appeared, was not a type of access that the broadcasters were accustomed to granting.

Naturally, a major reason for hesitation with giving access to an organisation may be the fear that the access will be used to reveal events and information that the organisations would prefer to keep hidden. Thus, a reason for being granted access by an organisation is that the gatekeeper has trust in the researcher to not do that.[5] This trust is no doubt strengthened if the researcher in question is seen as being 'one of us' – someone who is not out to question the very basis of existence of the people studied. Furthermore, if the researcher has been accepted by fellow organisations, in this case two news broadcasters to which DR considers themselves comparable, the trust is no doubt strengthened too.

By this rationale, it is no surprise that gaining access to the last newsroom of the four broadcasters, the TV2 in Odense, Denmark, did not take long. Meeting up with the newsroom head (Danish: *redaktionschef*) at TV2, I explained how the three other broadcasters had agreed to give me unlimited access to their newsroom and news workers for the study. Though the News Editor at first did think it an extensive access, he too agreed after being told of the other broadcasters' involvement.

Apart from the BBC, who later withdrew a substantial part of their access due to a surprise-announcement of staff cuts at the time of my fieldwork, the three other broadcasters kept their initial promise of access to all areas at all times. As will be highlighted in the following, during fieldwork I was not entirely sure of the unlimited access and felt that the process of negotiation was constant. However, looking back at the period, the access I was granted really did remain unlimited.

2.2 Conducting Fieldwork in Newsrooms

Traditionally, anthropologists have conducted fieldwork in places in which the field is limited by a village gate, a country or a language. In this defined space, the 'natives' have been thought to 'dwell, practicing traditional authentic culture' (Murphy 2011: 381). In this sense, the space of fieldwork has been viewed as a bounded entity that the researcher can go in and out of, such as an island, a village or a far-away tribe in a society disconnected from the researcher's own.

I have not been able to make such defined boundaries in what constitutes my field. Rather, I have chosen to view the TV journalists at work, from a specific selection of broadcasters, as my field, and therefore let the geographical areas of research be expanded at any time to wherever these journalists, employed by the BBC, ITV, DR and TV2, venture. In this sense, my field has no set tangible borders, but could be said to exist only in the mind of the journalists, as they set the limits to where they are able to venture in order to work.

Fieldwork as a strategy

Throughout this book, I make use of the term 'fieldwork' as a frame to encompass the methods, the time and the physical space within which I have conducted participant observation. But what research strategies are entailed when doing fieldwork from an anthropological perspective?

Venturing into a foreign field in order to 'evaluate people in terms of what they actually do, i.e. as material agents working in a material world, and not merely of what they say and do' (Miller 1997: 16–17 in Macdonald 2001: 86) and physically 'being there', is a fundamental ethnographic commitment. Historically, anthropologists have travelled to exotic, faraway places in order to write about foreign cultures for and to colleagues at home. This project has been done otherwise. Firstly, I have myself been a part of the culture that I am studying and do still feel part of the culture of journalists.[6] Secondly, the culture of newsrooms is not so different to the everyday culture of Denmark or Britain, as to make the lives of the news workers appear exotic. When fieldwork takes place among people of a different culture than that of the researcher, the relevance of anthropological theories and methods may seem most apparent (Hansen 1995: 118). However, when the culture, habits and everyday life studied are similar to one's own, it is equally important to apply theories and methods for finding out what can be understood, what meaning can be gained.

I had numerous experiences of confusion and frustration during this project. When sitting in at editorial meetings, I was often irritated by editors' and News Editor's constant use of the phrase '*that* is a good news story!', as it would generally stop all discussions about whether or not to select an event as news. I was frustrated by the extent to which this sentence could drain all discussion, and then I was further confused when I noticed that, even though staff might appear to be agreeing with an editor during a meeting, they might disagree with the same editor in practice and define what he saw as 'good' work as incorrect. Experiences such as these made me begin to consider how staff may use the editorial meetings as a stage for performance. In time, I decided to explore this phenomenon further, which made me conclude that the practice communities within the newsroom are the crucial forum for bonding and sharing values and ideals, whereas the editorial meetings were primarily a place for acting out already determined roles. Moreover, I decided to ask as many of the news staff as possible to explain to me what they saw as a 'good news story'.

Another frustration I encountered during fieldwork was the amount of repeated phrases staff gave me when asked the same question. First, when I asked staff to compare their news division to a news division from the competitor's broadcaster, I was told that the news divisions were entirely different from each other. They expressed an assumption of difference that I had expected, and therefore I felt in control of my research field when staff told me that they thought themselves very different from their competitors. As it had been key to my research that news staff at public service newsrooms worked differently, I had also expected staff to define their operational values, such as a 'good news story' and 'public service', entirely differently. But they did not. When I asked staff at the public service newsrooms the exact same questions as I had asked staff at the commercial broadcast newsrooms, I was often given the same replies. At first, I was frustrated by the fact that staff defined themselves as different and then in turn provided the same answers to my questions, and it made me consider not asking the same questions to all the news staff.

In situations like this one, we could either choose to think that the others are strange and irrational and overly sensitive, or we can use methods of anthropology to, as Ploug Hansen writes, 'note that we have not understood which rules and meaning (theories) are important among those we are right now together with' (1995: 119, my translation from Danish). The principle idea behind methods of anthropology, then, is that there is something to be understood (Hastrup 1992: 7), a meaning to be found and interpreted from the field in which one is situated, wherever that field may be and however obvious, irritating or strange the situation may seem at the time. In this sense, the strategy of fieldwork is to constantly work towards avoiding personal prejudice and preconceptions by trying to understand what is of matter to a group of people. To me, this approach meant that I began changing my fieldwork focus from one of looking for differences to one of accepting similarities and agreement between people from whom I had expected disagreement.

The round-dance

Fieldwork is a process, an education, and a theory in action.
(Gudeman and Rivera 1995: 244)

As shown in the examples above, through the ethnographic approach I have aimed to let the empirical findings lead to theories on how newsrooms work, rather than the other way around. Thus, I did not commence with a theory that I sought to apply to and confirm in the field. My execution of research did not progress in a straight line, but rather in lines that loop are interwoven and at times seem circular in their development forward (Ingold 2007), and neither my main focus nor my findings could have been predicted before research began. My strategy within fieldwork has been to work neither deductively or inductively but through a process of iteration. In this sense, as anthropologist Carl Cato Wadel (1991: 129) did, I have seen the qualitative research process as a 'round-dance' between theory, method and data while doing fieldwork. Wadel's frequently quoted circular description of the anthropological method has been an inspiration and an assurance that changing focus is not only an accepted but a necessary way of working methodologically during fieldwork.

The 'round-dance', as Wadel terms it, takes place due to many and varied factors. One factor could be that the researcher's method does not enable the study of what the researcher sets out to study. Another factor could be that the researcher's observations cannot be adequately described through the theories that the researcher set out with, and therefore the researcher may return to studying theories or think of an entirely new set of terms to work with. These, in turn, may lead the researcher to approach the fieldwork with a new interest or hypothesis.

Both my theories of the field and the method with which I collected data changed many times during my research. Thus, I have come to agree with Gudeman and Rivera's quote above, that the act of doing fieldwork in itself provides a theory, which is constantly being learned through the ongoing process of being in the field. When I began realising that news staff from all four different news divisions gave almost exactly the same answers to similar questions, I first thought there was no need to keep asking. But rather than stop asking people the same questions, I began taking note of the agreements that appeared to be expressed through their answers, and I employed these as key to creating a list of shared definitions (see Chapter 7 in which I illustrate one of these lists as Eight Key Factors to make a 'good news story'). Also, as I noticed similarities among the four different newsrooms, rather than the differences that I had expected, I decided to change my focus and be open to the possibility of the newsrooms being more similar than different. According to Becker (quoted in Wolcott 1995: 160), the essence of all qualitative research is that it is *designed in the doing*. This project is no exception to Becker's claim. It was formed on an assumption about what would be the focus, but then when my experiences in fieldwork falsified this first assumption, I let my field guide and educate me in changing and readjusting focus.

It was my constant challenge to not jump to conclusions. Rather, using different methods of data-collection during fieldwork such as (but not limited to) observation, personal experiences while participating, talking and interviewing, I have repeatedly tested my theories against each method, probing whether evidence and findings could be methodologically tested. In this way, I have constantly moved in a circular fashion, from experiences and observations in the field to theories and presentations of the field.

Participant observation – A balance act

Participant observation is the somewhat alluring umbrella term, which is primarily used to cover what an anthropologist does. The term implies that participant observation is a universally understood method. However, there is no universal consensus about its meaning, as anthropologist Ton Otto writes:

> [...] the term 'participant observation' is mystifying, because it suggests a straightforward and clear-cut methodology about which there is wide consensus, whereas in practice it covers quite different ways of data collection and correspondingly different kinds of knowledge. Moreover it elides the extremely important issue of the role of the real participants in the society under study, the local people, whose decision it really is as to what kind of participation the researcher will experience.
>
> (Otto 1997: 96)

If one overall definition of participant observation should be made, it could be that it is a term for collecting data among people, while the researcher to some extent participates in the social life of the researched. The venues for this participation are the fieldwork sites.[7] As the term implies, participant observation involves *both* participation and observation.

Participating while researching has provided me with a unique insight into the group of TV news workers that I studied. Additionally, I have felt that working practically together with journalists, cameramen and editors in their everyday work has made me complicit in the journalism produced at the time of fieldwork. As a researcher, this role of an accomplice has given me new experiences and insights rarely granted to academic researchers.[8] Historically, researchers (i.e. Tuchman 1973; Gans 1979) who have done ethnographies of newsrooms, have not been participating while observing. Although participant observation is taken to be the ideal method of research, with the exception of Hannerz's (2004) work on foreign news correspondents, actual participation by both past and recent researchers of news production has been scarce. As mentioned in a newly published overview of media ethnography, news production ethnography has emphasised the objective nature of data collection and thus leans towards observation and away from the emic-etic interpretive work necessitated where participation is given full partnership in methodological practice (Murphy 2011: 386). As I have strived to give participation a level partnership with observation, my study and methods thus differ from most other studies of news production practices.

As Otto describes it above, at each site of fieldwork, the participant gains a different role, a different access and thus a different type of participant observation. Moreover, in the relationship between different informants in the field, the researcher may play different roles, which enable different types of participation. During my fieldwork, the most dominant role I found myself in was that of *fellow-news-journalist-interested-in-how-you-do-things-here*, and within this role I was on the same level as the informants and was expected to understand their general language and their way of working, but I would also be expected to be interested in how things are done differently in this particular newsroom. This role enabled me to be attentive and engage with what the news workers found important and meaningful in their everyday work.

Another role I played was *The Student*, keen to learn from my informants. This role put my informants in the *Master* role, and meant that I was allowed to ask 'silly questions', such as asking for 'right ways of doing things' and definitions of the words and phrases that are often used in the newsroom, such as a 'SPIB', an 'Attack', the 'Dream Team' or a 'Just-Fucking-Do-It' reporter (see Figure 1). When out filming, I was in the role of *The Assistant*, helping a reporter by holding a camera or discussing how to edit a long interview. During the early stages of fieldwork, I was primarily in the role of *The Academic Researcher*, with whom few seemed keen to engage, so in time I found it most fruitful to stay in any other role. Indeed, as Wadel has expressed it, 'staying in different local roles makes it easier to be in the field *as* researcher' (1991: 62, own translation from Norwegian).

That I have myself been a journalist means that my role was more that of a colleague or a companion than a stranger. I can only speculate about others' perception of me. While I have listed a number of roles that I thought myself playing, there may also be roles that I was perceived to play of which I was unaware, but which influenced the way participants interacted with me. As I could take part in the everyday work with a sense of already knowing some of the daily practices in the newsroom, I was capable of participating in the everyday life actively, without the participants constantly feeling 'observed' (Wadel 1991: 28). The fact that the researcher can easily experience the role of the participant is a reason that some qualitative researchers argue that one should start research 'where you are – to use current situations or past involvement as a topic of research' (Lofland and Lofland 1984: 2).

During my fieldwork, which involved four different broadcasters and newsrooms, each environment provided a different kind of experience of participation. At some broadcasters, editors were keen for me to participate in the everyday work; at others, editors appeared more sceptical of my participation, and later some of that scepticism waned as I began to participate in discussions, and, to a greater extent, 'talking their language' (Lofland and Lofland 1984: 2).

Before commencing participant observation, I had planned that the participation part of my fieldwork would consist of any practical tasks that I could help journalists with in their everyday work. I mentioned this at my initial meetings with the newsroom editors of each broadcaster. Except for the editor at ITV News, who had known me as a journalist, the editors seemed puzzled at the suggestion that I should work while observing.

As it is crucial to participant observation to become involved in the practices of the people studied, being allowed to participate practically was important to me. As I had already had training and experience in TV journalism, I presumed it would feel natural for me to work and to be able to find elements in the daily work of the journalists that I could help with. Had I not had experience working as a TV journalist, I would have felt less certain that I would be able to participate while observing.

Although practically I felt able to work at a TV newsroom, I also felt challenged by the newsroom editors to explain why my participation would be valuable to them: 'Working with a journalist will make me understand much better how that journalist feels, what the realities are for the journalists and why the journalists work as they do', I said to the News Editor at DR. Still, he did not seem keen for me to work while observing. First, he told me that he would hire new journalists if more were needed – then he said he thought I could obtain a proper sense of what working at DR's TV Avisen was like just by being in their newsroom and maybe interviewing some of the journalists that knew most about working there. This discussion, which is indeed indicative of the fundamental differences between anthropology and journalism, ended as I acknowledged his way of seeing things, but emphasized that participating while observing was crucial to the academic method that I had been employed to put into practice. He finally told me that as long as I only participated and helped journalists who specifically asked me for help, I was welcome to participate in work while observing.

Having had this discussion meant that I was wary about asking to do practical work at DR, and I initially felt that all the editors were sceptical of my participation. However, in time, my experience of participation altered, and I became more and more included in the everyday work. The work I did on an everyday basis differed greatly, and included, for instance, me engaging in a discussion of a story during a newsroom meeting, suggesting people to interview for a story or, more practically, holding a camera, filming and discussing how to edit a news piece when a reporter asked for my opinion. Also, I often took part in discussing which parts of a recorded interview to use, and I was a part of the general discussions at debrief meetings. When I began participating publicly through, for instance, discussing news stories at larger meetings, the journalists changed their attitudes towards my participation, and they then invited me to work alongside them. As a female reporter on the business desk of DR Nyheder told me:

> In the beginning, I thought you were just someone who sat and stared at us. It is not that easy to understand that you are not an academic but a journalist. It has to be experienced to be understood.
>
> (DR Field Diary, 22 June 2007)

At DR, there was a group of reporters who had kept away from me in the first few weeks of my stay. Whenever I came near their desk, I was told they did not quite have the time for me to hang around. One day, I bumped into one of these reporters in the canteen and talked to her about a story I had worked on as a reporter, and afterwards she exclaimed: 'Oh, but I thought you were an academic!' and then promptly invited me to follow her work for a few days. After this, the entire group of reporters were keen for me to interview them. Among journalists, I found academic researchers to be viewed with suspicion.[9]

Thus, my experiences through participation changed greatly during fieldwork, as journalists began to view me as 'one of them' and I began to move from participation to observation of their everyday work. Both at TV2 and at DR it appeared that I began participating more with and in the field the longer I stayed. At my old newsroom, ITV News, my experience of participation was diametrically opposite: Here it seemed I participated more at the beginning of my fieldwork and gradually participated less.

Practically, the access to do fieldwork was very different at the different sites and newsrooms. At ITV News for instance, I was encouraged to participate in making the news already after the first editorial meeting I went to. During that first editorial meeting, which I took part in as a 'participant observer', I wrote in my field note book:

> An editor I used to work alongside in the newsroom suddenly turns round to me and asks: 'Are you *working* while observing?' At which the meeting suddenly stops and all eyes are on me. 'Yes, I'd love to help while I'm here', I say. Instantly, I get put on a story to work on and research for the day.
>
> (ITV Field Diary, 32)

During that first editorial meeting, I was given the task of researching facts to support a news story that the Programme Editor and News Editor had already decided to bring that same evening.[10] The facts and figures I was asked to supply were to be presented on the large electronic screen wall by the TV news reader after a news story. As it turned out, the story I was asked to research that day took up so much of my time that I had no time left for writing notes about what I was observing, or indeed to talk to people in the newsroom. As the day unfolded, I began feeling a sense of pressure from the Programme Editor to get the right facts to support their story by the time the evening news bulletin would be broadcast. This experience gave me a sense of participating and made me feel much closer to the lived experience of a journalist at work than an interview about the practice of researching stories could have provided – but it also made me feel overwhelmed with participation and unable to spend sufficient time observing and talking to the people I was in fact studying.

As I had already worked at ITV in the capacity of a journalist, I was given this task as I was accepted as an insider to the working practices in the newsroom already on the first day, a status that I had to work months to earn inside the newsrooms of the other broadcasters. However, at ITV News, it soon became challenging to find an equal balance between everyday participative work in the newsroom and observation of other journalists at work. The crucial difference from the ITV Newsroom and the others was of course that the people in the ITV Newsroom had previously known me as a participant solely. Therefore, the notion that I should suddenly return in the capacity of observer was odd. Rather than being participant observer, I began to feel like primarily a participant, albeit an observing participant. After having realised this, I talked to the editors of ITV about giving me slightly less responsibility and rather the opportunity to work alongside other journalists than work on a story alone. I had to negotiate a new role for my time of fieldwork at ITV, a role in which I should constantly work at stepping back from practicing and taking time talking to journalists and letting them work, thus apologising to my former editor that I could not work as if I was back to my old job. In this sense, at ITV, I was already known as a 'native'. Thus, returning to the newsroom I used to work in meant that I was expected to behave like one of them, not like an outsider. According to Clifford Geertz, what the anthropologist should be aiming for is not to become or get inside the heads of the studied people, for that is impossible. Rather, the anthropologist should aim to grasp and present the native's point of view (Geertz 1983). Or, if, as Geertz has expressed it, culture is a product of acting social beings 'trying to make sense of the world in which they find themselves' (Ortner 1984: 130), then we must try to grasp the actors' point of view. In presenting my fieldwork, I have chosen to use both the news workers' own descriptions of themselves and each other (in Chapter 3 especially) as well as my own experiences of how the different news divisions compare. Letting the news staff introduce their own values as compared to those of the competitor's news division, I have found a useful way to illustrate what I have found to be an institutional assumption of difference and originality. Using my own observations, I then proceed to illustrate how I have personally experienced there to be more similarities than differences across the four news divisions.

How best to 'get the joke'

How can a researcher claim to achieve an experience of what someone else feels? What I have aimed to do in connecting with news workers at all levels of the four news broadcasters resembles Geertz's idea of balancing between *experience-near* concepts and *experience-distant* ones. Writing about how to contemplate 'the native's point of view', Geertz makes use of these two distinctions (experience-near and experience-distant) first formulated by psychoanalyst

Heinz Kohut.[11] By Geertz's definitions, to capture the everyday life of people one should not begin to think that one has an omnipotent capability to 'think, feel and perceive' like the studied people (Geertz 1983: 56). The best a participant observer can aim to do instead, he argues, is to see things 'from the native's point of view' and describe them without being seeped in their worldview.[12] To Geertz, seeing and explaining things from the native's point of view involves a balancing act between what he defines as using both experience-near and experience-far concepts.

Where experience-distant concepts describe the way that specialists work through analysing and categorising phenomena, experience-near concepts are those which the studied people use. Again, borrowing from the language of psychoanalysis, Geertz gives the example of 'love' being an experience-near concept, which compares to the experience-distant concept 'object-cathexis' (1983). From the world of newsrooms one could add that the concept 'a good news story' is an experience-near concept, which in experience-distant terms can be described as 'a journalist's performance'. If one is to avoid getting accounts that are neither biased nor overly subjective, or blind to the language and feelings of the people, it is crucial for the participant observer to keep this balancing act in mind. Moreover, during fieldwork, a constant negotiation of positions takes place, a constant dialectic between self and other in making sense of the structures and meanings that comprise what is understood to constitute 'culture'. From this perspective, doing participant observation is a combination of comparable strategies. This balancing act is not dissimilar to what Gregor and Tuzin have described as 'illuminat[ing], at the same time, the phenomenon that we observe and the epistemological profile of our questions' (Gregor and Tuzin 2001: 15).

I have found this balancing act to be an ongoing struggle, which, much like Cato Wadel's round-dance, has needed constant consideration. My first challenge was to be able to approximate the TV journalists at work enough to understand how they experience their situation, and then to be able to find important elements in their life to see wider perspectives and to categorise their lived experience into meaningful concepts. As Geertz writes:

> To grasp concepts that, for another people, are experience-near, and to do so well enough to place them in illuminating connection with experience-distant concepts theorists have fashioned to capture the general features of social life, is clearly a task at least as delicate, if a bit less magical, as putting oneself into someone else's skin. [...] The trick is to figure out what the devil they think they are up to.
>
> (Geertz 1983: 58)

To me, the goal with participant observation is to be able to achieve an experience-near sense that could not be achieved through practice-distant research only. Using experience-distant concepts in turn ensures the reliability of the analysis. But to figure out what the people studied think they are up to, how does one manage to capture the most important elements within this particular group, the ones Geertz calls the 'general features of social life'? How does one know what is important to this particular group of people, and (crucially) what is not?

Upon realising that all staff members do not actually do what they say in an editorial meeting and that they do not always agree with the editor, how should I determine that this is interesting and worth including in an ethnographic account? When I attempted to explain participant observation as a method to journalists during fieldwork, I was often asked what exactly I was looking for. When I described the type of things I was making a note of, one reporter at DR asked me: 'How do you know what is important to look out for?' and 'How can you make sure you don't end up with a lot of uninteresting notes about what kind of shoes we wear? Don't you feel like you are wasting your time on some things?'. At first I found her questions irritating, a sign that she had simply not understood my method. Then I began thinking about the different messages implied within her question. I learned at least two things from her questions. Firstly, I understood that to this reporter, it was crucial to know exactly what her story should be before she went out into a field, and that spending time on information, which was not relevant to that one story, would be essentially a waste of time. Secondly, I began understanding that I should not expect the journalists I was studying to appreciate or agree with my methods. Additionally, as I will return to later, her question and those made by her colleagues, made me return and review the search list that I had compiled before beginning fieldwork.

Her questions also made me reconsider what exactly I was looking for, and whether she was, in fact, right that I was spending too much time jotting down uninteresting facts. I studied the notes I had made about conversations, times and numbers of things I had found interesting at the time. I found scribbled notes on how many cameramen were to be sent on a certain assignment, how many times a meeting was interrupted by a mobile phone call, and other apparently random facts and quotes. I re-read my initial plan for the fieldwork and remembered that what I was looking for was their everyday life, the culture of the news workers at work. The best way I could think of finding out what was most important elements in describing their everyday was to make a note of all that I thought important, and what I thought *they* found important during the time I spent among them.

'What is your story?' or: What I was looking for in the field

While doing this study, I have frequently been questioned by journalists about 'what story' I am writing. Initially, during the first meetings with news editors and other gatekeepers about whether I could get permission to study the newsroom, they would ask me 'what kind of angle' I was taking on the newsroom, 'what I wanted to study exactly'. Then, as described earlier, during the time I spent as a participant observer in the newsrooms, journalists would ask me what story 'I was looking for', and before an interview, journalists would ask 'what kind of quote I was interested in'. Finally, while writing up this book, journalists have queried: '[S]o…what *is* your story?'. Questions such as these lead me to the insight that the idea of having a story and being able to express it in one, easily graspable sentence is crucial to the people I studied.

Beginning this study, it was my aim to not have any one specific angle, before I entered the newsroom as a researcher. Rather, I aimed to let 'the story' arrive during the fieldwork, through living with the news workers in their everyday environment. From the very first moment of researching news workers I took notes on all experiences, relating to how journalists perceived themselves and their work. During fieldwork, I felt confused at times as to what exactly to look for in the everyday work, what to include in my Field Diary and what not to include.

Inspirational Search List – What I *could* look for inside the newsroom

INDIVIDUAL AND THE GROUP
- *How does the individual relate to the group in the newsroom?*
- *How are the borders between the individual, the viewers, the politicians etc. drawn?*
- *Who is important in terms of decision-making? The imagined viewer? The boss? The society?*

RELATION TO THE SELF AND OTHERS
- *How do individuals in the room relate themselves to people outside of the room?*
- *Through which images, metaphors and categories is society described?*
- *How is the line drawn, if any, between Us news workers and The Others?*

THE ROOM
- *How have rooms been organised in cultural terms?*
- *What is near/far, up/down, in/out, central/periphery in the room?*
- *How are possible border areas between being in/out of the room created?*

THE IDEA OF TIME
- *How is time defined and prioritised?*
- *How is time organised in the everyday, in weekday cycles, seasons etc.?*

LANGUAGE AND METAPHORS
- *What types of metaphors are used in the everyday? Are some repeated more than others?*

MORAL AND PRESTIGE
- *What is seen as right and wrong, good and bad?*
- *How is it tackled if an individual is seen as 'acting wrongly'?*
- *What is seen as prestigious and aspired to among news workers?*

FROM EVENT TO NEWS
- *How does a story appear, and how is it changed into being 'news'?*
- *How is the news flow formatted?*
- *Who decides what events are news? And how?*

Search List, constructed with inspiration from Ehn and Löfgren ([2001] 2006: 30–34).

These times of confusion I consider crucial to my process of fieldwork. At times, particularly in the early stages, I found it challenging to know where to look to take notes, and I felt intimidated by the questions about the story I was writing, and I worried that I could offer the enquiring journalists no reply. At such times, I found it inspiring to re-read research into fieldwork methods. I was particularly inspired in new ways of looking at the same phenomenon through researchers of culture such as Ehn and Löfgren ([2001] 2006). In their book on analysing culture, Ehn and Löfgren recommend making a *Search List*, with ideas for what to keep an interest in when being in the field. Inspired by their idea of a Search List, I made my own version, which I consulted whenever I felt confused or at a loss about things to look at and people to talk to in the newsroom. While I consider the feeling of confusion and boredom essential to achieving a near-experience to the everyday life of the people in the newsroom, having a Search List in the back of my mind aided me in seeing things in a new light, helping me to feel that I had 'a story' and a set of tangible questions I was seeking answers to.

At times, the above search list worked as a body of concrete questions that I could hold on to, while feeling swept away by diffuse and undefined experiences as a participant observer. As such, the search list was not a primary focus during fieldwork, but a few times, when I felt I needed to have something particular to search for, I consulted my list, which I initially compiled in early 2007.

2.3 Access: A Constant Negotiation

TV news workers in Public Service Broadcasters and at the two largest commercial broadcasters in Britain and Denmark are the focus of this research. In this sense, the setting for my research was not a pre-given place. Geographically, this took me as a participant observer to TV newsrooms in two different countries, a multitude of sites, events and journeys where news workers go in order to bring news back to the newsroom. Also, I went to places where staff go in their time off work – such as the smoking room, the canteen or the pub.

On the first day of fieldwork, I was given a pass in each newsroom so I could enter all the doors that other news staff could, I was given my own login to the computer system so I could enter the shared virtual network, and then I was told to find a desk. But as staff inside a newsroom rarely have a personal desk, neither did I. Rather, every day I arranged to work alongside a different person and follow his/her daily work, either while working on a screen or out of the newsroom to cover stories. When it seemed there was less interest in being observed, or when the journalists I was observing were primarily waiting for news to happen, I would find my own desk in the newsroom. On an everyday basis, I would turn up early for the first editorial meeting of the day, then ask a news worker if I could sit next to him/her for a while and stay alongside this person for an hour or for the entire day. At times, I would walk about in the newsroom and talk to different people, asking if they would mind me following them for a while. I would enter different rooms, such as the graphics room or the coffee room, or different places within the open office space of the newsroom.

I made some arrangements with reporters to follow them on set days, but generally I did not pre-arrange who I would be working along with on a given day, as the unpredictable nature of news work meant that staff did not feel able to plan a time or place they would be in beforehand.

As well as participant observation, I have conducted interviews, both recorded and written, collected material in the field, such as stylebooks and introduction videos to new staff, and kept hand-outs, such as running orders and idea lists from editorial meetings. Additionally, I have kept news numerous bulletins digitally and taken photos in the field, only some of which are included in this book. I worked along with journalists from all four newsrooms, spending first a full working month as a participant observer in each newsroom, and since returning to the newsrooms for follow-up interviews, day-long visits and filming of news reports or special news programmes outside of the newsroom. This method applies to the three newsrooms of ITV News, DR TV Avisen and TV2 Nyhederne. The BBC Newsroom, however, I spent only half the initial time inside, as my first week of fieldwork there coincided with the announcement that up to 10% of the BBC workforce was to lose their jobs. After this announcement, which came as a big surprise to staff, the newsroom mood and work environment was altered considerably, and my access and their openness to my study was affected.[13] After the fieldwork period, I returned to each newsroom in order to conduct follow-up interviews, and I stayed in touch with my field through other visits, both in and out of newsrooms and through Internet and phone. In summary, the main sources of data are:

- Long-term participant observation of an initial 18-month period, following the journalists at work in and out of the newsrooms. Thereafter, repeated visits and constant contact with the newsrooms. The last of these visits took place during two day-long shifts at the TV 2 newsroom in Copenhagen, December 2017.
- Over 100 interviews, both recorded and written, and both formal and semiformal.
- Material collected in the field, such as style books and introduction videos to new staff, and hand-outs, such as running orders and idea lists from editorial meetings.
- News products, news programming and news bulletins broadcasts.
- Photos of the newsroom and of the staff at work during my fieldwork.
- Five Field Diaries written during fieldwork

The above list is an attempt to explain and measure the different ways in which I have collected the information on which this book is based. However, this study relies on many other sources of data that have not been included here. Some types of data I believe cannot be adequately contained in a list such as the one above, as it derives primarily from memories or associations while being there. In the above, I have used the word 'data' for lack of a better word to express what I collected in the field.[14] However, I am not entirely satisfied with the term as a reflection of the entirety of intangible, hard-to-measure sources such as emotions or bodily experiences. For instance, my own exhaustion, excitement, boredom and a range of other emotions were indeed also part of my data sources.

In anthropological fieldwork there is no prescription as to how long one should stay among the people one intends to study. However, it is crucial to the method of anthropology that the researcher stays in the environment for so long that s/he can begin to get a grasp of what is everyday behaviour – and reaching this type of information and understanding will by definition take months or even years, rather than hours, days or weeks. Organisational researcher and anthropologist Bate (1997) suggests that good ethnography should reflect on the polyphony, the many different voices, of the real world, and offer a sense of 'being there' as well as providing unexpected details and conclusions. Goffman ([1959] 1990) would likely add that the researcher should stay long enough to be able to understand the performances and presentations of selves in the everyday life and to see beyond the front-stage-performances. Accordingly, Geertz (1983) would add that one should stay long enough in the field to be able to grasp not just the visitor's but the native's point of view. Arriving at this type of presentation necessarily requires a lengthy time spent in the field. According to Ehn and Löfgren, it is important to stay long enough to get to experience the everyday, as it is only then that the researcher can begin to note how the collective *we* thinks that it should act. Only then can the researcher attempt at mapping out what differs from the norm, and what conflicts and deviations there are to this everyday norm (2006: 164–67). To them, this is crucial for the analytical strategy of for instance making sense through contrasts, since 'what something means is closely connected to what it does not mean' (Ehn and Löfgren 2006: 164).

My primary aim has been to capture the everyday life of TV news journalists. In order to obtain the type of information, experiences and observations that I was interested in, it was therefore important to stay among the TV news journalists for a certain length of time. As it was also important to this research to compare the different practices of TV news journalists employed at different news broadcasters, I planned to stay for exactly the same amount of time at each broadcaster. Apart from BBC, I had the access and duration of stay, which I had planned and hoped for. Like other ethnographic researchers (Hirsch and Gellner 2001: 8), I wanted to stay longer at each place, worrying that I had not gathered enough 'data'. Paradoxically, I have also at times felt overwhelmed by having too much 'data' that was too diverse.

Who to include in observations?

When inside the newsroom, I was keen to talk to and spend time with many different news workers in different roles. Thus, though focusing on journalists rather than being limited to specific reporters, TV-hosts or news editors, my aim was to include everyone present inside the newsroom. My limitation, then, was the physical room rather than specific positions in the hierarchy of the newsroom. Although I started out spending time mainly inside each newsroom, I also followed news workers, e.g. photographers, stringers, journalists or reporters, out on jobs outside the room. Following news workers outside the newsroom, I would generally go for day long, sometimes only hour long, trips, and we returned to the newsroom with tapes of recorded interviews for the evening bulletin. On a few occasions, I spent time with a group of people, ranging from three to almost a hundred people, working together outside the newsroom to report on a live event.

My primary subject of research has been the journalists, a classification which can include Anchor Men, editors, reporters, producers, script writers and guest bookers. However, from the time where I myself worked inside a newsroom, I have brought with me a realisation that each individual news item broadcast is created and shaped by many different people at many levels of the newsroom. Thus, it was a given to the research that interpersonal relations in the newsroom between news workers from presenter to studio manager, director, the graphics department, programme journalist, cameraman and sub-editor to Programme Editor and News Editor, play a vital role in the final news broadcast. Therefore, although my analysis is focused on journalists, I include staff such as cameramen, graphic designers and editors in my observations. Likewise, those workers with less than full time contracts were also included. Thus, news workers such as freelance journalists, temporary staff and contracted staff are included much on the same level as their colleagues.[15] For a profession still relying on and consisting considerably of a freelance workforce, it is crucial to include freelancers, temps and contracted workers in any study. If researchers were to include only full-time permanently employed news staff in a study, the representation of the profession would be skewed if not simply incorrect. Since I have not been limited by job roles, positions or hierarchies within the organisations from the outset my study has had as its observational focus not only journalists, but everyone in the newsroom.

Following the journalist: The field is wherever the journalist goes

In constructing and carrying out this multi-sited and comparative approach to studying news making, I was at first inspired by anthropologist George Marcus' concept of strategically situated ethnography (Marcus 1995). In Marcus' view, there is a need for ethnographies in which the setting is not already determined; a space that is not fixed by the informants but by the subject or idea that the researcher wants to study. Marcus' concept of multi-sited ethnography calls for a strategically designed research following 'chains, paths, threads, conjunctions, or juxtapositions of locations in which the ethnographer establishes some form of literal, physical presence, with an explicit, posited logic of ethnography' (Marcus 1995: 105). My objective was to study the everyday work of journalists, and, as such, I let this idea decide where I went during fieldwork. If I should have continued along the ideals of Marcus, I would have not stayed among the news workers to follow their ideas and practice. Rather, I would have followed the idea of 'Public Service' in Britain, for instance, as it traverses from offices and corridors around the Department for Culture Media and Sport and at Ofcom, as they discuss the Public Service Broadcasting Charter Review, to public debates in newspapers and on the Internet about what is expected of 'Public Service', followed the idea of public service as it reaches the audiences watching news at home and discusses the news of today around their dinner table.

Although I have attended many hearings and meetings on Public Service Broadcasting in both the UK and Denmark, and I have been part of creating a public debate and a conference on Public Service, I do not aim to follow ethnographically the ideas and the practice further than the news workers.[16] In this sense, I parted with Marcus' ideals of multi-sited ethnography and drew my inspiration rather on methodologies of ethnographic comparison. However, I did use Marcus' techniques of 'following the people' as a guide in my fieldwork. This approach made me follow journalist out of the newsroom and into different locations, both in public places and in private homes looking for, filming, interviewing and researching stories. Additionally, I went to events such as *The Ultimate News Quiz*, or news award ceremonies attended by the news workers that I studied at the time. If a reporter I was following had a meeting, I would go to the same meeting, and, to the extent it was possible, I would stay with the same reporter as s/he left work and took the metro or bus home. On some occasions, I was also invited home to visit reporters, and on countless evenings I went out with reporters to the pub or a restaurant after work. My being open to invites led to many unexpected insights and opportunities that I could not have planned.

My methodological approach to studying staff working in the newsroom meant that I could not be too set on where to go, who to talk to, but allow new things gain precedence and to go down new paths if and when it seemed meaningful. This meant that working days were very long, as there were constant offers to go out shooting, going for a drink, going for lunch or turning up early the next morning to follow the early shift. In the time I had allocated to do fieldwork, I let the job be time consuming and take first priority at any time of the day – something which a number of news workers themselves told me that they did. At each of the fieldwork sites, I chose to find accommodation near the newsroom so that I could be flexible in regards to working hours, both staying late and arriving early in the mornings or in the middle of the night in order to follow the cycle of news work at all times of the day. The many shifts of work that I followed were generally ten to twelve hours long, which is similar to the daily working hours of the news workers. I primarily worked during the hours from 8am to 22pm, but as some of the early morning news bulletins invited me to work along with them, I also had shifts that began at midnight and ended with the first morning news bulletin. Getting physically exhausted after having worked weeks without a day off, or tired after long days of work together with the news workers, gave a clear feeling of being one with them; on a personal level it meant that I was unable to have much of a private life outside of the fieldwork.[17]

A field with no gate?

C. W. Anderson, who has conducted ethnographic fieldwork of journalists in what he terms the 'Philadelphia news ecosystem' (Anderson 2013), found it hard to limit the sites of his research. As he explains: '[A]s news production decentralizes, traditional methods of exploring the behaviour of journalists "at work" grow ever more problematic' (Anderson

2013: 153). During fieldwork, I had a similar struggle with determining the geographical limits of my study. As such, my field was limited to include the places where staff of the four newsrooms went. As news workers, such as reporters and cameramen, often left the physical space of the newsroom in order to cover a news story far from the confines of the newsroom, the space that I have included as my field is far from limited to the walls of the newsroom. When out covering stories along with the news workers, I have considered my field to consist of the space that they inhabit, which, by the very nature of the job, changes every day. So, although the majority of the time I spent working with news workers was spent inside the newsroom, the field of research has also covered a range of other sites that the news workers considered to be working spaces. To name a few sites, my field has included: A lawn outside parliament (when covering the Queen's Speech), venues of and around the London Fashion Show, a rapper's studio in London, the entire town of Møgeltønder (while covering a Royal Wedding in Denmark), a local school in Copenhagen and a Danish pensioner's living room.

Throughout this book, I primarily use quotes and observations gathered in fieldwork during the working hours of the news staff at each of the four broadcasters. However, as mentioned above, fieldwork has not been limited to the working hours of the news staff only, as I conducted fieldwork among journalists after work hours. While I do not frequently quote from or describe details of the time I spent with journalists outside of working hours, this level of fieldwork has nonetheless informed my study. Thus, a part of my understanding of what it means to be a news worker has been shaped by out-of-work experiences, such as when I took the underground with journalists, went to the local pub after work or visited news workers in their private homes outside of working hours.

Spending time with TV news journalists outside of their working hours gave me an insight into a side of news work that I would not have experienced had I conducted fieldwork only while staff was at work. It was during such out-of-hours fieldwork that I first began to notice a curious fact, namely that the scheduled working hours did not matter much to the TV news journalists, as they appeared to consider themselves at work at all hours of the day, and at any place, event or situation.

It was during one night out with the journalists from DR in Copenhagen that it became clear to me just how much journalists consider their job to be a calling, from which they are never off duty (see Chapter 6). Though the journalist leaves the job to go home or go to the pub, s/he never stops being a journalist. Rather, the journalists appeared to be constantly at work, often pulling out a notebook or writing down contact details and story ideas while out in bars or pubs. Among the British news workers, a few of the older, well-respected reporters and Anchor Men told me that they thought that the best stories arrive in the pub, out among 'the *real* people', so they considered going to the pub after work crucial. Similarly, the head of news at DR once told me that if he had staff enough, he would send a whole group of news workers out into the streets and bars in Denmark and hear 'what everyone is talking about, what matters to them, and then come back and make news covering the *real* stories of Denmark'.

Constant negotiations of access

Once I had negotiated access to each newsroom, I was not convinced I could rely on my access to remain unlimited. Rather, the negotiation of access was an everyday occurrence. At each newsroom, after having confirmed the date and time of my fieldwork, I was told to check that the arrangement would still be possible closer to the time of my arrival there. This was due to the nature of the job, I was told. If, for instance, there was an important news story, or something else important happening at the time I was due to arrive, then they would have to cancel my stay. Due to different circumstances, e.g. an editor being out of the office (at BBC), a redesign of the newsroom which got delayed (at TV2) and a round of job cuts (at DR), except for ITV every one of the four broadcasters in fact changed the scheduled day and time for my fieldwork.

Once inside the newsroom, it felt as if I was still negotiating access on a daily basis. Particularly during the first weeks at each newsroom, I would continually ask whether I could come along to a certain meeting, whether someone would mind me coming along for a filming or fancy eating with me at the canteen. As time went by, I gained access to different meetings, and I did not have to ask for permission to enter a specific room. But people who were initially comfortable with me being there could become less comfortable as time went by. Particularly in the newsrooms where staff cuts were under way, I felt it was necessary to continually explain my motives. At the DR newsrooms, in which rumours of staff cuts were circulating when I arrived, one group of journalists, centred on the politics desk, appeared to be particularly disinterested in talking to me. It was not until I spent my first day with the political journalists of Christiansborg (the Danish Parliament) that I understood why. When I introduced myself in person at their morning editorial meeting, one of the reporters exclaimed: 'So you are NOT working for the management?'. Because I had been introduced first in a staff email from the management, a rumour had started in the political journalists' circle that I was paid for by the management to investigate the efficiency of the staff. As Hirsch and Gellner write: 'Large organisations often have experience of management consultants. This may mean that the anthropologist is regarded as a potential enemy by staff, who assume that he or she is a management consultant whose report will recommend redundancies' (2001: 5). I had similar challenges at the other newsrooms that I went to after DR, but the experience from DR meant that I focused on continually eliminating such rumours by introducing myself as 'not working for management' and 'not doing a quality control'. In my introduction to all four newsrooms I also found it important to stress to staff that I was interested in 'not you, but the process of what you do'.

Though I did eventually gain the access I had aimed for, through the negotiating processes I learned to limit my expectations for what I was allowed to do inside the space of the newsroom as a participant observer. Thus, I had to make alterations to my initial plan for the fieldwork. Initially, for example, I hoped to film the newsrooms I visited, in order to make a visual anthropological account of my fieldwork. But the very idea of bringing a video camera to film inside a newsroom felt impossible after having struggled so much in order to get permission to be there with just a notepad. I did manage to take a photography camera into the newsrooms, but only after many months of staying in the same place, and then still with a less than warm reception by the news workers. Inside the newsrooms, as soon as the camera came out of the bag, people around me seemed to distance themselves. For instance, at DR one older reporter tapped me on my shoulder as I was looking through the lens and asked, 'are you a tourist?'.

An attempt to preserve the journalistic tribe?

> Journalists live in such a small, closed world and we protect and guard that world the best we can. I remember when we did a report about the use of drugs by politicians and X [name of a reporter] did this piece where he went into the toilets of a political party conference with a device which picked up residue from coke. And then Y [name of a journalist in the newsroom] went into our staff cubicles and found residue there too. But *that* was not a story.
> We can make stories about the politicians' drug use but not about us, when in fact we have the same problems ourselves. We don't question ourselves. That kind of reflection does not happen.
>
> (Studio manager at one of the four broadcasters, 29 August 2007)

> It is still a truism that the press engages in critical evaluation of every institution in society except itself.
>
> (Lule 1992: 92)

It is important for professionals of any profession to relate to their own practice and allow room for critical evaluation, but critical journalism about journalism is a rarity. Journalists are not the only ones who do not criticise themselves publicly. Indeed, a profession rarely criticises its own professional practices in public. Doctors, airplane pilots or bankers rarely criticise colleagues in public, and are even more rarely seen publicly questioning the foundations on which their professions rely. But expectations of critical rigour of the profession of news workers and journalists in particular are different to what is expected of pilots. As news workers are expected to be critical and inquisitive, the silence on issues of news making and lack of professional reflection is surprising.

In Britain, there is a market for critically assessing news by journalists (see for instance *Media Guardian* and the weekly Media pages of *The Independent*, the *Press Gazette* and *Media Week*), but rarely are the covered media stories critical of key professional values. Meanwhile, in Denmark, working as a journalist who wants to cover journalism is a challenging job. As one of Denmark's few media commentators has explained it: 'When one begins to dig in the journalistic products and thereby touch the process itself, the door is often quickly shut. Referring to editors in chief that go in automatic defence-position – or the silence is explained with reference to safeguarding the sources […] Journalism about journalism does not have many chances. Though it ought to' (Jensen 2009: 184, my translation from Danish). As journalist Nick Davies writes: 'Dog doesn't eat dog. That's always been the rule in Fleet Street. We dig into the world of politics and finance and sport and policing and entertainment. We dig wherever we like – but not in our own back garden' (Davies 2009: 1).

Entering any close-knit community as a researcher is a challenging affair, even if the participants of that community are willing to grant the researcher access. In his study of communities of practice, Wenger (1998a) defines the very existence of a community of people sharing practice as a boundary, which closes off for outsiders. According to Wenger, a shared working practice is a source of its own boundary, as:

1) Participants form close relationships and develop idiosyncratic ways of engaging with one another, which outsiders cannot easily enter.
2) They have a detailed and complex understanding of their enterprise as they define it, which outsiders may not share.
3) They have developed a repertoire for which outsiders miss shared references.

(Wenger 1998a: 113)

In my studies, I found Wenger's definition of the boundaries created by those sharing working practice to aptly describe the boundaries and the closeness of journalists and groups of news workers that I met. Thus, the reluctance to grant access to anyone studying news workers functions to further widen the gap between the community of those inside the journalistic profession and those outside of it.

As Buchanan et al. (1988) write on getting access to do research in organisations, the terms researchers use when getting in contact often have very negative connotations to the people within the organisation. Words such as 'research' and 'interview', they argue, have strong negative connotations, as they imply surveys and questionnaires that will be time consuming for the staff. Furthermore, words such as 'research published' can be understood as a threat that personal and commercial secrets may be printed in a leading national paper within the week. While I agree that there is a risk that the words and language used in trying to get access to organisations may instil fear within the organisation's management, I believe this fear is possibly even more accentuated among a group of people who use these same words with a different meaning. As will be shown later in this book (see Chapter 7), the very reason for doing what news workers term 'research' and 'interview' is often to 'scrutinize', to 'make organisations accountable' and to put 'dark things that happen out in the spotlight'. And of course, when work is published in a journalistic sense, this should be as far-reaching and as fast as possible. Thus, among journalists, the very idea of 'researching' and 'investigating' may instil notions of being put under more critical scrutiny than what the research is in fact aiming at. As seen in the quote from the Studio Manager above, the news staff that I worked among often talked of their community as a 'closed world', 'a tribe' or 'a family', which they liked to guard and protect. From this perspective, it seems to suit a general journalistic logic to not easily grant academic researchers entry into their world.

2.4 The Obstacle of Imagining Differences but Finding Similarities

Anthropologists are (in)famous for granting agencies for proposing one study and returning with an entirely different study (according to Agar 1986: 15). This book could no doubt reinforce that stereotype. During the ten years this book has been under way, it has undergone a change in hypothesis, theory and focus. According to Wadel (1991: 129), in qualitative research, a change of theories and hypothesis is the norm. This is of course a primary difference from quantitative research, in which the researcher sets out with a set hypothesis, theory and method and a clear assumption about the result.

As described above using Wadel's round-dance analogy, this study has employed empirical observations as the starting points for theories for understanding the culture of newsroom production – these in turn have been returned to the fieldwork and tested for empirical validity. Thus, consistencies and discrepancies between what I have experienced and seen in the field have constantly been pursued. This process, however long-winded, appears to me to be the closest I can get to a deep interpretation of the social life that I have experienced in and around the newsrooms.

It is important to stress, however, that the process of doing participant observation is not similar to going on a fishing expedition into an unknown sea. My time doing participant observation depended on prior research and identification of possible research questions. While I did not set out with an already constructed theory about the newsroom field, I did have a set of methodological starting points and sensitizing concepts from which I took the first steps into the field. These initial ideas then changed, as research focus changed during fieldwork.

Talking about differences, but acting similar

This study began with a set of sensitizing concepts made up of assumptions, expectations and personal interests. Initially, the intention of this research project was to do a comparative study of public service newsrooms and commercial ones. The intention was to use the British system by way of comparison to the Danish, and public service news institutions versus the commercially funded newsrooms. The notion of differences in working culture was a methodological starting point. Having worked in a national commercial newsroom, I approached the research with the sensitizing concept of difference between how the commercial newsroom and the way the public service newsroom works. I therefore thought it would be interesting to explicate the differences between working for a Public Service Broadcaster and a commercial one. However, though some differences between the commercial newsroom and the public service newsroom were found, I shortly began to see many more similarities than differences. Thus, initial fieldwork disproved the assumption that each newsroom and culture is very different. Rather, the more newsrooms I visited, the more similar they began to appear to me – culturally, in terms of working methods and regarding the physical newsroom layout.

The journalists that I have worked among did not imagine themselves as sharing working practices with journalists in other newsrooms. A recent study based on interviews with senior journalists in European newsrooms (including the newsrooms of ITV, BBC and DR) came to a similar conclusion, namely that there is no common or increasingly shared European journalistic culture. During in-depth interviews for the study, British journalists appeared to reject the notion of a shared journalist culture, mentioning the German and French media as being 'less vigorous, more reserved or "boring", and much less likely to deal with controversial stories than were the British media' (Preston 2009: 153).

Most journalists I have asked have told me that they work very differently compared to other journalists and colleagues in other newsrooms, and I do not find it surprising that they would reject the idea of sharing such a thing as a 'journalist culture' with any other newsrooms when asked by researchers. As my project relies on both interviews and time spent working among journalists as a participant observer, I have come to a different conclusion; namely that even though journalists say they work differently, they do in fact work very similarly, in similar settings, using similar methods.

As a former ITV journalist, I was used to talking about a certain 'ITV way of doing things', and imagined other news workers in other newsrooms as being entirely different, with a different culture to the one I came from. In the everyday work in the ITV Newsroom, and in the Channel 4 Newsroom too, we often talked about how differently we worked compared to 'The Beeb'. We would talk about how the BBC would have more and better equipment, much more money to spend. We never explicitly said it, but while working for a commercial national news broadcaster, I came to think of the rival public service journalists as having an entirely different way of behaving, thinking and being, and I assumed that their everyday working day looked entirely different compared to ours. I was therefore surprised, during my first fieldwork stay at DR's new newsroom in Ørestaden in Copenhagen, to find that the ways we worked at ITV were very similar to those of the public service journalists at DR. Not only did we have the same equipment and systems to work on, but we talked the same language, with the Danish news workers using English terms for describing news – and the layout of the room was strikingly similar (see Appendix). Then, when I reached my second fieldwork site, the BBC Newsroom, I was again surprised to see the similarities with the other two newsrooms, particularly as it turned out that the BBC Newsroom had in fact been styled according to the new newsroom at DR in Denmark. I was told that at the time of my fieldwork at the BBC, a delegation from the BBC had just returned from DR where they had been to get inspiration for the layout and design of their new multimedia newsroom.

At the BBC, I was also surprised to see so many old colleagues from ITV News, who I had before seen as staunch 'ITV men', now being just as staunch 'BBC men'. Throughout the last ten years, I have watched DR staff become TV2 staff and journalists at the ITV moving to the BBC and vice versa. Overall, it seemed the way that the BBC journalists were thinking, acting and behaving was very similar to all the other journalists I had worked along. So I began reconsidering my initial idea of the news workers and newsrooms being categorically different and began considering whether, in fact, the journalists I had viewed as 'ITV men' were above all 'news men', not dedicated to any particular broadcaster.

Thus, I began to consider the large TV newsrooms I visited and their news workers as connected, interlinked and similar. Additionally, I began exploring the notion of news workers, broadcasters, management and their newsrooms primarily as imitating each other rather than being inventive and original (Tardes 1903).[18] This made me consider how the newsrooms came to resemble each other physically, by sharing and copying methods and layout from inside other newsrooms.

After this experience, rather than assuming differences between the newsrooms and the ways in which they work, my focus changed dramatically to exploring the news workers' shared ideologies and shared ways of working within the different countries and newsrooms. The fact that I was searching out connections between the four newsrooms no doubt played a part in making me find more connections and shared practices than differences and divisions between the newsrooms. This alteration in my prejudice about the field changed my focus and gave me a new direction of research, a new approach to theory and different interview questions posed in the field. In order to study the shared ideology, for example, I decided that I would ask each news worker exactly the same four questions about news, and I was surprised to find that the questions, posed to around 100 different news workers in different newsrooms, received very similar replies in the two countries (see Chapter 7).

It must of course be noted that there *are* some differences in the ways of working at each newsroom, if not only because each is organised differently, is in a different country, each with different national culture and so forth. However, as I found the similarities more important than the differences, I kept a focus on what was shared among the four news divisions.

2.5 The Interview

The primary sources of material on which this study relies derive from time spent doing participant observation. When I found one specific subject interesting, I looked more intensely for it in the field, instead of asking the news workers directly. I have prioritised information derived from practice, offered or mentioned in passing, compared to information directly given as an answer to a question during a recorded interview. This distinction was made, as I do not believe that simply asking a person a question gives me the answer to that question. Rather, the answer that a person gives to my question simply shows how that person *chooses* to answer my question. And while that might answer some other interesting questions, such as 'what does this person perceive to be the best way of answering this question?' or 'how is this type of question primarily answered by the specific group of people that I see myself as belonging to?', it will not give the definitive answer to the question – as can be seen in the following, journalists are very aware of this fact themselves. When I began fieldwork, I hoped to be able to schedule hour-long meetings with news workers during their working day. However, when staff were asked in the newsroom if they could find the time for an interview, the response was apologetic – only very few of the news workers knew where they would be the coming week, and none of them knew whether they would have the time, as they could not know what they would be working on. Instead, I was often asked if I could begin an interview with them right away and then stop the interview if a new story or a job came up. I was reluctant to do this at first, as I thought it would be more beneficial for both the interviewee and myself to have a set time, place and date arranged in order to prepare and feel able to relax during the interview. However, as so many scheduled interviews had to be postponed or cancelled due to the unpredictable nature of news work, I decided to change the interview strategy.

Instead, in the spirit of what Buchanan et al. (1988: 53–55) have called the *opportunistic approach*, I began carrying my recorder with me every day, always ready to interview staff whenever they wanted to be interviewed. When I changed my interview plans in order to accommodate the spontaneous nature of their work processes, news workers seemed much keener for me to interview them. Reporters, cameramen and journalists were particularly keen to be interviewed when waiting for a news story, or at a time when they knew they did not have any scheduled news events but still had to be at work in case 'anything happened' for them to work on. Thus, I realised that if I readjusted my methods of interviewing, the interviewees were suddenly much more interested in participating.

Adjusting my method to accommodate not only my own terms but also those of the interviewees is central to the ideal of viewing the research field opportunistically. In fact, from Buchanan et al.'s perspective, being preoccupied with a set way of doing research will only serve to limit and disable research. Rather, they argue, 'the practice of field research is the art of the possible. It is necessary to exploit the opportunities offered in the circumstance' (1988: 55). Personally, I did not only feel limited and disabled by the initial approach to interviews, I also felt that limiting interviewees to a set time and place felt like such a different way of doing things that it could make the interviewees feel uneasy, restrained and uncomfortable. In this sense, changing my way of arranging and conducting interviews served to show the news workers that I understood their type of work and their everyday time constraints.

The interviews were primarily conducted outside the newsroom, as I wanted interviewees to feel a sense of privacy. Apart from the editors' offices and the meeting rooms, however, there are very few private spaces in and around the newsrooms. As the meeting rooms were primarily in use, I only conducted a handful of the 50 recorded interviews in meeting rooms. Thus, the only interviews I made within a room with closed doors were with editors who had their own offices.

The 'private spaces' I found for interviewing were the areas that news workers themselves suggested as being 'private' and 'a little away from the newsroom', which Goffman ([1959]

1990) would define as backstage from the front stage area of the newsroom. These include corridors or a staircase just outside the newsroom, editing suites, a smoking court, a dressing room or a corner of the newsroom where there were less people at a given time. In all these places, the interview could easily be interrupted by colleagues or work, as we were visible to newsroom staff, and the interviewee had his work phone turned on, often having to answer calls during the interview.

As I find the space of the interview to be an important context to the content of the interview, I have chosen to include the setting and place in which an interview was conducted whenever I quote an interview throughout this book.[19]

Planning the interview

I soon realised that different people gave different information at different times and settings in and around the newsroom. Formal interviews yielded a certain type of knowledge, and informal chats in the canteen or the smokers' yard, for instance, yielded another type of knowledge. Similarly, different roles in the news hierarchy gave different replies to my questions. Interviewing a manager or News Editor does not illicit the same type of replies to questions as when interviewing a runner, a reporter, a cameraman or a producer. When interviewing the management positions within the newsroom, such as News Editors or editors, it seemed they were giving me the 'official line' and an official version of how best to answer the questions I posed. These interviewees were often the ones who wanted to be named, rather than made anonymous, as they found it important to be able to track who had said what.[20] Both the informal and the formal interviews, both interviews with management and interviews with news workers, I have found important for a full understanding of what news workers 'think they are up to' (Geertz 1983: 58).

When planning who to ask for an interview, I therefore considered it important to include many different people and different locations and to conduct the interview at a time, which best suited each interviewee. My main subject of interest during fieldwork was the journalists at work; however, I found that I learned much about the relations that journalists make by talking to other news workers who work with, around and for the journalists in the everyday. It was in talking to a technical operator at DR, for instance, that I first began to notice the extent to which all news staff give similar reasons for working in the news business, and how much all staff appears to consider what they call the good news story as very important for guiding how they work. Interviewing a technical operator who works with repairing and maintaining technical equipment, I had not expected much interest in defining a news story. However, I was surprised to learn how much this particular news worker had thought of defining a good news story and public service. When I asked other members of staff, such as cameramen, graphics and Technical Directors, about how they would define the good news story, I began to realise the extent to which all news workers value the shared concept of good news story as an important motivational factor for their everyday work. Thus, I decided to include in my interviews news staff with different job descriptions.

Not only the different job descriptions, but also the different positions of authority were important to me when selecting whom to ask for an interview. A person employed as managing editor or Head of News often showed me the 'official line of reply' to questions. These 'official lines' were often referred to by news staff. After having talked to various members of staff with different levels of authority, it became clear to me that talking to those working in management was helpful for me to understand the conditions under which the journalists in the newsrooms worked, and to understand the everyday values and definitions of which management talked. At the BBC, for instance, in the management offices, I was shown a poster with drawings of different birds when I asked to the audience that they considered their news to be made for. Upon examining the poster further, I saw that under each drawn bird there was a descriptive text relating to different viewer segments, such as: 'Rare bird ... interested in foreign news'. The staff inside the managerial offices section expressed excitement with the poster and told me that they had hung it up at various key points around the newsroom. When I later heard journalists talk about how they considered their viewers, it was interesting to bear in mind the bird poster passed on by management. Similarly, during my time at DR, I often heard jokes by journalists and reporters about someone called 'Birte and René'. It was not until I spoke to the management at DR that I was told the 'official' description of who 'Birte and René' are. While talking to the Head of News at DR, he mentioned TV Avisen's prototype viewers, which were based on two real-life people called 'Birte and René'. These experiences taught me that management staff was helpful in finding the 'official version' of what should be valued, such as viewer segmentation. Thus, I considered it important to include in my interviews staff at all levels of the hierarchy in the newsroom; staff from managing positions, as well as staff who were employed full-time and those who were employed on trial basis only.

As I began to do recorded interviews, it became clear that some types of information, for instance what was revealed during the course of informal conversations, would not be mentioned during a recorded interview. Over lunch with staff in the canteen, journalists would joke about a certain editor, saying that s/he is very 'bossy', 'too demanding' and 'does not have the right sense of a good news story'. In a recorded interview, however, the same journalists would not share the same opinions, but instead told me that they like all their editors and think they work well together.

Due to the nature of this interview setting, the length of the interviews I conducted ranged from five minutes to two hours. The interviews were semi-structured, in the sense that each of them began with a few factual questions (title of job, department, time of employment and the agreement on anonymity or title of their job that we had reached). Thereafter, the interview would proceed with me asking the same four questions, after which the interview would become more like an informal chat. It was helpful to have the same four questions as a starting point for each interview, as they would often trigger other thoughts or opinions from the interviewee that would be explored afterwards. Also, the fact that I asked everyone the same four questions, that the questions were not secret or different when addressing other members of staff, meant that staff appeared to feel included in the interviewing process.

In planning the interviews, I have been inspired by Spradley's (1979) discussions on the ethnographic interview and Steinar Kvale's theories on qualitative interviewing (1996; Kvale and Brinkman 2009): Viewing the interview as a way of constructing knowledge through 'inter views' – an interchange of views between two persons. It was my aim, both during the interviews and during the participant observation, to build a rapport and a trust between the news workers, in which interviewees felt able to answer my questions openly. As Kvale has expressed it:

Creating trust through a personal relationship here serves as a means to efficiently obtain a disclosure of the interview subjects' world. The interviewer may, with a charming, gentle, and client-centred manner, create a close personal encounter where the subjects unveil their private worlds.

(Kvale 2006: 482)

It is important to stress, however, that this type of caring interview setting can mean that interviewees may say something so private that they later regret having agreed to make their assertions public. With his book on *InterViews* (1996), psychologist and qualitative researcher Steinar Kvale has been an influential proponent for the caring and emphatic qualitative interview. It was not until years after the book's publication, however, that Kvale directed attention to the dominant power structure implicit within this friendly and relaxed interview setting. The potentially oppressive use of interview-produced knowledge does not get much attention in literature on qualitative research. However, I believe, agreeing with Kvale (2006), that the setting of a qualitative interview is not a dialogue; rather, the interviewer has the dominant role over the interviewee, in what is arguably an asymmetrical power relation. This power relation I see as intrinsically connected to the constant and difficult balancing act between different and sometimes competing roles in the field – such as being a participant (friend, colleague) and being an observer (interviewer, data collector).

Early on in my fieldwork at DR, I came to experience the challenge of keeping trust after an interview, while at the same time noticing the stark difference in opinions expressed by news workers in and out of the newsroom, with or without colleagues listening. On one day, I had conducted an interview with a journalist outside in the smoking court while there had been a group of other smoking colleagues present. In the interview, he talked about the many different jobs he gets on an everyday basis at work in the newsroom. During the last few months, he told me he had been both editing the afternoon news bulletin show *and* been the on-screen host for the programme. This having to wear 'many different hats' within the same working day, he told me, felt a 'little head over heels' and was 'more an expression of rationalising than an optimal solution'.[21] He joked about his many different hats as we chatted after the interview, without seeming to care if anyone in the smoker's yard could hear him. He was happy for me to use all his quotes in my study, he said. Thus, I did not realise that what he had told me was something he would rather keep private and confidential from his colleagues.

The following day, I noticed that my interviewee had again been given the job of both editing and presenting two different news bulletins. When I saw him in the newsroom, I nodded to him in a friendly manner and said; 'I see you've got many hats on again today!' at which he stared at me oddly and seemed to pretend he could not understand what I was talking about. After that, this particular news worker seemed to distrust me and did not talk much to me. Though nobody else seemed to take any notice of my comment, I was left feeling as if I had betrayed and abused his openness. This experience taught me to be very careful not to mention in public any information, joke or insight that I was told during an interview.

Interviewing the interviewers

It is strange to be interviewed, because I can't help thinking in sound bites and deliver something that can be edited together well. I'm a damned bad person to interview, I am a little too messy in my views [...] I can't even make a formula for what is a good news story [...] I can't make a formula it is just a feeling in my guts.

(Lasse, reporter, formerly on the evening news, now at TV2 Praxis, in conversation in an editing suite after interview, 26 May 2008)

At first, it appeared to be a methodological advantage that the individuals I was interviewing use interviews in their everyday work as well. However, interviewing people who themselves are interviewers also made for added complications, reflections and discussion, often ending with a review of the interview and the way I carried out the interview.[22] While this was helpful at times, giving an insight into how journalists work, sometimes the interview seemed distant from the actual opinions and viewpoints of the interviewee but rather as a type of performance of 'how an interview should be', a making of quotes the journalists thought I was interested in. Particularly when I wrote down opinions and comments of the same person at work throughout a day, it was curious to experience how these opinions and views could change as soon as we began a recorded interview. Before I pressed record on my recorder, I would often get asked 'what kind of quote' I was particularly looking for and what quotes I already had, so that they could give me 'new' quotes that I did not already have.

During an interview, the journalists appeared very conscious of each word they said, making sure that each sentence was quotable – stopping at times and looking up at me saying things such as; 'oh, THAT was a bit of a long sentence there...' or 'maybe I'll try to explain myself a little more to-the-point... let's take the question again'. At times, during an interview, the journalist would glance at me and nod knowingly, as if to say 'this might be what you are interested in' or 'this quote is very useable'.

After an interview, my interviewees would often discuss how the interview went, and whether or not the quotes they had just given me would be of any use to me. As the reporter Lasse expresses it in the quote above, many journalists told me that being on the 'other side' of an interview situation made them feel odd. They could not help but constantly consider what I might 'be after' in the interview, and they worried about being able to 'deliver' something that could be 'edited together well'. As Lasse explains, he thinks it would be better for the interview if he could give me a definite definition, a 'formula' of what a good news story is, but he regrets that he cannot do that. Therefore, he thinks he is not a good interviewee for my project and recommends that I find someone else to talk to who is less 'messy'.

According to Goffman, the time after an interview represents a specific out-of-the-interview behaviour in which 'role gives way to person' (Goffman 1974: 273); a time of reflection which is more about the respondent's claims than the researcher's (Warren et al. 2003: 96). However, in the specific instance of news workers, the after-the-interview behaviour did not appear to reveal the person behind the role, who had just been interviewed. Rather, the comments after the interview, just as those before the interview, appeared to establish their role as a journalist, a type of ritual aimed at establishing their role rather than their person.

After an interview, journalists would often sympathise with me as an interviewer, pity me for having to transcribe their quotes and ask whether my recording equipment was any good. In this sense, the interview often worked as a bridge between me as a researcher and them as practitioners, in the sense that we were making use of the same methods and had the same challenges in our work.

At times, journalists appeared to find my interest in their everyday work curious. Journalists often suggested other paths that I should follow or other questions that I should ask. Mostly though, the journalists took my questions seriously, at times putting a more serious air to their reply than they would have when speaking about journalism amongst themselves. In this way, by the very fact that the recorded interviews were formal interviews, I was addressed differently and given different information compared to what I overheard when observing staff at work. In her study of letter editors in the US, Wahl-Jorgensen had a similar experience when comparing her interviews of staff to observations of staff, as she put it: '[…] the interviews constructed a somewhat artificial form of discourse, yet one that tells us useful things about the ideals of journalists, as well as their self-understanding' (Wahl-Jorgensen 2007: 64). Similarly, rather than view the interviews as objective truths, I see the interviews I have conducted as providing important insight into ideal values and ideal types existing within the journalism profession.

In 2016, as I returned to the newsrooms and spoke to some of the same staff that I first had met when I began fieldwork in 2007, most staff had moved to different, more senior positions. This made for interviews that could focus on the changes that have happened in the newsrooms over the last ten years – both in respect of personal, professional and broadcaster-level challenges. Returning to the interviewees over a ten-year period no doubt gives a special relation between interviewer and the interviewed. Another relation that the ten-year-research gave me was a sudden 'expert' role in the field of TV newsrooms. Thus, when I spoke to management in 2016 and 2017, I was viewed as someone who had also been around ten years ago and therefore had a special overview. After an interview, staff in management positions often asked into what I had found, some asking directly if I had 'found out how the TV news can secure an income' or 'which TV newsroom I would deem best able to survive in the current challenges'.

Anonymity

As it is not crucial for the study who said what, or did what, as a general rule I have kept all interviews and observations anonymous. During the process of gaining access to the newsroom, I made a promise to the gatekeeper who gave me access to keep staff anonymous as a rule and only name people who specifically asked to be named. What matters to my observations is the person's job title, gender, age or his/her length of employment, and therefore occasionally I provide such information.

In striving to make the participants in this study anonymous, I encountered a twofold challenge. First, keeping each interviewee anonymous is nearly impossible. As soon as I give the age, job title or gender of an employee who works at the BBC, for instance, it often becomes possible to make out the name of that person. As there is only one BBC, only one TV2, ITV and DR, I am of course already giving away much by revealing which of the broadcasters a specific interviewee is employed at. In this sense, full anonymity has not been possible. This, however, is much to the satisfaction of the interviewees themselves, as the second challenge to my policy of anonymity has been that the interviewees often have in fact not requested anonymity. During all interviews and introductions to my observations inside the newsrooms, I explained that I would make the individual journalists anonymous. The idea of anonymising, however, was far from well received by the journalists themselves.

In many areas of research, anonymity is seen as a shelter, which may supply the courage for the person to express opinions and viewpoints that s/he may otherwise be afraid to state openly. However, among the journalists I studied, the idea of anonymity appeared to have opposite, less positive connotations. Most news workers did not think it proper practice to make interviewees anonymous, as one reporter at DR asked me 'how can I make sure that you don't just make it all up?'. It troubled me at times that the people I studied disagreed with my method. However, as this study is made in the academic tradition, I have chosen to stay true to what I found the most academically valid way of quoting interviewees. In time, I found the promise of anonymity to make staff able to talk more freely and at times more critically than they would if they would have been named. As can be seen throughout this book, however, some interviewees were against anonymous interviews and therefore asked for their name to be used.

The four questions

1. What is a good news story?
2. Why do you work in news?
3. What is Public Service? – Do you ever think of it in the everyday work?
4. Do you see any difference between you and the nearest competing news bulletin? What do you see as the main differences?

During fieldwork, it was my aim to ask all staff the above four questions. I primarily asked the four questions in this exact order to staff during recorded interviews in sit-down interviews. Fifty such interviews were conducted during fieldwork. However, I also asked the questions during fieldwork at times where I was without recording equipment and then wrote down quotes in my field book. Forty such interviews were conducted. Lastly, as a couple of members of the news staff asked me to reply to my questions through email, I also mailed the questions and had replies from four news staff returned via email. In total I thus had 104 replies to the above questions from different news staff members, at different times and in different situations.

I planned the four questions to be both descriptive and using the 'native' language of the news workers (Spradley 1979: 78–90). While I do not believe that the replies to these questions give answers to what I asked, I do believe that the ways in which the replies are given are useful for understanding how news workers explain and describe themselves, their role and their work. It could be argued that the manners in which people replied to my questions simply resembled performances; a way of answering what they think is the 'right' answer catering to the type of researcher that I was perceived to be and the type of questions that I asked. I view this potential performance as a helpful way of learning what news workers consider the right and correct ways to best answer my questions. In reviewing the formal and informal interviews (as the chapter does not commence with interviews), I have used different techniques of emergent coding in order to group replies according to connected themes (see Charmaz 1983, for an overview). I further studied and analysed the themes that emerged from the initial coding of interviews. Lastly, I returned to each interview and re-read each transcript in order to study them closely and to see whether I could find more insights into the themes that emerged during initial coding. In this sense, I have let the news workers' assertions determine what themes to group the interview replies into. For instance, as I noticed that staff at commercial broadcasters talked about themselves metaphorically as working on the prairie, being like cowboys and arguing that to them everything is possible, I constructed themes that I termed 'Cowboys' or 'Everything is Possible!' and added different replies to my questions that I thought fitted these themes.

2.6 Presenting the Field

> What scares many research novices (and long-time practitioners!) is, to put it plainly, what to do with the collected data and how those data get written up. How do we translate, interpret and carry out our data into our writing and analysis?
>
> (Hoonard 1997: 22)

As I returned from having spent a year and a half in different newsrooms, I brought back a pile of handwritten Field Diaries, many hours worth of recorded interview material, files of hand-outs from editorial meetings and print-outs of future news ideas and running orders, a hard drive full of photos and DVDs with recorded news bulletins.[23] Where should I go next? How was I to make sense of all the differently shaped data I returned with? And how could I transfer and translate the notebooks of handwritten points, expressed in bold, or in sketches, drawings or in shorthand to a digital Word-processed format? Most importantly, how could all this differently shaped data combine to capture the everyday work of TV journalists, which is what I was hoping to do at the outset of my project?

When I returned from my fieldwork, at times I was confused and overwhelmed by the mass of differently shaped data collected from many different situations, places and newsrooms in two different countries. For a period, I felt the scare that Hoonard describes above. Stages of what some may experience as 'confusion', in fact, appear crucial to the method. Constantly being unsure, and thus open to new and unexpected findings appears to be part and parcel of a research method, which can be described as a 'round-dance' (Wadel 1991), 'a process', and an ongoing 'education' (Gudeman and Rivera 1995).

In a sense, I already began the 'translating and transferring' process during fieldwork, in the way that I shaped the Field Diary, allowing for a constant distancing and sensitizing of the field. I later found this a crucial help towards keeping at bay the methodological scare expressed by Hoonard. In the following, I discuss some of the methods deployed in the field for representing experiences. Subsequently, I explore how I have cut, edited and limited this data.

Everyday metaphors

While spending time among journalists at work, I began noticing how the work they did was often talked about in metaphors. The most commonly employed metaphors appeared to be repeated and shared so often among staff that no one seemed to question them. Sometimes metaphors were used in jest, such as when a reporter outside smoking with colleagues would stub out his cigarette, put on an exhausted grimace and say: 'Ah, well, I've got to go back to *The Machine*'. Other times metaphors would be used in all seriousness, such as when staff tells me they feel like they are deeply connected with their colleagues as they are all 'part of *one big family*', or when a reporter at TV2 told me during a recorded interview: '[W]e began out here on *the prairie* all alone [...]' (TV2 Reporter, Interview 38, 5 June 2008).

I have found the metaphors used in and around the everyday work of journalists relevant for exploring the everyday understandings that they have of their work. During fieldwork, I kept a list of all the different ways that news workers defined their work, and found that the metaphors staff used often encapsulated their opinions better than many phrases did. In this way, I have used the metaphors conveyed by workers as a way of ordering, systematising and focusing attention on specific themes expressed by news workers. Ordering words and themes in accordance with how I find them connected by different metaphors is helpful for systematising descriptions and ways of talking in the field. Ordering native peoples' utterances into different metaphors is risky, in that it is unavoidable for the researcher to choose, suppress and organise certain features. However, in the case of news workers, as metaphors are so often used when they describe themselves and their work, I believe much can be achieved by analysing these metaphors closer. Lakoff and Johnson have introduced metaphors as, essentially, ways of understanding one kind of thing in terms of another:

> Metaphor is one of our most important tools for trying to comprehend partially what cannot be comprehended totally: our feelings, aesthetic experiences, moral practices, and spiritual awareness. These endeavours of the imagination are not devoid of rationality; since they use the metaphor, they employ an imaginative rationality.
>
> (Lakoff and Johnson 1980: 193)

From the perspective of Lakoff and Johnson above, it can be seen as an expression of imaginative rationality when news workers used the metaphor *The Mchine* about the newsroom they worked in, as the word contains a richer description of how staff members perceive of their workplace, than if I asked them to describe how they felt about their workplace.

During my re-reading of interview transcripts, I came to realise that the metaphors staff used when describing their work were often consistent with each other across the different types of broadcasters, both the commercial and the public service ones. While re-reading and recalling the many different interviews I conducted during fieldwork, the metaphors were a helpful way of organising and remembering each interview. As Kvale and Brinkman (2009: 287) write, metaphors can aid post interview investigation as 'a study's main points may be more easily understood and remembered when worked into vivid metaphors'. I thus began ordering quotes, experiences and theories in categories related to each metaphor that I had found in the field. In this way, I became attentive to metaphors both during and after my interviews and talks in the field. When a runner at TV2, for instance, in a passing comment describes her work place like 'a family' (TV2 Runner, Interview 40, 9 June 2008), or when a TV Anchor Man at TV2 describes the way he became trained to be a good Anchor Man as 'like joining the army' (TV2 interview 41, 9 June 2008). Although not asserted in direct answer to how they define their jobs, these descriptive metaphors constitute definitions of how staff view their workplace.

Taking notes

Throughout fieldwork, I brought along a notebook everywhere I went. In the notebooks I wrote, scribbled, drew and sketched what I experienced, what was said and what was not said, what I saw and heard. Writing in a notebook was not very different from what most of the staff inside the newsroom did, so generally my note taking did not seem like a strange behaviour and I did not feel awkward taking notes in public. News workers use notebooks particularly during editorial meetings and planning meetings. At debrief meetings, however, or at times of waiting for news to come in, or when chatting in the coffee room or smoking outside, news workers were not busy jotting down in notebooks, and then it felt strange to be the only one writing. At such times, I would decide to write anyway and accept the comments directed at me, such as the smokers outside of ITV asking me jokingly what *exactly* I could be writing about them right now. Other times, I resorted to writing in more private places, such as the toilets or a quiet corner of the canteen, so as not to seem strange or unnatural in the company of the people I researched (Hammersley and Atkinson 1996: 205).

As I knew that the notebooks would be an important source of data later in the process, I spent a great deal of time contemplating how to take notes, before the actual note taking began. I made a few practical, rigid rules for my note taking: First, I divided each notebook into two themes. I was only allowed to write daily notes on the right side of each notebook. The left hand side of every notebook I kept blank for theoretical ideas – or ideas of theories of the field that I might come to think of during the fieldwork or after, when re-reading field notes.

For each entry in my daily notes in the notebook, I aimed to keep a rigid note of the date, time and place of each entry. Apart from these rules, I took notes on very different experiences, quotes, events, facts, emotions and actions as the fieldwork commenced, and my theoretical and empirical focus was shaped. I made notes of actions, but also of who performed the actions and connections with what was being said during which actions. Also, I made notes of other things that I observed, heard or experienced and otherwise thought interesting.

During meetings, for instance, I kept a note of who was present, including the gender of each person present at meetings, and I kept the lists of the story ideas that were discussed, and I wrote down quotes that related to each story discussion, and I often included a note on the tone of voice or the body language of staff during the meeting. Additionally, during a meeting, I would take count of actions I found interesting, such as: How many others apart from the editor talked, and how many times was an editor interrupted by a mobile phone.[24] Furthermore, I would draw the way we were seated during the meeting. Or, I would take notes similar to the notes that the others took at such a meeting, e.g. the time of day at which an interview would be arriving to the newsroom, or where a certain video feed from abroad was expected from EBU.

In time, I found that the notepad was a helpful tool in making me feel part of the group of journalists and for the journalists to understand my job. Taking note, and carrying a notepad with me everywhere I went was not unusual in the newsroom. Though it was not custom to be writing at all times during the working day, in fact I would have been standing out more among journalists if I did not carry a pen and paper. During meetings, I sometimes felt other journalists glancing at my notepad to see what I was writing; other times, staff would nod and smile to me after someone had said something, as if to say 'did you write *that one* down?'. Other times I would turn to a reporter after a meeting to ask if he got the exact time of an expected event, as I did not manage to write it down in time. Similarly, once in a while reporters asked me after a meeting if I might have made a note of when a certain event was expected to take place, and how many cameramen were out on stories. Thus, the notebook became a shared symbolic element between the researcher and the researched.

Writing up and transcribing

In the analysis of data, I have aimed to illustrate many different facets of facts, as I have found not just facts but the circumstances, emotions and other contexts crucial. Thus, I have strived to constantly follow ideals of 'thick description' (Geertz 1973: 3–30) putting onus on giving descriptive context and meaning to actions. Since Geertz first used the term, many have given different definitions of what exactly a thick description constitutes. In particular, I have been inspired by Denzin (1989), who compares thick description with what he terms 'thin description'. According to Denzin, thick description has the following features:

> (1) It gives the context of an act; (2) it states the intentions and meanings that organize the action; (3) it traces the evolution and development of the act; (4) it presents the action as a text that can then be interpreted. A thin description simply reports facts, independent of intentions or the circumstances that surround an action.
>
> (Denzin 1989: 33)

Looking at my notebooks upon returning from fieldwork, I found that not only were the words written important for remembering what I experienced during fieldwork. The way the words were written was important too – a sticky note, an underlining, a tired handwriting or a note written in capital letters and with a circle surrounding it all had different meanings. It was crucial that I would recall the exact situation of writing, every little detail of scribbling, drawing and sketching in the field notebooks. A small sticky note with a little goodbye note from a journalist to me, which I had stuck in my DR field book, reminded me of much more than what the note said. It reminded me that news workers wanted to stay in touch, and this particular note made me recall the last day of my fieldwork at DR where I suddenly felt part of the group; I was now someone who could get little letters on sticky notes, normally left on the screen of a good colleagues' desktop.

Similarly, when listening to an interview, the analysis was not merely influenced by what was actually said. As the head of TV2 banged the table, exclaiming: 'We have a very, very strong [bangs his hand on the table] top leadership which sits on things daily!' – I found the banging and laughing crucial to the interview.[25] Not only because the other actions he did, apart from using words, were important to understanding the words, but also because the sound of the banging triggers a memory for me of how I felt while interviewing this particular person.

Similarly, the muffled sound of busy people in the background of an interview has reminded me of how it feels to be inside a newsroom in ways that I could have not been reminded had I just written down words. An interview recorded with a certain echo to the sound reminds me that most interviews had to be done in hallways or atriums and makes me remember the feeling of sitting there in a way that I might not have considered had someone else transcribed the interview for me.

I agree with Kvale and Brinkmann (2009: 180) when they highlight the fruitful process of transcribing one's own interviews, as the 'social and emotional aspects of the interview situation [are] present or reawakened during transcription', meaning that the researcher will 'have already started the analysis of the meaning of what was said'. It has therefore been important to me to take the time to personally transcribe all the recorded interviews conducted.

2.7 Conclusions

Throughout this chapter, I have presented my methods of 'data' collection as a constant balancing act between participating and observing, being experience-near and experience-distant. A critique of the method I have chosen could be that it is subjective, personal and very time specific, and therefore not 'the true' depiction of the social life of TV news journalists of the news bulletins at DR, TV2, BBC and ITV. As I do not believe it possible ever to mirror one true depiction of social life, I do not claim to do so through this research. Rather, I believe I provide an interpretation of social life, which can add to current debates both among journalists and users of journalism.

Certainly, the way that I have conducted my research has been personal and very time specific. Firstly, the reason for commencing my study and the way I negotiated access was subjective and specific to me only. Others would have had different reasons, different sensitizing concepts, different interests and different ways of getting access, which would have led to a different starting point for the research and a different result. Secondly, other researchers would have acted differently in and around the newsrooms, participating more, less or differently. Moreover, others would possibly have chosen a different way of presenting their research. Others yet would likely conduct research at a different time, where the topics that I found interesting might be less interesting.

The method I have followed will not give *the* true depiction of *the* social lives that I studied. But I have striven for my method to give a depiction true to the place and time of my observations, the people included and the way I was a part of this. As Michael H. Agar writes, even ethnographies of the same groups by different ethnographers will always be different:

> [...] ethnographies of similar groups, or on similar topics, differ from one another. They differ because of differences in the audiences addressed, in the background of the ethnographers, or even in the groups themselves.
>
> (Agar 1986: 15)

From the perspective of Agar, ethnography is 'neither subjective nor objective, but interpretative, mediating two worlds through a third' (Agar 1986: 19). I agree with Agar in that it should be the aim of ethnography to mediate the two worlds, the researchers and the researched, in order to give an interpreted version of reality of the social life of those studied.

Due to the very different factors shaping the ethnographer and fieldwork, I believe the final ethnography will always have elements of subjectivity. Indeed, the very observation cannot take place without the researcher having an idea of what to look for, which in itself puts a subjective stance on the research (see Wolcott 1995: 163–66). It has been my aim throughout this chapter to present the elements that shape my subjectivity so much so that my experiences and viewpoints, such as sensitizing concepts, become evident to the reader. I make no claims to give *the* truth, but hope to show *a* truth that *I* have experienced and observed, and I highlight the different subjective ways and the time, the place and the people, who have led me to reach these interpretations. To give the truest depiction of the culture of the news workers I have studied, I have therefore aimed throughout this chapter, and in the next chapters, to lay as many intersubjective elements on the table, such as my personal interests, my history, my way of getting access into the field and discussions of the way I may have changed the field by being a part of it.

Notes

1   As discussed earlier, *gatekeeping* has been used to describe what journalists do (i.e. White 1950). Here, the term is used as a metaphor for those who are directly or indirectly in position to provide access to key resources needed to do research, be they logistical, human, institutional or informative. The relationship between the gatekeeper and researcher is not one-directional or static, but rather a dynamic, fluid and constant working process both before, during and after fieldwork (as discussed by Gellner and Hirsch 2001: 5; Campbell et al. 2010, among others).

2   Capital, from this perspective, refers to 'all the goods material and symbolic, without distinction, that present themselves as rare and worthy of being sought after in a particular social formation' (Bourdieu cited in Harker 1990: 13). I will discuss cultural capital and the notion of 'showing off' one's profession further in Chapter 8.

3   Although, in the case of sharing a satellite dish with a rival broadcaster, it is crucial that they do not get to transmit their story before the broadcaster who owns the satellite dish, and money may have to be exchanged for the favour.

4   As anthropologist Ruth Benedict expressed it in 1929, it is hard to see the lens through which one is looking. Any researcher puts a specific lens on what s/he studies (Goodall 2003). When the researcher has already been a part of the field that s/he researches, the lens may appear to be differently coloured to those for whom the culture is new and foreign.

5   Buchanan et al. (1988: 58) argue: 'Access will not be granted where it is felt that normal operations are likely to be disrupted, and where commercially sensitive material is likely to be disclosed. Gatekeepers in organizations often have views on these matters quite different from the expectations of researchers. The researcher thus has to respond positively to such fears, reservations and questions'.

6   I still today consider myself a journalist *as well as* an academic, since, while working on this study, I have had a few journalistic jobs working for different broadcasters than the ones included in this study. Also, my time working as a journalist means that I still find myself in journalistic circles of friendship, activities and interests.

7   The word 'data' is here used for lack of a better word describing the sum of understandings, observations, experiences, interviews and other documentations of the time spent among a group of people that a participant observer collects. In the following I will use the words 'field' and 'fieldwork-site' as the spatial site of participant observation.

8   See Marcus (1999) and Geertz (1973) for discussions on the uses of complicity, as an attempt to get a form of local knowledge which is not accessible by working out internal cultural logics.

9   Curiously, among academics, I have encountered a similar scepticism towards journalists. Shankman (2001) has written of journalism as often 'suspect in academic circles'. Being 'journalistic' is not necessarily a positive sign among academics. As Bird has put it: '[...] peer reviewers are known to dismiss ethnographies they dislike as "journalistic", meaning they are superficial or glib' (2010a: 4).

10 To back up the story that there was a huge increase in immigrants settling in the UK, with the town of Wrexham as a case study, I was given the job of finding the exact figures to present on the digital wall. The numbers I had to find for Wrexham included: *How many children do not have English as a first Language? – How many pounds are spent on translation by the council? How much more police staff has to be employed due to trouble with immigrants? – How many of the NHS employees are immigrants?* (ITV fieldwork notebook: p. 30).

11 Kohut used the term *experience-near* to introduce empathy as an abstract and operational way of helping clients with emotional suffering by, among other things, having 'the capacity to think and feel oneself into the inner life of another person' (Kohut et al. 1984: 82).

12　Who, indeed, would trust an 'ethnography of witchcraft as written by a witch'? as Geertz memorably puts it (Geertz 1983: 57).

13　During my first week of fieldwork at the BBC, the unrest among news staff caused controversy both around management and the public, as a private email from Peter Horrocks to the BBC's director of news, Helen Boaden, was leaked to the media. Reporting on the email, The Media Guardian wrote that the staff cuts could lead to 'militant behaviour' among news staff, who considered their battle a 'noble' one:

> There is 'strong support' for industrial action to fight potential cuts in BBC television news, the head of the division, Peter Horrocks, has privately warned. Many assistant editors in the department will be 'militant' as their jobs are under threat, Mr Horrocks said in an email to the BBC's director of news, Helen Boaden. 'The editors believe there will be strong support for action, obviously because of self-protection from job losses and excessive workload, but also because there is a feeling that the BBC's decision (as they see it) to spread pain fairly evenly does not fit with what the public most want from the BBC – i.e. news'.
>
> (*The Guardian* 2007)

14　I use the word 'data' for lack of a better word to cover the definitions of what I have considered relevant material for my analysis. As Hansen writes: 'Data is thus not "something" which is already waiting out there in the research field and awaits an ethnographer coming to collect it. Data is rather a construction in a scientific discourse. In other words, it is only when something is found and defined (as data) that it becomes data' (Hansen 1995: 124, my translation from Danish).

15　Indeed, experience working inside British newsrooms over the last decade has taught me that it is not unusual if a news worker is contracted for three months or six months repeatedly over a period of many years. According to the International Federation of Journalists, the practice of contract work and 'atypical' employment in the newsroom are increasing, making a paid position in the newsroom less 'secure and more intense' (IFJ and ILO 2006: vi).

16　Among other things, I was part of reading and commenting on the 2008 Ofcom review of Public Service Broadcasting in Britain. I was in the steering group responsible for organising the conference *Public Service – De Ti Bud*, held at CBS, 28 January 2009, in which media researchers invited media professionals to discuss the most important issues for Public Service Broadcasting today. In May 2017, I participated with a group of young media users in TV2's Public Service Hearing 'Et Medie Danmark I balance'.

17　One evening, after a few weeks of participant observation at DR, at the end of a shift where I had been working with the same journalist from 9AM till 9PM, I felt and looked exhausted. As I told the Programme Editor that I was going home, he said: 'Oh, are you going home already? Don't you want to see some more? How about the editing, the cutting? … alright I understand … those 13 hour days… Come in at 10 tomorrow so you can get some sleep' (Programme Editor's comment in DR notebook, 12 June 2007).

18　'All resemblances of social origin in society are the direct or indirect fruit of the various forms of imitation, custom-imitation or fashion-imitation, sympathy-imitation or obedience-imitation, precept-imitation or education-imitation, native imitation, deliberate imitation, etc. In this lies the excellence of the contemporaneous method of explaining doctrines and institutions through their history' (Tardes 1903: 14).

19 Gulløv and Højlund (2006: 240) state: '[...] the physical surroundings do not determine human action but they are circumstances implicit in practice. Place and social organization shall be considered connected in the analysis as a context for children's actions and relations; a context which is created through the children's (and the adult's) practices, and at the same time make the foundations for the possibilities they have' (my translation from the Danish).

20 Of course, as there is less management staff in a newsroom, it is easier to track references to the people in these roles.

21 Interview with Programme Editor and Host at DR Nyheder in smokers' yard in DR Byen, 28 July 2007.

22 Arguably, many people who are interviewed appear interested in how they fared, and whether the reply was the one the researcher wanted. In the past, I have conducted ethnographic fieldwork among passengers inside the London Underground and among members of religious cults in England (Thomsen 2001). Though the interviewees for these studies were keen to help me out with the quotes I wanted, they were far from as focused on the making of the interview as the journalists I have interviewed.

23 As described in Chapter 6.2, 'running order' is the term for the shared digital interface for all staff within a news division. I printed these digital news orders out every day during fieldwork, both early and late in the working day, in order to follow how the running order changed from morning to evening.

24 News Editors generally were interrupted by mobile phone calls 7–15 times during the meetings I attended.

25 Michael Dyrby, interviewed in his office overlooking the reporters' room, TV2 Kvægtorvet, 26 September 2008.

Part III

Introducing the Four News Divisions and a Relationship of Constant Competition

Chapter 3

Talking About Differences: How News Workers Define Themselves and Each Other

On real and imagined differences, and the idea that everyone is 'the best'

In Breed's (1955) study of newspapermen, conducted almost 60 years ago, he finds one of the key factors governing staff to be the policy set by the publisher. The learning of policy, Breed argues, is 'a process by which the recruit discovers and internalises the rights and obligations of his status and its norms and values' (1955: 328). During fieldwork, I too found each institution's declared policy important for how news workers understand the news division they work in. However, while I have found staff to talk of institutional policy as creating a key difference between their work and others, I have not found policy to be the main factor controlling journalists' work in the everyday. Rather, as shall be shown through this chapter, I have experienced the four newsrooms to have different identities but work within a shared consensus.

In the following chapter, I explore the differences in editorial policy at each of the four newsrooms from the perspective of the journalists, as well as the ways in which they define each other. Although I do not consider it entirely possible to distinguish rigidly between action and expression, as the two are always implicitly connected either knowingly or unknowingly, throughout the following chapter I will focus on how the news workers *say* they act, rather than *how* they act. For discussions on the design of the room I rely on interviews with management and editors who have played a vital part in the decision-making preceding the redesign. For discussions on identity, I rely on interviews with all news staff. In doing so, it is my aim here to let the news workers introduce themselves and the newscaster they work for in their own words. In order to keep focus primarily on how news workers in general and journalists in particular express their everyday work, I draw on more than 40 informal conversations as well as the 50 recorded interviews conducted during fieldwork as primary sources for this chapter (see Chapter 2.3). I will not include observations on the different news content that is produced by the four different broadcasters. However, as mentioned in the introduction, it is my firm conviction that what happens inside the newsroom significantly influences what can be seen on the TV as news – just as what is produced on the screen matters to how the news workers at each broadcaster perceive themselves. For as the Head of News at TV2 explained to me: '[W]hat we are on the outside, we'd also like to be on the inside' (Jacob Nybroe, recorded interview, 5 June 2008).

Initially, each of the four newsrooms I visited during fieldwork seemed different to each other, with different ways of working, different types of people, a different way of talking and behaving. At each of the four newsrooms, staff explained this difference as a 'difference in spirit'. The way staff talked about this 'spirit' appeared similar to the way one would describe two nations to be different, with different languages, different values and different groups of people. One news presenter, who has worked at many different broadcasters and describes himself as 'Denmark's longest serving' news presenter, explained when I asked if it feels any different to be employed at different news organisations:[1]

> It is a bit like a nationality feeling, you know? You see, if you live in Denmark, you are Danish, and then you can begin to decipher what it means to be Danish. If you are employed at TV2 then you are a 'TV2 national' one way or another. And ehmm… We can talk about it like a spirit. That may sound like a very fluffy kind of word in itself. You know, it is very spherical. But, but there is a TV2 spirit and I felt it as soon as I arrived here. We have some key values, which are in fact never talked about. We just know that they are there. And we very quickly get them under our skin. And if you don't like those key values, well then it's clear; you better find another place to work.
>
> (Anchor Man TV2, interviewed in studio after
> presenting the news, 9 June 2008)

Throughout this chapter, I explore the ways that staff at the four broadcasters have explained what the Anchor Man above describes as the broadcasters' 'spirit'. Furthermore, inspired by the above quote, I strive to 'decipher what it means' to the staff to work for each of the four broadcasters, TV2, ITV, DR and BBC. Anchor Man above told me that he sensed a special bond between all his news colleagues employed at the same broadcaster. Thus, the news workers' sense of belonging at first appeared defined by employment (I return to the issue of belonging in Chapter 6).

As will be seen in the following, the news workers I have talked to often describe themselves as working for 'the best' newscaster and express a fear of becoming like or resembling the other. For instance, at the commercial station TV2, staff told me both in interviews and informal chats that their way of making news was better than the way that the license-funded broadcaster, DR, made news. Similarly, at DR, staff told me that they worried whether their news-production style was becoming too similar to that of TV2, as the 'classic' DR way of working was much better than TV2's much 'more populist' way of news making.[2]

The four news divisions are different on many levels: historically, economically, politically, legally as well as culturally. With this chapter, the primary focus is on how journalists define themselves as different. While my empirical observations have found more similarities in ways of working than differences between the newsrooms this chapter introduces the way journalists define the daily work in terms of competition and difference. As such, this chapter illustrates the investigative route that I have taken during fieldwork, from differences to similarities between newsrooms. Crucial to the way journalists consider their way of working different at one institution to the others is the knowledge that their institution has a different history. Thus, in the following the historical foundations for the two different institutions of broadcasting, licence funded or commercially funded, are introduced.

3.1 Monopoly and Duopoly of Broadcasting

First, a brief introduction to the historical relations between news divisions of the licence funded and commercially funded broadcasters in Denmark and the UK shall be given. The newsrooms that I have visited are all part of a wider institution, a broadcast organisation to which they are connected as the *news division*. Of the four news divisions, BBC, ITV, DR and TV2, there is no doubt as to which organisation has set the standard for the rest. The concept of Public Service Broadcasting is larger than the BBC. Yet, as Born writes: '[T]he BBC has a special place in the history and the imagining of Public Service Broadcasting' (2005: 7). During my study, I have found that the BBC does not only have a special place in the conception of Public Service Broadcasting, but staff within all news divisions define good news work as very similar to how they define public service.

The British Broadcasting Corporation (BBC), the world's first public service corporation, was established in 1920. Today, it is the longest running and largest broadcaster in the history of broadcasting, with the largest broadcast news division in the world.[3] There was no news department in the BBC until 1934 (according to Scannell 2002: 204). The first BBC TV news broadcast with a presenter in view took place in 1955 just three weeks before the launch of the first news broadcast by their competitor ITN, who presented their first news bulletin on 21 September 1955. Before that, the BBC broadcasted Television Newsreels, which consisted of a ten-minute film with a voice-over, describing national and international events as well as sports and more 'quirky' human-interest stories.

In Europe, the BBC was viewed as the ideal prototype service broadcasting. Just as the broadcasting principles inspired the Europeans, so did the BBC ethics and values and the prioritising of an educational element in broadcasting. This resulted in a Public Service Broadcasting monopoly in which 'broadcast journalism was assumed to be oriented towards the values of universalism, objectivity as well as the defence of national values' (Hallin and Mancini 2004: 88). Greatly inspired by the BBC model, a host of Public Service Broadcasters emerged in Europe shortly after the establishment of BBC. The Danish Public Service Broadcaster *Danmarks Radio* (DR) was founded in 1925, as was the Public Service Broadcaster *Kringkastingselskapet* (now NRK) in Norway and *Radiotjänst* (Now Sveriges Radio and Sveriges Television) in Sweden.

In August 1926, Danmarks Radio (DR) began radio transmission of *Pressens Radioavis*, in which a presenter would read news telegrams edited by the newspapers. The DR radio staff did not have editorial responsibility of news coverage until 1964. That year, the radio staff created its own editorial news division and changed the title of the broadcast news programme to *Radioavisen* (translated: the radio paper). Not long after, on 15 October 1965, the first TV news bulletin was broadcast on DR, entitled *TV-Avisen*. In 1998, the different divisions from Radioavisen, TV Avisen, the actuality programmes Orientering and Horisont and DR-Online were united as one news division called DR Nyheder.

As with the British Public Service Broadcaster BBC, the European Public Service Broadcaster DR was then and now financed by licence fees. In both countries, by law, everyone who owns a television set, a radio, a computer or mobile phone with Internet access has to pay. Both broadcasters also receive an income from the selling of programmes.

Made to compete

Until 1955, the BBC held a monopoly of broadcasting both radio and television news. In 1955, Independent Television Network (ITN) was founded as a British commercial television network, referred to as 'Independent Television'. The ITN News (as it was then titled) arrived in Britain amidst a crisis of divided public opinion on the matter. The primary concern, expressed by a group consisting of Conservative MPs and members of the Church in particular, was that the commercially funded television content would 'erode traditional values and morals' (Johnson and Turnock 2005: 17). Concerns were also voiced that it would be wrong to challenge the then popular ideologies of the BBC, and John Reith's mission to 'inform, educate and entertain' and 'to bring the best of everything to the greatest number of homes' (BBC 2012: 1). BBC's first director John Reith was one of the very outspoken critics of the proposed commercial channel. A key to his visions for BBC had been what he had described as 'the brute force of monopoly' (Reith in Paulu 1981: 17). To Reith, monopoly made possible the creation of a moral responsibility. From his perspective, competition could not be made on morals. He charged that 'competition will be of cheapness, not of goodness' (Paulu 1981). Thus, initial debate surrounding the creation of a competitor to BBC centred on moral values and ethics. However, a group in favour of the new broadcaster, the pressure group Popular Television Association, argued strongly for commercial television as a much needed 'new way to distribute and deliver new programmes and services' (Paulu 1981: 17). The idea of competing with the already established news broadcaster was crucial to the foundation of ITN.

In Denmark, the monopoly of Public Service Broadcasting lasted somewhat longer than it did in the UK. In 1988, the commercial broadcaster TV2 was the first competing Danish broadcasting channel to emerge in Denmark. The new news bulletin, *TV2 Nyhederne*, was a key part of TV2's first day of broadcast on 1 October 1988. Most of the staff members, who were part of building the new competitor to DR in 1988, are still working at TV2 today. During fieldwork at TV2, the notion of being created to be different was often mentioned when I asked staff to describe their broadcaster. All staff exhibited visible pride and excitement when asked to describe the birth of their broadcaster and the breaking of the monopoly. One of them, an editor, looked excited when recalling his first day: '2 May 1988, that's when I began working here [...] I turned up and went for an interview in a small room with Rockwool and I thought 'what is this?' It was wild and it was exciting'

(TV2 editor, 23 May 2008). Another, more recently employed news worker at TV2 was keen to explain to me, during an interview about his everyday work, that he sees the very foundations of TV2 as competing with the Public Service Broadcaster DR in the manner of presenting news:

> I think one was very attentive, when we started TV2 in Denmark, that one wanted something which was very close to the people, you know, a bit more provincial, where for instance DR and BBC at that time were like very classic state broadcasters [...] And in that I think that one from the very start has put care into making TV2 different.
>
> (Reporter and Journalist at TV2 [employed at TV2 for 5 years
at the time of interview], interviewed in the reporter room,
Kvægtorvet, Odense, 24 June 2008)

As can be seen from the above two quotes, among TV2 staff the discourse of the emergence of their broadcaster is centred around 'being different' in ways that felt 'wild' and 'exciting', as opposed to what is defined as a 'very classic state broadcaster'.

3.2 Being 'Best' as Boundary-making

> [T]here's been a drive here, to goddammit be the best. There is an enormous drive to win here and I love that we are such a competitive people. We want to win! Even if I have to break the legs on my secretary then we want to win. And she would understand if I did it. [Laughter from the secretary, 'Yes!' she says.]
>
> (Michael Dyrby, Head of News TV2 interviewed in his office,
which he shares with a secretary, 26 September 2008)

When I asked news workers at the commercial broadcasters to describe the way they work, I was usually told that their main force was that they were *not* working for the licence-fee funded broadcaster. Likewise, when I asked news staff at BBC and DR to describe their way of working, staff told me that their primary strength was that they were *not* a commercial broadcaster. In this sense, both the commercial-funded news workers and the licence funded ones defined themselves to me by what they were not, rather than what they were, both saw the others' way of working as being not quite as good. During interviews, having established themselves as different to the other broadcaster, staff would proceed to explain to me that the way they practice journalism is better than the way staff at the other broadcaster practices journalism. The two following interview excerpts are typical of how staff members at each broadcaster define themselves and their competition:

LHT: Do you see any difference between TV2 Nyhederne and DR's TV Avisen?

TV2 Reporter, employed for 20 years: I think we are better. And I'm not just saying that because I'm employed here, I'm just as critical toward TV2 [...] But when we are in head on competition – the 19.00 News at TV2 and the 21.00 TV Avis [at DR], we are better than them. We are much more ambitious than them. Our cameramen... it is our journalists, they are better at telling good stories. [...] And they buy one editor after the other from us. It's also our popular appeal they want I think, for we go out into the country because of our own good heart, and they sit inside a glass cage and think 'oh, yes, that is right, there is also places in this country called Jylland and Fyn'.

(Male TV2 Reporter, interviewed in corridor outside newsroom,
Kvægtorvet, Odense, 5 June 2008)

LHT: What do you see as the difference between DR and TV2?

DR Graphic, employed for 19 years: Trustworthiness. Clearly the way we have of observing, I'd say. I, I do fear a little that DR is becoming, or at least it can seem like it at times, that they are trying to become like TV2, because TV2 is a little more eatable, but that is really not what I want. Because if I should turn on the news and watch something that I should trust, then I turn on Denmark's Radio [DR]. I don't turn on TV2 because I do believe I have experienced that the things they broadcast have been sexed up a little, and then I know they are not true. And I don't think that is good.

(Male DR Graphic, interviewed in the Graphic-corner,
DR Newsroom, Ørestaden, 26 June 2007)

The above quotes contain some of the most general comparisons of broadcasters, which I have heard expressed by staff at commercial and Public Service Broadcasters. During fieldwork, staff from all four different newsrooms told me often, both off and on record, that they consider their news 'the best', that they believe they are 'the winning news show' and that they believe there are many crucial skills that they just do 'particularly well' compared to their closest TV news rival.[4] News workers at all four newsrooms expressed a great deal of pride and satisfaction with their work, often using phrases such as 'we are better', 'we are the best!' or 'we are the winners'. Curiously, the feeling of being winners was not linked with which broadcaster had the highest viewer ratings, or online clicks – though the latter was a factor given much management attention during my 2017 fieldwork.

At the licence-funded broadcasters, this 'being better than the other' was often expressed while describing the commercial competitor, as 'sexing up stories' or 'making the reality more popular'. Meanwhile, staff at commercial broadcasters would describe their licence-funded competitors as 'sitting in a glass cage' and 'not making stories that real people care about'. Though all news workers talked about being better than the other, it was my impression that staff at the licence-funded broadcasters felt less of an urge to tell me that they were the best, as they appeared to expect me to think them better than the commercial rivals. Still, as there was an increased public debate about the need for Public Service Broadcasting at the time of fieldwork, staff within DR and BBC appeared keen on explaining to me the need not just for their news show but for public service by and large, and its superiority over commercial channels.

The institutional conversion

As discussed earlier (see Chapter 1), in his study of professionalism, Soloski finds institutional policies important to the controlling everyday work though he classifies a set of equally important values to be their professional norms, which are shared across organisations. Working for one broadcaster creates a practice-experience (Wenger 1998a) with which one learns and becomes accustomed to intra-organizational policies (Soloski 1989). When staff told me about their differences in working, it can be seen as a way of explaining to me that they have understood these intra-organisational expectations. Some journalists described the adaptation from one type of intra-organisational policy to another as 'a conversion'.

I did not in any conversations throughout fieldwork encounter someone who told me that the way they did things at another broadcaster than their own was 'best'. This sense of being better than the other channel appeared to be a feeling that all news staff adopted upon being employed. A female reporter, who had been employed for ten years at TV2, told me, the feeling of being best could be described as a type of conversion:

> You know, now I am totally converted, but before I came here I had greater… you know, I thought that DR's TV Avisen had a greater trustworthiness and I would rather watch their news programmes. TV2 Nyhederne didn't really do it for me. But now that I can see what we do, now that I'm kind of conscious of what we do, then I am 100 per cent sure that that's the way to do it. [Said with irony:] Now I am just as brainwashed as all the others.
>
> (Female TV2 reporter, interviewed in the reporter room,
> Kvægtorvet, Odense, 24 June 2008)

The cycle from disbelief to belief in an organisation is of course not atypical to how an employee might feel after having been working for a certain time with any employer. As Goffman described it in 1959, the same cycle can be seen in, for instance, an army recruit who initially only follows army etiquette in order to not be told off by his officers, but eventually he comes to follow the same rules, because he thinks he believes in them and worries whether or not only his superior but his entire organisation would be shamed if he did not act a certain way ([1959] 1990: 31). What is interesting in the above statement, however, is the way that the reporter appears aware of a conversion having taken place and is not ashamed to admit that she now has utterly changed her opinion of her current employer.

Though I asked staff to consider differences between broadcasters, I never ventured into questions about which broadcaster was 'the best'. Still, staff appeared to think me interested in measuring exactly that. During the working day, staff often offered me their opinion that they thought themselves 'the best' or 'better than the other one', or that their news station was 'the winner'. Also, it was not unusual for staff of all four broadcasters to express their fear of becoming like the other, often imagined to be due to some management scheming, which was not journalistically well founded, as shown in the quote from DR graphic above.

Apart from introducing this perceived fear among staff, the quote from the DR graphic worker above introduces the fact that there can be dissatisfaction with management ideas if they are seen as not being journalistically well founded – such as trying to be like TV2 as management consider their way of making news 'more eatable'. In this sense, what is journalistically well founded is more important to news workers than what management considers right. Thus, though editors and management have a dominant role within the newsroom, the communities of practice, which journalists and groups of news workers form, can play an even stronger role in the everyday news judgements (I will return to this in Chapter 6).

At times, the repeated statements of being better than the competitor seemed like a defence of a specific national TV news journalism towards an imagined critique that the other newsrooms makes news that is more trustworthy, more thorough or objective or just 'a better watch' and therefore has more viewers. I was confused at first as to how best to interpret the notion that employees at each of these TV newscasters consider themselves the best. I wondered whether it might be a way of legitimating themselves and their way of working; whether it might be a sign that news workers feel threatened by each other; or a sign that staff did, in fact, feel that their work was not up to standard and thus sought to convince themselves, and me, otherwise. Lastly, I wondered whether this constant assertion of being 'the best' could simply be explained by the fact that journalism is a very competitive profession, and therefore journalists would understand my research as an evaluation of who is better than who.

Interestingly, the notion of being best did not appear to be directly linked with which channel had a higher viewer rating than the other, or which channel had enjoyed more public praise. Though staff were very aware of which news bulletin had more viewers, since they would be told by management if a certain news bulletin had significantly fewer or more viewers than the rival TV news show, this did not appear to determine the feeling of their channel as 'being the best'.

After fieldwork, while re-studying field notes and interviews, I began listing all the different terms and oppositions through which news workers defined themselves at each broadcaster, as I wanted to understand how journalists construct identity through distinction from others. While doing so, I soon found that the concept *the way we work here is better than the way they work there* was often used when news workers were attempting to explain identity and make a distinction from others. Instead of considering why staff appeared so focused on telling me that they were better than staff at the other broadcasters, I began compiling a list of how staff described themselves using this shared concept. Using the first interview above, for instance, I put 'Popular Appeal, Good Heart' on the list opposite 'Glass

Cage'. As the list grew longer, I realised that rather than dwell on how best to interpret the fact that staff describe themselves as 'best' or 'better' than their rivals, it is interesting to use the concepts surrounding words such as 'best' or 'better' as a way of making boundaries between one broadcaster and another.

In this sense, I have come to use Frederik Barth's notion of a boundary as 'a particular conceptual construct that people sometimes impress on the world' (1969: 19). In the case of my fieldwork, I took boundary making to be the constant outward positioning of oneself as being 'better'. Thus, when I experienced journalists telling me that they were 'best' or 'better', I began to view the assertion as a metaphorical mapping performed in the service of constructing oneself, the newsroom, the broadcaster and the perceived competition. Inspired by Barth's concern with discovering 'the cognitive operations and imagery that people use to conceptualize their acts, social groups and environments' (1969: 25), I began to look for how TV news journalists as a profession conceptualise their work through expressing a constant competition in which they define themselves as winners. However, in coding the interviews, I was primarily interested in how the argument of difference was used rather than studying whether I found the argument to be true. Rather than searching for meaning in the content of what was expressed when staff told me they considered themselves 'better', I began searching for meaning in the way that the concept *the way we work here is better than the way they work there* was used. With this concept as a tool for understanding boundary distinctions, I began seeing differences in how news workers at the commercially funded newsrooms defined themselves in contrast to colleagues employed at Public Service Broadcasters. As will be seen in the following, a distinction between the two began to appear, through which I experienced that news workers from the two differently funded broadcasters define themselves differently. In the following, I introduce the key terms with which news workers at the four broadcasters defined each other as being different.

Talking about being different

In analysis of fieldwork interviews, using the term 'we are better because...' as a boundary definition, all recorded interviews were coded and a pattern of shared ways of talking became apparent among staff from TV2 and ITV and among staff from DR and BBC. As an illustration of some of the primary phrases and ideas with which staff described how they found their way of working better than the competitor's way of working, below I present a selection of key quotes.

Analysing the way staff compared their institutions' way of working with that of the nearest broadcast competitor below I only use interview-excerpts from recorded formal interviews, of which I made 50 in total. I choose to only use one type of interview for this analysis as the same type of setting and interview structure would make a better comparison than if I included all conversations and non-recorded chats I have had during fieldwork. However, the observations and non-recorded discussions with journalists have formed an

Theme	Commercial broadcast journalists defining how they are 'best'	Public service broadcast journalists defining how they are 'best'
Historical position	– 'We are lone riders' (iv. 45).	– 'We are the purest form of public service' (iv. 11). – 'We have more experience and know about best-practice' (iv. 16).
News presentation	– 'We are not afraid to be emotional' (iv. 21; iv. 22). – 'They talk down to their viewers. We talk up to ours' (iv. 42). – 'We engage our viewers more than they do, we are more accessible' (iv. 22; iv. 24; iv. 47). – 'We just tell stories better' (iv. 24)	– 'They are more "eatable" and popular' (iv. 4; iv. 17). – 'We are more trustworthy' (iv. 4; iv. 5). – 'We have a better specialised knowledge, they have all-round journalists'(iv. 5; iv. 7). – 'We think of reaching the broad spectre of viewers, the commercial broadcaster might think some of our stories too dry' (iv. 10; iv 18).
Organisational structure	– 'We are independent and free, they are a part of the establishment' (iv. 23). – 'Our structure is less hierarchical' (iv. 21; iv. 35; iv. 26; iv. 37; iv. 42).	– 'We are more free than if we had been a commercial media' (iv. 11). – 'All feel part of this organisation, the staff own this place more' (iv.5; iv. 16).
Economy	– 'We have less funding, they have ten times more of everything: They have many more channels, more staff, more news platforms' (iv. 21; iv 37). – 'Having less money keeps us on our toes' (Iv. 26)	– 'Whoever pays matters to the product' (iv. 1; iv 11). – 'They are a business, we are an organisation' (iv. 5). – 'They think in viewers, we think in public service' (iv. 1; iv. 5; iv. 10; iv. 11).
Competition	– 'We can be more aggressive, more combatant, more robust in our journalism culture' (iv. 26). – 'We are quicker than them' (iv. 35). – 'We are the underdog, so it makes us feel good when we win' (iv. 21).	– 'We are a much bigger news-machine' (iv. 5).

important background for analysis. During fieldwork observations, in the everyday work I have encountered a very similar framing of ways in which institutions are different as the ways in which I highlight below. In presenting interview excerpts above, I have strived to highlight the key metaphors and shared descriptive ways in which staff members talk about their differences (numbers in refer to specific interviews).

Re-reading and analysing interviews, I have found the above list of self-descriptions typical for the everyday boundaries expressed between staff at commercial broadcasters and staff at licence-fee funded broadcasters. It is not my interest here to discuss whether or not the descriptions about the two different types of news broadcasting are true. Rather, I am interested in illustrating the discourse staff at the two different types of broadcasters use when talking about each other, and how they appear to define their work in contrast to the work of the competitor. Nielsen (2012: 202–06) has shown how staff use self-descriptions and references to others' work as a way of positioning oneself professionally. In this way, the comparisons with competitors' ways of working can be seen as a way in which staff seeks affirmation of *institutional identity* (Gubrium and Holstein 2001).

Looking closely at the way staff compare themselves to the competitor, it becomes apparent that while some self-definitions differ, others are identical. All told me they thought their institution better than the other. The idea of the organisational structure being more free and united and all staff feeling 'part of the organisation' was mentioned by staff at both commercially funded and licence-funded media. Staff at both types of institution also shared the idea that the licence-funded broadcasters are bigger, while the competitor is quicker. It is important to note that the quotes above are primarily a presentation of how staff members talk about differences.

'Cowboys' and 'Dinosaurs'?

As I do not intend to engage in a discussion about whether the above definitions of newscasters are correct, I will not analyse the definitions further. Should one overarching discourse be highlighted however, the way staff at the two different broadcasters define each other can be said to allure metaphorically to ideas used by journalists in the everyday of new and fast 'cowboys' versus old, traditional and well-established but dying 'dinosaurs'. Among news workers, public service broadcast organisations are often perceived and referred to as either a 'mastodon', an 'organisation which is ten times bigger than everything', an 'Auntie' or a 'Dinosaur'.

It should be noted that the two different metaphors were not used equally. The idea of being 'the dinosaur broadcaster' was less used among staff at Public Service Broadcasters than commercial broadcasters, and then it appeared primarily in the hope of raising the issue of an imminent danger of extinction. Meanwhile, ITV and TV2, often describe themselves as being 'cowboys' or 'the quick and innovative newcomers', 'lone riders' who act decidedly different and in opposition to the Public Service Broadcasters. As the two metaphorical terms were not equally used by all staff, they cannot be used as a single self-definition of all staff. However, I find the two different metaphors useful explorative tools for how journalists view their competitive role in the media-sphere today.

As these two metaphors were used by staff during fieldwork, I began to find them interesting for exploring how public service and commercial news work could be understood among TV news workers. Viewing the traditional licence-fee funded broadcasters DR and BBC in metaphorical terms as a 'dinosaur' and the commercially funded broadcasters TV2 and ITV as 'cowboys' is thus both based on terms derived from experience-near findings of how the natives speak and ideas that I as a researcher find relevant as a distant-far concept (Geertz 1983).

It is not my purpose to evaluate whether or not the licence-fee funded broadcasters that I have studied in fact *are* like dinosaurs in their way of working. Rather, I have found it interesting to use the term as a prism to explore and introduce how news workers perceive differences among the Public Service Broadcasters I have studied. As Lakoff and Johnson illustrate (1980), understanding the metaphors used in the everyday are important for understanding the interaction between people using them. While those who repeat a certain metaphor every day may rarely consider the metaphor, it can become lived by as a structuring agent in the everyday. Using the example 'argument is war' Lakoff and Johnson illustrate how metaphors of war ('attack', 'strategy', 'wipe out', being 'right on target' or 'indefensible') are often used in the everyday. In this way, Lakoff and Johnson argue, 'the ARGUMENT IS WAR metaphor is one that we live by in this culture; it structures the actions we perform in arguing' (1980: 4, original capitalization). When a concept is metaphorically structured, they argue, an activity is metaphorically structured – which leads to the language being metaphorically structured. Metaphors, to Lakoff and Johnson are a way of making possible indirect understanding (1980: 177). When metaphors are at play, it can thus be a sign that what is being described is an abstract concept which can easier be expressed by referring to something else, which is considered less abstract.

Farmer boys on the prairie

The metaphor of being cowboys on the prairie was used among staff from all four news divisions both in everyday conversation and in recorded interviews to describe TV2 and ITV.

> We began out here on the prairie all alone, and the others said: 'Those farmer-boys they can't do anything at all'. And then five years went and we totally overtook TV Avisen [DR's News Bulletin] and we totally beat them, you know? We stick together here, against those people over in Copenhagen.
>
> (TV2 reporter with 20 years employment, interviewed in the hallway between newsroom and reporters room, 5 June 2008)

The above quote, from one of the many journalists who have worked at TV2 since its very first day in 1988, aptly describes the way staff members feel about the relationship they have with the public service news-rival, TV Avisen. DR was first, then TV2 broke their monopoly, and against all odds this new, smaller channel soon had more news-viewers than DR had, and now they stick together against the licence-fee funded channel. At ITV, though the channel was not winning the ratings battle at the time of my research, I experienced a very similar sense among staff of 'sticking together' against the big licence funded broadcaster. ITV news staff appeared to have a shared memory of winning the ratings battle in the past and perceive themselves as united in the battle to win viewers in the present too. At ITV too, staff felt that they treated stories in new ways, more exciting and engaging than how the traditional Public Service Broadcaster worked.

Both the news division at TV2 and at ITV have a public service remit, but as the news bulletin is scheduled within a commercial broadcasting system, the news product takes on character of a commercial commodity, in relation to commercial functions demanded by the channel in which it is broadcast (a point also raised about the Norwegian TV2, in Helland 2001: 254). As highlighted above, however, the idea of using the news as commercial goods to be sold and packaged for a certain viewer segment has arguably found its way to the traditional Public Service Broadcasters, BBC and DR, as they describe an aim to engage the viewer and keep the viewer tuned in (see for instance Dyke in Arlidge 2002; DR TV Avisen online 18 May 2011).

Comparing themselves to the Public Service Broadcasters staff both at TV2 and ITV would at times talk of themselves in terms of 'cowboys', 'riding the prairie', fighting the bigger, more established other broadcaster. I believe there are many other metaphors that one could use to describe the commercial newscasters, but the mythical idea of a cowboy conveys many of the ideas and ideologies that I have observed among commercial broadcast staff. As such, sticking with the metaphor of cowboys helps to provide an illustration for the sense of being new and different, being smaller in number than the traditional broadcaster, using new technological measures, battling, constantly moving forward and being lone riders – which I have experienced among news staff at both ITV and TV2.

Both ITV and TV2 broke the monopoly of Public Service Broadcasting in their respective countries, with the aim to make news different to how the traditional broadcaster presented it. It is perhaps this historic fact, which most of all determines commercial news journalists' will to be different at all times, to present stories in an exciting and innovative way. Making a news programme that is 'different' and 'nearer to the people' than the licence-fee funded rival is an expression that is used at both commercial channels. At TV2 one of the channel's declared missions has been to reach 'Maren by the Dam' (in Danish: 'Maren i Kæret'), which is a common Danish saying referring to a 'common, average person without any special educational prerequisites'.[5] In editorial meetings, while discussing how to present a specific story, reporters and editors often interrupt a discussion, saying 'but we need to convey this story to Maren i Kæret!'. At ITV, there were similar expressions, such as 'we need to make this story *accessible!*' put when discussing how best to 'treat' a story to make sure everyone could understand, and be engaged with it. ITV staff talked of BBC as 'less engaging with *real* people' and as 'not representing the establishment' compared to their own news content which did. In the tone of ITV, referring to the engaging of real people, a News Editor at TV2 told me 'there is media which talks down to the audience and media that talks up to the viewer – and we talk more upwards to the viewer' – hinting that the licence-paid broadcasters veer towards arrogance. Meanwhile, at the licence-paid broadcasters, staff described their commercially funded rival as 'untrustworthy', 'poppy' and as making more 'eatable news' by 'thinking in viewers'.

3.3 A Shared Struggle

The four different news divisions in this study all work to a public service remit, but have different histories. Still, at the time of my study all share the same challenge. In their country, all four broadcasters were, and are still today, competing to provide news in a media environment continuously reshaped by increasing competition, globalisation, digitisation and convergence. Though the journalists I talked to were concerned with explaining how they were better than their nearest competitor, at times I found them talking of sharing a crucial battle with the same nearest competitor. This battle was often talked about as the battle to keep public service alive.

The idea that Public Service Broadcasting is dead or dying was often talked about among all news workers. When Public Service Broadcasting talked of the death of public service, it was often in connection with the cuts in jobs expected by staff within the news division. Thus, it appeared staff at all broadcasters defined a cut in jobs as a cut in public service values. I had a very visual example of this at my first day of fieldwork at DR in 2007. On the short walk from the metro station at DR Byen to the newly constructed DR building housing the news division, I was met by a makeshift sign (Fig. 3.1).

The sign, which I later found out had been erected on that same day by a group of staff from different departments inside DR, read: 'PUBLIC SERVICE BORN 1926 – DEAD ??'.[6] Apart from this wooden sign erected for all staff and the public to see, at DR, staff had collaborated on a music video about how public service was being killed off, which was shared through the DR intranet. Also, in the kitchen adjacent to the newsroom, staff had cut out and hung satirical drawings from the print press, which were critical of the expected job cuts. One such drawing was an illustration entitled 'Room for excitement', depicting the large new DR building with two comparatively small people standing outside and the caption: 'Right, now there's only us two left, and we just have to make the very best TV Avis' (see Fig. 3.2). Thus, from the very first day of fieldwork, I noticed how staff were using different means to express to both management and the public that the cuts in jobs at DR would make it impossible to meet the high standards and expectations of a public service news division.

Among all four national news divisions, it has been the aim to maintain a brand identity as a trusted and valued source of information because of their commitment to an impartial and accurate news and current affairs provision. Trustworthiness is a frequently

Fig. 3.1: Translated: 'PUBLIC SERVICE BORN 1926 – DEAD? (erected outside the DR newsroom, June 2017).

Fig. 3.2: Translated: 'Right, now there's only us two left and we just have to make the world's best TV Avis!'. Entitled 'Room for excitement'. (DR news division kitchen, DR Byen, June 2007).

used argument for prioritising the national news bulletin. Particularly among the Public Service Broadcasters, the argument is made that public service broadcast news is thorough, trustworthy and sensible, rather than subjective, opinionated and sensational. In 2011, describing the evening news bulletin, TV Avisen, DR thus writes:

> The news flow has never been stronger. Communication has happened faster. Anyone can share an opinion with others through Facebook or the Internet. But the news flow is also confusing, and sometimes full of errors or indifferent gossip. For a newscaster it is tempting to use all the effort on drama, war, fire and crime. There are 'good' pictures in such stories.
>   TV Avisen is much more than that. We try to clean up. We show the people behind the story and analyse the perspectives and the consequences, so we don't just tell what has happened, but also give a suggestion as to why it happened. Therefore we spend time on stories which are not necessarily full of drama, but which are significant in the long run.
>
> (DR TV Avisen online, 18 May 2011, my translation from Danish)

The values outlined above are not unique to DR alone; rather, they suit traditional notions of public service. In 2017, the argument put above is still referred to among journalists at the four broadcasters: while new social media may bring more news, it can be confusing, sensational and less trustworthy. Among all journalists, I found the notion of 'trustworthiness' as outlined above, one of the most often used arguments for fighting the shared challenge of new media. Editorially, at all four newsrooms two other words where used when talking about essential tools for combating the new media challenge: to 'engage' and 'entice' the viewer. In the following I illustrate how these ideas were presented and worked towards.

To inform, educate, entertain *and* engage

While the national broadcasters (such as TV Avisen above) may want to signal to their audience that they offer a reliable alternative to the 'confusing' Internet, they are at the same time forced to use the Internet and other media platforms if they are to engage a broad spectrum of viewers as required in their public service remit. Additionally, the use of the Internet in a media strategy can aid Public Service Broadcasters in maintaining audience share – an element which not only the commercial broadcasters have to consider. As McNair has remarked: 'Even the BBC, free of the direct commercial pressures felt by ITN and Sky News in Britain, must pay attention to its audience share if it is to maintain political and public support for its licence fee funding' (McNair 2005: 29).

As Public Service Broadcasters like the BBC and DR have moved online, they have celebrated a new role: engaging audiences in public conversations – on the web, by mobile phone and IPTV, on Facebook, Twitter and YouTube. Today, when a reporter is in Syria to report back from the war, s/he will be expected to do a lot more than the evening broadcast. S/he is expected and very much encouraged to use social media actively throughout the entire journey of the report. And a successful report will have engaged viewers on platforms such as Facebook, Twitter, Snapchat and Instagram. At the beginning of this Millennium, the then BBC Director-General Greg Dyke announced plans to update the old mission to 'inform, educate and entertain' to also include the word 'connect' (Arlidge 2002). Similarly, at DR's 60-year anniversary of television broadcast in September 2011, DR presented themselves as having moved 'from information to interaction' (Mølgaard 2011).

At DR, I was present doing fieldwork on 7 June 2007 as the new online news platform Update was launched. The launch was celebrated with champagne corks going off in the newsroom and speeches held by, among others, Ulrik Haagerup, the newly appointed Head of News for all the different DR news platforms. Members of staff from all sections of the news division were present at the launch, as was the Director General, Kenneth Plummer. 'This is the biggest innovation since the colour TV! In the midst of a hard time we bring something new, something good', said the Head of News in his introductory speech, which was one of the first in-house presentations by Haagerup. By March 2013, the online news broadcast platform Update was closed down as it was deemed not to fit DR's future news priorities.

Among some of the members of staff who have worked at the Public Service Broadcasters for many decades, this shift towards having to engage the viewer is at times referred to as problematic, as it brings too many changes too fast. One of the most critical members of staff I met at DR, a long-time employed graphic news worker, complained: 'There was a time when it went well [...] Everything is being changed all the time around here. Just like a container ship that is being moved with a big jerk – you just can't do that. It needs to take a quiet, steady, safe course. I think it will sink'.

Enticing viewers

> The fear of boring the viewer has changed a delicate balance, and Mr and Mrs Denmark
> will be wise to put on the critical glasses for their evening coffee and the news.
> (Journalist Lasse Jensen, in Prent 2007)

In 2007, at a time when interactivity, standing newsreaders and innovative news walls were on the increase at broadcasters in both Britain and Denmark, critics such as Lasse Jensen above expressed a worry that news was becoming more about the show than about the presentation of balanced views and information. This type of critique was often aimed at the commercially funded broadcasters, ITV and TV2, as their news bulletins were deemed more popular and keen on using new technology in broadcast news. But, as broadcasters followed suit with their commercial counterparts in terms of using both standing news readers, interactivity and 3D news walls, the critique of choosing style over content fell on the licence-fee funded broadcasters. At DR, there was a particular urgency for enticing and keeping viewers, as TV2 were perceived to be stealing their viewers – a fact which was often discussed both inside the newsroom and outside of it when socializing with colleagues after work.

As described previously, the news divisions of all four broadcasters work under a public service remit. Thus, the commitment of public service values is one that all four news divisions share: The two licence-fee funded broadcasters (DR and BBC) are bound by the public service contract, and the two commercial broadcasters are bound to broadcast public service content in their scheduling, which they define as synonymous with their news bulletin. Thus, as Cushion has described it, both national commercial and national Public Service Broadcasters work towards the same shared public service ideal: 'Those values associated with well-resourced and high quality journalism lie at the heart of public service values, informing not only public but also some commercial broadcasters in this new millennium' (Cushion 2012: 21). Among researchers, in the new age of media use and new media content, the need for Public Service Broadcasting is highlighted to a greater extent than before, as public service values are important in order to sidestep or avoid what is often described as an otherwise capitalist and commercial media landscape (see for instance Preston 2009).

Enticing emotions

When I asked staff to define the way they work, at both commercial broadcasters replies mainly centred on the content they produce. At TV2, content is primarily compared to that of the DR, with the argument that viewers choose to watch the commercial channel as their news is 'easier to watch', 'more accessible', 'engaging' and just 'more interesting' compared to the licence-fee funded newscaster, which 'makes less of a story'. Responses expressed by employees at ITV about their news content compared to BBC's were similar, even despite the fact that the channel was not winning the ratings battle at the time of my fieldwork. Similar to the way staff at TV2 talked of themselves, staff at ITV told me that ITV 'tries to engage the people more than BBC does'.[7]

'Engaging the viewer' is a phrase often used among staff at commercially funded institutions, and one that I found less frequently mentioned inside the license-funded newsrooms. During morning editorial meetings, when a certain story had been chosen, there was much more debate at the commercially funded channels compared to the license-fee funded channels over how a story was to be told *as well as* how to make it 'engaging', 'fascinating' and 'interesting' to the busy layman viewer. At both commercially funded stations, it appeared that members of staff were seeking to portray and entice emotions, often through a case study. I have found this use of a case study to suit what Arpi researching the use of cases at TV2 has described as: '[A] technique of presentation using a person or a group of people as an illustration of a greater societal connection and an important character in the presentation of the journalistic story' (Arpi 2004: 62, my translation from Danish).

At both ITV and TV2, I experienced cases to be a crucial part of telling a story, to the extent that some stories were dropped if there was no case to tell it. At DR and the BBC, cases were similarly viewed as important for the presentation of a story, and at both places I saw stories dropped if there was no case. Flemming Svith's study (2008) into the use of cases at DR compared to TV2 in Denmark has reached a similar conclusion. Svith found every fifth of TV2's news stories to be based on cases, and there 'was no significant difference between DR's and TV2's use of case based stories, though one could have expected it' (Svith 2008: 90, my translation from Danish).[8] I did not count how many of the stories I observed were based around case stories; however, it became clear through fieldwork that finding cases and encouraging sources to tell their stories through emotions was a significant part of the job for reporters and journalists at all the four broadcasters. The only difference that I could sense was that staff at the commercially funded broadcasters appeared keener to talk about the necessity for cases and less prone to questioning their daily work with finding cases. As a reporter doing work experience at TV2 told me:

> […] it is a part of everything we do in the TV2 system, that we are case based and closeness-based. I've been to a meeting where I was told about this […] but it's also written in this book we've got […] and then it's something you're brought up to do, we talk about it, and then there is the debrief every day, and it's obvious that the boss prizes that type of stories, they like it when we've done it that way. On the other hand, there's beatings when we've done it the expert-way or the bureaucracy-way.
> (TV2 reporter, interviewed in reporter room, outside news management offices, Kvægtorvet, Odense, 24 June 2008)

During the interview above, when I enquired about the 'expert way' and the 'bureaucracy way', the reporter explained that it meant telling a story using 'a talking head', an expert or someone from within the bureaucracy – a method which at both commercial broadcasters is generally seen as a type of storytelling that distances the story from the people. Over the ten years of this study, the Internet and specifically social media have been taken more and more seriously as a news medium. Today, all broadcasters consider Facebook, Twitter and to some extent Instagram and Snapchat as crucial for their everyday work. Case studies are talked about as vital for a story to make it to online versions. 'Sometimes a story will do great on Facebook but not that great on TV. Facebook is a very important platform for us, but if a story does not have a case it will never make it on Facebook at all', a TV2 journalist told me in November 2016.

The Theatre of News

Just as DR and BBC are inspired by each other, so are ITV and TV2 – and one of the most visible ways is the manner in which both broadcasters focus on illustrating news stories. At both commercial broadcast newsrooms I have found one of the crucial ways that staff members aim to be different to be how news is presented, illustrated, explained and visualised.[9] A recent case study of this aim to be visually different to the licence-funded

Fig. 3.3: ITV's Theatre of News: Health and Science editor Lawrence McGinty presenting from the studio. The screen-grab illustrates ITV's 3D wall and floor effects in the 2007 studio nicknamed 'The Theatre of News'.

broadcast news is the 'Theatre of News', a concept that was first invented at ITV News in London (see Figs. 3.3 and 3.4 for illustration). Introducing the studio in 2004, the editor of the ITV News Channel highlighted one of the key worries that journalists talked about in relation to the new studio: That all the gadgets and the graphics would overtake what they saw as 'good journalism'.

> The design is perfect for news channels that need to look busy even when there's little going on. But it remains a huge challenge for presenters and directors to use the wall live and unrehearsed 24 hours a day. We also have to be constantly vigilant to make sure we don't get carried away and let over-production get in the way of the journalism.
> (Dominic Crossley-Holland, writing in Press Gazette, 27 February 2004)

Since 2004, ITV News has been famous among broadcasters and news researchers for its new and innovative 'virtual studio'. The 1 million pound studio, nicknamed 'The Theatre of News' or 'The Virtual Newsroom', which features a floor-to-ceiling sized curved green screen for presenters to stand up in front of and present graphics to viewers, became an attraction for broadcast staff from all around the world. Presenters will wander along the very large green screen, pausing to point out images or graphics, all in an attempt to make more 'accessible' news. Editor of ITV News, Debora Turness, who was responsible for the new virtual studio, complained that the traditional way of working with pictures was becoming boring, arguing that: '[p]ictures are our base material, yet newscasters traditionally sit at desks with static windows behind them' (Turness in Robinson 2004). The aims of the new studio were aptly

Fig. 3.4: ITV's Theatre of News: Alastair Stewart presents from the studio, with a pre-recorded newsroom as background. The screen-grab illustrates ITV's 3D wall and floor effects in the 2007 studio nicknamed 'The Theatre of News'.

summarized by Chief Executive of the ITV News Group, Clive Jones, as an attempt 'to try and break the gap that has always existed between the formal atmosphere of a traditional studio and the pictures gathered in the field and the computer generated graphics deployed to explain and analyse the news' (Jones 2004 in Johnson and Turnock 2005: 134). On top of the interest from competitors, the innovative new ITV News studio won ITV News a Royal Television Society Award in the category 'technical innovation' in 2004.

After ITV introduced the Theatre of News, the practice of including 3D graphics and letting presenters stand up to present was soon used at all four broadcasters and many others internationally. Another feature of the Theatre of News was to use props to tell and explain a story, a way of explaining nicknamed by ITV staff as 'Show and Tell'. One of Turness' favourite examples of a Show and Tell was how ITV presenters would tell the story of rising fuel tax: Rather than do a graphic, a litre of fuel would be poured out onto the studio floor.

When Hallin in 1992 criticised the new types of broadcast TV news, he pointed to the presentation of news as the most dramatic sign of a commercialisation of news. According to him, the new type of evening news meant a change for the worse in which 'the pace has come to resemble more closely the pace of the rest of commercial television, with 10-second sound bites and tightly packaged stories' (Hallin 1992: 21). In order to produce more commercial news, Hallin found journalists to be pressurised more than ever to present stories that have both narrative and visual values containing both drama, emotion, good video and 'tug at the heart strings' (1992: 22). The Theatre of News can be said to represent all these values.

At the BBC, the secretary to the Head of News asked me how it 'really felt' to work inside the Theatre of News. 'Of course I've been there too... that's where they've got the Theatre of

News!', said Michael Dyrby, the Head of News at TV2, when I told him I had worked at ITV News. Together with a group of news managers, he had been to visit the ITV News studio in 2005 when the studio had become famous around newsrooms across Europe and the rest of the world. He told me that the way ITV had created their newsroom and news bulletin was a crucial inspiration to the renewed 22 o'clock TV2 news bulletin, and that he thought Debora (Head of News at ITV) very courageous for daring to create such an innovative way of presenting news.

> I think it [the Theatre of News] is pretty far out, but also fantastic. [...] And it is ITV who has been the inspiration for us taking the step we have taken. But I just didn't want to go as far as she did, to go into the virtual, because I would like to have real reality. [...] So therefore we said, we'd like to have those big screens, we'd like to have those hosts that walk [...] The 22 news bulletin has actually been created a little in its image, and then we shaped it to fit our model.
>
> (Michael Dyrby, interviewed in his office,
> 26 September 2008)

During my fieldwork I have met staff at all three other channels in Denmark and Britain, who have been to visit the virtual studio at ITV to learn and be inspired. In 2009, ITV reworked the virtual studio to make a new set once again, hailed by Editor-in-Chief David Mannion as created to 'put the human element at the heart of our journalism' (in *Broadcast Magazine* 2009).

3.4 When Broadcasters Agree

The values and missions of the broadcaster are taken into account when a journalist shapes, illustrates and presents stories. But during fieldwork I did not find these values to play a deciding factor in the selection of which events should be taken up as stories. Among the commercial broadcast news workers, I only very rarely observed that a unique case led to the broadcasting of a story they would have otherwise not brought. Thus, in the everyday, it is not the values and declared mission statements of each broadcaster that are the primary motivations for bringing a story. For, though the values and mission statements differ at each broadcaster, within all four broadcasters, I saw that it was very much the same type of events that were chosen to be story material on any given day.

What management and editors do not control

As discussed earlier, Breed's (1955) study of newspapermen finds publisher policy one of the key factors controlling staff inside the newsroom. The learning of policy, Breed argues, is key for new recruits to understand institutional norms and values (1955: 328). During the study,

I found broadcaster policies and missions to be important for how news workers talk about the way they work in the everyday. I found the perceived policy of an editor significant to how news items were presented to specific editors, and how news stories were talked about with the editorial staff. Additionally, I found the broadcaster's policies, mission statements and official values to have some importance for how news stories were presented: At the commercially funded broadcasters, for instance, 3D graphics were often considered key to a news story, while at the licence-funded broadcasters 3D graphics had lower priority both among editorial staff and journalists. I have come to agree with Breed in that an editor's reprimands are important for signifying what the boss favours and what he does not favour. However, although I found policy important, I have found ideals of the profession rather than ideas of institutional policy to play a key part in the everyday decisions about what is news and what is a good news story (this issue is explored further in Chapter 7).

In deviating from the notion that policy works as a key factor in social control of the newsroom, my study deviates from that of Breed. It is not broadcaster policy, editorial policy, nor organisational values that steer the selection process when facing a list of events and deciding which should be a news story; rather, the process is guided by values of the journalistic profession: A shared ideal that I found to be dominant among staff at all four broadcasters. Though I spoke to news workers from four different newsrooms with different mission statements, different management and different broadcasters, during fieldwork I met more agreement than disagreement with values and ideas in the everyday work. Thus, though I found news workers to share an institutional consensus that each news division was unique and different to the other news divisions, within time, I began to notice similarities rather than differences across newsrooms. This finding made me interested in researching what I found to be a shared ideal, and to consider journalism as an ideology. Comparing journalists in Holland, Germany, Britain, Australia and the US, Mark Deuze (2002) has come to a similar conclusion: That a shared ideology exists between journalists from elective democracies across borders of newsroom and nationality. As Deuze concludes:

> [J]ournalists in elective democracies share similar characteristics and speak of similar values in context of their daily work, but apply these in a variety of ways to give meaning to what they do. Journalists in all media types, genres and formats carry the ideology of journalism. It is therefore possible to speak of a dominant occupational ideology of journalism on which most newsworkers base their professional perceptions and praxis, but which is interpreted, used and applied differently among journalists across media.
>
> (Deuze 2011: 19)

Deuze's study referred to above is survey-based and focuses on Holland. Arguably, his study is primarily a study of how journalists *talk about* their work, rather than *how* they work. However, during my fieldwork, studying the everyday practices of journalists, I have come to agree with his above conclusions.[10] From this point of view, a broadcaster's declared mission statements can be seen as important primarily to how the story is presented, rather than how it is selected, angled and created in the everyday. Realising that staff at the different news divisions appeared to have more values in common than I had first assumed, I began to ask staff who had worked at both license-funded and commercially funded broadcast news to explain to me what they saw as the main difference. One presenter, who had worked at both a license-funded broadcaster (the BBC) and a commercially funded broadcaster (ITV), told me that he saw all news journalists as connected, belonging to a shared community of practice, which is united in a shared public service responsibility:

> Well I was trained at BBC, where there is a real feeling about Public Service, that is their raison d'être [...]. But I do think, whether you are a journalist working for a state broadcaster or working for a commercial broadcaster, I do think that if you are working in news you do have a public service responsibility. And I think it is one of the most important roles of a broadcaster. It does not matter how it is funded.
>
> (Presenter, ITV News, interviewed in his office overlooking the newsroom, 31 October 2007)

The talk I had with the ITV presenter above made me realise that staff who had been working at different broadcasters were important informants on how the key differences between the different broadcasters were perceived. Talking to staff members who had worked across the different broadcasters made me realise that these members of staff, like me, saw license-funded news divisions and commercially funded news divisions as having central similarities and agreements. Throughout the following chapters, I will take a closer look at similarities and agreements among the four different news divisions, and in Chapter 7 one of the key shared values is explored, that of the 'good news story'.

3.5 Conclusions

In this chapter, I have introduced some of the ways that members of staff at TV2, ITV, DR and BBC describe their way of working. News staff talk about themselves as being 'the best', in what is perceived to be a constant competition between themselves and the other national TV news makers. Following Barth, I have used the way staff talk of being the best as a boundary, which defines and distinguishes how staff members at a given broadcaster consider themselves in relation to their closest rival.

In order to provide an illustrative metaphor portraying the way that commercial news staff perceive themselves, I have introduced the mythological idea of Cowboys and Dinosaurs. Firstly, the metaphor of Cowboys and Dinosaurs has been introduced as it is an *experience-near* concept, which the staff used to describe themselves. Secondly, the metaphor is used as it captures part of the essential sense of broadcaster identity that I have experienced among news workers.

With this chapter, it has been shown how staff at all four different news divisions share values resembling those articulated in public service regulations. As such, I have found the organisational values to form only part of the many challenges that news workers have to negotiate in their everyday struggle to reach what they see as the ideal news work. This realisation was a surprise to me. However, in time, I found studying the shared values of the four newsrooms to be much more meaningful than studying the differences. In the following chapters, I explore the shared values among all news workers by illustrating the ways in which the four different newsrooms are connected and work in a very similar daily routine.

Notes

1   At the time of the interview, the presenter told me he held the Danish record in presented news shows, as he was soon to round 10,000 presented shows.

2   The Danish word 'Poppet' (stemming from the English 'pop') is often used at DR about the way TV2 presents news.

3   With currently over 6300 staff employed in the news division and 20,753 staff employed in total – a figure which can only act as a lower guideline as it does not take into account the number of permanent or fixed-term contract workers, nor freelancers and short-contracted staff (according to BBC Freedom of Information Request, 2 February 2011).

4   '[…] brilliant at ideas, treatments for stories, and that is, you know something ITV News does particularly well. It is part of the culture here […]' (ITV interview 19, Programme Editor, 19 October 2007).

5   According to the Danish dictionary, *Den Danske Ordbog*.

6   'Public Service – Født 1926, død??'

7   ITV newsreader and journalist, interviewed 23 October 2007.

8   When Svith set out to study the use of cases among the public service broadcast news, DR compared to the use at the commercially funded TV2, he expected for the commercial broadcaster to be keener on case use than the public service one. His expectations, however, were proven wrong. His study, conducted with fellow colleagues at the Danish School of Media and Journalism, analysed a total of 45 news bulletins broadcasts from January to April 2007.

9   Incidentally, media researcher Knut Helland points to a similar argument in the 1992 upstart of Norway's commercial rival to the Public Service Broadcaster, NRK. In the early days of TV2 in Norway, management at TV2 saw it as crucial to profile the channel as being 'different' to the public service rival by focusing on having a visual profile that was more 'delicious and elegant' to watch (Helland 2001: 247).

10   While Deuze bases his research on surveys of journalists from five different nationalities, it is beyond the scope of my study to include journalists from other countries, just as I do not include journalists from any other media platforms than the national TV news division.

Part IV

Inside the New Newsrooms

Chapter 4

A New Design of the Old Newsroom

On newsrooms turning circular, and how meetings act as a show of who is in control

The previous chapter illustrated how journalists *talk* about institutional differences. This chapter will focus less on how journalists say they act and more on how I have observed news work to be structured. Exploring the structure within which journalists work, this chapter describes and analyses key similarities between the four newsrooms. In structuring this and the following chapter, I have been inspired by Wenger's (1998a) view of an organisation. According to Wenger, there are two views of an organisation:

1) *The designed organisation*, such as the place where staff works, and the structure of space and time within that place.
2) *The practice* (or, more accurately, the constellation of practices), which gives life to the organisation and is often a response to the designed organisation.

(1998a: 241)

Though it is problematic to single out the designed organisation from the practice within the organisation, with this chapter I aim to introduce the designated organisation, with a particular focus on the newsroom. Already in 1979, in their comparative study of news casting, Golding and Elliot pointed towards the necessity of focusing on organisational structures of work when studying ideals of journalists at work. Golding and Elliot define the structure of work space and work routines as a key factor for what journalists produce as news. More recently, Fenton (2010) has defined news journalism as intrinsically dependent on the complex structures within which journalists work, in that 'how journalists make news, depends on their working environment' (Fenton 2010: 3). In his studies of professions, Freidson (2001) defines the structure of everyday work as an important element for analysis:

Most, if not all, disciplines are part of a particular division of labor organized, established, and enforced by some power external to it. The actual jurisdictional boundaries between concrete specialisations, even when managerial authority rather than free occupational interaction organize them, can be bitterly contested (in firms this is called 'office politics') and may by no means be taken for granted. [...]

No doubt other features of knowledge commanded by a discipline may be related to variation in the structure of the division of labor and the processes taking place within it, but the topic must be approached with caution because it cannot be separated from the character of the labor market upon which the very existence of labor inevitably depends.

(Freidson 2001: 163–64)

The lengthy quote by Freidson above illustrates two key arguments of this chapter. First, the structure of everyday work is an important not-to-be-taken-for-granted element in the everyday work of journalists. Studying the structure of work is also a study of how boundaries between concrete specialisations are created and kept in place. Second, the structure of working practices can be seen as inevitably connected to market forces, in this instance the increasingly competitive media market. Thus, the journalism profession is inextricably linked to a market logic. From this perspective, the journalistic product is a result of both a professional and a market logic.[1] The newsroom can be seen as a bounded entity within which both the professional logic and the market logic meet and compete for attention.

Inspired by Freidson (2001), Golding and Elliot (1979) and Wenger (1998a), through this chapter, I focus on the structure and organisation of news work, specifically the temporal and spatial organisation of the newsroom. Analysis will thus be twofold: focusing on both the structure of place and the structure of time within the newsroom. In the chapter following this one, I delve into further analysis of practice, which gives life to the designed organisation. As introduced earlier (see Chapter 2.6), in analysis of fieldwork, I am inspired by Denzin's (1989) definitions of 'thick description'. Thus, I aim to not only describe action within the room but also explore the context, the intentions and meanings that organize the action, trace evolution and development of the action and present this as a text that can then be interpreted (Denzin 2001: 33). This approach makes a descriptive account necessary for analysis. With this approach in mind, this chapter will present empirical findings through descriptive-attentive discussions.

Why structure matters

In September 2017, when I visited the regional TV newsroom of DR Østjylland, I noticed that two very big TV screens were now enjoying a prominent space in the staff coffee area. The two screens showed the currently most shared news sites in Denmark and the current trending online posts across Denmark. This new design of the coffee area undoubtedly signals management interest in staff being aware of stories trending online. Arguably, it also shows how management encourages a type of stories that may trend online. During 2016 and 2017, I saw similar screens put up in and around the newsrooms at all four newsrooms. Space structures how people can act. Delaney and Kaspin define space as 'perhaps our primary means of orientation in the world – physically, socially and cosmologically' (Delaney and Kaspin 2011: 35). Physical space, they argue, is not only that which is visible, rather it is 'filled with things and with meanings' and 'encodes social meanings and values' (2011: 35). With this definition in mind, I believe that looking closer at the structure of space can give an understanding of the values and ideals with and within the newsroom. During fieldwork, I have found the physical space of the newsroom to be a contested space in which ideals of both journalists, management and institutions meet.

Other studies of the first wave of newsroom studies (see Schlesinger 1978 and Gans 1979) have paid attention to everyday routines and the division of labour as key to defining journalists' activities, thus providing a descriptive insight into professional constraints of news production at the time such as deadlines, the organisation of news gathering and competition. Recent research on news production has found the structure of work, primarily the temporal and spatial layout to be important to the news product. Through fieldwork at Nordjyske Medier and DR Byen, Bechmann describes how a change in physical rooms and physical layout has a 'signal value' (2009: 140) to the journalists, which in turn makes the product and practice change. Introducing the three largest broadcast newscasters in Britain, Harrison (2000: 79–107) has shown how different organisational hierarchies are evident in different layouts of newsrooms. Viewing the structure at BBC news as 'inherently complex' (2000: 79), she illustrates how the physical space of the BBC newsroom is also complex. Describing the close relationship between the input desk and the output desk within the ITN newsroom, Harrison shows how the physical layout of the ITN newsroom has made it possible for the editors of Intake and Output to 'shout across to each other constantly as well as to laugh and joke with each other' (2000: 91). In this way, Harrison shows how the ideology of the room is linked to the structure of the room. In studying journalists at work, Harrison finds it 'important to understand the physical geography of the newsroom structure as an organisation as well as the formal and informal dynamics created by this environment' (Harrison 2000: 86–87).

While both Bechmann (2008) and Harrison (2000) describe the importance of physical layout for the working practices, the comparison of structural, spatial and temporal settings is not a direct focus of their research. Through keeping a more concrete focus on the structural organisation of the newsroom, with this and the following chapter I explore and illustrate the importance of structure to the production of news work. Moreover, I analyse how professional values and ideals are challenged by constraints in the spatial and temporal layout.

4.1 The Market Logic of Changing the Newsroom

As discussed previously, the newsroom can be seen as a site in which both professional ideals of journalists and market logics of management and media owners vie for attention. Even if professional ideals between journalists and management are not the same, journalists are closely connected to the labour market upon which the very existence of journalistic work inevitably depends (see Freidson 2001: 163–64). According to Freidson, the market logic is steered towards economic gains and organised around consumption 'with consumer preference and choice determining whose services will succeed' (2001: 1). Within this logic value is measured 'primarily by cost' (2001). While management and editors may have other professional values, their work is linked to a market logic. During fieldwork within the newsrooms, journalists referred to such market logics as the primary reason for restructuring their ways of working, often hinting how this type of logic is far from that of their own professional values.

As discussed earlier (see Chapter 3.3), at the time of study all four newsrooms were facing the challenge of a media environment being reshaped by increased competition, globalisation, digitisation and convergence. The shape, function and ideals of the new newsrooms must be seen in this light, as they were reorganised as part of a general trend towards coping with these changes and as part of broadcasters' constant battle against competitors.

Time for a new room

The structural redesign, changing the workplace of journalists from one of small units and closed offices to larger open office newsrooms where more people can hear and see each other at work, is not unique for the journalistic profession. Indeed, over the last two decades, researchers of professions have pointed towards changes in managerial practices and technology as being so profound that 'the fundamental bureaucratic principle of hierarchical control realized by formal supervisory and personnel policies has been displaced by new forms of organization and employment' (Freidson 2001: 8; see also Kalleberg 1996; Littek and Charles 1995). Thus, the move towards open plan office structures can be seen as part of a general re-organisation of professions at work. Arguably, for a profession so devoted to ideals of self-control, the notion of being under surveillance is experienced as particularly challenging.

In 2007, with the growth of ever more media platforms, staff at the four news divisions, BBC, ITV, DR and TV2, who had before considered themselves to be the prime news sources of the nation, felt they were under increasing threat from new media platforms, such as the mobile phone and the Internet, as well as novel sources, such as citizen journalists and bloggers. Among management at the traditional national broadcasters, this perceived challenge led to the idea that the news division should think 'out of the box' and use the new media available to maintain their viewers (or 'the users', as they were increasingly described). At management level, collaboration and multitasking were seen as a way of combating the new threats facing their news division. In 2007, younger reporters from the online news desk would visit editorial meetings in order to pick up stories they could share or premiere online. If one of these online reporters would be interested in using a broadcast story first online, there would be much aggression and annoyance among TV staff. Today, TV news staff are much more accustomed to their TV story-ideas being shared online before broadcast on the evening news. For, ten years later in 2017, each newsroom has reporters employed solely to publish stories on social media and news apps, as soon as a news story unfolds.

Initially, one of the managerial hopes linked to multi-skilling staff was that of using the same content for many different media platforms simultaneously, thereby creating new business models and new ways of engaging the users. When I asked the Chief Executive at ITN how he thought ITV could compete in the new media market, he seemed very proud of the new ideals ITN management had just set in place, namely to provide news and entertainment content for media platforms such as YouTube, MSN, Telegraph Media Group and Yahoo! – a move which in 2007 was seen as an innovative and new way of approaching the new challenges facing traditional news divisions:

We are a fast moving place, and we have to be. ITN has done well in developing new businesses. That is the only way to survive in broadcasting, otherwise we'll stagnate and be overtaken.

(Mark Wood, ITN Chief Executive. Speaking outside his office, 20 October 2007)[2]

Among both news staff and management, 'stagnation' was referred to as something to be feared immensely. Stagnation, naturally does not suit the market logic of constant consumer competition. Thus, the change in room works to signal a position of not-stagnating towards management, the competitor and media owners and the public. This leads to another reason for management to create a new layout for the newsroom: It was simply time to show a change. And as one broadcaster began to change the newsroom layout, so did the others, and thus none of the newsrooms could be said to be stagnant, and all the newsrooms signalled that they were a fast moving and fast changing place. In this way, to the journalists in the room, the restructure of working routines and physical boundaries took on a signal value that suited market logics.

During fieldwork, I observed news workers discussing the restructuring of their news routines and newsroom as both 'wrong', 'dangerous' and 'exciting'. Though opinions were divided, it was clear that all thought the new newsroom structure would make a big change. As the head of BBC's new newsrooms, Peter Horrocks, expressed it on the first day of the new Multimedia Newsroom, 12 November 2007, in his blog on *The Editors*:[3]

> For thousands of journalists in BBC News, today is the start of one of the biggest changes we have ever been through. Many of the people who bring you the news are uncertain of their own futures, but I know that all of us are determined to improve further the service we bring to you. BBC News wants to be the most successful multimedia news operation in the world – competing with and excelling against the best newspapers, broadcasters and news aggregators on the globe. [...]
>
> This new structure will help us to be more efficient and so save money to invest in improvements to BBC News. We will be putting more into on-demand news – for instance developing content for new platforms such as mobile and IPTV; increasing personalisation and providing purpose-made audio/video for the web. The new organisation also allows for our journalism to be used more dynamically across our three main existing platforms – web, radio and TV.
>
> (Horrocks 2007: 1)

The above text illustrates how market arguments are used by management when describing the structural changes to the room and to the news product. The argument that the new newsroom would make staff benefit from collaborations between all the broadcasters' many platforms was one that I found to be echoed at all the four newsrooms during fieldwork. To the BBC, the new multimedia newsroom was only the first step towards the ideally integrational newsroom, which was not scheduled to be finished until 2012. The new newsroom, which is part of an over £1.03 billion BBC building project, has been underway since the turn of the millennium and can today be said to be one of the biggest of its kind in the world. By 2017, the new newsroom integrates even more different platforms, with all staff having been transferred from the BBC Television Centre and Bush House. This new building is an exercise in putting even more diverse parts of the news division together in the same room.

4.2 Inside the Newsroom: Spatial Layout

During fieldwork, the first and most obvious similarity between the newsrooms that struck me was how similarly the newsrooms and news studios were designed. I began fieldwork at DR's recently constructed newsroom DR Byen in Ørestaden, a few metro stops from the centre of Copenhagen. I was impressed with the new newsroom, which seemed to me to be innovative in many ways. It was new to me to experience one room shared by representatives from each news medium, both radio, TV and the online news feed – who all appeared to be within eye contact of each other.

Another thing that struck me was how all the desks were arranged in a circular fashion, meaning that the different media representatives appeared more connected and in contact with each other than they would be in the more classic square, divided newsroom that I had experienced as a journalist in Britain.[4] As I ended fieldwork, however, all four newsrooms had come to resemble the DR newsroom as it was in May 2007. In fact, during the time of my fieldwork, though there were some exceptions, by and large all of the four newsrooms underwent a remodelling, in which the furniture, the editing systems, equipment and entire interior design came to look very much the same at all four broadcasters. In order to get a sense of the general structure and design of the four newsrooms, in the following I give a brief description of the DR newsroom.

Introducing the newsroom

You enter through a big glass reception, take the elegant escalator upwards and open the big doors. Here you find the large shared working space for all DR's news journalists, the multimedia newsroom. Lit in bright light, the room is made up of rows of desks put together in a circular system with desks neatly mapped out according to the role of those who are seated at them.

At one side of the circle, towards the middle, sits the Programme Editors who decide what news will be used and how it will be presented on today's show. There are two Programme Editors, one for each of the news bulletins of the evening. Just next to them in the circle are the assistants, then their producers. Next in the circular shape sit the technical directors and their assistants. At the table right next to them is the foreign desk, which at the nearest side has the editor, who decides what foreign news to pass on to the Programme Editor, and further away sits the journalist who works closely with the foreign News Editor.

At the other end of the circular shape sits the editor of Update, the 24-hour Internet news desk and her assistants. One desk further away sits the Programme Editor for the radio news and their assistants. Just above this room, overlooking it, in another bright room are the reporters. Even further away, in a different, smaller space altogether, not overlooking or being overlooked by anyone, sits the Graphic Team. These are all output desks, concerned with putting news out today.

On the first floor are the Input Desks. Here, the people are seated who only concern themselves with events either two weeks ahead or two days ahead. If these events are news, they will be given over to the Programme Editor at one of the Output Desks. Just above the newsroom, overlooking it, sits the Head of News. He has the final say in what is news, how to cover it and who can cover it when. Above the Head of News, also overlooking the newsroom, sits the Director General who has the ultimate say in what any of the people below him do.

Watching everyone in the newsroom from an even closer angle is the public. For when the news bulletin is broadcast, the newsroom is visible through a large glass backdrop, making anyone inside the newsroom constantly on watch, from either their closest editor, their Head of News, the Director General or the general public.

Inside the room, people walk faster than they do outside, they talk faster than they do outside and their sentences are short, precise and to the point. Though they deal with death, tragedy and conflict every day, they never cry, but often laugh and joke about stories and their people. The extent of news, destruction, tragedy or sensation on any given day can be read on the pace of the people in the room. When a big tragedy happens in a place that has their interest, these people will be running. But people inside this room look alert and busy at all times, even if the day is what they call a 'no-news day'. They speak their own language, they have their own special terms and values, and per instinct they all know what events are news and what are not. Though there are no written rules for how to act in the room, its inhabitants seem to all act in unison. Every day has different stories, different treatments, different Programme Editors, different reporters, but the newsroom and the roles within it stay the same.

(DR Field notes, May 2007, quoted in Thomsen 2007a)

The above is a description of DR's newsroom as it functioned in May 2007. But this newsroom setup is far from unique to DR. After I spent the summer of 2007 working inside this newsroom, it was a curious experience to go to the BBC newsroom in London. For when I entered the BBC, I found a newsroom not much different to DR's. The newsroom at BBC was not strictly circular in design, but the same structural setup of people in power, watching over those working on the daily news prevailed, just as the BBC had recently arrived at the idea of integrating many different news platforms into one room. And more similarities were to arise.

Fig. 4.1: DR Newsroom, seen from the office of the Head of News, May 2007. (Photo: Line Hassall Thomsen, during fieldwork.)

After having been to see the two very similarly styled newsrooms of DR and BBC, I arrived back at my old work environment, the ITV Newsroom. When I had been to see the newsroom earlier that year, the room had been square, with clear divisions between desks. In the traditional, square newsroom of ITV, the different desks, presenters and planners for the daily news show sat at a distance where they could not see or hear each other, unless they yelled very loudly, or walked quite far across the room. Another factor in ITV's former, square newsroom was that some staff, such as the graphic team and the news PR and publicity employee, would sit outside of the newsroom, far from able to see or hear what was happening among their colleagues.

By October 2007 when I began fieldwork at ITV, to my great surprise, the old newsroom I returned to had now adopted the new trend in newsroom design. The newsroom I arrived at in ITNs building on Grays Inn Road in London was just about to turn round, moving all news staff, such as the graphic and the PR employees, to sit inside the newsroom. The week I arrived, the rebuilding was only just beginning, with months of drilling, moving and installing of circular desks to the traditional square newsroom, and everyone within the news division preparing to be sat in the same room. For an illustration of how the ITV Newsroom went from square to circle see Fig. 4.2 to 4.5.

Fig. 4.2: The ITV Newsroom in the process of turning circular, Autumn 2007: Before… (Photo: Line Hassall Thomsen, during fieldwork).

Fig. 4.3: The ITV Newsroom in the process of turning circular, Autumn 2007: During…(Photo: Line Hassall Thomsen, during fieldwork).

Fig. 4.4: And after: The new ITV Newsroom, 2011 (Photo: ITV Press Office, with permission).

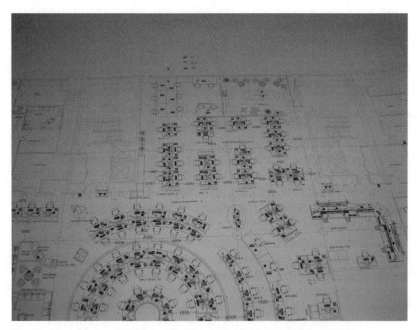

Fig. 4.5: Map of the new ITV Newsroom (Photo: Lincoln Hooper, with permission).

A circulation of managerial practices

When I asked the Editor-in-Chief at ITV News why they were reorganising the furniture of the room, his argument was not far from the arguments I had heard at BBC:

LHT: Everything seems to be going circular…

ITV Editor-in-chief: Oh, really? It is probably the fashion. It is simply because, having looked at various options and because, as we wanted to bring, as I said, different parts of the newsroom together, like the international desk, which works very closely with the news desk […] So, we designed it in such a way that people who need to be closer together, to hear what is happening and what each other is doing can do so in this new circular horseshoe shape. It is just more practical.

(ITV editor in Chief, interviewed in his office overlooking the newsroom, 30 October 2007)

To the Editor-in-Chief at ITV, the reorganising of the furniture in the room was a way of keeping ahead of the game, though he was fully aware that the rest of the industry was doing exactly the same. One member of the newsroom staff, Newsroom Technology Manager Lincoln Hooper, who had been part of the planning group behind the refurbished ITV Newsroom, told me that ITV News had been particularly inspired by the newsroom of *The Daily Telegraph*, which incidentally was the same newsroom inspiring the BBC News.[5] In turn, the BBC's newsroom appeared similar to the newsroom of DR. Lincoln Hooper, who was ITV's project leader in the group responsible for the 'updated newsroom' project, told me that they had been inspired by 'the newest in newsrooms'.

On the first day of fieldwork at the BBC, when I went upstairs to the management office above the BBC newsroom to introduce myself, one of the members of the management team from the department of Head of News exclaimed: 'DR is very interesting! We have in fact stolen their idea of sharing the room […] and some of the ideas of multi-skilling!'. He told me that a group from the Head of News department had been to see DR's newsroom and been very inspired by the design. The focus of the BBC management field trip had been to learn from DR's interior design, in order for the BBC to redesign their digital newsroom. After this trip, in November 2007, the BBC decided to follow suit with DR's trend of newsroom design and move all their news division, including online news desks, radio news and TV news bulletin staff to desks in one large Multimedia Newsroom. Inspired by DR's newsroom in Denmark and the newly constructed circular design of *The Daily Telegraph* newsroom, the BBC made their own similarly designed room. Thus, I found the BBC to be very keen to learn from its Danish counterpart DR, and the designer team behind DR's new look, Fridbjørg Design, the BBC conceded to there being some validity in the claim that the designer's work with the DR newsroom had created 'results which are still setting the standard, in the business of connecting communication, branding and physical settings for the TV media'.

Later, I was told at TV2 that management staff at TV2 had been inspired to redesign their newsroom and news studio after a visit to ITV. While talking to editors or management staff, I was often told how they had been to see the other broadcasters' newsrooms to gain inspiration, or had invitations from other broadcasters to share experiences. At ITV, the Editor-in-Chief told me he had had one such invitation from DR as they were researching how they could 'make their news more exciting to watch'.[6] Thus, the inspiration across broadcasters and countries appears to move in a circular fashion, both between license-funded broadcasters and their commercially funded counterparts.

Realising the close contact and constant inspiration among managers at national newsrooms across Europe, I came to see the new newsrooms as the image of a new ideal shared among managers: an ideal of collaboration, multi-skilling and increased control of content and staff. Moreover, the new circular room can be seen as an example of a mutual influence and of circulation of managerial practices among leading European broadcasters, particularly those in the core public service territories. More specifically, what the round newsroom seems to encapsulate is that when one newsroom practice has become fashionable, then within a very short amount of time, this newsroom practice spreads. It is interesting that this sphere of circulation in which, typically but not only, the BBC's latest managerial fashions spread within months through Europe to Denmark, Norway, Finland, Sweden and vice versa. I find this kind of mutual influence in office design to be an important phenomenon in the transnationalisation of management techniques across different broadcasters. As I will suggest, this transnationalisation of design, in fact, tacitly created work processes the similarity between which is shrouded by a general ideology among journalists about 'cultural differences'. While such circulation of spatial layout may have taken place among different news organisations in the past, today the management personnel have more ways of communicating, meet more often and appear to visit each other's newsrooms to get inspiration more than ever before.[7] The result, I suggest, is the tacit transnationalisation of certain office designs and workflows, which have the effect of making the news industry more homogenous than ever before. In the globalisation of news, homogenisation happens in spite of, perhaps even in conjunction with, an explicit ideology of difference.

The main difference brought about by these new, circular shaped newsrooms was the idea that all news desks should be represented in one room. At both DR and BBC, management told me that they believed it would help the efficiency of the newsroom and make working together more 'natural' by seating staff from many different media platforms as close to one another as possible. Among management personnel, the collaborative element was often mentioned when discussing the new newsroom. Thus, it appeared, among management, the new room was discussed as signalling a hope that the news workers would feel united, able to share not only a room but also desks, technology and, crucially, content.[8] With the new design came an expressed hope from management that the different units such as radio news, TV news, online news and other factual programme departments, which had before been divided into individual often competitive units, should now consider themselves closer – not only in spatial terms but in terms of identity as well.

As illustrated, the new newsroom layout brought about an increased possibility of seeing-without-being-seen for the news management and the Director General and for fellow colleagues within the room. I have now highlighted how this ability of surveillance is made possible by the design and structure of the newsroom. In the following, I introduce another element of observation, impacting the way staff inside the newsroom work, namely the design and structure of the computer interface system, the running order, crucial to all news bulletins produced.

A virtual room for seeing-without-being-seen

A second level of everyday observation of employees in the newsroom has less to do with the physical design of the room. As this level of observation is digital rather than spatial, it enables observation of staff who are not in the same building, but abroad or out on a reporting job.

As mentioned earlier, the computer system that news staff use to create the evening's digital running order, containing film clips, script and lead-ins for presenters, is viewable by editors and management. In the everyday work, News Editors and Programme Editors are constantly making use of this type of observation, using special rights within the system for them only, so that they can see what different news workers are adding to the running order at all times, and they can change it without the consent or knowledge of other members of staff. Thus, in Foucault's terms, the news management and Director General can easily obtain knowledge of the other, that the other can never obtain, and the editors and management at all times oversee what everyone else adds to the digital shared space and edit content without news workers knowing. Before I explain the functions of the shared digital interface, the running order of the daily news bulletin, see Figs. 4.6 and 4.7 that show what it looks like on the screen.

The screen grabs show the two different types of digital running order interfaces that I experienced during fieldwork, Newstar (used at DR and TV2) and ENPS (used at ITV and BBC). Additionally, it shows the different views and differences in access granted to the running order depending on whether the screen is logged on with rights of an intern or a Programme Editor.

There are a few differences to the layout between the two different systems. ENPS, for instance, has a space right at the top centre which 'flashes' big news stories and events as they come in from the news agencies (in the illustration from BBC above, the text 'PAN-3 MEDIA GMTV' refers to one such news story). Apart from differences in layout, both systems have the same structure based on the idea that different users have different levels of access and editing abilities in the shared interface. For every news bulletin on any day, a digital running order is created, such as the above. All text read by the presenter is inserted into the running order throughout the day, which is constantly surveyed by the Programme Editor. Likewise, any film clip, edited film packages or suggestions for

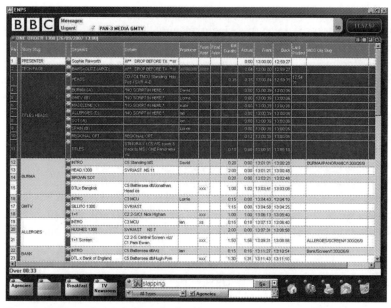

Fig. 4.6: ENPS interface. Running order for the BBC News. Logged on with the rights of a Programme Editor (Photo: screen grab made during fieldwork, 26 September 2007).

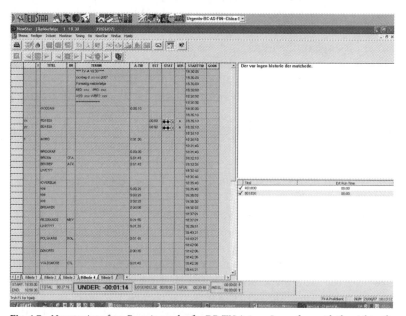

Fig. 4.7: Newstar interface. Running order for DR TV Avisen. Logged on with the rights of an intern (Photo: screen grab made during fieldwork, 29 June 2007).

questions for the newsreader to ask an interviewee are inserted into this shared running order. While watching over what arrives on the digital interface, the Programme Editor constantly makes corrections, edits, deletes or moves a news item up or down in the running order of pieces for the final news programme. In the ENPS system (as illustrated from BBC News above) there is a column in the system in which different editors (either deemed a 'Team Approval' or a 'Final Approval') sign off each segment in the running order before it can go to air. Similarly, in the Newstar system, Programme Editors mark their approval of a news story by changing the colour of a story's field in the running order from red to yellow or green.

Without this digital approval from editors above the reporters, journalists and scriptwriters, the news items created cannot be broadcast. Journalists, reporters and scriptwriters inserting news stories into the running order are aware that their work is under constant watch from those with more access to the digital interface than themselves. Thus, all news staff members are very much aware that from the second something is entered into the interface they can expect it to be edited, deleted or moved around in the digital list of news. In this sense, much like those working in the newsroom are constantly watched over by management, so the digital interface is constantly making it possible for *some* to see what all others are working on, without anyone knowing.

I have now introduced two different levels of observation of staff, which I found to exist in all the four newsrooms I visited: Physical observation of staff inside the newsroom and digital observation made possible through a computer interface that gives editors unique access to content and editing of content without the consent or knowledge of the journalists whose content they edit. Additionally, I have described how the many editorial meetings and constant phone calls from editors to journalists function as a controlling and correcting mechanism.

A third level of observation of staff inside the newsroom comes from another angle, namely that of the news viewer and the imagined idea of the viewer. As I will introduce in the following, this level plays a crucial part in making a news worker perceive him/herself as 'the face' of a broadcaster.

4.3 Inside the Newsroom: Editorial Meetings

Having noticed how similar the four rooms were and how similar the shared digital working platforms were, I began to notice another parallel between the four broadcasters, namely the way that time is managed and structured. As I began making lists timing when meetings were held, who would attend which meeting and what would be discussed, a very similar pattern between broadcasters began to emerge. Centred on editorial meetings, the way that each news worker's day was organised did not appear very different from licence-funded to commercially funded broadcaster, or from England to Denmark.

Why study meetings?

In Breed's (1955) study of newspaper staff, he highlights meetings, news conferences and debriefs as important ways of management exercising social control of staff. With this in mind, I found it interesting to follow the discussions in meetings in order to explore how meetings were part of the everyday structure of news work. I believe much can be gaged about the news division, the strategies of news gathering and the internal prioritising of time and staff by studying the structure of editorial meetings. As such, I believe the fact that a meeting time and place is set aside for such things as forward planning and debrief gives a good insight into the priorities of each news organisation. But not only the time and place of each meeting matter; for an understanding of who has a say in the newsroom, it is also relevant to consider *who* is expected (or allowed) to go to the meeting, and who is expected to chair the meeting or talk back to the one chairing the meeting.

Within the disciplines of anthropology, psychology, sociology, management studies and others, the general interest in meetings has been threefold. Firstly, the meeting has been seen as a tool for tasks (see for instance Zuckerman 1970; Janis 1972); secondly, the meeting has been explored and analysed as an ineffective 'waste of time' (Drucker 1974; Alvehus 1999; Bjerlöf 1999); and lastly, the function of the meeting has been sought improved by scholars (i.e. Drucker 1966; Kawakita 1991).[9] Recently, with a self-professed aim of 'exploring the boring' inspired by Schwartzman (1989), *Meeting Ethnography* has become a new subfield of anthropology (see for instance Sandler and Thedvall 2017).

There are not many theories of how to study or analyse meetings yet. However, I have come to agree with Sandler and Thedvall (2017: 1) that the meeting is 'arguably the most important and under-theorized phenomenon that ethnographers encounter'. In reviewing research related to meetings, it appears 'the meeting' has primarily been used as a method for researching something else, as a tool for conducting research about that which the meeting is said to be about. According to anthropologist Helen Schwartzman, the meeting should rather have a central role in studies of an organisation, of which she has developed theories of *Ethnography in Organisations* (1993). Schwartzman points out the distinction among researchers in using the meeting as a 'tool' with which to do analysis, or viewing the meeting as a 'topic' itself worthy of investigation. In looking at the list of meetings as both a topic worthy of analysis *and* a tool for understanding how the working day is structured, I hope to be able to be open to the multitude of understandings, which can be gained from studying an organisation through its meetings.

The importance of viewing the meeting as a 'topic', Schwartzman argues, is that the ritual-like quality of meetings comes to the foreground. Thus, the meeting can be viewed as not only what it appears at first glance, such as an editorial meeting discussing story ideas and news events, but as a frame in which the organisation of hierarchies and relations between individuals is confirmed and reaffirmed. Looking at the meeting as a 'frame' makes it possible to read more from the meeting than if one just studies what is being said and discussed, as Schwartzman puts it:

One of the most important aspects of the transformation that the meeting frame produces is that it creates the possibility for individual and group social relationships, agreements and disagreements to be discussed and 'framed' as a discussion of business.

(Schwartzman 1989: 78)

From this perspective, when a reporter asks for something to be discussed at the editorial meeting, this may not necessarily be because he would like the story to be discussed. Rather, a reporter may add to the discussion in the editorial meeting in order to engage in the power struggle of reporter and editor. Thus, simply by saying that he has *a* story that is worth discussing, the reporter shows himself as engaged, willing to take responsibility and be independent in the role of reporter.

A show of who is in control

Inspired by Schwartzman (1989), I have come to view the many editorial meetings taking place during the course of the day as a frame through which one can explore power structures within the news division. While editors tend to see journalists as wild, journalists appear to view editors as strict and 'dictatorish' (see quote below) – these very different ideologies express the power structures, which are all at play within the daily editorial meetings. Thus, though the many editorial meetings *are* forums for planning, discussing and creating news stories, I have come to see them as also a signalling of who is in control within the news division. This signal, as I have experienced it, is primarily given by the News Editor who has influence on who gets time to talk in meetings and whose story ideas are accepted. During meetings, I have experienced the well-respected journalists, reporters and Programme Editors to be accepted to interrupt others mid-sentence. Meanwhile, I noticed that among news reporters there appears to be a correlation between suggesting news stories and being given more time to work on a story. In turn, those who got more time to work on a story appeared to find more contacts within a niche field and thus came up with even more unique story ideas and got more time to work on original stories.

If the editorial meeting provides a frame for exploring who is in control of the news agenda, so the many phone calls conducted by the Programme Editor to his team throughout the day can be seen as a way of constantly surveying the work of journalists. The Programme Editor, and at some news divisions the News Editor too, is in constant touch on the phone with the news workers. I experienced many of these phone calls both at the receiving end when doing participant observation with reporters and from the editor-end when I was doing participant observation in the newsroom. One example of these phone calls happened at 6PM in the TV Avisen Newsroom, just half an hour before the programme was broadcast. A reporter who the Programme Editor had not talked to much during the day called up to say that his news piece was one minute longer in duration than they had agreed on at the morning meeting. Upon hearing this, the Programme Editor looked flustered and told the reporter off loudly. When he finished his phone call, he turned to me and said: 'Yes, that is the danger when you don't talk to them all the time [...] You just goddammit don't do this!'.[10] This experience serves to confirm that editors tend to view reporters as people who may run wild, and who therefore need constant supervision. Programme Editors told me that they have to constantly check up on their journalists in order to avoid such surprises. Through phone calls, the editorial staff is constantly checking up on what the news workers are working on, how they angle a story and what quotes they are getting from interviewees. Through a combination of preventive and corrective practices (Goffman 1990: 25) on behalf of the editorial team, this strategy works to constantly remind the news worker of who is in control.

Among the newest recruits of reporters, cameramen and producers, the phone calls from Programme Editors are talked about as 'helpful' and as 'giving good guidance' on how to make the news piece. But many of the reporters, cameramen and producers that I worked alongside appeared frustrated by the constant phone calls from Programme Editors wanting to check up on them and appeared to see the calls as a sign that editors did not 'trust' their work.[11] At ITV News, where the Programme Editor and the News Editor called reporters more than 10 times an hour on average, some defined the calls as a sign of strong editorial 'dictatorship'. As an ITV News reporter expressed it:

> There have always been pretty dictatorish leaders while I've been working here. There has never been time for reporters to argue back or for any other opinions than those of the editor to be taken seriously. That is a shame, because there are so many knowledgeable people in this newsroom. We do not question it. I suppose it would be better if this place were a little more democratic.
>
> (ITV News reporter, employed at ITV for approximately ten years, in conversation in the atrium outside newsroom, 23 November 2007)

A day of meetings

In the following I explain the day of meetings at DR, focusing on the scheduled meetings related to the two evening news bulletins at TV Avisen.

The table in Fig. 4.8 lists the daily meetings related to the two evening news bulletins (broadcast at 6.30PM and at 9PM every day) at the time of my first visit to DR in 2007. I have chosen to use DR as a case study to continue the insight into the DR newsroom that was commenced in the introduction of this chapter. It should be noted that I could just as well have chosen one of the other three newsrooms, as the type of meetings and the timings of them are very similar. At each newsroom, the staff appeared to believe that they had many more meetings than they would have had they been working at the other newsrooms. At ITV, for instance, one of the PAs responsible for the roster told me that all the meetings

Time	Name of Meeting	Place for Meeting	Present at Meeting
8.30–8.50	*Morning Meeting*	Meeting Room 1, Ground Floor	TV Avisen News Editor, Radio 1 Editor, Programme Editor, Foreign Editor, Radio 3 Editor, Actualities (Orientering)[12] Editor.
8.55–9.15	*Pre-meeting*	Meeting Room 2, Ground Floor	TV Avisen News Editor, TV News and Actualities Editors, other news management, Regional News Editor from Aarhus via phone link.
9.15–9.45	*Editorial meeting*	Meeting Room 3, 1st floor	TV Avisen News Editor, 18.30 and 21.00 Programme Editors, reporters, if available; 'Dream Team'[13] cameraman, Regional News Editor from Aarhus via phone link.
12.30–13.00	*Editorial meeting*	Meeting Room 3, 1st floor	TV Avisen News Editor, 21.00 Programme Editor, reporters, dream team cameraman if available.
14.30–15.00	*Daily planning*	Meeting Room 2, Ground Floor	TV Avisen News Editor, Programme Editor for 18.30 and 21.00 news, TV Presenters if arrived.
15.00–15.30	*Tomorrow planning*	Meeting Room 2, Ground Floor	TV Avisen News Editor and Programme Editors for tomorrow.
16.00–16.20	*Graphics meeting*	Glass Room, Ground Floor	Graphic, Programme Editor and Producer Assistant.
19.10–19.30	*Debrief*	Meeting Room 3, 1st floor	TV Avisen News Editor, Programme Editor and reporters.
21.40–22.00	*Debrief*	Meeting Room 3, 1st floor	TV Avisen News Editor, Programme Editor and reporters.

Fig. 4.8: Daily meetings at the DR news division over the course of May, 2007, including staff typically present.

at ITV and BBC are 'a British thing for sure. Nowhere else, internationally do they have so many meetings. The reason we have a lot of meetings here is that a lot of people who work here used to work at BBC and so they just carried on the structure' (ITV Newsroom, 22 October 2007, ITV Field Diary 1: 75). However, the list of the average amount of everyday editorial meetings related to the news bulletin revealed there to be eight to ten meetings a day at all the newsrooms.

As can be seen in the table above, on an everyday basis at least nine different meetings were held. The above table only lists the planned daily meetings and does not include ad hoc meetings discussing, for instance, troubles with deployment of trucks and reporters, cross promotion, a story idea, planning stories a week ahead or other forward planning issues. Thus, nine daily meetings in or around the newsroom appeared to be an absolute minimum at the news divisions I studied. Among the journalists at all broadcasters, the meetings were sometimes talked about as 'too long' and 'hard to get your opinion heard' but 'really important to go to'. It was particularly new members of staff who told me that they felt it was important to come up with ideas at the meeting, in order to 'show that you are active, and that you have ideas for good stories'.[14] Though some complained about the meetings being too long, only a few of the News Editors told me that at times there were too many meetings in the day, but that they were 'essential'.[15] While employee opinion was that meetings are long and boring and may detract from the real work, I have found the meetings crucial in maintaining cooperate hierarchy. While the meetings serve as a forum to hand out stories to reporters, I have found the primary function of editorial meetings to be that of maintaining hierarchy and order between news workers, journalists, producers, cameramen, editors and management.

I have designed the list of meetings above to illustrate both the amount of time spent on meetings, the spatial setting of the meetings and an insight into who attends the editorial meetings during the day. From the above table, I find it particularly interesting to note which parts of the news division are represented at the daily meetings, as it gives an insight into the crucial issue of who is allowed and who is expected to be part of the everyday decision-making. As can be seen from the list of meetings, admission and representation are determined by the different roles within the newsroom; only the News Editor can go to all nine meetings. At DR, the only scheduled meeting that the News Editor does not attend, is the graphic meeting, which has a more practical focus than the editorial meetings. Meanwhile, cameramen are rarely present; they only enter an editorial meeting if they happen to be deemed part of a 'dream team' and thus attached to a reporter.

At the other broadcasters, BBC, ITV and TV2, I found the structure of who should go to what meetings strikingly similar to that of DR, just as the number of meetings and topics discussed were similar by and large. Of the differences that I observed, I noticed that the commercial broadcasters had one or two fewer scheduled meetings, as meetings with other news platforms, such as radio and actuality programmes, were not relevant.[16] Where other news platforms were involved, such as ITV's online news and TV2's 24-hour news channel, a representative would be present at the editorial meeting for the evening news.[17] Other differences were that reporters at some broadcasters seemed to be more talkative during meetings than at others. Lastly, during fieldwork, I experienced the debrief meeting to have lower priority at the licence-funded broadcasters. Thus, when I was at DR and BBC I did not experience the same need for all staff to stay on for the debrief, as was the case at ITV and TV2. During my stay at DR, debrief meetings were cancelled a few times due to the fact that the TVA News Editor, who usually chairs the meeting, had gone home by the time the late news had finished – this, I was told, was due to there not being a need for a debrief as everything was in order and not much needed to be said. At both ITV and TV2, however, the debrief meetings were seen as vital to the everyday work, and attendance from all involved news workers was expected – if a reporter, for instance, had been working on a news story but did not turn up to the debrief, this would be questioned by management.[18] As the News Editor was not present every night after the evening news, someone else from the management team would always cover, and I never experienced a debrief meeting to be cancelled at ITV or TV2. These differences taken into consideration, I find the above list of daily scheduled meetings connected to DR's TV Avisen a useful guide to how the everyday work is structured across all four newscasters.

Work as 'Guessing what the News Editor wants'

Throughout all the daily meetings in and around the newsroom, either the News Editor or the Programme Editor is responsible for chairing the meeting. What sets the agenda for the meeting is *The List* of events that the News Editor brings to each of the daily meetings, which he runs through when suggesting events as news stories on any day.[19] The agenda for the meeting, however, is not created by the News Editor, but by planning staff employed at departments within the news divisions entitled The Research Unit ('Nyheder Research' at DR) or The Forward Planning Desk (at ITV). Thus, the members of staff responsible for making The List have a significant say in what events are selected as news stories on any given day.

As I realised the important role of the planning staff in the everyday list of news available to the news division, I decided to spend time during fieldwork working alongside the planning desk at the different newsrooms. In working with these planners I was shown just how important other media are in selecting news for TV, as Planners often begin their day with reading other news both through papers and online news sites, and research stories through a database of archived newspaper articles. At DR's planning desk (DR Nyheder Research), staff told me that they use a search tool provided by the article database, Infomedia, as the first tool for creating their daily lists of planned news events.[20] Only after having used stories from this media database do the planners use news agencies such as the Danish news agency, Ritzau. In 2017, planners have added TweetDecks with lists of key Twitter-profiles as a priority source.

When I asked the planners at the different broadcasters how they judged what stories to put on The List of events to pass on as story ideas, many planners told me that the best way of finding out whether events would be a story, was to 'guess' whether the News Editor would like the story. Not surprisingly, when I asked the planners what made a successful list of events, they told me that the best lists of events are those that have most events on them that the news team is happy with. Or, as a planner from ITV told me more bluntly: 'I don't watch the news bulletins; I just keep planning for tomorrow. If I don't get bollocked, then it probably went ok'.[21] When I asked different members from the planning team how they defined a good story, most did not have a personal definition of a good news story, other than that it would be one that the News Editor likes and the news workers use. Working alongside the planners and seeing the way the list of events was created in the everyday, the likes and dislikes of the News Editor was often used as an argument for adding certain events to The List. Thus, though the planners make The List, they do it with the News Editor in mind, and with the aim of not being told off by him.

4.4 Conclusions

In this chapter, the new newsrooms of all four broadcasters have been introduced. While introducing one newsroom I have also portrayed the look of many others: as highlighted throughout this chapter, all the newsrooms included in my study were all reshaped and restructured to look very much the same. In describing the new newsrooms, I have shown how the design of the room is linked to a rethinking of the news units, which to journalists were seen as driven by market logic. One example of such rethinking is the idea that staff should collaborate more across platforms and be able to 'multi-skill' in everyday work.

This chapter further shows how the new circular room can be seen as an example of a mutual influence and circulation of managerial practices among leading European broadcasters, particularly those in the core public service territories. At the management and editorial level of the newsrooms, a close contact prevails enabling newsroom management to follow the development of ideas at the competing broadcaster and change ways of working to follow what may be considered the 'latest trend' in the TV-news business. To me, the physical similarities between the newsrooms were what first made me begin to reconsider my expectations to differences of working culture.

Two key issues have been introduced. Firstly, I describe how the four newsrooms of BBC, ITV, DR and TV2 have a physical similarity, which is designed with ideas of surveillance, control, collaboration and multi-media work in mind. Secondly, it has been shown how news work is structured around meetings. I have focused on the daily planned meetings related to the news divisions. Viewing meetings as both a tool for analysis and a topic for research, empirical findings have been used as a frame for exploring the everyday routines of TV news workers. Through describing the routines of a working day, I have illustrated how Programme Editors and News Editors are in constant contact with their journalists. This constant contact I have introduced as enabling the Programme Editor to shape, correct and control each news item.

In studying the structure of spatial and temporal layout within the newsroom it has been highlighted how a market logic can be seen as underlining the design focus on surveillance, control, collaboration and multi-media work. In the following chapter, I explore how such ideas in design can be experienced as a mismatch between ideals of journalists and ideals of management. By describing the organisation of news work, focusing on the structure of space within the newsroom, I have aimed to show the first of what Wenger (1998a: 241) defines as two views of an organisation, the designed organisation. In the following chapter focus will be on describing what Wenger defines as the second view of an organisation: the practice as it happens within the designed organisation.

Notes

1 As an example of another profession relying on the market logic, Freidson describes the work of architects: 'while the practice of architecture may begin with a drawing, a design created by an independent individual, the design ordinarily has no exchange value unless it is realized. Only personal time and expense may be expended to create a design, yet realizing it in a building requires a considerable amount of capital. Dependence on the wealthy and powerful to commission a design for a building is intrinsic to the labor market of most architects' (Freidson 2001: 165).

2 (ITV Field Diary 2, p. 10).

3 *The Editors* is a BBC-site in which editors from across BBC News share what they term 'our dilemmas and issues'.

4 As mentioned previously, I worked as a journalist before commencing fieldwork. The newsrooms that I had worked in before this project include the ITV Newsroom, the Channel 4 Newsroom, the More4 Newsroom and the newsroom of the newspaper *The Independent*, all based in London.

5 'We went to many meetings at *Telegraph* to learn about their newsroom', explains Lincoln Hooper and draws the two different types of newsrooms, the 'Concentric' and the 'Radial' they were interested in (30 October 2007, Drawing and quote in ITV notebook 1: 21).

6 David Mannion in conversation, ITV field book 1: 77.

7 I am indebted to professor Georgina Born for pointing me towards the relevance of this phenomenon to my findings.

8 These arguments for redesigning the newsroom corresponds with arguments used by management at other news divisions who have made very similar redesigns (see for instance Bechmann 2011; Domingo and Paterson 2011).

9 According to Furnham, for instance: 'A meeting is a group of people that keep minutes and waste hours' (Furnham in Westling 2002: 9). Business management theorist Peter F. Drucker argues that organisations would be better off without any meetings at all, as: '[…] the human dynamics of meetings are so complex as to make them very poor tools for getting any work done' (1974: 548).

10 DR Field notes, 18 June 2007.

11 DR Field notes, 18 June 2007.

12 'Orientering' is the title of an in-depth current affairs programme, which often runs stories and discussions on the back of what has been broadcast at the daily news bulletin.

13 At DR, some of the well-established reporters had been appointed a set cameraman to work with, and the two were coupled and called 'dream team'. Only cameramen who were part of a dream team would go to editorial meetings.

14 TV2 News, girl in work experience, in conversation after taped interview, 18 June 2008.

15 News Editor, talking to me as we hurry out of the 8.30 meeting to the next meeting, 27 June 2007 (DR Field book 1).

16 Neither ITV nor TV2 has a radio news contract and neither of the broadcasters have as close a collaboration with actuality programmes as the two licence-funded broadcasters.

17 In the case of TV2, he would most often be present via videoconference.

18 Of course, if the reporter was filing back stories from out of town, s/he would not be expected to attend the debrief meeting. However, generally reporters who had been deployed out of the house would return to the building by the afternoon or early evening to edit and finish their news piece and story for the debrief.

19 Within newsrooms, the list of events planned as stories referred to simply as 'The List'. At DR it was nicknamed 'The Yellow List' as the News Editor printed it on yellow paper.

20 Apart from newspaper articles, the media database also contains summaries of media content from radio and TV-programmes, as well both Danish and national websites (according to Infomedia.dk 2011).

21 ITV News planner, 23 November 2007 (ITV field book 1: 84).

Chapter 5

Negotiating the Newsroom

On newsrooms being like a stage, and how staff leave if they are not
performing correctly

In the previous chapter, the newsroom was introduced from an organisational perspective, focusing on what Wenger (1998a) defines as 'the designed organisation'. With this chapter, I turn to explore how design affects the practice of work within the four news divisions studied. Thus, I set out to view the organisation from a second perspective, which Wenger (1998a: 241) defines as 'the practice', which often happens as a response to the designed organisation.

The central focus of this chapter is on how staff members inside the newsroom appear to negotiate the room on an everyday basis. I explore the notion that staff members inside the newsroom feel under constant observation. In discussing practice within the designed organisation, I explore how journalists' professional values and ideals appear to clash with the ideologies behind the new newsroom. Furthermore, it is shown how journalists are able to negotiate and manage performances within the room to suit their everyday lives. In conclusion, I introduce the notion that staff constantly works towards negotiating a professional ideal and a sense of privacy in their everyday work within the newsroom.

I believe that exploring the structure of time and place within which staff are organised is fruitful for understanding the working conditions for news workers today. However, I agree with Lefebvre (1974) that a place is much more than its functions and physical framework. A place is where space is 'practised' in a certain way; people make 'place' by living, being and acting spatially. Just as a place is defined by the framework of spatial layout and timed meetings, a place is made up of the life, the traditions, the unspoken rules and the rhythm of people who inhabit the place.

5.1 Negotiating the Stage

> Houses don't always reflect the way we really live, often they represent fantasies of the way we'd like to live.
>
> (New York architect Robert Stern speaking in 1987, quoted in Delaney and Kaspin 2011: 57)

Considering the above quote, one could view the fantasy of the new newsrooms to be defined as a dream of more multi-skilling, collaboration and control of those working inside the newsroom. In practice, staff may collaborate more within the new newsrooms than before, but whether the dream, to which the room aspires, has come true can be questioned. Though certain people structure place in a certain way, all people may not necessarily act in the way intended by the design. When architects create a fine public lawn with a path encircling it, the public will more often than not create a new path crossing directly over the lawn (Gehl 2010). In similar ways, staff members working within the newsroom use the newly designed room as a starting point for negotiations with, in and around the room.

According to Beeman, broadcast journalists can be categorised along with 'super-salesmen, politicians, orators, actors, folk artists, writers, comedians, journalists' and others 'who depend on their performance skills to achieve success and fulfilment in life. The most successful of these communication specialists know [...] how to exploit the ideational shapes of their culture in order to generate powerful, effective communication' (Beeman, in Peterson 2003: 163). This approach, like the early newsroom studies (Tuchman 1972; Gans 1979, among others), tends to view journalists as merely acting out already predetermined roles. While I see the newsroom, particularly the newly designed newsrooms that I encountered during fieldwork, as a very public working place akin to a stage, I see journalists as able to constantly negotiate and manage their performance within the room to suit their everyday lives. In the following, I introduce the idea that news workers negotiate the place within which they work. This negotiation can be viewed as a tension between an imagined role and the reality within which staff members find themselves in their everyday work.

Exiting performance means exiting the newsroom

> The staffer, especially the new staffer, identifies himself [...] with the executives and veteran staffers. Although not yet one of them, he shares their norms, and thus his performance comes to resemble theirs. He conforms to the norms of policy rather than to whatever personal beliefs he brought to the job, or to ethical ideals.
>
> (Breed 1955: 332)

Above, Warren Breed describes the way news workers act inside a newsroom as a performance adapting to the policy of the news management. Studying news workers in relation to the newsroom they work in, I have come to agree with Breed in that news workers inside the newsroom are constantly performing a role. During my study, however, I have found staff to be *aware* of the fact that they are performing. Therefore, while the constant observation, corrections and controlling elements are at play inside the newsroom, so is a constant negotiating process in which news staff struggle to negotiate the policy to suit their own and professional ideals. Thus, the news staff I have studied may appear to conform to policy, but this conforming is a performance of the self of which staff are aware, and one which I have found staff to negotiate individually rather than as a group. In this way, I see journalists as able to constantly negotiate and manage their performance within the room to suit their everyday lives. To construct this performance best, each news worker is aware that when exiting the performance, s/he should exit the newsroom.[1]

At all four broadcasters, news staff expressed unease and unhappiness with the lack of private areas in or near the new newsrooms. Delaney and Kaspin write of people who feel unease when others get too close physically that proximity can be felt as 'invading our "bubble" of private space – that pocket of air surrounding our body' (2011: 35–36). For staff within the newsroom, the lack of private 'bubbles' in the newsroom meant that they would make efforts to create such 'bubbles' elsewhere. Not having places designed for staff to be seen and heard did not mean that they did not find places in which they felt more private and less 'on'. In practice, as illustrated in the prologue of this book, I found that staff needing a private place would find other spatial sites to be, such as the toilets, an empty editing suite or a corridor. At DR, a reporter one day told me to tell the editor that she could be found in one of the empty editing suites if needed, as she needed to make a phone call to her boyfriend. At ITV, a scriptwriter asked me to interview him inside an empty editing suite, as that was one of the only places he felt he could 'talk freely'. At the BBC, one of the Head of News staff talked much more openly about the economic struggles within the BBC news division when we sat in a secluded corner of the canteen than when we were in the newsroom. At TV2 News, one reporter told me that she thought the lack of place and time where staff could be 'off' during a working day was the reason why so many of her colleagues had to leave the job with stress-related symptoms. During fieldwork, I had countless experiences of how place mattered to the people I talked to, and experienced how staff established areas where they could be private, though no such areas had been planned in the design of the working space.[2]

Whenever inside the shared newsroom, staff did generally not discuss their personal lives, conduct private phone conversations or go on websites considered private on their computer.[3] Similarly, I never observed emotional reactions to news stories taking place inside the newsroom. Rather, when inside the newsroom, news workers appeared to behave alike and touch on similar subjects in a shared language. From this perspective, the design of the room could be seen as the making of a stage on which the news workers perform, act and talk in the manner that is expected of them as journalists and employees at a certain broadcaster.[4] For the journalists I worked alongside, being inside the newsroom meant that they constantly had to look for spatial areas where they did not have to perform the front stage role so necessary when being in the newsroom. This constant managing can be seen as a negotiating of tensions between the imagined idea of news work and the actual realities within which staff work. While the negotiation of the newsroom is crucial for keeping a sense of self and a sense of privacy, I have also experienced the design of the room as a specific challenge for the professional ideals of journalists.

When professional ideals do not match the newsroom

In the previous chapter, studying the design of the newsroom it has been illustrated how the temporal and spatial organisation of work has undergone a restructure. I have described how the new more open plan newsrooms makes possible more management-observation and more collaboration across media platforms than previously. Using market logic, news management talk about this restructure as a necessary strategy to 'keep ahead of the game' (ITV Editor in Chief, 30 October 2007). Meanwhile, journalists talk about the new newsroom as 'challenging' for their professional ideals and for their private life. The challenges to staff privacy that large open plan offices create are no doubt an important critique of the new newsrooms (Jensen 2009). Moreover, it is worthwhile to consider the ideals of the profession in order to evaluate why the new newsrooms are experienced as problematic for journalists. With this chapter I begin such considerations, while in Chapters 6 and 7 I explore key ideals also challenged by the new demands of journalists such as those of doing 'good work' and making 'good news story'.

Today, news broadcasters have increasing competition in the shape of news and information being accessible from more and more new media platforms (such as the Internet or the mobile phone) and in new and untraditional formats (such as Twitter, Facebook or mobile news updates). As Hallin (1992) has argued, this modernised pressure coupled with economic pressure on the newscasters is key to management's decision to restructure the newsroom and the organisation of news work. Writing about what he describes as the 'Passing of the "High Modernism" of American Journalism' (1992) Hallin characterises the mid-1960s as an important time in American journalism, where journalists were no longer political tools of their owners. According to Hallin, since this fundamental change, journalists began to be 'committed more strongly to the norms of the profession than to political ideas' (Hallin 1992: 15). Due to issues such as an economic security of media at the time, 'journalists could think of themselves more as public servants or as keepers of the sacred flame of journalism itself than as employees of a profit making enterprise' (1992: 15–16). Hallin sees this position of journalists today as changing in favour of the profit-making business model. From this perspective, news can be seen as just one of many different types of 'software' (Bogart 1991) offered by the television broadcaster in a media system driven primarily by market forces (Bogart 2000). According to Hallin (1992), this commercialisation of news can be seen in a change of pace in the presentation of news, a tabloidization of hard news and an increased pressure on the journalist to produce stories that 'tug at the heart strings' (1992: 22) and have high production values, 'both narrative and visual, drama, emotion and good video' (1992: 22). The values of professionalism which Hallin describes journalists as driven by in the mid-1960s can no longer fit the structures within which they work. Rather, the commercialisation of news means that economics has 'eroded the barrier between journalism and the profit making business of selling audiences to advertisers' (1992: 21). While the journalists I have talked to express interest in 'winning the viewer battle' between direct competitors, in the everyday work, arguments of the professional ideals such as the good news story are what matters to journalists, not whether the news has commercial value or meets demands of multi-platform work. As Klinenberg (2005) writes in his study of the newsroom changes at the organisation Metro News in New York: 'Digital technologies have changed journalistic production, but not according to the journalists' preferences – the goal is productivity, efficiency, and profitability' (Klinenberg 2005: 229). To Klinenberg, the increase of market logic on the structure of journalism work makes for a dramatic change to the structure of journalism work: 'The penetration of market principles and marketing projects into the editorial divisions of news organizations is one of the most dramatic changes in journalism' (2005: 229).

During fieldwork, I too have found journalists to be committed more strongly to values of the profession than to political ideas. However, I have found economic values such as multi-skilling and faster production to be encouraged by editors in the everyday work and by the very design of the newsroom. In this way, I have found journalists to experience a sense of mismatch of logics, the market logic versus the professional logic of journalism.

According to Freidson's (2001) definitions, professionalism among workers is characterized by elements such as specialised knowledge, working knowledge and skill (Freidson 2001: 1–2, 31, 33–34). These elements of professionalism are all linked to the belief that workers gain special insights and practical experience that they are themselves able to use to the best potential through self-control (2001). In this sense, the ideal of professionalism relies on a notion of self-control. To Freidson (2001), professionalism among workers 'cannot exist unless it is believed that the particular tasks they perform are so different from those of most workers that self-control is essential' (2001: 17). Thus, being professional and being part of a profession can be seen as linked to the expectations by other members of the profession to journalists' ability to maintain individual self-control and self-governance. In this way, journalists who consider themselves part of a profession may believe that their individual self-control renders any other form of management control unnecessary. As journalists see their shared ideals as basis for a professional self-control in their everyday work, they may not see the need for controlling elements such as the temporal and spatial control that I have described. In this sense, the very structure of space and time may make journalists sense a mismatch between their own ideals of being professionals and those of management.

In discussing professionalism, I find the ideal of being 'dedicated to do good work' (Freidson 2001) crucial to defining journalists. Central to this ideal is the notion that doing good work for the benefit of others and for their own satisfaction is more important than doing work in order to maximise income. When I asked staff why they choose to work in news only one of the over 100 news workers I interviewed responded that money was the motivation.[5] Some journalists told me that if they were interested in making money they would be working somewhere else, in PR or marketing. A few journalists told me that they had been offered jobs from the private sector with more pay, but had turned the job down as it was not as 'meaningful' as working for a national broadcaster. Indeed, considering the working hours the monthly wage for a broadcast journalist is not exceptional. Rather than being motivated by the monthly pay, I found journalists to be driven by an ideological wish to better the world and to act like 'a scout' for the benefit of the people (for a discussion of private motivators for working in news in, see Chapter 8). The primary motivation for journalists to work in news is thus neither connected to competition nor to the general market logic with which management has restructured the newsroom.

I have found the new ideals of adapting work to suit many media platforms to be problematic for journalists' professional ideal of doing good journalistic work based on specialised knowledge. The ideal of adapting work to suit many platforms is talked about among journalists as counterproductive to producing good journalism. Thus, the new newsroom organised around the ideal of multi-platform journalism is experienced as a sign that management does not understand the ideals of journalism. To the journalists I have studied it matters whether management appears to understand the values that are the very foundation of their work. In the documentary *Page One inside the New York Times* (Rossi, 2011), talking about management not having respect for journalists, an editor remarks: '[P]eople start despairing because their company is being run by people who just don't share their values'. Potentially, the division between management ideals of market logic and news workers ideals of journalistic professionalism is particularly strong at a time when the job of both management and journalists are threatened by competition. Further, as my fieldwork was conducted immediately after the newsrooms had been restructured, it is likely that journalist staff were more critical to the new structure, while management who had been responsible for the restructure had a more positive approach. However, I believe that analysing the newsroom as a shared contested space can illustrate some of the key differences that journalists experience towards management, while making concrete some of the tangible challenges which journalists face in their everyday work today.

5.2 A Room Where Someone Is Always Watching

> I don't want everyone to see me all the time… I don't know what I'll do about that in the new newsroom!
>> (Producer, ITV News – as he finds a seat next to mine in a corner of the square newsroom, now undergoing a redesign. ITV Newsroom, 17 October 2007)

Among staff in the newsroom, while it was mentioned that the newsroom had a number of positive effects on news content and collaboration, some staff members pointed to other less positive elements of the new room, but only when management staff was at a distance. Staff worried how they were to find the private space needed, as the quote above illustrates. This concern with the new newsroom, which was not voiced in public, focused on the way that staff inside the newsroom felt they had much less room for privacy in the new room. In the following, I will explore some of the challenges felt by staff working inside the new newsrooms, using my own experiences of being a participant observer working inside the same rooms.

A room for watching others

When I began my fieldwork at DR in Denmark, I was very impressed with their new newsroom, which had only recently been built, while some of the connected DR buildings, such as the DR Koncertsal, were still under construction.[6] Their newsroom was very big, bright and new compared to the one I was used to at ITN. And then it was circular. This meant, as illustrated previously, that everyone in the room was constantly watching each other and that the decision-makers on the daily news bulletin became a natural centre of attention for all news workers in the room – and those who decide less are spread out from that centre. Management and the Director General's office are placed on the first and top floor overlooking the newsroom, thus making it easy to observe the news workers without the news workers being able to see management offices or know when they are being watched. As staff within the newsroom are aware of this constant possibility for surveillance, the newsroom becomes a place in which they are prepared to be seen at all times.

After a few days of working inside the DR newsroom, the large multimedia newsroom began to make me consider the room as a modern-day panopticon (Foucault 1977). For Foucault, the essence of power itself can be summarized by the ability to see-without-being-seen, an architectural structure within which those being seen know that they may always be observed. Using Jeremy Bentham's vision of a prison, called a panopticon, in which guards could watch prisoners without them knowing that they were being watched, Foucault argued that the panopticon model was used more abstractly to exercise power over society. Studying professions from a perspective of power theories, Vågan and Grimen use the panopticon as an example of what they call 'power technology' (from the Norwegian 'Maktteknologi'). To Vågan and Grimen, structuring a room in the fashion of a panopticon is 'on one hand a way of exercising power where the architecture plays a central role. On the other hand, it makes it possible to collect knowledge of a specific type' (Vågan and Grimen 2008: 420, my translation from the Norwegian). The knowledge that can be said to be collected within the newsroom is at least twofold. Management may gain knowledge of how staff is working and staff will gain the knowledge that they may at all times be observed by management.

During my very first week of fieldwork at DR, I personally experienced how this observation from management affected my everyday work. During the first few days of fieldwork at DR I felt nervous about disturbing employees who looked busy. And as most staff in those first few days appeared busy to me, I found it hard to walk around the room and ask people if I could work alongside them. Then, when one of the Programme Editors at TV Avisen appeared more friendly and open to my questions than others, I decided to spend the first two days mainly working alongside him. On the third day, as I was leaving the morning editorial meeting, the Head of News at DR took me aside onto the balcony where management can keep an eye on the newsroom: 'You've been talking a lot to that guy', he said, pointing at the Programme Editor I had been working with, seated at his desk in the newsroom. I agreed that I had spent a lot of time shadowing him in these first two days. 'Well, you shouldn't spend your time talking to him, he's not really part of the DR spirit!' – the Head of News then explained, smiling though his eyes looked serious, so I had no doubt that he meant what he had said. 'Oh', I replied, 'then who *is* part of the DR spirit?'. He pointed out a few other younger news workers, who had all worked at DR for a shorter while, and suggested that I talk to them, smiled and then walked off.

The experience first left me confused. Later, I felt I had learned at least three important things from what the Head of News had told me. Firstly, I was confused by the fact that the Programme Editor I had been spending time with, who had been employed by DR for over ten years and appeared to be well-liked and well-known in the newsroom, was not part of what the Head of News deemed the 'spirit of DR'. And it puzzled me what exactly made the other employees more part of this 'spirit'. Indeed this incidence was the first instance where I heard of the 'DR spirit', and after having become aware of the term, I chose to use it when talking to all news workers, asking them each to define what they found part of their spirit.

Secondly, I learned that the Head of News had not given me as free access as first promised, as he thought himself able to tell me who to spend time with and who not to spend time with. I did, however, chose not to follow his instructions, and talked and lunched with the said Programme Editor as much as I believe I would have done had the Head of News not instructed me to do anything. Indeed, I became more interested in the Programme Editor after this experience, and tried constantly to figure out why he would not be deemed good to talk to – and the only conclusion I came to was that he at times did things a little differently, seemed less busy and had more time to chat than most other news workers did.

Thirdly, and crucially for understanding how it feels to work inside the newsroom on an everyday basis, I realised that the management was guarding my actions from above without me knowing. I further learned that the Head of News was not embarrassed to admit to his constant guarding over me; rather, it seemed natural to him to tell me that he had been watching me. After this experience, I felt surveyed when inside the newsroom, constantly sensing that someone was watching me from upstairs.

While the experience of being watched by the Head of News made me worry about what others saw me doing, I also received less threatening comments on who I was seen talking to and where I sat in the newsroom. Often, other news workers, reporters and staff at the input desk sitting at the level above the central newsroom made references to something they had seen me do in the newsroom. In this sense, it appeared that the ability to observe my actions was helpful for other news workers to understand what my work consisted of. In some instances, it was also helpful to me that people on the levels above had seen who I spoke to below; if someone saw me talking to a friend of theirs for instance, it felt as if they warmed to me more quickly and found time to talk to me too.

In the everyday work, I noticed many times how daily work was eased because staff could see each other. A Programme Editor would exclaim: 'THAT is a good story!' and news workers in the near vicinity would instantly be interested in the story. But it was not very often that a news story from one platform would move to another platform, even though both the radio news, the online news and the TV news could see each other. When I asked staff what they thought of their new newsroom, the ability to work better together across media platforms was often mentioned. If I talked to news workers in a space outside the newsroom, staff would tell me something else: 'There is no place to be private – we have to be constantly on', one reporter told me, explaining that the only place she could go to make a private phone call, for instance, would be an empty editing suite or the toilets. Getting them to voice their negative opinions about the newsroom was not easy when inside it. So in order to get critical comments on the newsroom, I had to be placed outside the room itself.

When inside the newsroom and in close proximity to peers, staff appeared to be of very much the same opinion, and no one was critical of the room, the news organisation or management. That staff should feel watched over may in fact be one of the reasons for not sharing emotions that work against management's idea of what is the best practice in the newsroom (as illustrated in the Prologue). Realising this, I came to notice how the same people would tell me entirely contradictory things inside the newsroom to what they would tell me outside the newsroom, in the smoking yard, the coffee room or in the train leaving work, for instance. It is therefore no surprise that it is mostly those members of staff who have been interviewed outside of the newsroom who have been critical towards the organisation they work for.

Being 'the face' of a broadcaster

The TV journalists that I worked alongside during fieldwork often referred to themselves as the 'face' of their broadcaster, a 'TV2 person' or a 'BBC man'. Rather than define oneself as working for the *Evening News at TV2 Nyhederne* or *BBC Ten O'clock News*, for instance, a journalist would refer to the broadcaster when describing oneself and a personal working-style. News workers can be said to see themselves as embodying the broadcaster they work for, understanding themselves as representing their broadcaster and imagining viewers to see them as that too.

That news workers perceive themselves to be representing the broadcaster as a whole is founded on at least three different ideas concerned with how they feel watched by all colleagues working in the same building, and how they feel visible to the public and perceive of themselves as being at the centre of public debates surrounding the values of the broadcaster they work for.

Firstly, when the merits of a certain broadcaster are being discussed publicly, news staff perceives this discussion to be centred on how that broadcaster makes news. As the lawyer for ITN's news content, John Battle, expressed it:

In this country in the last year, there has been a massive issue of trust about regulations and whether on screen the viewers are being duped or conned in some way by what they have seen. [...] news, I think, is the gold stamp and I do think within public service broadcasting, there is probably a higher duty on us here to ensure accuracy and integrity and honesty than any other area of broadcast media.

(John Battle, interviewed in his office, overlooking the newsroom, 30 October 2007)

This quote from a lawyer whose job it is to check all legal issues with news stories before they are broadcast shows how public debates on whether to trust TV content is seen by staff as closely linked to the news they produce. This leads to the perceived idea of news being like a 'gold stamp' for an entire broadcaster's reputation, thus putting a 'higher duty' on news staff than on any other member of staff at the broadcaster. Among news journalists, I found there to be a general agreement with this idea. Journalists would often reflect on a specific job they worked on individually or communally as being an important asset for the entire broadcaster.

Furthermore, the quote above introduces the idea often expressed among commercial broadcast news workers that BBC are not the only ones to work in public service, commercial broadcasting news staff consider themselves to be doing a public service too. At the BBC, I observed a similar attitude towards news and actuality programmes as particularly important for the organisation. I do not believe this sense of self-importance among newsmakers to be a recent development within the news division. Looking back, in an annual BBC report written a few decades ago, it is explicitly expressed that news is what the people judge BBC by: '[...] whatever lies ahead, the BBC will always be judged in large measure by the quality of its news and current affairs output' (BBC 1986–87 annual report in Syvertsen 1993: 224).

Secondly, news staff see themselves as playing a more significant role in the corporation compared to their colleagues from different departments at the broadcaster. At all four broadcasters I have visited, the place where news workers work, the newsroom, is put in a primary spatial position that is very visible compared to the rest of the working offices belonging to staff working for the same broadcaster on different programmes. Thus, architecturally and spatially, the newsrooms and news workers are given a prime position. Each newsroom that I have worked at for this study has large and elegant entrance halls, leading easily to the newsroom, as that is the way guests, dignitaries, politicians and other people on the national agenda will be led to their interview inside the news-studio. Thus, internally among fellow workers at the broadcaster, by the very structure of the building the staff work within, their newsroom is the centre.

Thirdly, news workers see themselves as representing the whole broadcaster as they perceive themselves to be the group of staff within the broadcaster who are most visible to the public. News workers travel the country with a camera, a car, jackets and bag with the name of their broadcaster. When a big event happens in their country, a van with the name of one of the national broadcasters will be at the scene. And when you turn on the TV to watch the news, you see the newsroom. By comparison, staff working at making drama, children's TV or cooking programmes do not get to have their everyday working offices on TV. As a reporter at DR explains:

We are very exposed, and then we become a little like that for many viewers and listeners, therefore we simply are Denmark's Radio. It is also always our studio one sees, and in this way we become very exposed, and that is both good and bad, also internally in this house.

(DR reporter employed at TV Avisen for 20 years, interviewed in the open reporter room, DR Newsroom, 1st floor, 29 June 2007)

The practice of using images of working journalists as a backdrop to the news show was first introduced by the BBC in the mid-1970s, as the evening news began to be broadcast from the BBC newsroom itself rather than from the news studios. As part of a revamped news bulletin, the newsreader would present to a camera while sitting on the edge of a desk; behind him staff could be seen working busily at their desks. Meanwhile, at ITV, the practice of using working staff as a backdrop was not fully introduced until 1991, when the broadcaster moved to its present location at Grays Inn Road, at which time they began presenting the news from inside their newly purchased newsroom. In Denmark, the trend of showing the newsroom with working journalists during the news bulletin was not introduced until TV2 Nyhederne began broadcasting in 1988. When viewers tuned in to watch TV2's first news broadcast in 1988, they were met by a presenter who read the news from the so-called News Room (TV2 chose to use the English word rather than the Danish), in which there was a flurry of TV screens and journalists busy both running and typing in the background behind the presenter.

The primary idea behind using the newsroom as a backdrop to news shows is no doubt to convey certain signals to the viewer. To convey these signals, e.g. the journalists working busily at their desks, can in the terms of Goffman be described as an aid to upholding a 'front' for the newscaster to make the performance of constantly working busily, thus making the viewer believe that the news bulletin is up to date with the latest events worldwide. As Hjarvard has put it: By putting the newsroom on show during the news broadcast, 'one wants to give the illusion that the news presenter is right there where the news is being made and has his hand on the pulse of news' (Hjarvard in Ahrens and Selliken 2007). This illusion, or perception, is exactly what the architects of the new newsrooms intended with the design of newsrooms that are visible as a backdrop during the news programme. Creator and designer of DR's newsroom architecture and layout has described, his idea behind using the DR newsroom during broadcast: 'Every time a new TV Avis starts, the viewer gets another look into the working news staff, which underlines values such as trustworthiness, authenticity and sharpness' (Fridbjørg in Munch-Nielsen 2007: 14, my translation).

Another crucial cause for broadcasting live from the newsroom as explained by the DR reporter above is that journalists and news workers also come to feel they are constantly 'on', since their everyday working space is being watched, not just by colleagues but by the viewers.

When fieldwork commenced, all four broadcasters either began the evening news broadcast with a shot of their newsroom including staff busily working, or had a constant camera shot of a busy newsroom at the back of the news presenter during the entire news show (see Figs 5.1 to 5.3 for an illustration). Except for ITV News, which used year-old footage of a busy newsroom recorded at the time when they shared the newsroom with the ITV News Channel and had a very busy newsroom, all four news broadcasters used live footage from the newsroom as a part of the daily news show.

The members of staff that are visible during the evening news bulletins busily working away in the newsroom are primarily responsible for producing or editing the news bulletin. According to Goffman ([1959] 1990), it is possible to describe the area in which these staff members reside during a TV news bulletin as being 'backstage'. Having these workers as part of the 'front stage' performance of the TV news bulletin thus renders the backstage front stage and presents staff who are not accustomed to being on live TV together with the rest of the news bulletin. I was present as this type of filming was re-introduced at ITV, and I could indeed be seen working busily at a desk during the introduction to the ITV Evening News bulletins during 2007 and 2008. At that time, we, the news workers, were anxious and nervous about having a camera film how we work, and we were not very happy with the prospects of our busy computer working habits being broadcast live to the nation. We noticed that it was those of us who were most busy working by the screen, who were caught

Fig. 5.1: TV2 Nyhederne: Anchor Man Per Christiansen is here placed in the studio at the front of the newsroom (which is on this occasion not so busy), with a backdrop shot of the long corridor of Kvægtorvet, the building from which TV2 broadcasts.

Fig. 5.2: ITV News: A filmed loop from the newsroom is shown in the video wall behind news presenters. This looped film is shown between stories making the illusion that the news studio is placed right outside the newsroom. (2007 ITV Evening News, presented by Mark Austin and Mary Nightingale).

Fig. 5.3: BBC News: While presenters are on screen so are the live actions in the newsroom.

on film. When we asked the cameramen what they wanted us to do on camera, we were told the brief was to 'look busy' and we were asked to 'continue doing what you are already doing, without taking any notice of the camera'.

At the time when the practice of filming news workers and using the working staff as part of the news show was introduced at ITV News Channel, there was a general discontent with the idea among those who ended up being broadcast live while typing at a computer. But as we, the newsroom staff, became used to the practice of being included visually in the news bulletins, we learned how to 'perform', we joked about the performance and no longer cared about appearing and performing like a busy TV news worker.

Though the staff sat busily at work by a computer live on TV every night appear unaware of the camera, most are very aware of being filmed. Many of the news workers I talked to seemed unhappy with the public performance, some turned to comic relief to ease the sense of unhappiness with the performance role. Thus, at times, just before the live filming began inside the newsroom, I heard news-staff shout: 'Now the camera is rolling!', 'no nose-picking, we're on TV!', or make a loud countdown such as: '3, 2, 1 – Let's all act like monkeys!'. Others use the recording of the newsroom as an opportunity to perform in a coded language in front of the camera to friends outside of the newsroom. For instance, I have met news workers, reporters, journalists and producers who use the filming as a platform for sending messages to families watching at home, for instance by walking past the camera in the newsroom in a certain way, or wearing a certain top while being filmed. Thus, the news workers have found ways to subvert the performance from one controlled by the management to one of which they retain some control themselves.

It is interesting to reconsider the performance of news workers in front of the cameras in the newsroom during the evening news bulletins from the perspective of a Panopticon. The difference between being observed by the newsroom cameras at a certain time, and by management within the newsroom at all times, is that when the cameras start rolling, staff are aware of being observed, while inside the newsroom staff can never fully know when they are being watched. Crucially, by performing and using the camera to their own needs, staff have an opportunity to take control of the room; for some this is also an opportunity to show discontent with being watched.

5.3 The Stage Is Set

As has been described previously, the TV newsrooms of this study had recently undergone a change in both the structure of space (the newsroom and the digital interface) and the structure of time, such as arranging new meetings for different news departments to meet and collaborate. In the following, I will analyse some of the impacts that this new newsroom has had on the staff working in it. The new joint meetings introduced at the time of my research coupled with the new layout of the room made possible both more collaboration amongst staff and more observation and control of staff. The newly designed circular layout of the newsrooms enables other levels of collaboration, observation and control.

During my own research, being observed from above made me feel different in the room. Experiences such as when the Head of News at DR told me that he had observed me talking to a member of staff who was not entirely representative of the established values made me take into account how the Head of News would like me to behave during my fieldwork, and thus at times it felt as if I was performing this idea of how I *should* behave when in the newsroom. This experience made me consider the newsroom through Goffman's ideas of positioning on stage and off stage (Goffman 1959, 1967). I found it particularly interesting to map out the boundaries of the newsroom, where the habits and rituals of the room began and where they appeared to end. With these questions in mind, I drew maps in my field notebook and encountered a number of spaces at all four newscasters, where news workers appeared to be more relaxed and able to talk more openly: Places such as the kitchen, the corridors outside the newsroom or the smokers' area outside the broadcast building.

When ideology shows in design

> When we meet, it always happens in specific physical surroundings – surroundings, which we view selectively and classify culturally, as a possible stage for specific, and only certain types of activities.
>
> (Barth 1994: 91, my translation from Norwegian)

As Barth describes in the quote above, any place is designed already with certain ideas in mind. I believe that, in any encounter between different people, the spatial setting and the expectations to this setting are of crucial importance. Studying practices through the structure which keeps it in place, I have come to agree with cultural geographer Tim Creswell that 'place is not just a thing in the world but a way of understanding the world' (Creswell 2004: 11). The structure of a room can be seen as a structure which enables actions. When editors designed new newsrooms in which all staff should be in closer proximity to one-another, this is closely connected to management hopes of multi-skilling and collaboration. Which in turn, as shown by From et al. (2016), can be compared to the arguments put forward by car manufacturer Henry Ford when optimizing work processes and limiting what he termed 'wasted motion and misspent energy' (Ford 1922: 77). Generally, the structure of room is fixed. A room has rules, which are both practical (such as not standing but sitting on chairs) and social (such as the rule that one behaves appropriately and, for instance, does not talk loudly or yell when an interview is being conducted in the newsroom). As Gulløv and Højlund have argued in their description of the *pedagogical force of the material*: '[S]ituations yield opportunities for certain forms of behaviour and status; not because they are already defined, but because people often act in accordance with expectations placed in certain places' (2006: 24, my translation from Danish. See also Barth 1994: 91). Thus, for the staff within the room (except for the few in managerial positions who can decide on redesigns of the room), the newsroom structure is fixed and must be negotiated daily in order to work. Like language, however, some structures may be changed slightly over time, such as when the camera staff at DR found themselves a place within the building to sit and share a coffee, although they had not been considered part of the design. As the camera crew repeatedly turned up inside the newsroom staff coffee kitchen, the room came to be the place for the camera crew. While in the beginning journalists complained that the camera crew took up all the seats in the coffee kitchen and took all the cups meant for journalists, after a few weeks there was no longer any debate over who belonged there. As Creswell aptly puts it: 'The point is that human agency is not so easily structured and structures themselves are made through repetition of practices by agents' (2004: 36).

When the social room is visible in the physical room

'When you enter a large office, aren't you immediately aware of the status of the person sitting at the desk?' This question is posed by anthropologists Delaney and Kaspin (2011: 48) in illustrating how spatial arrangements can convey social status and social order: 'The status is not just communicated by the plush carpets, the view, the furnishings, but from the sheer size of the office' (2011: 48), they argue.[7] In the case of TV news workers, I have found status to be conveyed in two ways among staff: If you are within management, status is conveyed in the privacy you have within a room and the ability you have to watch over the working staff within the newsroom; and if you are among the general news workers, status is communicated by the position you have inside the newsroom – and indeed by the very fact that your role has been considered a central part in the new newsroom.

Most of the newly designed newsrooms I worked in during fieldwork were very similarly designed, putting journalists, producers, Programme Editors and other staff working directly with producing the content of the evening news in viewing distance of each other. Still, of course, all the four different rooms did not look exactly the same. At each broadcaster, the newsroom was situated in different buildings, which made for different spatial designs. At both DR and BBC the newsroom had one or many levels above it, making it possible to look down on the news workers as described in my representation of the DR newsroom. Both TV2 and ITV, on the other hand, only work on one floor, which is partitioned with glass walls, thus giving a similar panopticon-style opportunity to look at the news workers while they work, without the news worker being able to see the person observing.

The circular-shaped Daily Telegraph newsroom, in which representatives from all news output operations are seated close enough to each other to be seen or heard, was a great inspiration both for the rebuilding of the newsroom of ITV and BBC. TV2 was the only of the four newsrooms that did not opt for a strictly circular newsroom in their redesign of the newsroom, which took place just before I began fieldwork there in May 2008. Still, however, the newly designed TV2 newsroom was shaped so that representatives from online news, Text TV and the foreign desk could see and hear the rest of the news division working on the daily news bulletins. Apart from TV2's newsroom, all four newsrooms had offices at the side, in which the editors and news managers could constantly watch over the news workers. At TV2, the management and Head of News was easily able to observe the staff at work inside the newsroom through a glass wall either side of the glass hallway, which divided the newsroom and the news management. Thus, the design of the newsrooms was similar across all four newscasters.

Every room is designed to suit certain ideas, hopes and ideologies.[8] In the design process of the new newsrooms, different management agendas made for a few differences in the priorities of design. For instance, at the time when the new room was designed, it was considered best for cameramen to be primarily out of the building, out filming. Also it was not considered important for camera crew to be a part of the journalistic debates over stories. Therefore, cameramen were not given a physical place to work within the new layout of the four newsrooms I visited. Instead, a room was allocated for the cameramen outside of the newsroom, or in the case of ITV News on Grays Inn Road, a room in the basement of a building opposite the newsroom. Thus, as Bechmann has pointed out in her study of a cross media newsroom in Northern Jutland, Denmark, a centralisation of news desks into one closed super desk excludes those parts of the news division who are not placed centrally (Bechmann 2009: 145; see also Bechmann 2011).[9]

At DR, cameramen were told that they should consider their working place to be 'the road'. Thus, when cameramen moved with the rest of the news workers to their new building in 2007, there was no space allocated for them to sit within the new newsroom. Consequently, the five cameramen at work every day at DR could be found in the small coffee kitchen next to the large multimedia newsroom, when not out on the road. This lack of a physical space within the room created discontent among camera operators who perceived themselves and their camera work to be neglected in favour of an economic strategy behind the newly designed building. As one camera operator told me, before the rebuilding the cameramen had a place to sit – with the new newsroom the ideal is for cameramen to be out of the room, therefore they have not got a space allocated to sit in the newsroom.[10]

Those who did not have a space inside the new newsroom often communicated the feeling of not being an integral part of the news division. To them, sitting inside the new newsroom, having a space (even if only a hot-desk to share with a colleague from the same unit), were a crucial signal as to how much they were considered a part of the decision-making in the daily work – so not having been a part of the design-plan of the new newsroom made them feel neglected. Those news workers who did not have a space within the newsroom or the reporters' room appeared to perceive of themselves as distant from the others and less connected with the daily decision-making. At DR's research unit, for instance, which is placed on a floor above the newsroom where news workers rarely come except when they pass by for a meeting, the Head of Research described his team as 'the dark room in the newsroom [...] which just sits and delivers to the others'. Describing the layout of the news division, he told me: 'There is a hierarchical build, which is just [...] which is just there. And that one cannot really change'.

It has been my experience that those who had not been designated a seat centrally in the newsroom felt that they were not considered as important a part of the news division as those who *were* placed centrally in the room. Bourdieu has described this idea of a link between a physical place in the room and a symbolic place in the order of the people in the room as a 'symbolic power' (1996), with which the social room can be interpreted from studying a physical room. As the cameramen and researchers at DR, for instance, are in the periphery, and not the centre of the newsroom, they view themselves as peripheral to the everyday work of the news division and believe that others view them as that too. In discussing the importance of a physical place Bourdieu writes that:

> The social room shows in the physical room, but always in a more or less messy way: The power over the room, which ownership of different forms of capital yields, is shown in the physical room in the shape of a certain relation between the structure in the spatial distribution of actors and the spatial distribution of goods and services, private or public. An actor's position in the social room is expressed by the place in which the actor is placed [...]
>
> (Bourdieu 1996: 153, my translation from Norwegian)

Bourdieu's description of the connection between a social order and a physical order of a room matches my observations of the way that news workers talk about the importance of a central place for a central role in news making. In exploring the importance of positions in a room, it is interesting to study where different working groups are placed within the room. Realising how the idea that camera crew should be on the road results in camera crew not having a place within the room, for instance, one can begin to see the organisation of place as important for the organisation of people, of ideals and of working practices among people in the room. In this sense, to my research, studying the place where news workers work has been key to studying the way they work.

A room of front stage performances

As Bourdieu (1996) has described, the power structure of the social world can be visible in the very design and structure of a room. Within the new room, there are less backstage (Goffman 1959) areas where staff can act differently to what they believe is expected of them. As illustrated, the entire newsroom is not only watched by colleagues at the same level and at management levels, but by the nation, watching the newsroom as a backdrop to the news bulletin. This constant sense of 'being on', combined with the physical moving together and taking down of walls dividing news staff, can be defined as the creation of a room that for its inhabitants may feel like a large stage. It is my experience that the newsrooms of today are experienced as more public than ever. Thus, the newsroom can be viewed as a stage, which has already been set for staff to act 'front stage' (Goffman 1959) in the way that they believe is expected of them. That the working positions within the newsroom have become more public can thus be seen as creating a work environment that is more like a stage than before. Using metaphors from the world of theatre, Goffman describes public space as a stage in which people act as they believe they should act in order to convince others of the validity of the role s/he is playing:

> To *be* a given kind of person, then, is not merely to possess the required attributes, but also to sustain the standards of conduct and appearance that one's social grouping attaches thereto. The unthinking ease with which performers consistently carry off such standard-maintaining routines does not deny that a performance has occurred, merely that the participants have been aware of it.
>
> (Goffman 1959: 81, original emphasis)

From this perspective, the breaking down of those barriers which were made for a less public working environment can be likened to what Sartre has called a precaution to 'imprison a man in what he is' (Sartre 1957, quoted in Goffman 1990: 82).[11] As Goffman points out in the quote above, the people inside such a room may not necessarily consider their own actions a performance, but may appear to act out a 'standard-maintaining routine', or what Goffman has called 'impression management' with ease. I will not go into deeper explorations of whether or not journalists consider themselves to be 'actors' within the given room. In fact, I have no doubt that some journalists would disagree with the idea that their behaviour inside the newsroom is mere performance. One of the critiques of Goffman's social theory has been that his emphasis on role and performance creates an impression of cynical and strategic actors. I do not consider journalists cynical, but I do believe that there may be a strategic reasoning behind the actions that take place inside work places, such as the newsrooms that I have studied. As illustrated previously in this chapter, one example of everyday performance in the newsroom can be found in the way that newsroom staff members behave while they are filmed during the live broadcast.

5.4 'Multi-skilling' as the Term for What Went Wrong

Recent studies of the impact of technology on journalism (see for instance Pavlik 2000; Klinenberg and Fayer 2005; IFJ and ILO 2006) suggest that the boundaries between editorial and economic interests are becoming increasingly blurred. A report made by the International Federation of Journalists and the International Labour Organisation on the changing nature of news work around the world writes that the journalism profession's classical 'good' journalistic content, such as investigative work, appears heavily challenged by economic demands in that 'journalists' workloads have increased – many of them work for digital media as well as traditional media, but are not paid for the additional labour (IFJ and ILO 2006: 5).

Today, all levels of staff in the newsroom are aware of the constant competition from other news outlets, and news workers are expected to provide content for multiple platforms and to consider things such as cross promotions and tie-ins in order to reach as large an audience as possible. Add to this the economic crisis, which hit journalism in the years my fieldwork took place, and it is clear that the everyday demands of news workers have increased over the last decade. How are these new demands visible in the restructured newsroom? As shown in the previous chapter, the new newsroom has been designed with the aim of encouraging multi-media collaboration and multi-skilling journalists. With this new room, a new way of working has been encouraged by management within the four newsrooms, and a new type of journalist has been introduced: the multiskilled journalist. Unlike the traditional journalist, this type of journalist is not defined by the media for which he works but by his capability of working for multiple media platforms and the speed by which he works.

Early newsroom researchers, such as Tuchman (1972, 1973) and Breed (1955), have described urgency and speed as the very essence of news making. As Tuchman put it in the early 1970s, 'the need for speed is so overarching that it influences characteristics of news stories' (Tuchman 1973: 116). Recent research establishes that this tendency of putting an overarching value on speed has increased rather than declined since Tuchman and Breed's studies (see Deuze 2005: 457–59, for a discussion of this, see also Lewis et al. 2008).

'It is not the same shop that I work in now'

Researching production routines in four online newsrooms in Spain, Domingo (2008) has illustrated how 'immediacy rules', with the primacy of immediacy in the newsroom being 'overwhelming' (2008: 115). Today, it is particularly in TV newsrooms with an online news department that the urgency of publishing news is felt. Jannie Hartley, who has studied online news desks in Denmark, writes of the shared news stories that 'the online journalists cannot procrastinate – precisely because the competitors could press "publicise" at any minute' (Hartley 2011: 279). The emergence of Internet news has no doubt furthered a priority of speed among journalists. As the four broadcasters each have an online news platform as part of the news division, they publish stories as soon as they happen, and then count the seconds until their competitor posts the same story. In December 2017, when staff at the TV2 newsroom first learnt that another body part of Kim Wahl had been found at sea, they published the story online and linked to it on their Facebook page, then kept a triumphant watch over how much slower DR was in broadcasting the story. Urgency is no doubt more important today than it was in the newsrooms in the early 1970s. In this sense, 'being fast', 'working fast' and 'being a quick thinker' are all important skills of the ideal news journalist. Some of the challenges created by the necessity of this skill are that staff have less time to work on specific stories, giving way to what critics have called 'churnalism' (Davies

2009).[12] Most of the journalists I worked alongside during fieldwork complained that they had less time today to do their work than they used to have. A prioritising of working fast, a decrease of news room staff and an increase in expectations to each news worker were some of the most frequently mentioned reasons for why journalists felt they had less time to do their work today than they used to have.

At all four newsrooms, staff numbers were being reduced during or just before I came to do fieldwork, so the number of news workers was rapidly decreasing. This, at a time where the newsrooms were engaging in more interactive ways of presenting, encouraging reporters to take up many new tasks such as doing their own editing, making a blog on the broadcaster's website and work on making TV interviews available on many more platforms. This combination of events made many of the news workers I talked to worried that fewer members of staff were now being asked to do more work. Particularly those members of staff who had been employed over a long period of time described the changes in the organisation as drastic challenges to their ideal of good journalism work, as the following quote shows:

> It is not the same shop that I work in now compared to that which I was employed by 39 years ago. It has the same name, but that is the only thing, which is still the same. [...]. At that time we had a camera each, and of course that camera was lying idle on a day off. [...] Now the idea is that we must not let a camera stand idle for a day, no computer or table should be standing unused for an hour. Therefore we get no place where we can sit.
> (DR camera operator and editor, employed at DR for 39 years, in conversation in the DR newsroom kitchen, 18 June 2007)[13]

Just like the camera operator above, at the time of my fieldwork many of the news staff with whom I worked spoke of how things used to be better. They particularly spoke of a time free of threats to their job, their news bulletin and their broadcaster. At all broadcasters I visited, there had either just been cuts in jobs (at ITV and TV2) or cuts to the number of staff were announced while I was there (at DR and BBC). News workers at all newsrooms I visited referred to these constant job cuts and constant worries of job cuts as making the everyday work 'harder', 'more lonely', 'more busy' and creating an increased need for 'multiskilled' staff. The term 'multi-skilling' appeared among many of the journalists I spoke to, as a defining term for what they considered to be going wrong within their newsroom. When discussing the ideas behind 'multi-skilling', journalists particularly talked of how it would mean a 'downgrading of news quality and news content'.

The idea of requiring more technical abilities from the same journalists were introduced to the news divisions a few years before the new converging newsrooms were designed, during the year 2000 (Bechmann 2009; Erdal 2008; Deuze 2007, Bechmann 2007). Thus from 2000 and onwards, TV journalists have been increasingly encouraged to film, edit and produce their own news stories and share content across the news desks. In 2012, at DR for instance, a project known as 'the news engine' was set in motion, which was to change the everyday routines of each news worker drastically. Crucial to this new way of working was collaboration and multi-skilling, which led journalists to feel less personally responsible for stories. The new way of working required each journalist and cameraman to contribute to stories of the day and share pictures, stories and quotes with the entire news organisation of DR. As From et al. (2016) have highlighted, this led to journalists feeling unhappy and while they were involved in many stories, they did not feel fully involved in any specific stories on an everyday basis – resulting in some journalists describing themselves as 'feeling amputated as a journalist'.

With the emerging research into convergence newsrooms, attention has primarily centred on the effects on how journalists make news (cf. Quandt and Singer 2009: 134; see also Bardoel and Deuze 2001; Singer 2004; Ursell 2001; Blankenship 2016). During my study, I have had a similar interest, although I have focused specifically on the journalist's point of view and how the converged newsrooms may function in relation to professional values of journalism. As put forward by Deuze: 'Every aspect of the professional identity of multimedia journalism will […] entail a critical discussion on the various meanings it can have for the journalists involved, indicating the bandwidth of issues involved in the convergence process which facilitate the journalists' agency' (Deuze 2004: 139; see also van Zoonen 1998).

The transition of journalism roles has been described by Robinson (2011) as threatening to 'fragment journalistic identity' (Robinson 2011: 41). During fieldwork at the newsroom of the once-print paper now online-only media *The Capital Times*, Robinson finds journalists to be confused by new demands of being competent in many different identities. This confusion, he found, 'created tensions among this staff' (2011: 41). In her study of converged newsrooms in the US, Singer found that although some journalists were unhappy with certain aspects of convergence, they generally supported the idea, with some expressing the belief that 'converged operations could enhance their public service mission' (Quandt and Singer 2009: 134). I have found journalists to express a similar optimism towards the idea of producing content in multiple media formats. However, only very few journalists (primarily the younger generation) agreed with their editors that they should personally be expected to create this multiple media content as an additional job to their usual one. Rather, the journalists I met expressed resistance towards working with multiple media formats and working as 'multiskilled' journalists. As discussed by Shoemaker and Reese (1996), the foundations of cultural resistance against convergence start with the differences between online journalism and the print journalism practice – not to mention the differences between online and broadcast journalism practices. Additionally, I believe the resistance towards producing journalism for multiple platforms has roots in a pressure caused by the diverging ideals of the profession.

Many of the journalists I have studied described themselves as having a specialised knowledge akin to what Freidson (2001) defines as a characteristic of ideal values of professionalism (see Chapter 1.2). Some talked of being particularly good at human interest stories, others talked of politics or immigration as a special expertise. Most journalists talked of themselves as 'good at interviews' and quick at 'getting the story'. Journalists talked of using both practical and formal knowledge (Freidson 2001: 30), but in none of their self-descriptions regarding working knowledge did they mention being able to work with different media nor having technical skills. In this sense, the very expectation of journalists to want to work with different media and use different technologies can be seen as contradictory to already established professional values.

Within all four broadcast newsrooms I have studied, the new management requirements, which were introduced as 'multi-skilling', had a cold reception among journalists. In Britain, the National Union of Journalists engaged in a continuous discussion with the BBC for two years, since the English regions drew up plans to extend the use of video cameras and laptop editing equipment for journalists. One of the arguments put forward by the National Union of Journalists was that there was a concern 'about the impact on editorial standards of multi-skilling and the ad-hoc introduction of new working practices' (according the Press Gazette 2002). In April 2002, BBC news workers threatened strike action over the new ways of working, particularly the requirement of journalists to film and edit their own news stories, which was not coupled with an increase in pay. While staff expressed worries over the working time that multi-skilling tasks would require, another concern among the traditional news journalists was the worry that the excitement about new media platforms took focus away from the traditional journalistic values. As one long-time journalist, the investigations editor at *The Guardian*, expressed it:

My fear is that today everybody is rather too obsessed with new platforms. But not enough people are talking about values. [...] I fear that these developments will endanger the role of the reporter. Of course there'll always be room for news bunnies – to dash in front of the camera and breathlessly describe a lorry crash, or to bash out a press release in 10 minutes. There'll probably be a lot more news bunnies in the future: High-speed, short legged creatures of the internet age. There will probably also be hyper-local sites: postcode journalism fuelled cheaply by neighbourhood bloggers. But not proper reporters.

(Leigh 2007)[14]

Within all four newsrooms, I heard journalists express discomfort and disagreement with multi-skilling journalism similar to the critique of the new 'Internet age' above. None of the interviewees I spoke to at the four broadcasters were willing to be quoted talking so directly against the new demands however. The unhappiness with the new requirements were particularly explicit among staff who had been employed for a few years, while among the younger and more recently employed staff, I did meet journalists and reporters who appeared genuinely interested in learning to film and edit *as well as* working as a journalist. As it is particularly the long-term employed journalists who have acquired a certain specialism, specialist areas in the newsroom appear to be threatened most by the new ideals of multi-skilling journalists. As one trainee broadcast journalist expressed it:

Gone are the days of specialism in print, broadcast or even online. Today's journalists must be multiplatform wonders and those who fail to adapt to these new expectations will find it increasingly difficult to compete. [...] By lacking a particular specialism, are today's journalists in danger of sacrificing quality by spreading themselves too thinly? Are we willing to trade in excellent print journalists and broadcasters who have honed their craft for years in exchange for cohort of adequate journalists who can multi-skill? Do we have a choice?

(Whelan writing in *The Guardian*, 16 June 2008)

In answer to her question, I would argue that the journalists of today do not have much choice but to follow the new requirements in order to suit the wants of the times.[15] However, I believe it is important that not only the staff within the newsroom but also the public watching the news discuss what multi-skilling requirements may take away from the news bulletins.

During fieldwork, I experienced journalists talk critically about the new newsroom when talking among themselves during work and in breaks. Further, I saw journalists physically move away from the new newsroom to find spaces where they could work without being observed. And almost daily, I overheard journalists talk about the expectations of journalists to multi-skill and do multi-media work as 'not real journalism', 'too gimmicky' or 'commercial'. However, in recorded interviews, when I asked journalists to tell me what they thought about the restructure of their news work and the reorganisation of their newsroom, no one was openly critical to the changes or to their editors. On record, the journalists rather told me that they thought the new room was helpful for keeping eye contact with colleagues. The usefulness of calling on other colleagues to help in try meet the new demands of editing one's own packages on the personal computer was mentioned when talking about the new newsroom. All these new challenges, journalists told me, meant that they found it particularly helpful to be in the close proximity of colleagues with the same difficulties – as they could be able to help with the editing, be alert to good clips on the server that could be used in a news piece or help with the new tasks in any other way. This shows how the positive aspects of the new newsroom were very much present in the consciousness of staff. Moreover, it shows how positive connotations were primarily given when staff discussed the room publicly. The new newsroom was talked about as signalling a new way of working, in which staff should collaborate more, be able to multi-skill more – and, just as the new room connected desks which had before been disconnected, staff expected that they would come to connect and collaborate more with their colleagues in the room.

The continued pressure on newsroom staffing, such as the demands to produce more in less time and 'to multi-skill' has been described as an attempted 'coping strategy' for old media in a digital age (see for instance Freedman 2010). According to Freedman, continued pressure on journalists is not a tenable solution but a sign that the professional values of journalism are being underprioritised in favour of a market logic:

The internet has the potential to expand the diversity of news sources, to improve the quality and breath of news coverage, and to deepen the interaction between news providers and their audiences. Yet, given today's hard economic circumstances, the internet has instead contributed to a possibility that the news of the future is going to be sustained by a declining number of specialist news organizations, a growing band of generalist news and information businesses, and a handful of parasitatal aggregators supplemented by an army of contributors working for free. Market logic, in this scenario, is set to prevail over news logic.

(Freedman 2010: 50)

Witschge (2013) describes the pressure on newsroom staff as 'what forms the real challenge to journalism'. Witschge (2013) sees investment in public-service journalism as crucial for escaping what she describes as negative cycle of old news. In this, she agrees with Nossek (2009) in that the most imminent 'threat facing journalism is de-professionalization, which means that everyone can be a journalist and nobody actually is one' (Nossek 2009: 358). Freedman (2010) also points towards underinvestment as the biggest threat to old media. To Freedman there is an urgent need of investment 'in technology, in resources and, especially, in journalists themselves' (Freedman 2010: 50). From this perspective, considering new trends of demanding more media skills from the broadcast news staff and more content in less time, the journalists' fear of the idea of 'the multiskilled journalist' appears well founded. While the many new ways of communicating news stories may seem exciting for broadcast management, there is a danger that they will lose what is, in comparison with new media competitors, one of their most valuable elements, namely specialised knowledge. In this sense, by favouring multiskilled journalists over those with a specific specialism, the national broadcast media may just lose the most competitive element they have. Not only could this lose a winning element in the competition to keep the audience, the trend of prioritising multiskilled journalists may also cause them to lose good journalists. As I will discuss in the coming chapters (see Chapters 6 and 7) 'specialism' and the idea of being particularly good at one's specific craft are central ideals of journalists today, which are seen as threatened by the new structure of news work.

Increased reliance on agency copy

Don't look at agency copy as you write. Make a note of any facts you might need. Clear away the agency copy from the screen, then write the script from your head.
(An advice headlined 'Top Tip', – sent by email from ITV scriptwriter and Programme Editor to other scriptwriters, 30 October 2007)[16]

The above advice sent to all scriptwriters at ITV indicates one of the primary challenges to news writers, both in 2007 and 2017: copying from agencies. In the following, I will look closer at this issue, which is important to journalists not only in broadcast news but on all media platforms today. In the everyday working practices, I experienced journalists being frustrated by lack of time to work on stories, which in turn led to an increased copy of agency stories, cases and sources. With the sharing of news agencies among all national broadcasters comes not only the risk that staff copy blindly what the agency writes, but also that news divisions share content, images and news sources between broadcasters in the everyday news work.

At all the four broadcasters, the primary sources of everyday news and news footage were mostly the same: the news agencies and other media sources such as online news or newspapers. Online news and newspapers are of course sources of news that are available to all and not exclusive to news workers. Still, however, other media, such as newspapers, are vital sources for news stories (see Lund et al. 2009). Reading through the stack of morning papers waiting for him/her on his/her desk, flicking through online news pages and listening to the radio in the morning, a Programme Editor starts every day by establishing what stories other media choose to lead with. If the Programme Editor finds one such story interesting, s/he may forward it to a reporter, who will take the information, sources and cases that the newspaper article uses as a starting point. Thus, it is not surprising that many of the stories broadcast on TV news often use the exact same case studies and sources as the newspaper article that inspired the story (Lund et al. 2009). Particularly on days when time is short and case studies are hard to find, contacting the same source found in another medium is often used to speed up the story process, as the time it would take to find another case is simply not available. I found that this practice was used to a similar extent at all four newsrooms.

Other visual elements, which the newsrooms share, are video feeds, pictures and stories from news agencies. Inside the newsroom, each newsroom worker sits by a desk with at least one screen on it continually updating the most recent news stories from the news wires (see for instance the top 'flash' of a news story on the ENPS interface in Chapter 4.2 as seen by staff at BBC News). The news wires with video feeds attached, which appear on this screen, arrive at BBC, ITV, DR and TV2 from either of the same primary sources: Reuters and APTN. These two news agencies both provide video feeds of news events, which, with a voice-over and simple 'cut and tail', make for a fast ready-to-broadcast news piece.[17]

Each national newscaster has different national news agencies that they prioritise for local stories, such as Ritzau in Denmark and PA in the UK. But for video footage of events, each of the four broadcasters subscribe to either Reuters or APTN. Due to economic constraints, the broadcasters today tend to subscribe to *either* news agency's video feed and not both as has been practiced in the past.[18] Still, though a broadcaster only subscribes to one agency, such as APTN, staff do have access to read about which feed Reuters can offer at any given moment. During fieldwork, I noticed that a widely used practice was to check both news agencies for information and facts about a story but only use video feed from the one with which the broadcaster had a contract.

The sharing of news agency pictures is a crucial explanation of one of the most visible similarities between the news bulletins across the four different broadcasters: the similar images used to illustrate news. As one of the staff who works in TV news and archive footage, Robert Baldwin, Business Development Manager at ITN Source, told me: 'When you go abroad, you see very similar footage everywhere. The news content today is becoming more and more homogenised. Every news provider either has a contract with Reuters or APTN, and little money to spend, so they use the footage they get with their contract, which then means the footage used in news is very generic'.[19] In the everyday work, I have seen the news agencies as playing a dominant role in the selection of what video feeds to run with, and hence what stories to take on a given day. Thus, I do believe that the contracts, which broadcasters have signed with news agencies, are crucial in determining which footage is shown to illustrate a news story.

When journalists are given less time to work, key professional values, such as those of the 'good news story', and do 'good work' are being challenged. This dissatisfaction comes across in the following quote from an Anchor Man at ITV:

There is no question that real, pure journalism is being out and about with a cameraman, I mean for television news you know. With a blank canvas and putting something together yourself, making, filling in this canvas. So, starting from scratch and then coming back having a story that is completely self-generated, that is what I consider to be pure journalism.

Ehmm... Quite often now, you see stories which are basically comprised on pictures that are available to everyone, so there is a great sort of... there is a very generic feel about the coverage. Take 24-hour news channels. It is quite often that you can turn on two 24 hour news channels side by side and you can see the same pictures, the same stories, different presenters, different reporters.
(Anchor Man at the *ITV News at 10.30,* interviewed in his private office overlooking newsroom, with blinds pulled down, 31 October 2007)

As expressed in the quote from ITV's Anchor Man above, 'self-generated' investigative reporting and investigative journalism is valued as an ideal model for journalistic work, and as such, can be seen as the very reason for why journalism exists – according to journalists.[20] According to ex-journalist Nick Davies, however, not having enough time is the reason for the current decline in journalism standards. With his book *Flat Earth News* (2009), Davies aims to 'expose' the British print media's lack of time to think and therefore lack of in-depth analysis and lack of original news. This reduction in time to work leads to a favouring of what he calls 'churnalism over journalism' – reducing a journalist's job to the practice of continually regurgitating unchecked stories and press releases that may or may not be true. In his book, he cites among others a research conducted by Lewis et al. from

Cardiff University (see Lewis et al. 2008), which found that 80% of the stories in Britain's quality press were not original and that reporters generated only 12% of stories. This, according to Davies, shows just how quality and accuracy have been reduced in print journalism today.

The notion that journalists do not have enough time to check the stories that they read from news wires or in the newspapers was not frequently talked about directly during everyday work, though staff were often complaining that they did not have time to make as 'good' a story as they felt they should. During my research, I did not find evidence that the lack of perceived time to do the job should lead to a dominance of spin and press releases being increasingly reported as news, as claimed by Nick Davies. However, I did find that the news stories coming to the journalists through wires from primarily AP, PA, Reuters and Ritzau's news agencies were trusted, unquestioned and employed as sources, and their validity was hardly ever checked. I talked to one reporter at TV2 who told me that he found it incredibly hard to fight off the mass of press releases that land in his email inbox every day, as they are so easy to use and simple to lift into a news item, particularly if he had little time to produce a story. Working off press releases, he told me, is particularly tempting if one is new in the field and is not able to see through the spin. This particular reporter, who had at the time worked five years at TV2, told me that he had now determined to avoid press releases and press officers and had made it his rule to always interrogate a press release before considering it to be of any use. This type of approach to press releases and PR was not uncommon in all four newsrooms that I worked in. Using a press release entirely as a news source was not a respected practice among news workers and their editors, and it was thus a source of news that news workers did their utmost to avoid.

Doyle's (2006) research of financial journalism came to a similar conclusion, namely that spin is a well-recognised threat among financial journalists and business reporting. According to Doyle's research, even though journalists are aware of this challenge from press releases, they are also acutely aware that the little time they have makes it hard, if not impossible, to conduct the in-depth research that is their ideal. In my time among news workers, I have found this understanding of press releases and spin apparent among reporters on all levels; an understanding which can make the everyday work seem like a constant negotiation between the real and the ideal news work. In his analysis of economic and financial news production in the UK, Doyle quotes one financial journalist, who defines this constant struggle as 'working within the constraints of reality':

> In terms of economic development, we write about, say, whether countries have been successful in reducing their debt level, but we don't ask why we have a system whereby countries have debts in the first place. We don't challenge – but I'm afraid that's the deal... We are not campaigning but we are working within the constraints of reality.
>
> (Financial reporter quoted in Doyle 2006: 447)

5.5 Conclusions

One day in the canteen of DR, while lunching with a group of journalists and producers, I mentioned that I thought it would be interesting to study the newsroom in order to understand how the TV news staff work. As I told them that my Ph.D. thesis (Thomsen 2013) would be at least 200 pages long, the staff I sat with warned me that they did not think I could write many pages about their newsroom: 'There's not much to say about our big shared office – it is not easy to concentrate and it is hard to be personal. Full stop', said one reporter, informing me that she did not think there was any other story that one could write about the newsroom.[21] I should like to think that with the last two chapters I have refuted this DR reporter's assertions, as I have suggested many more and different ways to study the TV newsrooms of today in order to give an understanding of the conditions under which TV journalists work and the effect on staff these conditions may have.

With the previous chapter, through my descriptions of the room, the digital working space and the structure of editorial meetings I have illustrated how news journalists are constantly experiencing being corrected, controlled and surveyed by editors in the everyday. With this chapter, I have analysed the empirical findings with a focus on place in order to explore how the setting of a room can matter to the people in it. I have shown how staff aim to negotiate the designed room in order to suit their own sense of self and professional ideals. I have illustrated how staff talk of the restructure of news work as 'a different shop' to work in and how the demands of multi-skilling is talked about as not suiting journalistic ideals. During this discussion, I have illustrated how the social world can be said to be visible in the physical world, as argued by Bourdieu (1996). Further, I have shown how the 'designed' room influences the 'practice' within that room (Wenger 1998a). As shown throughout this chapter, I have found that the way that newsrooms are structured matters to the way that people experience their role within the room and the way in which they work within the room.

With this chapter, I have described the working practices of the newsroom and the effects that I have observed the newsroom to have on staff. Underlining the practices of journalists I have come to see shared ideals of the profession to be important to the everyday work. In the following two chapters I will explore and analyse these ideals further.

Notes

1 The notion that the individual actively negotiates behaviour to suit his own self can, as Hochchild ([1983] 2003: 224–32) argues, be seen as a departure from Goffman's (1959) definition of a less active individual, who is often unknowingly acting out a presentation of himself.

2 It should be mentioned that some broadcasters had attempted at making more private places near the newsroom in order to satisfy a request from staff, but often the areas created were

not closed off enough to be experienced as private. When TV2 News' news department in Copenhagen created a 'relaxing area' for news staff, it came in the guise of a group of plush sofas placed right outside the News Editor' offices. As the walls of these offices are of glass and often have an open door, when seated in the sofas the staff felt more seen and heard there by their editor than anywhere else. As a result, I found the sofas hardly ever used.

3   Within some newsrooms, staff members do not have the choice to access private websites. In 2007, within some of the four newsrooms, use of social network websites such as Facebook, MySpace or Twitter was restricted by the broadcaster, making it impossible to access them inside the newsroom. By 2017, there were no such restrictions.

4   This idea may support earlier notions of media ritual (see Carey 1998; Tuchman 1973; Couldry 2005).

5   The person who did mention money as being a motivation for working had a managerial position.

6   *Copenhagen Concert Hall* is the English term for DR's concert venue.

7   Using academia as a case, the anthropologists continue to describe how among university lecturers, professors and assistant professors there is a certain pecking order, which is visible in the size of their offices, pointing out that '[t]he size of an office, even if the difference is only a few square feet can create all kinds of personnel issues and conflicts' (Delaney and Kaspin, 2011: 48).

8   As Gulløv and Højlund write of nurseries and children's institutions: 'It is rooms which are built on the background of political, economical, ideological and professional interests in children, childhood, upbringing, education and society' (2006: 21, my translation from Danish).

9   Bechmann's (2004–06) study of cross media work focused on *Nordjyske Medier* and *DR Ung*.

10 DR camera operator and editor, employed at DR for 39 years, talking in newsroom kitchen (18 June 2007, DR Field book 1, p. 91).

11 'There are indeed many precautions to imprison a man in what he is, as if we lived in perpetual fear that he might escape from it, that he might break away and suddenly elude his condition' (Sartre 1957, quoted in Goffman 1959: 82).

12 See also www.churnalism.com, an independent website built by the Media Standards Trust, inspired by Nick Davies's book, to 'help the public distinguish between original journalism and *churnalism*' (churnalism.com 2012).

13 DR Field Diary 1, p. 91.

14 In line with the BBC and ITV News, *The Guardian* newsroom has also taken inspiration from *The Daily Telegraph* newsroom in its embracing of convergence (according to conversation with editors as I was on a newsroom visit, January, 2009).

15 Journalism is of course not the only profession facing the challenge of adapting to and using new media in this new Millennium (for studies of organisations and professions adapting to change see for example Hoff and McAffrey, 1996 and Stacey, 2007).

16 I received this staff email as the sender of the email, ITV Programme Editor and one of the most celebrated scriptwriters at ITN, forwarded me emails that he thought I might find useful for my study.

17 'Cut and tail' is a phrase journalists often use for the job of cutting the beginning and the end of a video feed – this most simple of news editing practices can today be done by news workers at their desk, as all computers are equipped with basic editing tools.

18 This limitation of news sources no doubt works to limit the variation of news stories and images. Of course, if an agency that the broadcaster does not subscribe to has essential footage then arrangements are made for the broadcaster to pay a one-off fee for buying the footage. Additionally, short-term subscription is often arranged with a news agency, during times and events when the video feeds of the agency are deemed particularly useful for a broadcaster.

19 Phone interview conducted 7 October 2011.

20 Ettema and Glasser make a similar conclusion on the relationship between daily reporting and investigative reporting, in their book *Custodians of Conscience*, on investigative journalism and public virtue (Ettema and Glasser 1998: 155).

21 11 June 2007 in the DR canteen (DR Field book 1, p. 31).

Part V

New Struggles and Old Ideals

Chapter 6

The Unity and Community of Journalists

On connections between the newsrooms, journalists as parts of a
community of practice, and how this unites

Throughout the previous chapters, the four different newsrooms of BBC, ITV, DR and TV2 have been introduced as having different values in terms of how to present news, though working within a very similar structure of time and space. Though staff at the four different broadcasters have appeared keen to define their way of working as different from how staff at the other broadcasters worked, I have found the way of working across all four broadcasters to be very much alike. As described, all four newsrooms of my study had a similar look and design, a similar meeting structure of the day, used the same news agencies and similar equipment and systems to create news content. I have described how the newsrooms matter to the staff working in them. With this chapter, I would like to highlight the fact that even though the structural framework is important, it is not the structure within the room, that plays the primary part in making news staff feel connected and united in their everyday work.

Having noticed the many similarities between the four different newsrooms, I began considering what reasons there might be for the newsrooms looking and functioning so similarly. In order to explore how connected the four newsrooms are, I began considering relations of what is core and what is periphery to staff within the newsroom. What I found through researching the correlations among staff was that each newsroom is very much connected to the other newsrooms, by way of everyday practice communities, both real and imagined. I found that these practice communities construct a core relation of strong friendship bonds across broadcasters. In this way, the realisation that all the newsrooms and TV studios I conducted fieldwork in were designed and structured so alike was a starting point for exploring and attempting to map out connections and relations linking each of the four newsrooms.

In the following chapter, I will illustrate the many different levels of practice-related connections existing among news workers, with a specific focus on those employed as journalists. As will be described, some of the connections across broadcasters are perceived as being as strong as those of family bonds. Journalists may consider such bonds to be much stronger than the imagined bond felt by the employee working for a specific broadcaster or media platform. Above all, I argue, journalists across broadcasters perceive themselves to be connected and related across broadcasters and media platforms in a shared community consisting of all the people working in journalism.

How one redundancy can anger an entire profession

In September 2014, after over 30 years working for Danish Public Service Broadcaster DR, a well-known journalist and presenter was fired. He was one of over 650 staff members from DR who was made redundant due to economic problems at the broadcaster. However, this particular journalist, Niels Lindvig, decided he did not want to leave. Instead, he chose to keep doing his presenting and journalism jobs for the broadcaster. 'As long as I don't get thrown out of the building I will stay working here, because I like my work', said Lindvig (Lindvig in Bruun-Hansen 2014). Lindvig was not alone in his denial of management decisions. Outpours of support came from journalist colleagues from competing news organisations across Denmark. A few days after he lost his job, journalists from competing news organisations began supporting a nationwide petition for Lindvig to stay working at DR, stating that: 'Niels Lindvig is an extremely good journalist, who makes an incredibly thorough, in-depth job' (according to the petition text, Skrivunder.net 2014). Shortly after (13 October 2014), Lindvig was told by his superiors to leave the building. This instantly caused his colleagues at DR's programme *Orientering* and a number of other DR programme staff to go on a day-long strike. After this strike, staff called the Executive Director of DR for a meeting in which she was asked to explain the values behind making a good journalist redundant. Soon after, a competing radio station, *Radio 24 syv*, began using Lindvig as a guest-commentator. In 2017, there is still an active group of journalists and radio listeners campaigning to have Niels Lindvig back at DR. The group has brought his case to the Ombudsman, which they lost. However, they are still campaigning for Lindvig to return to the Public Service Broadcaster, on the counts of him being a 'good' journalist.[1]

Lindvig's case highlights some of the key findings I have made during my study of journalism culture: journalists share a bond, stronger than any bonds created by management rules and organisational competition. One of the key values within the practice community of journalists is that of being a good journalist. When the practice community sees their core value as being threatened, journalists unite in order to protect their practice community and their profession. As this chapter explores, staff may experience a sense of threat to their entire profession, if a colleague that they deem 'good' is being made redundant.

The controversy surrounding DR journalist Niels Lindvig being made redundant have made public the many practice-community bonds existing between broadcasters. The case is particularly interesting as it has made news journalists openly declare that they see a mismatch between management ideals and the ideals of their profession (see also Thomsen forthcoming).

6.1 Following Connections Between the Newsrooms

As described previously, management staff members within each newsroom often visit each other in order to get inspiration and learn about the latest newsroom trends. These trips were one of the first connections between newsrooms and newscasters that I took note of.

Having found this connection between the four broadcasters, I decided to look out for any other connections, follow them, enquire about them and concentrate my research on the similarities that had at first so surprised me.

Following the different relations between newscasters, I thought it helpful to map out the boundaries between those inside the practice of news work and those outside it. In doing so, I was particularly inspired by the idea of mapping relations in complex societies introduced by Wolf (1966) and the onus of focusing on boundaries put forward by Etienne Wenger (1998a: 253–55). In Wolf's discussion of friendship relations, he notes that the formal structure of large institutions or a state 'exists alongside or intermingled with various other kinds of informal structure which are interstitial, supplementary, parallel to it' (Wolf 1966: 2). I find interesting Wolf's use of the term 'interstitial' in relation to the ties of friendship particularly. Apt for describing the important, yet mostly unseen connections, which the different broadcasters gain through friendship links, is this medical term referring to that which is not seen with the naked eye but exists within or in relation to parts of an organ or between groups or cells.

From this perspective, the mapping of relations existing across different media and different broadcasters is crucial when wanting to view the full structure of each broadcaster's news division. As I found that friendships construct a boundary between those inside the community of news workers and those outside of it, I began to explore these friendships across broadcasters. In time, I came to view journalists' friendships as community builders *as well as* border makers for those outside of the profession. As I will illustrate in the following, looking out for connections between the broadcasters meant that I came to see many more ways of reaching across the different newsrooms and broadcasters than merely management going on inspiration trips to see each other's newsroom designs.

'It's like a family!'

It was during one lunch hour in the early summer of 2007, as I was walking through the Danish Parliament with one of DR's reporters, that I first took notice of the warm friendships existing between journalists from rival networks. At every corridor we passed, another politician or reporter would greet us, some politicians shared a joke, and some reporters shared a story or gave a tip to a political story of the day. Then, as we reached Snapsetinget, which was introduced to me as the canteen where DR staff had lunch, I noticed that all political journalists as well as politicians on all levels were using this as their canteen too. As we had our lunch, different DR journalists, editors and cameramen came to eat with us and have a chat, as did journalists from both print and TV news. When I asked him for the reason why there did not seem to be a very strong boundary neither between journalists from rival networks nor between the different politicians, he responded:

We are a little family here. We know each other so well. And then of course, when journalists go on holidays with politicians, that relationship is strengthened. [...] Those at TV2 are all friends of ours. The only fight we have with each other is about being first with the questions and pictures.

(DR Christiansborg Reporter – in conversation, the Danish Parliament, Christiansborg after having had lunch in Snapsetinget, 21 June 2007)[2]

At Christiansborg, I met another reporter from DR, who had worked both at TV2 and the Danish broadsheet newspaper *Berlingske Tidende*, who expressed a similar opinion when I asked him about DR's culture:

There is no DR culture. We are all the same, journalists, who I have worked with in many different newsrooms in Denmark.

(DR Reporter Christiansborg, Copenhagen, 6 June 2007)[3]

The time I spent at Christiansborg, DR's political bureau was my host, but the people I met and talked to were journalists, reporters, cameramen and editors from across all the different news media in Denmark. The friendly and intimate relationship among journalists and politicians, much akin to the descriptions given by Krause-Kjær (2003), was new to me. What was also new to me was to see so many different journalists across different media platforms working together in such a friendly, collaborative and united way. Though the friendships with politicians did appear genuine, with journalists telling me that they often met with politicians socially, the community feeling between all the different journalists seemed even warmer and more collegial.[4] During fieldwork, I waited hours outside meeting rooms in the large, long corridors of Christiansborg for the Prime Minister and his spin-doctor to exit a room.[5] On such occasions, which could take hours, a group of about fifteen news workers from both radio news, the news agency Ritzau, TV2, TV2 News, DR and sometimes all the print news journalists too were gathered, and there did not appear to be any limit to the camaraderie, and the sharing of both journalistic advice and ideas and also technical equipment such as leads between all journalists present.[6]

During these moments of waiting, there would be general banter between all news workers, only broken by a reporter from TV2 News making a 'live update' from outside the closed door. This TV2 News reporter would, as soon as she had a break from live broadcasting, often get friendly, internal jokes and encouraging comments from journalists employed at rival broadcasters – such as 'you're getting better and better at talking about what might be happening behind this closed door!', or sharing tips to what else the reporters could include in reports from Christiansborg today. It was occasions such as these that made me first notice the connections, friendships and collaborations between news workers in their everyday work.[7]

When colleagues feel like siblings

The notion that a community of journalists is akin to a family unit was one that I heard not only among the political journalists at the Danish Parliament *Christiansborg*, but from many different groups of journalists. The crime reporters of BBC told me that they saw the group of crime journalists from different media as a small family in which members often meet and of course help each other on the job. Likewise, I met correspondents and war-reporters from ITV and DR who spoke of their friendship with other correspondents whom they meet when out on a job in ways that one would describe family or kinship relations – such as another correspondent being 'like a brother to me' or describing very private relations of sharing hotel room, dinners, stories, translators or camera equipment when in a warzone with correspondents from other broadcast networks. Through sharing practices, obstacles, threats and dangers of working in a war zone, these journalists appeared to form particularly close bonds, which far outweigh the fact that they are employed by rival networks. Adhering to the metaphor of a family, through listening to the stories of shared experiences from correspondents covering shared subjects such as war, crime, sport or politics, news workers define themselves as connected across networks through a blood relation, which is stronger than the allegiance demanded by the individual employer.

A specific bond is made between the news staff who work together on a daily basis, often in close-knit unites and under sharp deadlines. I experienced divisions in all newsrooms talk about their specific area as a special unit which would just not be the same on days where one of the usual staffers was exchanged by a temp or a new employee. In newsrooms this special bond can exist between a producer and a journalist working close together, or a scriptwriter or a presenter for instance. Foreign correspondents describe a similar kind of camaraderie and sibling-like connection with the producer that they travel with. When a news worker leaves a position this special bond between fellow staff is often expressed as the biggest loss. As DR photographer Bettina Johnbeck left a position working closely with correspondent Puk Damsgaard she said: 'the one thing I miss is the camaraderie one gets with the journalist. We are together all day long and discuss stories from we meet at the breakfast till we go to bed at night' (Johnbeck in Bruun-Hansen 2016, my translation from Danish).

The friendship and sense of community that I experienced among Denmark's political journalists, who are all working in the same buildings, sharing the same canteen and mostly work on the same stories with the same interviewees, may not be so surprising. The many shared interests and working spaces taken into account, it only seems natural that these journalists appear more like a closely knit family unit than rival colleagues. As the political bureaux of the many different media are located within parliament, most of the political news workers see much more of their colleagues from rival broadcasters than they see of their colleagues employed by the same broadcaster. Thus, the family-like feeling may not be so surprising, but the close friendships between news workers at Christiansborg serves as a good illustration of the same type of friendships that I noticed at different levels across news media from many other parts of the news divisions. Further, these types of friendships across newsrooms and broadcasters that I saw at Christiansborg made me notice that the assumption about what other journalists will consider 'good' is an important aspect of the everyday work of journalists. As I will explore in the following, the friendships across broadcasters existing at Christiansborg can be viewed as a community of practice in which all share the identity, practices, interests and ideals of working in journalism.

6.2 Communities of Practice and the Imagined Colleagues

As discussed earlier (see Chapter 3), news workers told me that at each broadcaster members of staff have their own shared language, a shared history and share certain definitions of what good practice is. Working at the same broadcaster, I was told, is much like sharing a nationality. In time, experiencing friendships and community between staff from rival broadcasters, such as the ones described at Christiansborg, I came to wonder whether there was another relation that made news staff across broadcasters perceive there to be a bond much stronger than that of sharing nationality. Thus, I return to a critical exploration of an idea I have introduced earlier, expressed by one of TV2's Anchor Men, namely that news workers perceive there to be a shared nationality feeling by employees working within the same broadcaster:

> It is a bit like a nationality feeling, you know? You see, if you live in Denmark, you are Danish, and then you can begin to decipher what it means to be Danish. If you are employed at TV2 then you are a 'TV2-national' one way or another. [...]
>
> (TV2 Anchor Man, interviewed in news studio
> just after presenting the news, 9 June 2008)

During fieldwork, I found each news worker I worked alongside to have a sense of belonging to the rest of the colleagues in the newsroom akin to what the TV2 Anchor Man above describes as a 'nationality feeling'. Though reporters, cameramen and Programme Editors may spend long hours working alone, outside of the newsroom or inside a small, dark editing room they do not consider themselves to be working alone, but as an important part of a wider community. This community, as I see it, consists first and foremost of the perceived community of all people working with making news. On a more physical and practical level, however, news workers' sense of belonging is connected to all news workers employed at the same broadcaster, then with news workers outside of the broadcaster. Within this entire community, much like a nationality, members of staff have their own shared language (see Appendix), have a shared history and share definitions of what good practice is. This type of belonging is not dissimilar to Etienne Wenger's definition of *communities of practice* (1998a), which has at its core the mutual engagement and 'shared repertoire of communal resources (routines, sensibilities, artefacts, vocabulary, styles, etc.)' (Wenger 1998b: 2), which only a shared practice can bring about.

A map of perceived communities of practice

A community of practice in Wenger's definition, comes into being when a group of people share learning practices, such as the practice of editing, the practice of working for the news, the practice of eating lunch together or sharing a certain hobby together – common to all these practices is that they matter to the people doing them, and from this starting point, a group sharing practice is produced (Wenger 1998b: 2). Some communities have a name; others do not. But most importantly, according to Wenger, the community of practice creates bonds that are stronger than those of the broader organisation or group of other people with whom one has not physically shared the practice. At the strongest level of connection, Wenger's definitions of a community of practice resemble the description of friendships across broadcasters, which journalists have described in terms of strong family relations.

Thus, using Wenger's theory, I find it worthwhile to consider what he terms a 'community of practice' to be a practice community that has the ability to generate a close, family-like relation. Each individual news worker in a newsroom needs to be considered: One could view the news workers from one newsroom as sharing practice, and thus being in a community of practice with the fellow news workers in the room. This general sense of belonging can be said to create a home for identities and making the people within the group experience a nationality feeling akin to the description provided by TV2's Anchor Man above. These local identities, however, like the practice of work, are closely linked to the global identity of one's practice, in a constant 'local-global' interplay (Wenger 1998a: 161–63) – such as the interplay of being a news reporter working inside a particular BBC newsroom and that of working as a journalist. According to Wenger, the local-global interplay is an important aspect of the work of any community, as it connects a local practice to a broader context in which practice is located.

In this sense, from Wenger's perspective, the local, i.e. the newsroom, is equally important to that of the global, i.e. belonging to the journalism profession. Thus, I find Wenger's theories interesting in order to explore how the community feeling among journalists goes much further than the newsroom they are working in. However, among journalists, I have found the global to be at times more important than the local. That is to say, I have found news workers to primarily identify themselves with their global identity, of being 'A Journalist', or 'working in news'. Thus, I have found the interplay of the two categories, which Wenger terms the local and the global, to be led by the least tangible and less physical of the two. I find particularly fruitful the idea of connecting the local and the global in defining the work of journalists, as I see journalists as never only engaged in creating media but also always engaged in producing themselves as social persons in relation to others. Peterson (2003) has aptly described the many layers of connection a journalist has: 'Media production always and everywhere involves epistemologies, heuristics, competences, and aesthetics, as well as social organizations, hierarchies, rituals, and technologies, and all of these together constitute the worlds in which these producers live and work' (Peterson 2003: 162).

In Wenger's definition of communities of practice, the imagined communities, such as those of other workers doing a similar job, in a similar profession are important. It is this connectedness with a greater mission, a greater role in society, a shared ideal of the journalism profession that I have found to be present among news workers at all levels in the four newsrooms. News workers within one newsroom thus feel a connection with news workers at other broadcasters with whom they may never have worked. This connection can be viewed as a community of practice shared with imagined colleagues. Adding the importance of imagined communities to news workers' identity feeling, the sense of belonging to a nationality, is just one of many multi-communities of practice to which news workers have a sense of belonging.

In order to attempt an illustration of the communities of practice in which I have found news workers participate, ranging from the local to the global, at least seven different layers of communities of practice should be highlighted. These seven different layers consist of groups, such as 'Co-workers in the newsroom', 'All staff in the newsroom' and those in the 'Same role as another broadcaster', and above all, 'all working in journalism' – all groups that news staff talk about as important parts of their community. In exploring the way members of staff talk about their community in the everyday, I have found there to be seven such groups working in a constant closely knit interplay among all news staff. In the seven layers illustrated below, levels 1 and 2 encompass the local, levels 3–6 consist of the global on a

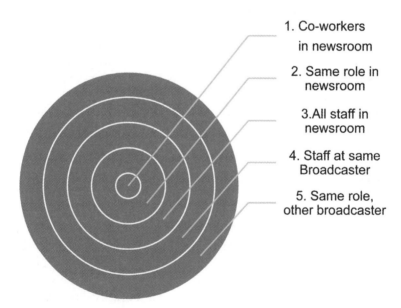

Fig. 6.1: Mapping of multiple layers of community that each news worker perceives to belong to.

physical level and the seventh level encompasses a less tangible factor, namely the entire journalism profession comprising shared crafts of journalism.

It is of course not possible to map the entire group of people that news workers may experience a sense of community with, as a sense of community feeling is a personal matter, which is different to different people. Female journalists, for instance, may feel a sense of community with other female journalists, just as news workers from a particular journalism school may experience a sense of community with those who have graduated from the same school. The above figure should only serve as an illustration of some of the primary connections that I have heard news workers express in their everyday work – connections which, when perceived as being particularly strong, were described as akin to family bonds.

Studying the above attempt at mapping the levels of belonging, it is interesting to note how many of the levels are imagined (i.e. not physical or tangible). It is also interesting to see the extent to which each individual news worker connects to global others, such as news workers at different broadcasters (level 5), and those employed at different types of media, such as print and radio (level 7). From this illustration, it is only the first four levels of staff that the TV2 Anchor Man describes as *a nationality*. Staying with his metaphor, the next two levels (5 and 6) can be referred to as *the world*, and the last (level 7) can be viewed as the *entire universe*, in which news workers see themselves and their shared larger community of belonging. I do not see all of the levels as connecting staff in family-like ties, but have found that across each of these perceived communities talked of as family-like, ties may develop which are much stronger than those of any of the individual first 1–6 categories of practice-communities.

As illustrated in my figure of perceived levels of practice communities above, the one overarching practice community within which all define themselves is that of 'working in journalism'. During my time within the newsrooms and within editorial meetings, I have found this shared category to be used in arguments of how to behave, act and work in the everyday. When spending time with journalists and news workers, it was not uncommon to hear members of staff explain their behaviour with the fact that they belong to the profession of journalism: 'I had to had to do it, I am *a journalist*', a news worker would say to explain why she had to interrogate her boyfriend upon returning home late at night. Similarly, a reporter at DR told me that the way she talked to her friends was mostly with a lack of patience and she was preoccupied with the ideas of a news story in her mind, for as she said: 'I am *a journalist!*'.

As the illustration above conveys, I have experienced staff to feel a sense of belonging, which thereby links the individual workers to many more people than those they meet in their everyday, thus having what Wenger would term 'multiple modes of belonging'. Being with news workers I have found all the different layers to be important for the everyday work, but one over-arching layer, that of 'working in journalism' (level 7), is talked about in the everyday much more than all the other layers together. As 'working in journalism' is a description that all the news workers I have studied use to categorise their work, this is a practice definition that they all share. Often, I have found this shared category to be used in arguments of how to behave, act and work in the everyday. I shall return to this issue shortly. Firstly, I would like to illustrate the above figure through a case study.

Case study: A BBC crime reporter's communities of practice

In order to describe further the above figure of layers of community, I will illustrate the connections perceived by a reporter at BBC News, who specialises in crime stories. First, the reporter experiences a sense of belonging to those in the newsroom whom he works with and shares practice with on an everyday basis, much like Wenger's definition of communities of practice. These colleagues may be producers, editors, runners, cameramen and other reporters. Together they share a vocabulary, e.g. related to the BBC News Division's mission statements, and at the end of the day it is their collaborative practice which creates the news bulletin. As some members of this community repeatedly share working practice and history of practice, this bond may begin to be perceived as forming ties that are referred to in metaphors of family relations.

Additionally, a BBC crime reporter experiences a sense of belonging to the group of reporters with another specialism, such as health, sport, politics or entertainment. These fellow reporters do not work together physically, but they have the same challenges in their everyday, sometimes they meet after work to discuss their work, they share practices, vocabulary and everyday traditions.

Apart from the sense of belonging he feels with those employed by the same broadcaster, the BBC crime reporter experiences a sense of belonging to a specific group of crime reporters from other broadcasters and from the newspapers that he often meets near crime scenes that he reports on around the UK. These reporters share vocabularies, they help each other and discuss their practical work, again much like Wenger's definition of communities of practice. Though these reporters come from different media platforms and different newsrooms, during repeated sharing of practice they may form strong bonds of friendship, which they perceive as being as close as they believe family bonds to be.

However, this BBC crime reporter feels a sense of belonging to at least two other groups that he never or rarely meets in the everyday, namely the entire group of people working for BBC and the entire group of people who work as reporters and journalists, not only in the UK but worldwide. Being employed at BBC, the reporter feels a sense of belonging with staff from the entire broadcaster. Therefore, should he meet a person employed at BBC's drama department, the two may connect in sharing what it feels like to work 'for the beeb'[8]; thus sharing a community of practice between them, which is imagined as it is not experienced in the everyday. Similarly to the other communities, the communities of all staff working for the BBC to a certain extent help each other and share a language and history.

Another group of people that this BBC reporter feels an imagined sense of belonging to is even less tangible, namely the entire community of people who work in the same profession of journalism, worldwide. This group of people consists literally of any person, who works as a journalist, and the reporter feels a strong sense of belonging to this group and he defines himself according to this group at all times. When this BBC crime reporter goes on holiday and happens to meet a person who works as a journalist, he will instantly sense a feeling of belonging to a shared community. Particularly if the journalist he meets is a TV journalist working for an established national broadcaster, our BBC crime reporter will feel a bond of practice and identity. Though he has never before met this journalist, he will find that they share a vocabulary using the same British words in the everyday such as 'OB', 'VO', 'ATTACK' and 'SYNC' (see Appendix). Also, these two journalists have similar operational values such as the importance of making a 'good news story', and the BBC crime reporter expects to be helped and feels happy to help this person as they are in a shared professional community.[9]

As illustrated in the example above, the practice of work, working together or working in relating fields all foster a community between the journalists and news workers across different broadcasters. From this perspective, I find Wenger's definitions of communities of practice apt for illustrating some of the core connections and boundaries that I have observed among news workers. According to Wenger's definitions, shared practice works as an exclusive and excluding connection, as '[p]articipants form close relationships and develop idiosyncratic ways of engaging with one another, which outsiders cannot easily enter' (1998a: 113). I have discussed this particular type of boundary making previously in my descriptions of the challenges in getting access to study news workers (see Chapter 2.3). Just as I have experienced that the shared working practices act as a boundary keeping others, such as academic researchers, out, I have seen the shared working practice working as a boundary for keeping staff in. It is this strengthened practice community that journalists describe using metaphors of family relations. Keeping those sharing the practice in and others out is a key element in Wenger's notion of communities of practice. According to Wenger, the mechanism that keeps participants inside the community is constantly reinforced – as the repeatedly shared practice reinforces the shared language, strengthens practice-based relationships and further deepens communities of practice (Wenger, 1998a 114, 253–54).

The feeling of always being at work

As illustrated in the figure of perceived levels of practice communities above, the one overarching practice community within which all define themselves is that of all staff 'working in journalism'. I have found the shared role of 'working in journalism' to be an identity, which all the news workers I have studied see as central to their life both in and out of work hours. Thus, the role of 'journalist' is one that staff members appear to take on at all times. As a journalist who had presented the news at TV2 for the last ten years told me:

> The problem for a journalist is that you never hang up your brain on a hook [as you leave work], and say 'I am non-existing to the world'. One is always a little at work.
>
> (Anchorman at TV2, interviewed at his desk in the studio right after the news bulletin, 9 June 2008)

A few years later, in October 2017, another TV2 Anchor Man told me that he was so glad his son had joined the local Optimist sailing club because the environment he met while watching the son sailing led him to find a wealth of local news stories. The idea that staff should always consider themselves at work was often talked about among journalists. They shared these stories of never being out of the role of a journalist both among each other in the everyday and with me in recorded interviews. It appeared that most of the news workers I studied had stories of how they give high priority to their role as a journalist in their everyday lives. They told me how they would be on holiday and come across a news story, or how an experience they had had outside of work was made into a news story. The staff members who told these stories appeared proud of how they used their time off work to do journalism. As such, the stories appeared to work to share the ideal of being in a closely knit community with all others working in journalism; a community in which all share the idea that once one works in journalism then one is always a journalist.

These stories were encouraged, laughed about and appeared to be prestigious to share among colleagues. For instance, during a lunch break, one DR reporter told me and a few of her colleagues of how she had had to cut short this year's New Year's party as a story had emerged near the venue for her New Year's party. During the festive dinner at her friend's house, she had heard noise from the street. The noise came from a group of youths throwing bricks they had collected from the pavement. Soon the police arrived and the youth hurled bricks at them. Resolutely, the DR reporter had left the party, called her newsroom and within minutes she was reporting live from the clash between youth and police to all DR's media platforms. Thus, the story of the DR reporter's off-duty live reporting was suggestive of her giving high priority to the role of being a journalist rather than that of being a private individual and friend celebrating New Year's Eve.

In the vein of the story from the DR reporter, staff at all four broadcasters likened their duty to be always at work to a doctor's oath, in that they felt obliged to work on a news story at any time they saw a 'good news story'. When I asked staff what their partners thought of this priority, some told me that if friends or partners did not understand this obligation to journalism they would have to leave. Others suggested that if their partners did not understand how much journalism meant to them, then they did not understand each other – thus hinting that the profession of journalism had become a part of their very identity. During fieldwork, I did meet a couple of reporters who had recently started a family, who expressed frustration with the fact that working in news made for such unstable working hours – thus contradicting the ideal of thinking oneself always a journalist and always potentially at work. The staff members who told me of their frustrations with the idea of constantly being at work told me so always in privacy and never in the newsroom with other colleagues able to hear.

Management often encouraged staff to collect news stories when outside the work place. At ITV, a News Editor told me that it would be ideal if all staff would go to their local pub and collect stories from the people, and listen out for what stories people cared about. At DR, the Head of News encouraged his staff to look for stories when on holiday (according to news staff). The Head of News at TV2 told me in a recorded interview that for a journalist it is crucial to 'open up one's ears when at confirmations, silver weddings and weddings and funerals and whatever one attends'. To him, being curious at all times is the journalist's 'damned duty and privilege'. To him, this duty to always be at work is not just one that he expects the TV2 news staff to take on, as the duty is one which *all* working in journalism have.

When I visited the private homes of some of the news journalists I studied, I found the decoration of their homes to revolve around TV sets. Some had TV sets in the bathroom, the living room and the kitchen. Most journalists I visited subscribed to international news channels at home. When I asked why there was so many TV sets in their home, journalists would tell me that they felt they 'had to be updated' and 'didn't want to miss a story'.[10] Furthermore, staff told me that it was important for them to be constantly updated, as they were always preparing to go to work the following day. In this sense, the fact that TV sets take up so much private space in the homes of news workers illustrates how these members of staff consider their role of a journalist to be constant; they are at work even when at home. Though staff did not talk of their many TV sets in their private homes as work-related, the presence of TV sets illustrates how staff perceived their role as a journalist to require that they are *always at work* and *always preparing for the next news story*.

As social outings were common at most of the newsrooms I spent time in, I was soon invited to join staff for a drink after work. Though other more personal topics of conversation would arise during a night in the pub with journalist colleagues, and though journalists would share drinks with other pub goers who were not journalists, there was always a sense that the journalists were at work, planning and scouting for good stories to be worked on the following day. Thus, if a fellow pub goer mentioned something that the journalists present considered a good story, however drunk the journalists might appear, they would swiftly begin taking notes on notepads brought along for that purpose, or take phone numbers for leads for a story. I witnessed a few news stories emerge through this practice, and many more stories were inspired from such conversations in the pub. In this sense, when journalists went out after work, it appeared they were still journalists at work, together in the search for new stories and new insights to topics that engaged the public. In this way, I noticed that news workers defined themselves, their private homes and their actions by their profession, whether at work or outside of work. Such practices made me regard the journalists as always perceiving themselves to be at work and sharing an identity feeling that goes beyond the newsroom and the broadcaster and is made up of ideals of what it means to be a journalist.

Effects of family-like bonds across broadcasters

As illustrated in my description of the communities of practice, which a BBC crime reporter may experience, I see the networks of community of news workers to be much stronger and more extensive; the network extends further than just to the colleagues they meet every day. To illustrate the closeness among news workers, who are not employed at the same broadcaster, I find the metaphor of a family interesting. At first sight, the community feeling may appear to only comprise those in the near vicinity, such as the journalist's colleague's, and the broadcaster for which s/he works, particularly considering the fact that the members of staff who I have worked alongside appear to be so proud of the specific broadcaster they work for. However, when a specific group of cameramen from TV2 regularly meet a specific group of cameramen from DR when out filming, these cameramen soon form a friendship shaped around their shared work and shared practices of work. Similarly, when the same war correspondents from different broadcasters find each other doing similar reporting jobs in warzones around the world, these correspondents soon develop a bond, which often grows to be close friendship and a shared community of practice, which extends beyond their being employed at rival broadcasters.

I have found these different connections, made across broadcasters and across media platforms, to be very important in the everyday life of news staff in many ways. Among those employed within the news division as journalists, with whom I have spent most of my fieldwork, I have experienced the contact and connections with journalists of other media to be crucial to the work produced.[11] First, the many friendships established across newsrooms mean that journalists in one newsroom are very aware of what stories journalists at other newsrooms are working on or take an interest in at any time. If one broadcaster has a journalistic scoop one day, journalists at the rival broadcaster will find out about it before the story is broadcast. Such information would often arrive at one newsroom through a journalist receiving a text message or call from a friend working at another broadcaster. Attaining this knowledge of the other broadcaster's work influences the journalists' judgment of what stories should be considered important. Other studies of news making have focused on such connections and mutual inspiration among newsmakers from different news divisions as a 'striking routine reliance on other media', with strong tendencies towards 'pack' or 'copycat journalism' (Preston 2009: 57). Introduced by Timothy Crouch in 1973, 'pack journalism' is seen as synonymous with all that the journalism profession aspires not to be: homogeneous, unoriginal and non-exclusive. Studies on 'pack' journalism have pointed towards consistency as a 'distinct and unspoken industrial routine and norm whereby copycat news making minimises risk and uncertainty in defining what is newsworthy' (Preston 2009: 57, see also Shoemaker and Reese 1996: 123–25).

In her study of terrestrial TV news culture and content, Harrison (2000) describes how the similarity in planning processes and a similar everyday working routine makes for a homogenous product. However, among journalists, the very notion that the similar ways of working generate similar content is seen as 'toxic' (Porter 2005). The close connection between journalists and the apparent agreement with the ideals of the journalism profession, which I encountered during my research, stands in stark contrast to the occupational myth of originality and exclusivity. As American newspaper journalist Tim Porter writes: 'Pack journalism is toxic. It is an addiction to faux news and lazy reporting. But **it is also easily corrected** because it requires no additional resources, news hole or time – the Holy Trinity of rationalizations for why newspapers don't change. To kick the pack, all that's needed is the will to do it' (Porter 2005, original emphasis). The argument that journalists should stay critical and open-minded in order to constantly combat the critical effects of journalists being and working in similar ways is one that I frequently encountered when discussing the everyday work of journalists.

Apart from the risk of pack journalism, I have observed a second impact that friendships and contacts between broadcasters can have on individual journalists, namely that friendships across broadcasters can become a closed forum for sharing, testing and confirming whether a news story is good. This sharing may inform their work and help define what is newsworthy, while also strengthening the shared notion of professionalism among journalists. In his study on professionalism, Freidson (2001) describes the sharing of knowledge among practitioners as crucial to strengthening the profession. The alternative, according to Freidson, is destructive. As he states:

> It is even more destructive when knowledge or technique is withheld as a legally defined and protected trade secret rather than becoming part of the common body of knowledge held by all practitioners. Secrecy is the anathema to the growth of knowledge and technique […].
>
> (Freidson 2001: 219)

Case study: When a source is shared and kept secret

In Denmark, a controversial case centring on the friendships of a journalist from TV2 Nyhederne and a journalist from DR TV Avisen, one from the newspaper *Politiken* and a documentary filmmaker, illustrates just how much contacts across broadcasters mean to the everyday work. From the perspective of Freidson (2001), the case provides an example of how journalists strengthen their professional work by sharing key knowledge, and how much these strong professional ties matter in the everyday.

In 2007, a source from inside the Danish Ministry of Defence contacted a TV2 reporter to tell him, even though it was confidential information, that Denmark had just sent elite troops to Iraq.[12] The TV2 reporter then shared the information with his two journalist friends who often met socially, a journalist from DR's TV Avisen and a journalist at *Politiken*.

After TV2, most other Danish media brought the story revealing that the elite troops were on their way to Iraq. The lives of the soldiers and their mission in Iraq were said to have been greatly compromised by the news stories. Consequently, a police enquiry was initiated to locate the source of the information. During the ensuing enquiry, journalists and editors from DR, TV2 and other Danish media were called to witness. None of the news workers revealed the source for their story. The three journalist friends from different media, TV2, DR and *Politiken*, however, were all aware of the source, and one of them was later revealed to have shared the name of the source with another friend of his, a documentary maker. Not until three and a half years later, in December 2011, in a recording of a conversation between the TV2 reporter and his journalist friend at DR he provided a hint that could reveal the source of the story.

The case, which made public some of the many friendships, interrelations and contacts between media platforms, is controversial on many counts. Firstly, not having to disclose sources is one of the most valued rights and promises within the journalism profession. As TV2 News Editor Michael Dyrby expressed it in his testimony to the enquiry into the story of the elite soldiers in Iraq: '[P]rotection of sources is a crucial element in the Danish media work. Without the protection of sources, the media would in many cases not receive vitally important information' (Dyrby in Højesteret 2011). The case has revealed that within the community of journalists, confidential sources are at times shared among journalistic friends. Secondly, the case and the police enquiry that came in its aftermath have revealed how the community of journalists can stand together as a unit against government and police pressure towards not revealing their sources.

Additionally, the case has shown that when a member of this closely knit community breaks the unity and reveals that which they have kept quiet, members of the community may exclude them. In February 2010, when it was revealed that the DR journalist had been recording a conversation with his reporter friend at TV2 in which he disclosed the source of the elite soldier story, he was promptly fired. The sound file of the recording, in which the TV2 reporter talks of the source, was not to be heard by the public and was said to be 'kept within the Director General's pockets' (see Pedersen and Rasmussen 2010). When in December 2011 a redtop newspaper finally did get hold of the recording of the two friends' conversation and put it online, this caused an angry outcry from other journalists within the community. One of TV2's most prominent elder Anchor Men, Jes Dorph, spoke openly about the publicising and recording of friendly conversations among journalists as a form of betrayal, declaring the DR journalist responsible for the recording 'an absolute asshole' (Dorph in Kirkbak and Bakalus 2011).

6.3 The Constant Peer Review

As described earlier, I attempted to speak to as many different groups of news workers as possible during my fieldwork. Though most of the people I spoke to were journalists, I also spoke to many other groups of practice within the news division. During the time I spent among journalists, I was keen to not only be among those in high-profile jobs, or interview those who were mostly on TV. This approach meant that I found myself doing participant observation in many and different communities of practice of news workers, a fact which was noticed and talked about among staff within all the newsrooms I visited.

After having spent time with one person in the newsroom, someone else or an entire group of people from the same newsroom would approach me to tell me their opinion of this specific person's news work. At times, I was told that a person whom I had talked to did not have a good history of work, and that I should not take very seriously what s/he had told me. At other times, staff would approach me to say that they had seen that I had been talking to their colleagues and that they therefore also wanted to spend time with me. In this way, I became used to constantly being watched, and my contact with different groups of people in the room was constantly evaluated by all staff. This way of talking about each other did not appear to be foreign to news workers. Rather, I observed many different groups of people from different layers of the communities of practice within a news division to be talked about by other groups of practice. In this way, it appeared that all colleagues were constantly being watched, and their work was reviewed by their peers within the newsroom, but also outside of it and across different broadcasters.

No one, it appeared, was exempt from being criticised and evaluated in his or her everyday work. Different practice communities discussed each other often, but never or very rarely is the talk about private behaviour or personality; rather, the constant evaluation of colleagues was centred on the way people practiced their work. Reporters would talk of other reporters' work, but also about different editors' work, their News Editors' history of work or a specific producer's way of working. An anchorwoman and Anchor Man from one broadcaster once took me aside to tell me that the scriptwriter that I had just interviewed did not have a good history of work and that, though he had worked in the newsroom for over twenty years, they did not consider him to be 'good'. At one broadcaster, journalists and reporters talked of a specific editor as not being 'good', and explained to me that they therefore did not feel that they should take seriously what this editor told them to do, but rather act on their own initiative, while of course outwardly acting as if they did take notice of what the editor said. At another broadcaster I experienced two reporters wanting to talk to me because another reporter that I had just talked to was 'good'. At three of the four broadcasters, producers told me that some of the presenters and Anchor Men had 'star whims' and were problematic to work with. These experiences made me consider the different communities of practice as important forums for sharing evaluations of other people's work.

Among journalists, there did not necessarily seem to be a connection between having a superior job title and enjoying more respect by colleagues. Thus, a News Editor, Programme Editor or Anchor Man's opinions in how to cover a story will not necessarily be listened to or obeyed just because of the nature of his/her formal status within the news division. Rather, what I have found to be of primary importance among news workers is the history of practicing journalism and news that a colleague has. When discussing the merits of a colleague, the history of her/his work would be recounted with emphasis on what stories s/he had covered and how. Thus, the stories that one has worked on appear to be continuously recalled and reviewed by colleagues within the different communities of practice that news workers are linked to. Having worked on stories considered by peers to be 'big' – such as events that are particularly historical or ground-breaking – will be talked about and remembered by colleagues. When a colleague has a practice history of working on big stories and making what staff will describe as 'good' news stories, this person is often talked about in awe, as being 'a good news journalist', having 'a journalistic heart', a 'nouse' or a 'nose for news'.[13] In this way, those who were looked up to by their peers seemed to embody the ideals of journalism. Likewise, however long one has worked as a news worker, if one has neither worked on stories considered 'big', nor been known to make particularly ground-breaking news work, then this will be remembered and taken into account by the news workers, who may not trust one's opinions as much as someone else with a better history of practice.

During my fieldwork, I noticed how the opinion of some Programme Editors and News Editors appeared to be taken much more seriously than the opinions of others. During editorial meetings, I saw news workers agree with certain Programme Editors during the meeting, but as soon as the meeting was over, the same news workers would talk ironically of the Programme Editor's story ideas or opinions on stories, describing the Programme Editor as 'not being a good journalist'. Such disagreements with the editor could, I witnessed, lead to staff not entirely following the guidance given by their superiors if the superior was defined as not having proper journalistic abilities.

When broadcasting a story becomes a stamp of approval

As introduced, one of the effects of family-like bonds across broadcasters is that a friendship can become a closed forum for sharing, testing and confirming whether a news story is good. Within the newsroom, certain members of staff only rarely meet, but still consider themselves members of a shared working practice community. When a guest booker at ITV News sees that BBC news has a certain topical guest in the newsroom, he will take note of it and use the knowledge either in order to contact the same guest himself or to learn of the experience for next time ITV is covering a similar story. If the guest booker at ITV knows one of the guest bookers at BBC, he may contact this person in order to obtain the contact details for the guest he would like to use. Therefore, the guest bookers from all broadcasters keep a close watch over which guests appear in the studios at other broadcasters. Likewise, news workers in different roles within each newsroom watch the other broadcasters' news in order to learn from the way staff doing the same practice are working on a specific story.

Each of the four newsrooms I have visited are equipped with screens that are visible to all news division staff, either on their desks or placed in a central spot within the newsroom, which show broadcast news from rival networks.[14] Particularly when the most direct rival, the other national news broadcaster, is broadcasting the evening news, this will be closely watched within each newsroom, and often discussed loudly among members of staff. Throughout the day, however, other news broadcasters' shows are shown on the shared TV screens.

In all four newsrooms, I found that the direct competitor as well as the 24-hour news channels CNN, SKY News and Al Jazeera were broadcast on a central screen, either constantly or frequently (a factor which adds to the compilation of shared sources described in Chapter 5.3).[15] By studying the competitor's news content, all members of news staff always keep an eye on what the competitors are doing. When viewing other broadcasters' news output, the focus was on both the physical on screen presentation and the ways of presenting. But I have also noticed the news staff members' curiosity in looking out for which stories the other broadcasters will bring, which interviews they have got, where they have sent their key reporters and where they have sent most cameras on a given day. I found that journalists consider the fact those colleagues at other broadcasters work on a specific story to be a confirmation of the story's validity. If the competitor's news division runs with a story, it appears journalists sense a type of confirmation that the story is a good one – an argument that I have heard in all four newsrooms. In her observations of online newsrooms in Denmark, Hartley has made similar observations, stating that: '[B]y quoting stories they credit other news sites and by being quoted they confirm their own judgement' (Hartley 2013: 8).

The trouble with family-like practice communities

[...] journalists are in an underdog position compared to editors, owners, and sources. This underdog position, coupled with a firm belief amongst journalists that they are (and should be) free and autonomous agents, cause tensions within the organisation.

(Melin 2008: 24)

Above, Melin describes how the idea of being an 'underdog' compared to editors, owners and sources conflicts with a shared ideal among journalists of being free and autonomous. Among the news journalists I have worked alongside, I have found a similar tension between being asked to do tasks by an editor they do not consider good and their own ideal of being a good journalist. Due to some editors or producers not being considered good among their practice sharing colleagues, I have thus experienced journalists to intentionally neglect to do what an editor has told them to do. In this way, journalists negotiate the type of tensions described by Melin above.

As I have experienced the different communities of practice among journalists, it is when a practice community is perceived to be particularly strong that staff members of begin to describe relations to be as strong as family relations. I have found this depth in relations to be gained by repeated sharing of practice by the same group of people – a definition akin to Wenger's notion of deep relations within practice communities.

That staff members care about practices is no doubt in the interest of the broadcasters and news divisions at large. When the interest in practice makes staff become closely connected across broadcasters, this may also be in the interest of the broadcasters, who can learn from the deep connections with other staff and other news stories from other media. However, when in time these connections become strong practice communities, which may be perceived to share bonds as strong as those of a family, this may not be in the individual broadcaster's interest. Indeed, the close family-like bonds may become stronger than the bonds perceived to exist between individual staff and the broadcaster, and what these communities define as good practice may not necessarily be the same as what the broadcaster defines as good practice. Similarly, it is likely that not all practice communities will agree with the editors employed to manage news staff.

The trouble with communities of practice becoming so closely united that they may describe their connection like that of a familyis that the practice community may begin to exclude or distance itself from those outside of the group. This fragmentation within a news division or across a larger group of news workers is what Wenger has discussed as the coupling of an 'organisational asset and organisational liabilities, but in complementary ways' (Wenger 1998a: 256). To Wenger, the organisation will benefit from the created boundaries between different practice communities, as boundaries become learning opportunities. Wenger's research of practice communities is centred on fieldwork he has done among medical claims processors operated by a large US insurance company. Among these professionals, the idea of boundaries being a useful learning tool may be relevant. However, regarding journalists, I have found boundaries and ideas of certain individuals not accepted as 'good' among specific communities of practice to be problematic and at times obstructive to the shared work.

Though the boundaries defined by a specific group of people may function as a fruitful tool for learning about what is defined as 'good' and what is seen as 'bad' news work, I have at times seen the boundaries of a group as compromising the everyday work and create unproductive fragments and divisions within the newsroom. When one group of reporters does not accept a specific editor as part of their community, or when an Anchor Man does not like the work of a certain scriptwriter, this is not advantageous to the everyday work. For Wenger's more positive idea of boundaries between practice communities to be considered, it would be worthwhile for journalists from the different communities to openly share what they define as good work and what they define as bad – thus openly discussing the internal disagreements with certain news staff, rather than keeping them secret within the closely knit groups of news staff. To begin such a discussion, in the following chapter I will look closer at what staff within the different news divisions define as 'good work'.

By opening up towards other communities of practice than that which they have a strong connection with, staff may open up to understanding the whole of the organisation rather than concentrating on the fragment within the news division to which they have a strong sense of belonging. A graphic at DR who asked to go visit the radio news staff for a day told me that his day-long visit to this entirely different community really opened his perspective on the 'wholeness of DR'. This experience, he told me, made him consider the extent to which the different groups, such as cameramen, graphics, foreign desk staff and reporters, mainly 'think of their own little world': 'If only the journalists could use three minutes with us graphics, we could tell them a lot about the use of images. But we don't really work *together*. It is only because I choose to visit Radio Avisen that I now know how the radio functions', he said. Such cross-field experiences could no doubt open up some of the closed boundaries between practice communities within the newsroom and help create a more united news division across platforms and practices.

6.4 How Pride and a Distance to *The Others* Unites

While I have found newsrooms to be divided at times, as different practice communities would disagree with the opinions of management or News Editor, above all, I have found staff to be closely united in their shared practice of working in journalism (level 7 above). I have found this closed unity, which appears linked to a pride in one's job, to be both strengthening for the news divisions and distancing for the relationship with 'others' outside of the journalistic profession. In the following, I will illustrate and explore how I have found staff to be both proud of their jobs and distanced from those outside of the journalistic profession.

Showing off and being proud of one's job

The journalists and other news workers that I worked alongside and talked to during fieldwork appeared primarily proud, very satisfied and happy with working for the broadcaster in question. Though some expressed irritation with particular editors or management, the general attitude about working for the broadcaster was one of pride of being the best. When talk fell on the threats from the national competitor, it appeared the biggest worry from staff at each broadcaster was that they would begin to be in any way similar to the other one (as described in Chapter 3). As shown in the map of perceived communities of practice above, staff appear primarily attached to the notion of being part of the entire journalism profession, viewing themselves as professionals.

Aldridge and Evetts (2003) discuss the attraction in viewing oneself as professional in that 'discourse is being used as a framework of occupational and self-identity which could be interpreted as a form of cultural capital' (2003: 555, with reference to Bourdieu). Aldridge and Evetts thus characterise the feeling of being part of a profession and working as 'a professional':

> a discourse of self-control, even self-belief, an occupational badge or marker which gives meaning to the work and enables workers to justify and emphasize the importance of their work to themselves and others.
>
> (2003: 555)

During empirical observations I noticed different ways in which staff appeared to show off and emphasise their role as a professional journalist in the everyday, akin to the way Aldridge and Evetts describe it. Spending time with news workers after work, I began to notice how staff appeared to show off pride in their employer in public, particularly the extent to which news workers adorned themselves with logos and other paraphernalia connected to their broadcaster. During working hours, news workers had to carry ID badges, which must be shown or inserted into entry points in order to get access to the building and editing suites. These badges were often worn in lanyards with the broadcaster's logo printed on it in bright colours.

When out filming, reporters, cameramen and producers would wear these ID cards in their lanyards, thus making their work relation and connection to fellow colleagues visible. However, when not working, on the train on the way home or socialising in the pub or a wine bar after work, staff would often keep wearing their ID cards and broadcaster lanyards in a visible position. Similarly, I noticed news workers were wearing bags, umbrellas, caps and jackets adorned with their broadcaster's bright logo at all times, whether on or off duty. Furthermore, at DR, I noticed news workers would signal their position as news journalists audibly: Most news staff had changed their mobile ringtone to that of the introductory jingle from the DR TV Avisen news bulletin.[16] From the perspective of Goffman's study on presentation of self in the everyday life (1959), this type of sign-carrying could be interpreted as a minor cue of something important about a person's performance, such as the fact that this person is employed by a certain established broadcaster.

When studying the ID cards worn by news workers, there is a great difference in status and connection linked to each type of ID card. A plastic coated one, for instance, signifies a connection to the broadcaster that is more permanent in nature than a paper one with the lettering 'VISITOR' on it. Meanwhile, if the ID card has a picture of the bearer (used at most of the four broadcasters I visited), this signals an even more permanent position. New employees may not get their picture ID card until after some time of employment; some may only receive one upon having finished a trial period of employment, and thus are quite excited when getting a picture ID. When an employee receives a picture ID card, this may well be remarked by the people s/he works with, who will ask to see it up close, and often supply ironic comments about the photo. This card gives entry through a number of doors and rooms that are shut to the public and shut to those who only have a paper ID card; for instance, the entrance to the entire building, the newsroom and editing suites. Additionally, the picture card makes it possible for the bearer to venture into different parts of the broadcast building, such as the vaults or the top of the building with its gigantic satellite dishes. Some ID cards are also used as a Press Card, giving free entrance to sites and events, which the public otherwise have to pay for. At specific events, such as a royal wedding, the Queen's Speech or a press conference, ID cards may give entrance to sites that are closed off to the public at a time when this particular site is particularly newsworthy (such as the church where the royal wedding took place). Thus, the ID card is a sign of cultural capital (Bourdieu [1977] 2000).[17] The ID cards, badges, bags and jackets and even the pens with logos on are much more than their physical appearance, as they have a significant importance and signify importance to other news workers as well as to the public.

At later stages in my fieldwork, I saw staff from different broadcasters spotting each other due to the lanyards, or logos on bags, thus using the shared sign of broadcast employment to connect and find communities of the journalism profession, whether working for the same broadcaster or not. In time, I found the pride expressed by wearing an ID badge or a jacket with the broadcaster's logo on it to be less related to the broadcaster than to the entire profession of journalism and news. In this sense, though staff members were proud of their broadcaster, above all, I have found staff more generally to be proud to work in news.

How news workers view *The Others*

It is an old cliché, but it still rings true: When you look inside a TV newsroom you will mostly find white middle class university graduates with male editors. According to a recent study of 700 news workers in the UK (see Thurman et al. 2016), the British journalism industry is 94% white, 86% university-educated and 55% male of which most hold managerial positions. The fact that a newsroom is made up of such a homogenous group of people no doubt has an impact on how they define and view those outside of their close-knit group. Exploring the many different communities that news workers expressed a feeling of belonging to, I began noticing how news workers define a border between themselves and *The Others*, those outside of the newsroom, the broadcaster and the journalism profession as a whole – outside of what could be termed the entire universe of news workers.

Previously (in Chapter 2), I quoted a studio manager who describes news workers as living in 'a small, closed world', which they want to protect and guard to the best of their ability.[18] In my discussion of how I gained access to do fieldwork inside the four newsrooms I highlighted one way of protecting and guarding the community of people working in the news profession, namely the reluctance to let those outside of the profession in to study them. Another way of keeping firm boundaries between those *in* the journalism profession and those *outside* of it that I have experienced is the way the insiders talk about the people outside of journalism from whom they are constantly distancing themselves. Often when watching people on the screen in the newsroom, in an editing suite or somewhere else, news workers would discuss ironically what was on screen. This kind of ironic commentary could include how a person looked (a celebrity wearing the same sunglasses for the tenth time on screen, an interviewee with a peculiar face or wearing a strange combination of clothes), the name or identity of a person (a man whose name looks funny on the screen) or the way a person was talking (in an unusual accent or using long-winded sentences) or behaving on screen. At all four newsrooms, when watching the news made by us or a competitor, it was customary to comment on what appeared on screen, referring to the person's looks, a peculiar name or way of behaving on screen.[19]

This commentating did generally not include news staff, such as reporters or presenters from one's own broadcaster, but apart from that, there did not seem to be limitations as to who among news staff would be ironically mocked. One example of such commentary that I overheard in the newsroom at ITV illustrates how ruling parties, including the prime minister, can often be the laughing stock inside the newsroom:

Reporter: That David Cameron is SO cocky!

[To Gordon Brown, as he appears on screen:] Say something, you are the Prime Minister! Ha, ha!

[General laughter from colleagues in the newsroom][20]
(12AM Wednesday, in the ITV Newsroom as PMQs play out on each TV screen in the room, some senior news workers commentate, 17 October 2011)[21]

Arguably, the verbal distancing to others, as illustrated above, helps make the often very emotional events that journalists have to report on seem distant and less traumatic (see Richards and Rees 2011). Another effect of the ironic distancing to those outside of the journalism profession is that it can help shape a solidarity feeling among those within the journalism profession against those outside of it. Additionally, the ironic commentating works to show the less senior news workers and those recently employed how senior news staff members believe news should be presented.

At all four newsrooms, I experienced a cynical distancing to those Others who were not journalists, similar to the ITV Newsroom quote above. Following Goffman, this distancing is a typical way of treating the absent in everyday life. In his study of *The Presentation of Self in Everyday Life* ([1959] 1990), Goffman writes:

When the members of a team go backstage where the audience cannot see or hear them, they very regularly derogate the audience in a way that is inconsistent with the face-to-face treatment that is given to the audience. In service trades, for example, customers who are treated respectfully during the performance are often ridiculed, gossiped about, caricatured, cursed and criticized when the performers are backstage; here too, plans may be worked out for 'selling' them, or employing 'angles' against them, or pacifying them.
(Goffmann [1959] 1990: 168–69)

News staff members, it appeared, were perfectly aware that they should not be seen talking down to, ridiculing or caricaturing the very individuals who they make a living off of. As the union representative at DR told me one day, looking very serious: 'Some of us have been talking about the fact that it is someone like you who can be dangerous. You can for instance reveal how we swear and whether how we talk can be deemed racist. So we need to talk nicely when you are around'.[22] After she had told me this, I looked a bit worried at which she laughed and said; 'I'm only teasing you, of course!'

But the idea that staff considered me 'dangerous' persisted, and I began to notice how some of the louder and ruder jokes were downplayed when I was near, not only at DR but at all the newsrooms I worked in. Thus, at a few times during fieldwork, when a joke was told about specific high-powered authorities or celebrities, staff would look to me as if to see whether I took note, and at times I was asked not to include certain critical comments about specific people in my study. It is not my intention to describe further the ways that staff at times talked critically and cynically about their interview subjects. Suffice to say that at times a critical distancing is evident among news workers, and this way of talking about The Others, who are not employed in the news business, no doubt helps to further the gap between those in the news profession and those outside. Interestingly, I have observed a similar cynicism and scepticism towards journalists from those outside of the profession.

The UK election in 2017 is a prime example of just how much newsroom opinion and politics can influence broadcast news – and how the group of white, middle class, university educated staff can get the national opinion wrong. As Channel 4 news presenter Jon Snow said in the opening of the broadcasters election special on 9 June 2017: 'We, the media, the experts, the media pundits know nothing. We simply did not spot it'. In a broadside to the media after the election, Journalist George Monbiot of *The Guardian* wrote of newsrooms: 'But the biggest problem, I believe, is that we spend too much time in each other's company, a tendency that is fatal in an industry that is meant to reflect the world. [...] There is a lack of contact not only with most of the population, but also with the material world and its physical parameters' (Monbiot 2017).

Journalists, as I have experienced them, consider themselves markedly different to people who are not journalists. This difference was at times expressed through the notion of journalists 'being outsiders' themselves; neither belonging to the public, nor belonging to the establishment. The idea of being an outsider, not belonging to neither the people for whom they make news nor the authorities that they interview, leads to some news workers characterising themselves as 'viewed with suspicion'. At ITV News, a writer and producer gave me the following reply when I asked him to tell me why he liked working in news:

They are not respectable people, journalists, they are viewed with suspicion by a lot of people, especially those who are in authority. A bit like actors too and artists, they are also outsiders, and I love that kind of outsider element. You know there is something kind of almost, not subversive, but it is... you are not part of the establishment, and I like that.

(Producer and writer, ITV News, regular freelancer at ITV for
6 years, interviewed in empty editing suite, 25 October 2007)

Among journalists, I often heard opinions, such as the one above, that journalists are a special breed, a special group, who neither belong to the public nor belong to the authorities. This opinion no doubt reinforces news journalists' perception of their world of work as closed, enclosed by both the ideas of the others and the imagined idea of other people's perceptions of them.

6.5 Conclusions

Throughout this chapter, I have illustrated some of the many connections and relations existing across media platforms and broadcasters. As has been illustrated, at all levels within the newsroom a close contact and connection is constantly at work with other colleagues in the news business. I have explored some of the specific connections between newsrooms and introduced the idea that when news workers across different broadcasters are connected and constantly in touch with one another, it influences the way they work. Returning to the notion of a nationality feeling among staff employed at the same broadcaster, I have introduced a bond stronger than that of a nationality, which is shared among news workers across broadcasters, namely that of being in a shared family. I introduced this unity as connected to a shared pride in working as a journalist, a pride that both unites all staff and distances them from those outside of the journalism profession.

Across different newsrooms, journalists and news workers in general meet when out covering stories, and at these meetings staff form friendships that they describe through metaphors of family relations. I have argued that these imagined bonds of blood relation are perceived to be much stronger than the bonds established between employees of the same broadcaster. Using Wenger's definitions of communities of practice I have illustrated how news workers from one broadcaster recognise a relation to many different groups of news staff across broadcasters and media platforms. It is when these communities of practice are perceived to be particularly strong that staff may consider the relations to be as strong as they imagine family relations to be.

I have described the friendship relations across broadcasters as affecting the way staff work, and the way the community of journalists may stand together against pressure from those outside of the profession. Additionally, I have highlighted some of the problematic consequences of strong bonds perceived to be family-like within practice communities for the news divisions. I have identified the central challenge for the news management to be the potential that bonds between news workers can become stronger than those between employee and his/her broadcaster and management. Analysing the practice communities, I have highlighted how the shared group of journalists are united in distancing themselves from others outside of the profession. Members of a certain practice communities may not always agree with the values of an editor, as they may not consider him/her a 'good journalist'. As I will discuss in the following chapter, when the individual journalist perceives his/her values of good journalism to be different to those of the management, the everyday work is considered a struggle to negotiate individual values of good journalism.

Notes

1 See for instance the active Facebook group entitled 'Niels Lindvig back on P1'.
2 DR notebook, p. 117.
3 DR Field book 1, p. 10.
4 Though interesting, to adhere to the topic of the thesis, the friendship between politicians and journalists within Danish Parliament will not be explored further here.
5 In 2007, it appeared to be common practice for the Prime Minister Anders Fogh's spin doctor to exit a meeting room in advance of the Prime Minister, telling the gathered journalists the outcome of the meeting and giving guidelines as to what kind of questions Anders Fogh would answer.
6 At times, the print journalists would be allowed to attend meetings that the broadcast journalists were not allowed to go to, as talk during the meetings were allowed to be quoted in tomorrow's papers but not broadcast on the day.
7 DR Field book 1, p. 113.
8 A nickname by which staff at the BBC often refers to the broadcaster.
9 See Appendix for descriptions of these English words and phrases, which I found were used in the everyday in both Denmark and the UK inside all four newsrooms.
10 The tendency to decorate the home with news media as the central element relates to the journalistic traits of what I have termed the 'News Junkie' (see Chapter 7).
11 As mentioned previously, among those employed as journalists inside the TV newsroom are news staff with many and different roles and titles, such as producers, reporters, script-writers, guest-bookers, editors, presenters and hosts.
12 According to interpretations of a recording of a phone conversation between the two reporters put online by Danish media early December 2011, the source was former Ministry of Defence Søren Gade's spin-doctor, Jacob Winther (see Ritzau 2011).
13 The word 'nouse' is a somewhat ambiguous term which I heard used among English news staff. Being a pun on the word 'news' and 'nose', it is used as a term for someone with a very good feel for news stories. The word does not appear to be known outside the journalism profession, but in this profession, the term is highly valued. Interestingly, I have found the word 'nouse' defined in a study of a regional BBC newsroom, as referring to 'an instinctive knowledge of how to get to the heart of a news story' (Hemmingway 2008: 221).
14 The TV screens can be seen on some of the illustrations from inside the newsroom that I have used within this book. On the picture of ITV's newsroom in the year 2011 on the cover of this book, the TV screens showing other broadcasters' news are placed in a circle just above the circle in which staff sit. In the former design of ITV's newsroom, the same screens were less central, placed on each news worker's desk.
15 Following from my earlier observations about the connection between room structure and ideals of structure of peoples, the fact that these screens are placed very centrally in a

newsroom shows that management encourages the constant observation, competition and inspiration among news divisions.

16   DR notebook 1, p. 132.

17   As referred to within Chapter 2, 'capital' here refers to 'all the goods material and symbolic, without distinction, that present themselves as rare and worthy of being sought after in a particular social formation' (Bourdieu cited in Harker 1990: 13).

18   Interview with studio manager, 29 August 2007.

19   During fieldwork, this constant distancing from what appears on the screen became a habit of my own. I too would comment if I saw something on screen that I thought ironic, or thought my fellow news colleagues would find ironic.

20   Though the people being talked about in the above quote are key politicians, I do not intend to portray news workers as political; rather, it is my impression that news workers and journalists in particular aim to be a-political and not show any political bias in their everyday work. Thus, I view the commentary above as primarily connected with the politician's role and performance on screen during this particular showing of The PMQ's.

21   In the UK, 'The PMQ's' is a constitutional convention that takes place every Wednesday (when the House of Commons is sitting), wherein the Prime Minister spends half an hour answering questions from Members of Parliament (MPs) (ITV Notebook, p. 41).

22   DR Field Diary 1, p. 45.

Chapter 7

The 'Good' Journalist: An Old Ideal

On how journalists define 'good' work, and how this shared definition matters in their everyday work

As introduced in the previous chapter, the news workers I have worked among appear driven by what they define as 'good' work. In the everyday negotiations about which stories to run, I often heard phrases such as 'This is *good* journalism', 'I want to do a *good* job', 'I want to make a *good* news story' or simply: 'I want to be a *good* journalist!'. Though seemingly a central drive for journalists, the definitions of these moral values are rarely talked about in the everyday work.

Within the first wave of newsroom studies, many researchers were keen to study what they termed 'the values' of journalists. These values were seen as key to the everyday judgement and selection process, for as Gans (1979: 38) noted: '[R]eality judgements are never altogether divorced from values'. With this chapter, I focus on values, particularly those expressed by journalists in their definitions of what good news work is. I aim to illustrate and explore the moral codes of doing 'good work' that I have found to be crucial to all the journalists inside every one of the four newsrooms of BBC, ITV, TV2 and DR. In order to investigate this notion, which appears so central to all the news workers I have worked among, I aim to describe and define, through the natives' own language and point of view, what it means to do 'good' work and what a 'good news story' is according to the news staff. I will explore some of these shared perspectives on work, and reasons for doing work, as expressed among journalists both in interviews and in their everyday work. In conclusion, I introduce the notion of a shared expressed ideology of news journalists.

An old ideal

The basic thing that drives one here is that outside this house there is somebody who is sitting with something, and doesn't want that thing out. Outside this house there is somebody who does something they actually shouldn't be doing. Or: outside this house there is somebody who does something good, which actually deserves to be told.

(DR Reporter, employed at DR for over 20 years, interviewed in
1st floor meeting room, DR Byen, 29 June 2007)

The biggest public service that we can do as an independent news journalistically based organisation, is to ferret out the truth, where people are trying to stop it from being published and tell the world – if it is in the public interest, and that is what we are trying to do. And that is a great privilege that we have as journalists, the ability to do that – to tell the world something that the world would not otherwise know if it wasn't for us uncovering it.

(ITV News Editor-in-Chief, David Mannion, interviewed in his office, overlooking the newsroom, 30 October 2007)

I tooke [*sic*] up my pen for disabusing his Majesty, and for disbishoping and dispopping his good subjects, and for taking off vizards and vailes and disguises.

(Marchmont Nedham on why he became a journalist, writing in the 1650s)[1]

It was never for egoistic reasons that I wanted to make stories, but because of a sense of justice, an indignation on behalf of the people.

(Per, former TV2 journalist for 25 years, reminiscing about the job he no longer works in, in interview, 20 June 2017)

During fieldwork, I was overwhelmed by quotes like those above. The quotes derive from journalists in different countries, different times and with different employers – a licence-fee funded broadcast news worker, a commercial broadcast news worker, a journalist who worked in print a few hundred years ago and one who worked in broadcasting a few years ago. All four agree on what the main purpose of being a journalist is: to be a watchdog for the public, 'revealing' to them what is good and what is bad in society. The four quotes above, though each expressed by journalists working in different realities, give a similar impression of news journalism: It is above all a profession of moral values regarding what is right and what is wrong. I see the idea of journalists being able to ferret out the truth objectively as an ideal of doing good, which is stronger than political, organisational or broadcaster bias. Thus, I have come to agree with Hallin in that '[t]hey [journalists, LHT] are committed more strongly to the norms of the profession than to political ideas' (1992: 15).

Though conditions and challenges for news workers today are very different to those centuries or even a decade ago, it appears that the reasoning for working in the news and the belief that journalism can function as a guard for the public against wrongdoings by authorities have stayed much the same. Comparing the first two quotes above with that of Marchmont Nedham, though they are 350 years apart, the expressed reason for working in journalism appears very similar. I find the idea expressed by Marchmont Nedham that journalists strive to take off 'vizards and vailes and disguises' to be strikingly similar to the aspirations of TV journalists today. Furthermore, when talking to journalists and editors alike, they often describe their values as being 'old', 'old fashioned', 'classic' and 'as old as journalism itself'. In this sense, journalists today can be said to perceive their key professional values as closely connected to key professional values in the past.

Among the staff I worked with, the key values are not only perceived as being connected to past broadcast journalism values, but to an essential set of journalism values inherent in all journalism, central to which are the factors implicit in what staff deem a 'good news story'. Though journalists appeared keen to tell me how unique their news division was to others, when I asked those who had been working for two different broadcasters what difference this made to their journalistic work, they told me that the way of working is fundamentally the same at all news divisions. When I interviewed the News Editor at DR, who had been working 13 years at TV2, I expected him to tell me about the differences in culture, but he did not:

LHT: So, do you see any difference in working for DR and working for TV2? And what is that difference?

News Editor, DR: Nah, […] [i]t is exactly the same criteria which I use to make news here.
(News Editor at DR, interviewed in ground floor
meeting room, DR Byen, 26 June 2007)

TV2 Journalist: There is no real difference between working at a newspaper and working in TV news. All the places I have ever been working, we all look for good news stories!
(Journalist at *Jyllands Posten* [10 years] and TV2 [25 years].
Currently in regional TV, 20 June 2017)

At ITV, I met a scriptwriter who had worked for ITV in the early 1990s and then left the newsroom to work for a range of other broadcasters before he was reemployed by ITV. When I asked him to describe the changes between the newsrooms, and the different ways of working he replied:

[…] here we are in the middle of a technological, technical revolution, and things are changing very quickly […] And I thought the technology is a bit different, but basically no, it's not changed at all. There are fewer people doing more things, but it hasn't changed. And it doesn't change because although our treatment of news changes, the way we do it, the amount of news we do, how we dress it up, how we present it, how we paint it – I don't think the product changes very much. The stories change, but it is still the same underlining guiding principles.
(Scriptwriter, ITV news, interviewed in an editing suite,
Grays Inn Road, 25 October 2007)

The above quotes aptly illustrate how news staff, when pressed to explain differences at the four different news divisions, instead talked of shared values, shared criteria or shared guiding principles. As my focus is on broadcast journalists, I was primarily asking staff to identify differences observed upon changing employer to or from the directly competitive news division; however, staff also expressed there to be shared guiding values between broadcast and print news journalism. As an example, the Head of News at DR who had previously been working for the newspapers *Berlingske* and *Politiken* told me: 'It is exactly the same basic idea of what a good story is at all serious media.'[2]

7.1 A Shared Value

As I have accounted for earlier, the similarities between the different newsrooms surprised me, as I had imagined journalists from the different newscasters to be of a different type, a different culture than the others. When I began to consider the similarities between newsrooms and news workers rather than the differences, I began to notice a range of perspectives that the news workers that I worked alongside appear to have in common. During my time of working with news journalists, it seemed that in the everyday, these shared perspectives collectively represented a shared ideal with which everyone positions themselves and their news work.

In his comparative study of journalists in Holland, Germany, Britain, Australia and the US, Mark Deuze (2002) has concluded that a shared ideology exists between journalists from elective democracies across borders of newsrooms and nationalities. Deuze defines this shared ideology as an 'occupational ideology of journalism' (Deuze 2002, 2011: 19). During fieldwork, I too have come to consider journalists to be sharing an ideology. To Deuze, the ideology of journalists is defined as 'an (intellectual) process over time, through which the sum of ideas and views – notably on social and political issues – of a particular group is shaped, but also as a process by which other ideas and views are excluded or marginalized' (Deuze 2011: 19, with reference to Stevenson 1995: 37–41; Van Ginneken 1997: 73). While the notion of a shared ideology has been much discussed among journalism researchers (as discussed in Chapter 1), as Deuze points out: '[E]ven though scholars are comfortable to refer to journalism as an occupational ideology, *the distinct building blocks of such an ideology are sometimes left to the imagination of the reader*' (2011: 20, emphasis added).

As shown in previous chapters, I do not view news workers as solely controlled and governed by management and editors, and thus I have come to disagree with the notion of 'intraorganisational' control as put forward by Soloski (1989). However, I agree with researchers in that a shared ideology, which I define as ideal typical values of the profession, prevails among news workers. In response to Deuze's call for 'distinct building blocks' of an ideology, I would like to describe in the following what I have found to be the key shared value among news staff: The idea of 'being a good journalist', which is closely linked to that of making 'good news stories'. Shared value is seen here as explicit or implicit fundamental beliefs, concepts and principles, which underlie the culture of a group and guide decisions and behaviours of the group.

As illustrated in the previous chapter, journalists are grouped in practice communities, with bonds that are strengthened through working together. Within these communities of practice, I have found the shared value of 'being a good journalist' to be governing the practices of each individual news worker, thus functioning as a key building block in what can be defined as a an occupational ideology. Members of practice communities within a news division often talk about how they review other people's work. Such ongoing evaluation, which I have described as a constant peer review, contributes to the impression that staff members have an agreement about what constitutes good work. Indeed, I never heard discussed the definitions of what to classify as good working practice. Rather, each news worker appeared convinced that those within his/her practice community were in agreement with the definitions.

When journalists talk about 'good'

I first noticed how similar the expressed ideals of news workers were when I began paying attention to how similar the arguments for bringing a story were at editorial meetings in all four newsrooms. Moving from one newscaster to another and finding here the exact same reasons for bringing a story as I had observed at the rival newsroom surprised me at first. I had expected differently financed Public Service Broadcasters to have very different reasons for deciding which story to take – reasons that I thought were primarily guided by the different values and guidelines that each broadcaster had defined in policies and mission statements (such as to 'engage', to 'entice the viewer' or to 'make public service news' as described in Chapter 3). After having attended countless editorial meetings at each broadcaster, I found that the same argument, whether expressed directly or not, was used in most discussions about a story; namely whether the story was a 'good news story.'

Thus, the definition, of what is 'good' and what event news workers define as 'good news story', plays a deciding factor in the everyday making and decision-making inside the TV newsroom. I am not the only one to have come to this conclusion. Recently, for example, David M. Ryfe concluded fieldwork inside a mid-sized daily American newspaper, describing the journalists he studied as having a clear idea of what is good and what is bad. As a result of sharing the practice of newsgathering, Ryfe writes, 'like any such community, the community of journalists contains conceptions of what "good" journalism is, and what it requires, and who a "good" journalist is, and how she might be distinguished from a bad one' (2011: 166).

During fieldwork, primarily, when I asked a journalist to describe what makes a good journalist, s/he would tell me what a good journalist does and give examples of work that s/he considered good. This was a fact I noticed shortly after beginning fieldwork, as my questions were often answered with long anecdotes and historical references. Gaye Tuchman (1973) had similar experiences while doing fieldwork in newspaper newsrooms in the early 1970s and David M. Ryfe (2006) had the same kind of experience during his fieldwork. This constant referring to practice, Ryfe has suggested, is because 'the identity of journalists is tightly bound to its practice' (Ryfe 2011: 170). As I too have found the practice communities central to the news divisions, I agree with Ryfe in that journalists perceive their identity, and the identity of their colleagues, as closely bound to their everyday working practices. Thus, when I attempt an exploration of what news workers define as 'good', this definition is deducted from lengthy stories and anecdotes of practical news work retold to me in formal interviews, informal conversations as well as experiences and observations I have made while working alongside news workers. Before entering into an exploration of what constitutes the good news story, I will explore the definitions of another central element in the everyday work at the four newsrooms I have studied: What is public service?

7.2 Good Work as a Public Service

In August 2007, the key people from the Danish journalism profession were gathered at the School of Media and Journalism in Aarhus to celebrate the annual 'Journalism Day'. The special theme of the day was 'public service'. During the day, broadcast management, editors and media researchers discussed the values of public service for journalism. As the day came to an end, it appeared there was a disagreement among the delegates over how to define 'public service'. More precisely, there was a disagreement between how those *researching* journalism defined public service and how those *working in* journalism defined public service.[3] Among those working in journalism (print or broadcast, commercial or public service), 'public service' and 'good journalism' appeared to mean one and the same thing. Among journalism researchers, public service was defined by being that which Public Service Broadcasters make and by those public service regulations that govern Public Service Broadcasters. The different views of the idea of public service came to a head when the head of the journalism school Anne-Marie Dohm summed up the day saying that she had thought the journalism practitioners a 'tad fluffy' when it came to the definition of public service'. In her critique of the journalism industry's definitions, she singled out DR's Head of News Ulrik Haagerup particularly.[4] To this Haagerup replied:

> There are a lot of demands, it is very specific things. It would be healthy if good judgement, common sense and an urge to make the good story was the same as 'public service'.
> (Haagerup talking on Journalistikkens Dag, DJH, 2007)

During the course of study I encountered a similar schism between the definition of public service by practitioners and researchers of journalism. Among the researchers studying public service journalism there appeared to be a set definition of what public service is, while among the public service journalists, the definition was less rigid and more connected with values of what they considered 'good journalism'. In the everyday work, I found much the same reasoning for selecting events as news at commercially funded Public Service Broadcasters as at licence-fee funded Public Service Broadcasters. When I asked staff to define public service to me, the most typical answer was as a presenter at TV2 told me:

'I find it hard to define public service, but to me it is very closely connected to the definitions I have of journalism and of what my mission is as a journalist [...]'. At all broadcasters, public service was talked about as crucial for quality in news production. In 2016, as the online news site and social media had become increasingly important, public service values were often mentioned as a primary argument for why 'TV news has better values than online news'. As the newly appointed Head of News at TV2 told me in autumn 2016, the values of public service and online news are far from the same:

> We have these old journalistic ideals, such as public service-values, objectivity and in-depth reporting. Should these values stand aside for online values such as being quick, funny, sensational and case-driven? No.
>
> (Jacob Kwon, Head of News, TV2, 27 October 2016)

As introduced previously (see Chapter 3), the regulations of all four news divisions are guided by ideals of public service, with the notion of doing a public good, and the Reithian moral values to 'inform, educate and entertain' as key. Even though all four news divisions are working to a public service remit, before commencing fieldwork I had expected the ideals of public service to be more outspoken at DR and BBC than at TV2 and ITV. As will be illustrated in the following, however, staff at both the traditional Public Service Broadcasters and at the commercial broadcasters appeared to have similar ideals of working towards 'bettering the world', much akin to the values of Public Service Broadcasters.

When public service staff define public service

LHT: Do you think of Public Service every day?

News Editor, BBC: Not merely 'every day', I think about it *every* day. And I don't think you'd survive long here if you didn't.

> (Male BBC News Editor, *Ten O'Clock News,* in the newsroom, by his desk, The BBC Newsroom, 26 September 2007)

When studying Public Service Broadcasting, I believe it is crucial to include a study of the broadcast staff's key definitions of public service. This is why I included the questions 'what is public service?' and 'do you think about public service in the everyday?' in questions to staff.

The role of a Public Service Broadcaster has arguably been one of the most well-defined tasks of the media landscapes in almost all European countries since the early or mid-twentieth century: to educate, inform and entertain the public, through morally correct broadcasting. As Moe and Syvertsen (2009) have remarked, the growth of research on Public Service Broadcasting must be seen as related to the growth of public service institutions. As the first public service corporation was established in Britain, the BBC and British researchers have played a prominent role in research and in debates of Public Service Broadcasting (Moe and Syvertsen 2009: 399).

While there have been extensive discussions by academic researchers on how to define public service, and there have been discussions about the value of public service, I have not found any studies of how public service staff tend to define public service. Only few empirical studies compare licence-fee funded news production with commercially funded television news production (see for instance Helland 1995). Neither have I encountered studies that explore how staff at licence-fee funded broadcast news divisions define public service compared to the definitions of staff at commercial broadcasters with a public service remit. In my study, which has given access to perform this comparison, I have been surprised by the apparent shared definition of what public service is. Moreover, I have been surprised to find that staff members at licence-fee funded broadcasters and commercially funded broadcasters define public service in terms similar to a definition of good news work.

Though only the two broadcasters – DR and BBC – are traditional Public Service Broadcasters, definitions of the public service values of broadcast news were echoed at ITV and TV2. During my fieldwork among journalists at ITV and TV2 Nyhederne, the notion of being a public service provider was often mentioned when news workers were discussing the importance of their news division. The ideals of a 'good news story', which I found among news staff at all four newsrooms, appeared closely linked with values of public service.

During my study, I asked as many staff as possible two questions relating to public service. This amounted to over 70 different replies, which I received in form of taped interviews, written interviews and in conversations. First, I asked staff whether they ever considered 'public service' in their everyday work.[5] At this question, all but two of the staff I asked replied that they thought about public service in their work every day. Of course, these closed questions may have led the news workers to feel that it was expected of them to answer in the affirmative. Again, I find the replies that I was given primarily relevant as a study of how news workers talk about and express their work. When being asked about their reasons for working in news, they often referred to the importance of working to do a public service. Among staff at all four broadcasters, a primary definition of public service centred on the notion of 'dressing people up' to better understand the world. While this moral ideal is perceived to be linked to ideals of public service, it also appears to be linked to the key news factors of being able to 'better the world' and 'inform and educate' the viewers: factors which staff talked of as important to making a good news story (I will return to this in Chapter 7.3).

Though BBC's declared mission of public service is nearing 100 years of age, the central definitions of its public service mission, first heralded by BBC's first Director-General in the late 1920s, appears largely unchanged today. As always, in the 2017 BBC Charter it is outlined that the broadcaster sees it as its overall mission to 'inform, educate and entertain'. Thus, the mission of BBC's founding figure, the influential, charismatic first director of the BBC, John Reith, is still central to the values of BBC today. And, as the BBC ideology later to be termed 'Reithianism' spread across Europe, just as the inspiration to form national Public Service Broadcasters spread in the first years after the success of the BBC, today the ideologies of public service have spread to the other broadcasters I have studied.

The idea that a broadcaster has the ability to select and disseminate information as education, while at the same time entertaining its audience, supports a notion of the broadcast staff of public service institutions as having excellent moral judgement. To sustain such high morals of being able to judge what is news worthy *and* educational puts a particular pressure on news division staff within a Public Service Broadcaster. When reviewing research on public service, the role of news divisions within a Public Service Broadcaster is often seen as a key guardian of the public good. As Preston puts it:

> PSB (Public Service Broadcasters) has been frequently characterised as framed around a specific editorial culture and attendant journalistic ethos ('to educate, inform and entertain' as the BBC's first director general defined it) combined with a commitment to a diversity of both programming content and universal service with respect to the national audience.
>
> (Preston 2009: 156)

'Dressing up the viewer to understand the world'

> I think that I'd like to dress people up so they can have an opinion in their everyday, both politically and in consumer issues, and give them knowledge. That is really what I see as public service [...] So they are able to act.
>
> (Reporter, DR Business Desk, interviewed in the sofa corner,
> 1st floor by Business Desk, 19 June 2007)

The above quote illustrates one of the key definitions of public service, which staff gave when asked directly for a definition of 'public service'. The idea of 'dressing the viewer up' was often mentioned explicitly. Similarly, in the everyday work, the ideas of giving the viewer knowledge that would enable him or her to act were key to journalists and reporters in their jobs of editing and presenting events. 'What can the viewer do to get involved?', 'What is the most important thing to tell the viewer?' were questions often posed among journalists and producers working together during the process of filming and editing a news piece.

Where the focus on DR and BBC centred on *being a Public Service Broadcaster*, the focus for news staff at the commercial broadcasters ITV and TV2 was on *doing a public service*. At the licence-fee funded broadcasters, the idea of public service was often talked about as 'being in the walls' or 'grown into us', as a very physical foundation for their work place and their work.[6] Among commercial broadcast journalists, the definitions of what public service were not much different from the definitions expressed among licence-fee funded broadcast journalists. However, when asked to define public service, the journalists at ITV and TV2 often appeared to feel a need to assert themselves as 'doing a public service'. Thus, commercial broadcast journalists appeared to feel misunderstood by journalism researchers such as myself, who assume that they tend to give higher priority to a story that sells over a story that provides a public service. As the Editor-in-Chief of ITV expressed it:

> People always see the BBC as the ultimate Public Service Broadcaster in the UK, or DR in Denmark. And that is true to some degree, but *we* provide a public service. We are not publicly funded, but we do provide a public service, I mean, we tell people what is happening. And that is a service. And more directly, if there were to be some disaster affecting London or Birmingham, or Manchester or wherever it might be, people need to know about it, they need to know how to avoid certain areas, they need to know what to do. And they need to have information passed to them from government departments, all that kind of stuff. So, in those occasions, on very major events, that is a public service that we are more than happy to provide. The biggest public service that we can do as an independent news journalistically based organisation, is to ferret out the truth, where people are trying to stop it from being published and tell the world – if it is in the public interest, and that is what we are trying to do. And that is a great privilege that we have as journalists, the ability to do that – to tell the world something that the world would not otherwise know if it wasn't for us uncovering it.
>
> (David Mannion, Editor-in-Chief, ITV News,
> interviewed in his office, 30 October 2008)

The definition of public service expressed in the quote above centres on two key parts: to inform the viewer and to ferret out the truth. As I will illustrate in the following, among the journalists I have talked to, these two elements are central factors for creating a good news story.

The moral role of journalists expressed in the quotes above each appear similar to what James Ettema and Theodore Glasser (1998) introduced in their book on investigative journalists with the notion of journalists being *Custodians of Conscience*. But the news workers above are not investigative reporters; in fact, in their everyday work, they have hardly ever had more than half a day to investigate a story and often rely on news wires and news feeds for their news content. Thus, as these quotes show, the lofty ideals of being a watchdog and a Fourth Estate for the people are not only expressed among investigative journalists. Rather, as Martin Eide suggests in his edited book on journalism, power and democracy (Eide 2001b: 16), other journalistic genres take legitimacy from the investigative journalism and from the idea of journalism as an educator of society.

Following on from the quotes above, news workers consider themselves both responsible for pointing a spotlight on the wrongs in the world *and* being able to know exactly where to point that spotlight. In the view of the news workers I have worked alongside, this knowledge of what is good and what is wrong is inherent in a good journalist who can use the ideal factors inherent in a 'good news story' to better the world. According to Marcus, it is not unsurprising to find among different sites of what he terms a 'so-called system' a 'shared cultural logic':

> Cultural logics so much sought after in anthropology are always multiply produced, and an ethnographic account of these logics finds that they are at least partly constituted within sites of the so-called system (i.e. modern interlocking institutions of media, markets, states, industries, universities – the worlds of the elites, experts and middle classes). Strategies of quite literally following connections, associations, and putative relationships are thus at the very heart of designing multi-sited ethnographic research.
>
> (Marcus 1995: 97)

7.3 The 'Good News Story'

After a few weeks of fieldwork, I soon began noticing that among all levels of news staff the key reason for bringing a story was the argument: '*That's* a good news story!'. Among staff, the exact definitions of a good story were not discussed in detail, but the argument '*That's* a good story!' was accepted among news staff as a valid reason to bring a story. Particularly in the different practice communities, staff agreed on what constituted a good news story and what did not. Staff within the Graphic Department would agree when a member of the graphic staff exclaimed 'That's a good story!' – and reporters at the parliament would agree when a fellow reporter exclaimed the same. Across the different communities of practice I began to notice a central agreement on what factors are essential to a 'good' event. In order to explore how members of staff define a 'good news story', I decided to ask as many staff as possible to define it.

'… it's like riding a bike!'

When asking staff what they saw as a good news story, I would rarely get a direct answer. Rather than tell me what they saw as a good news story, staff would tell me that a good news story is just something that a journalist can 'feel in the backbone' and not something that can be explained theoretically. As an Anchor Man at TV2 told me:

> You know I was educated in 1988, then I spent four years learning an incredible amount of parameters, news triangles and all sorts of theoretical ehm… and all that shit I've since

happily forgotten. I don't go around thinking about it. For me, and that I can feel, one just becomes one with ones working life. When one has been here as many years as me, then one just has to feel that it gives a shiver or a jump somewhere or something else – a feeling in the body, which tells me 'goddamnit something is happening here!' So for me, a good news story is something which I can feel. [...] Yeah it's a bit like riding a bike, you know you don't sit and think in those news triangles, or you just don't sit and think. [...] When you've learnt to ride a bike then you no longer concentrate on keeping the balance, you just do it.

(Anchor Man at TV2, interviewed at his desk in the studio after broadcast, 9 June 2008)

The above quote illustrates how staff appeared to view the idea of a good news story as something very physical, which in time becomes a part of one's self. This idea suits the notion put forward by Wenger (1998a) that practice communities are strengthened the longer participants work together. From the perspective of the Anchor Man above, the bonds between the news worker and his/her news division can become so strong that it is no longer thought about, but has become a very part of his/her body.

Other researchers of practical professions and of practicing journalists have been similarly unable to make journalists describe their practice in what Geertz (1983) would term experience-distant terms (see Chapter 2.2). Within journalism research, and indeed research on professions in general, staff are often talked about as unable to describe what they do in their job. As Gans wrote in 1979, journalists 'act on the basis of quick virtually intuitive judgments, which some ascribe to "feel"' (1979: 82). In her study of broadcast news values, Ida Schultz (2006) defines the feelings such as those described by the TV2 Anchor Man above as 'the journalistic gut feeling' (2007: 190). Studying print journalists in Denmark, Gitte Gravengaard (2010) had a similar experience of journalists not feeling able to talk about what they do, thus having an unspoken practical knowledge of how they act in the social world in the newsroom (2010: 57).

According to Wenger (1998a), the sharing of practical work is the glue that unites and strengthens practice communities. As the nature of this type of knowledge is practical, and often experienced as bodily, it is naturally hard to explain it to outsiders in words. In his study of organisational knowledge creation, Nonaka (1994) describes such practice-based knowledge as a 'tacit knowledge'. Much akin to the above Anchor Man's reply to what a good news story is, the definition of 'tacit knowledge' according to Nonaka is that which is 'unarticulated and tied to the senses, movement skills, physical experiences, intuition, or implicit rules of thumb' (Nonaka and von Krogh 2009). From the perspective of Nonaka, tacit knowledge becomes explicit in the everyday through articulation or expression of one's tacit knowledge (2009: 139). Thus, to study what news workers see as a good news story it is both important to encourage articulation of the practice based tacit knowledge that staff have of the *good story* and to be present to experience the way of expressing these values at work.

Two definitions of 'good'

When talking about 'good' in relation to news work, I came to see two key interpretations. I found both definitions apparent in observations of everyday work and in recorded interviews with news workers:

1) 'Good' as that which journalism colleagues from the same practice community define as the best working practice.
2) 'Good' as work which does good for society, informs, educates and helps better the world.

The above two definitions of 'good' are the result of both discussions about good work and observations of when staff talk about their work in the everyday. The two definitions are not dissimilar to how Gardner et al. (2001) have categorised 'good' as either work that is deemed to be 'of high quality' or work that is 'socially responsible'. As staff appeared to view both factors above as 'good' and equally important to news work, it becomes apparent that staff may become dissatisfied with their everyday work if both two definitions cannot be said to be fulfilled.

When ideals of peers from within a practice community and one's own ideals of doing work that 'does good' do not correspond, doing work can be felt as a struggle. Such disconnection between a superior's expectations of what is deemed good and one's own perception of what is good is what Gardner et al. terms a 'misalignment' (2001: 6). When a news reporter at TV2 News tells me that she sometimes feels stressed, as her superiors do not seem interested in 'the best' news work but rather in the 'quickest' news work, it is an example of how staff may perceive their own professional values to be conflicting with those of management in the everyday.

Gardner et al., who have studied different professions, found journalism to be a 'textbook example' of a profession that must continually face new challenges. In 2001, the journalists they talked to as part of their 'good work project' explained themselves as:

> [...] working at a time when the profession is wracked by confusion and doubt – that is a time when the relevant forces are massively misaligned. Journalists may feel the need to take time to investigate a complex story, but the public is calling instead for gossip and scandal, while management is seeking greater profits in the next quarter.
>
> (Gardner et al. 2001: 6)

As I have found the two differing definitions of 'good' both equally important to staff, reasons for working on a story often appeared driven by a determination to do work that would fit both definitions of the term. When talking of a 'good news story' it appeared both definitions of 'good' were hoped to be achieved within the work. Thus, to explore the key ideas of both 'good practice' and work that 'betters the world', in the following I will discuss the notion of the 'good news story'.

Researching news values

It has been key to journalism research ever since its emergence to define what constitutes a good news story or which 'news values' guide the selection process. While one part of the first wave of newsroom studies described the newsroom as a factory floor (Bantz et al. 1980), governed by management and editors at the individual newsroom (White 1950; Breed 1955) and official source channels (Sigal 1973), another part of the early newsroom studies focused on listing news values used in order to select an event as news. Termed invariably *news values* (for instance Gans 1979; Asmussen and Meilby 1977), *newsworthiness* (Epstein 1973; Lester 1980), *news judgement* (Fishman 1980) or *factors that seem particularly important* (Galtung and Ruge 1965), journalists' definitions of a good news story have been central to journalism research. In Danish journalism research and journalism practice handbooks, the discussion of news values (Asmussen and Meilby 1977; Olsson and Poulsen 1995; Tverskov and Tverskov 2004; Kabel 2009) has centred on five key criteria:

The five Danish news criteria

1. *Actuality*, the more current an event the more actuality.[7]
2. *Relevance*, a qualitative judgement of relevance to the public and to other news.
3. *Conflict*, between causes, organisations, events or people.
4. *Identification*, a judgement of what events the public will identify with.
5. *Sensation*, prioritising the unusual and spectacular element in an event.

Within international research into how journalists define a good news story, the study 'The structure of foreign news' by Galtung and Ruge (1965) has been particularly dominant. The two peace researchers Johan Galtung and Mari Holmboe Ruge wished to study how events become news. Through an analysis of four Norwegian newspapers' coverage of foreign stories, they concluded that the more of the below twelve factors were included in an event, the more likely it is that the event is deemed a good news story. Galtung and Ruge introduce these twelve factors as 'a systematic presentation of factors that seem to be particularly important' (1965: 64) in creating what they termed 'newsworthiness'. Presenting these factors, Galtung and Ruge state that 'the more factors an event satisfies, the higher the probability that it becomes news' (1965: 90):

How events become news: Galtung and Ruge's twelve factors

1. Frequency
2. Threshold
   2.1 Absolute intensity
   2.2 Intensity increase
3. Unambiguity

4. Meaningfulness
    4.1 Cultural proximity
    4.2 Relevance
5. Consonance
    5.1 Predictability
    5.2 Demand
6. Unexpectedness
    6.1 Unpredictability
    6.2 Scarcity
7. Continuity
8. Composition
9. Reference to elite nations
10. Reference to elite people
11. Reference to persons
12. Reference to something negative

While the focus of Galtung and Ruge's research was to study how foreign news is structured in Norwegian newspapers, my interest in defining the factors that are central to a good news story came about after I had found the phrase *'that's* a good news story' as central to the decision-making process within the newsroom.

Eight Key Factors to make a 'good news story'

What is a 'good news story'? – This was the first question that became essential for me to ask during fieldwork. This type of question is what James Spradley has called a 'typical sentence question', made up by a folk term, or a 'native-language' question, which 'asks for typical sentences that contain a word or phrase' (Spradley 1979: 90). I included the question in my four primary questions posed to all staff as I was genuinely bewildered about what exactly the term 'good news story' meant to the news workers.

During fieldwork, if there ever was debate over whether to bring a story, say between a reporter who was keen on doing a certain story and an editor who did not seem to find it interesting, discussion would be drawn to a halt if the editor uttered, with authority: 'this is simply *not* a good news story!'. When an event had received that stamp, there did not seem to be any chance of pushing the story. Generally, when a story had been defined a 'good news story', it appeared to stay one. But at times, a story that had been defined a 'good news story' one day was not seen as 'a good story' the day after even by the same staff. This, I was told, was because the 'good story' is always seen in relation to all other events and stories available on a given day.

Personally, I soon became confused as to what exactly the term meant and felt I needed to ask staff themselves to define it. As the term was heard so frequently in the everyday work of the news workers, I felt it would be crucial to understand the definition if I was to understand what the journalists appeared to share, value and use most in their everyday work. In the interview situation, sometimes I would begin my question by explaining that I often heard the phrase 'that is a good news story!' in the newsroom and therefore wondered exactly what was meant by it. Most interviewees agreed that they use the phrase often, and many interviewees thought they had a very unique interpretation of the word. But in fact, almost all the journalists I spoke to at the different practice communities and at all four different newscasters gave me almost the exact same explanations of what constitutes a 'good news story'. Analysing the different descriptions, it appeared that eight key definitions were prevalent. I do not find it possible to quantitatively measure which of the definitions were more key than the others, so suffice to say that all eight factors below were central to the definition. As each of the factors was mentioned as important to a good news story, just like Galtung and Ruge (1965) I present the definitions as 'factors', which are each important to the selection of events as news. Some of the news workers I spoke to mentioned all eight points, others mentioned some of the eight points and some focused only on one of the central definitions in their reply to me. When mapping the different responses to my question 'what is a "good news story"?', the following pattern of factors emerged:

A 'good news story': Eight Key Factors according to news journalists

1. Brings something new
2. Is interesting to a broad spectre of the people
   2.1 Can make people talk
   2.2 A story which I imagine people will relate to
3. A story with which I can personally relate
   3.1 A story which I think my mother and my friends will relate to
4. Has the ability to inform and educate the viewer
   4.1 Has good values
   4.2 Is important
5. Is relative to other events
   5.1 Relative to what else happens on the day
   5.2 Relative to the other stories covered on the day
6. Is geographically dependent
   6.1 Events from 'our' culture prioritised
7. Is unique
   7.1 A story which the competitors do not have
8. Can help better the world
   8.1 Can encourage the viewer to make a positive change

In methodology, my list of news values differs fundamentally from the way journalism research has primarily come to list journalistic news values. While Galtung and Ruge's

(1965) study was based on a content analysis of four Norwegian newspapers' coverage, my list of factors that make an event newsworthy is a list created from what journalists themselves express. Thus, the above list can be seen as a list of how the news journalists I worked alongside talked about their working process. As such, it can be argued that these criteria are an expression of what the journalists perceive to be their news criteria, but they may not necessarily be the criteria they use in their everyday work.

In these discussions about events, news workers mentioned some of the above factors. However, all factors were objects of discussion and news workers at all four newsrooms aspired towards them in their everyday work. In a debrief from management at the end of the day, it appeared, both explicitly and implicitly, that many of the factors above were also agreed on by management. At DR for instance, a new News Editor introduced the reward of a bottle of wine in the evening to any journalist who produced what she deemed a 'solo' story, which (as in factor 7.1 above) is a story which 'the competitors do not have'.[8] Likewise, when an editor told me that he thought it would be best to send journalists out into the pubs to see what the people in the country are talking about, he expressed agreement with factor 2 and 2.1 above as an important news value.

While I have found some of the above factors mentioned during everyday work, news workers never entered into explicit discussions about the implied meaning of the phrase 'that is a good news story!'. Thus, rather than viewing the list above as an *absolute definition* of the values that make an event newsworthy, I find it interesting to study the list as an illustration of what staff *express* as being central to their work.

In the editorial meeting, one of the key elements to a good news story appeared to be the journalists' own engagement with a story (factor 3 above). In the everyday work, most journalists would be given a story to work on for the day by the editor at the morning meeting. The process of giving a story to a journalist at times appeared to be a process led by negotiation and convincing tactics. Before presenting a specific journalist with a story idea, an editor would tell a journalist 'this is one for you', or 'this story is just up your street!'. In this way, it appeared the handing out of stories at the morning meeting centred on making journalists engaged and awakening a personal interest in a story.[9]

The idea that an event should bring something new appeared to be implicit in all news staff members' definitions of not only a good news story but any 'story' at all. While news and events from what was perceived as *Our* culture were often prioritised over the culture of *Others* during editorial meetings, staff talked of the importance of the news bulletin reaching a 'broad spectre' of viewers.[10] The notion that an event should be 'interesting to a broad spectre of the people' (factor 2 above) was explained with equal importance both among licence-fee funded and commercially-funded broadcast staff. Within the idea of the 'broad spectre of the people', however, it appeared that they gave higher priority to the number of people than to the broadness of the spectre. As the News Editor of DR put it:

My criterion is just that it should be a story which is placed where I would call it the middle of the road. That is a story which is interesting to a broad spectre of the Danish people. I am not interested in fine arts, which might interest 5000 people in this country, or a sports event that might interest 20,000. I am interested in a sports event or a piece of fine art, which interests one million people. Then I don't care whatever the topic is.

(News Editor, DR, interviewed in ground floor meeting room, 26 June 2007)

In journalism studies and practical journalism handbooks, the notion that news is relative to other events and other news stories (factor 5 above) is often mentioned (see for instance Harcup 2011: 47). In the everyday work, I noticed stories being taken or being dropped on account of not fitting in with the other stories in the news bulletin, or simply being 'too small a story' on a given day, where there were already many bigger stories. As one of TV2's long-standing reporters replied when I asked him what a good news story is:

That one can never know. It all depends on supply and demand, you know? If a serious accident has happened, then we'll take that, but we won't take the serious accident if a large explosion with many dead happens. Sometimes there's a killing in Iraq, which doesn't fit in, because something more serious has happened. That's news. It is always supply and demand.

(Reporter, TV2, interviewed in corridor outside newsroom,
Kvægtorvet, Odense, 5 June 2008)

One of the key people responsible for the pictures used in a news bulletin, a female news worker whose task it is to constantly keep an eye on the video feeds arriving from abroad, told me that she could easily make a world map of where in the world events are considered most newsworthy. Key to such a map, she argued, was the fact that events from what she perceives to be 'our' own culture are prioritised. As she was employed with a news division in Denmark, she felt that 'the closer you get to Denmark, the less dead people you need. And the nearer you come to places where a lot is happening, the Middle East for instance, there we need a higher death rate before it will be interesting, because we are simply so used to people dying down there'.

When I asked staff to explain what a good news story is, most people mentioned the fact that it should be an event which s/he could relate to personally (factor 3 above). Many also mentioned the importance of close family and friends relating to the stories they made.[11] The possibility of imagining friends and family to relate to a story was often closely connected to the idea that a broad spectre of viewers (factor 2 above) would identify with it. As when TV2 News Editor, Jacob Nybroe, told me about a good news story: '[...] Will it impact on my children or my parents, me or my car garage or something like that?'.

Explaining the importance of a news story relating to viewers, it was often mentioned that the ultimate news story should make viewers relate while learning. This was often described as 'widening' an issue, using for instance case studies to make people relate and identify with a 'wider' story. Thus, a good news story was described as containing a mix of something one can relate to and a greater issue. The notion of educating the viewer while making possible a relation to the story was often mentioned in connection with what I have identified as factor 8 above, to help better the world. An example of such a connection of the different factors, with a focus on educating and informing viewers with what is seen as 'good values', can be seen in the below comment from a female reporter at TV2:

> To me, I get turned on by values like, for instance [...] there was this morning where it was a running story that Karen Jespersen [Danish Minister for Equal Rights] encourages relatives to take more care of the elderly in care homes. It was before the strike and all that, so like on a very general level, that one should get more engaged in one's own elderly. Well, when I got to work I felt like: 'That story, I'd like to make today!' because I think it is important, it is an important issue, it is an important discussion, it is about some values in society, which we could learn something from. It's things like that which I think about. And that it has a great importance because it is politics but it has a closer importance too, I think. That is a value-story!
>
> (Reporter, TV2, interviewed in the reporters' newsroom, Kvægtorvet, Odense, 24 June 2008)

Comparing the Eight Key Factors which staff have described to me as key to a good news story, in essence they appear to be primarily similar or the same to those of the Danish news criteria and those of Galtung and Ruge (1965) above.[12] However, a key difference is evident, namely the last element (factor 8 above): that a news story should 'help better the world'.

Crucially, all eight factors above indicate that news staff believe themselves able to know and judge an event well enough to deem it 'new', 'important', 'educational', as having 'good values' and as able to 'better the world'. In my interviews, this last ideal, of being able to better the world through one's work, appeared particularly important to staff. Thus, I became interested in studying whether the ideal of 'bettering the world' appeared to play a part in the everyday work of journalists. Furthermore, I was keen to explore whether the ideals were more or less as strong at the differently financed broadcast news divisions. In the following, I will look closer at the key values for good work as they were discussed and employed by news journalists in their everyday work.

7.4 Good Work as 'Very Scout-Like'

> Why I work in news? That's your question? Ehm... It is very much because I want to make journalism in the service of the public, so you know it is very old fashioned. It may sound a little religious, but it is [...] being a part of dressing people up to understand the world we live in, being a part of telling what is happening. Be a part of putting the critical questions, so that the ones in power, yes, all kinds of powerful people and decision-makers

and so forth can explain themselves. [...] I really like the idea that I'm a part of telling the ordinary people what is happening in the world around them. So it is very scout-like.

(Reporter, DR, interviewed in meeting room, 1st floor, DR Byen, 28 July 2007)

I work in news because I like to educate the viewers. And if there are any wrongdoings happening, I would like to help stick them to the authorities. The elderly people who need money for instance, they cannot say that to the authorities themselves, so we say it for them.

(TV2 Regional Anchor Man, Jacob Rytz, interviewed in the studio right after broadcast, 5 October 2017)

The above quotes illustrate a key point expressed during interviews and also in the everyday work inside the newsrooms: News work and good news stories are important to better the world. Thus, by the very position of being employed as a news journalist, staff members perceive themselves to be responsible for what was often expressed in terms of 'putting spotlight on all that's dark in the world'. I noticed news stories that matched the description above and were prioritised over other news stories. I have included the quote above as I find it particularly illustrative of how staff talked about news events and crucial to how staff would instantly frame events, keeping in mind their role as 'very scout-like'. As the following example shows, this perceived role of helping the ordinary people in a 'very scout-like' way made staff feel responsible for holding others accountable on *behalf of* the people.

'It's like ringing a bell for the authorities to take notice'

While attending an editorial meeting for the 9 o'clock news at TV Avisen one afternoon in early June 2007, I noticed that the Programme Editor and News Editor seemed particularly eager to bring a certain story. That day, a report had just been released by The Danish Refugee Council (Dansk Flygtningehjælp) that showed that suicide attempts among asylum seekers in Denmark had tripled in number since 2001. Even though one of the Programme Editors had tried and failed to get case studies to illustrate the story, particularly the Programme Editor for the late news appeared very keen to bring the story. The main storyline up for discussion was how bad the conditions for asylum seekers were in Denmark, and how badly asylum seekers were being treated in the Danish asylum centres. 'I did this exact story twelve years ago!', said the Programme Editor and looked frustrated. 'That's a proof that we have tried to ring the bell for years and still nothing has been changed', he continued.[13] That night, the story of the drastic rise in asylum seeker suicides was broadcast as a long item in the news bulletin, even though there was no case study available nor any asylum seekers who wanted to talk to the press. TV2 also brought the story, as did a number of the daily newspapers the day after. As the story was not suited to do 3D graphics, had no case studies, nor any of the people implicated wanting to talk to the press, the story did not fit many of the ideals expressed in the broadcasters' mission statements and broadcast values. Still, the story was deemed so important for 'bettering the world' and making a difference that it was selected anyway and presented as a long news item. In this way, the ideals of 'bettering the world' appeared more important than the broadcasters' expressed ideals and mission statements.

The notion that journalists are responsible for 'ringing a bell' in order for the authorities to take notice of wrongdoings within the country aptly corresponds with news workers' explanations of their reasons for working in the news. However, while I found ideals of 'bettering the world' key to the determination of good stories, I also found staff to be driven less by moral ideals and more by personal agendas related to their work, such as feeling powerful and getting an adrenalin kick from finding themselves at the centre of historic events.

The Scout, the Power Tripper and the News Junkie

As introduced previously, I have found journalists to be led by a desire to reach shared ideal typical values. These normative professional values are central to creating a shared newsroom culture. As I have highlighted previously, a central ideal typical value among journalists is that of 'bettering the world'. While the ideals of bettering the world were central to most staff members within the newsroom, I noticed at least two other central reasons for working in news: the adrenalin kick and the feeling of power. When stories were scarce, staff would often talk dreamingly of days when they were busier. During a busy news day, staff would seem excited, at times almost high on the importance and significance of the events they were covering. Looking at news staff at work, during the many different events, it appeared different staff were personally excited about work for at least three different reasons, which I have identified as three journalistic character traits: The Scout, the Power Tripper and the News Junkie:

The Scout: Is driven by what he sees as a *duty* to help the viewer, find the educational and democracy-supporting aspect of a story. Sees himself/herself as playing an important part in 'bettering the world' and feels able to choose what values are good and what values are less good on behalf of the viewer. While working, the Scout aims to 'take the viewer by the hand' and 'dress people up' to better understand the world.

The Power Tripper: Feels important in shaping and creating history. Is excited about the constant contact with people of fame and power. Expresses his/her work as being 'in the front row of history'. Remembers a time when s/he was not working in news and was unable to talk to authorities in the same way.

The News Junkie: Gets a kick out of stories that are deemed big. Might talk about bombs and tragedy as 'fun'. Enjoys the fast pace and has an adrenalin kick on days where big news happen. Right after having worked on such big stories, s/he feels particularly good. Spends the quiet news days waiting and wishing for big events to happen, in order to feel like something 'real' is happening.

While the above list identifies what I have seen as three primary reasons for working in news, the list does not exhaust the different motives that staff may have. I present the list only as an illustration of the three primary reasons I have observed and experienced staff to both express to me and to their colleagues in their everyday work. I have found the reasons listed above to work as private motivators for working, not to be confused with the shared professional ideals which I have found predominant among all news staff.

While I have defined three different types above, I have found staff to primarily show traits of what I term the Scout. The traits of the Scout outlined above thus, in my experience, constitute the primary driving forces among all the news staff studied. However, while the ideologies of helping the public, bettering the world and supporting democracy are central to news staff, other ideas, such as the adrenalin kick and the feeling of self-importance (which I term the Power Tripper and the News Junkie above), are also central to motivating staff. Thus, one news worker may at the same time be driven by motives from all three of the categories above.

The News Junkie characteristics were sometimes talked about when staff members were to explain what they liked in their work and some staff explicitly used the term 'news junkie' as a self-description. But more than being expressed verbally, I noticed the traits of what I identify as the News Junkie in the everyday. Most staff appeared more excited, happy and eager to work when big news happened, and if there was not a lot of big events happening on a day, people inside the newsroom would be waiting eagerly for big events to happen. When bombs dropped, politicians were arguing, an election was called or other unplanned events happened, most staff in the newsroom would be more active, excited and keen to be at work. With these experiences in mind, I find the following two comments from staff at both TV2 in Denmark and ITV in the UK representative for how staff in the everyday perceived events from what I have termed a 'News Junkie's' perspective:

> Last Monday, when the bombs came, THAT was fun! Well, I'm sorry to say it in that way, but we were just sitting there, a quiet Monday, and then it happened, at 9.20AM. [...] then goddamnit something suddenly happened.
>
> (Host of the *Breakfast News*, in conversation in corner of newsroom, at 5.10AM on 9 June 2008)

> It is just this tremendous feeling of being a team, and the adrenalin is flowing, everybody knows what they are doing and then gets on and does it. And then, you know, you are judged by the product at 10 o'clock 10.30 or 6.30 or whenever it is. And then also, there is nothing quite like the feeling when that product has ended, it's finished. You've done it,

it's all over, you can't go back and do it again. You don't take it over. You know, it's gone, that is it. And next day you wake up and do it all again.

(Host of the then *ITV News at 10.30*, interviewed
in his private office overlooking the newsroom, 31 October 2007)

Just like the host of TV2's Breakfast News quoted above, staff from all four news divisions studied often used the word 'fun' when describing news days with unexpected tragedy, war or conflict. My time working inside the newsroom made me aware of just how different the staff members behave inside the room when a big news story happened, all seeming more eager and excited to be working on stories such as bombs or natural disasters. After the event they would call it a 'big' news story. The majority of days I spent in the newsrooms during fieldwork were not Big News Days. However, among staff there was always the feeling of a chance of something big happening, making even the most eventless day feel exciting. The excitement I experienced in the newsroom when 'big' news stories happened, and the feeling of 'fun' which staff talked about in relation to 'big' events, may be due to staff feeling what some, such as the host from ITV above, termed an 'adrenalin kick'.[14] However, the feeling of excitement that I witnessed among news staff when big stories broke can also be connected to the feeling of power, which staff perceived as they were now placed in the 'front row of history' and could meet all the key players in a big national or international event.

The journalistic characters, the News Junkie, the Power Tripper or the Scout identified above, should not be seen as exhaustive of all the different motives existing among the news workers in the four newsrooms I have studied. However, I have found the three different character types as typical of the primary motives, which I experienced staff to have for working in news. In the everyday, during an editorial meeting or in interviews when talking about their work, staff often said they were motivated by all three or a couple of the three primary journalistic characters. When I asked the Head of News at TV2 to tell me his main drive for working in news, for instance, he expressed ideals comprised in all three journalistic characters above:

There is a feeling of absolute joy in saying: 'this is goddamnit too bad, don't you think Denmark?' 'Yes we think!' […] It also gives a big feeling of power and I dare to take that upon myself, that of course I think it is interesting to be a mouthpiece, which is of course not my personal mouth piece because it is journalism we're making, but we do have a number of priorities […]. If I should lift my head a bit I would say it is an important profession for democracy. And I like it to feel a bit like that sometimes. It is ok if it feels as if one is a part of something important. And ehm… that is what I feel we are.

(TV2 Head of News, Jacob Nybroe, interviewed in his
office overlooking the news division sofa area, 5 June 2008)

Upon explaining the reasons for working in news, the ideological definition of 'good' as a way of bettering the world was often mentioned. Above, the Head of News at TV2 aptly illustrates some of the central elements to being a journalist. The idea of being 'powerful' was not always expressed as explicitly as above. The notion of journalism as 'important for democracy', however, was expressed in most of the more than 100 interviews conducted. Furthermore, during editorial meetings and negotiations between editors and journalists, ideas of 'bettering the world' appeared central to news journalists selecting stories, just as the ideals of bettering the world were central to a 'good news story'.

As I have found character traits of what I identify as the Scout above to be primarily dominant among the news staff, I have come to consider this role as particularly important to the news journalists I have studied. The notion that work can 'help the people', 'better the world' and 'take the viewer by the hand' is central to what I have described as the eighth factor for a 'good news story' above. As I have shown, staff appeared to use values and traits that can be metaphorically described as 'scout-like' within the everyday work of deciding, selecting and framing events.

In the everyday work, journalists could often seen to be motivated by goals either suiting the stereotypes of the Scout, the Power Tripper or the News Junkie. When I met journalists who had left their job, they would talk in terms suiting some or all of these journalistic character traits – as when I asked a former TV2 reporter and News Editor what he missed the most:

> I miss the pulse. Whenever a news event with a relevant perspective happens today then I really go off like a rocket. I miss putting things on the agenda for politicians and the world. I miss being part of shaping history.
>
> It was never for egoistic reasons that I wanted to make stories, but it was because of a sense of justice – an indignation on behalf of all people.
>
> (Per, TV2 journalist for 25 years,
> talking 15 years after he left the job, 20 June 2017)

As journalists appeared to perceive their jobs as very closely connected to their practice, many would refer to a practical job they had done rather than describe their work to me in an interview. In the following, I will illustrate one such example of practical work, which was often highlighted as exemplary among news staff.

'Bettering the world': A case study

When I asked staff to describe to me exactly what makes a 'good' news story, most staff gave me examples of actual stories that they had worked on, which they considered to be 'good'. Many of these stories appeared to have a motive of changing the world in a positive way by highlighting what they deemed as 'bad' or 'wrongdoings' in society. One such example was the news from Zimbabwe that staff at all levels at ITV often told me about when describing 'good' news stories they had worked on.

The September 2007 reports from Zimbabwe, presented from the border of Zimbabwe, were something they were proud of. During a week of special ITV News programming, the broadcaster put a focus on Zimbabwe by presenting the late evening news from a studio by the border between Zimbabwe and South Africa. From this linked up studio, ITV News' former Africa correspondent Mark Austin presented the evening news bulletin for the entire week. To illustrate the way the presenter described the situation in Zimbabwe, below is a copy of the script read by the presenter from Zimbabwe during the week:

<u>17 September 2007, ITV News at Ten Thirty</u>

PRESENTER: Good Evening from the border of what should be one of the richest countries in Africa. In fact Zimbabwe – behind me here – is now amongst its most desperate. Ruined by the man running it, President Robert Mugabe. It is a country on the cusp of collapse.

And these are a people shown **no** mercy by their President. This is a country crying out in pain, crying out for help. But those cries are smothered by Robert Mugabe's brutal henchmen. Tonight we have exclusive evidence that he has set up camps to train teenage hit squads. Their job: to suppress opposition to the President in the run up to next year's elections.

<u>18 September 2007, ITV News at Ten Thirty</u>

PRESENTER: Good Evening from Zimbabwe's border with South Africa – where tonight we reveal the risks Zimbabweans are taking to escape the tyranny and the tragedy taking place on the other side of the fence behind me. These rows of chain-links and that spaghetti of razor wire, is meant to be a barrier. But to the desperate and the destitute of Zimbabwe it is a magnet – attracting those prepared to risk all they have left – their lives.

<u>19 September 2007, ITV News at Ten Thirty</u>

PRESENTER: Good Evening again from Zimbabwe's border with South Africa. Behind me, across that bridge, is a country whose president is at war with many of his own people – determined to suppress opposition to his regime in almost any way he can. It is a country desperate for change – nowhere more so than in its second city Bulawayo – home of the opposition party. But the people who live there are being deprived of the essence of life – punished with water shortages because of their thirst for change. Many are resorting to drinking dirty water from holes in the ground – risking disease, even death. To see this for myself, I travelled to Bulawayo – a broken city.

<u>20 September 2007, ITV News at Ten Thirty</u>

PRESENTER: Good Evening again from Zimbabwe's border with South Africa. As we've reported this week, over that bridge, Zimbabwe's people are crying out for help. Today in an exclusive interview with ITV News Gordon Brown told us he'd seen our reports, heard that cry and promised Britain would answer it. He talked of sending more aid, of more UN checks on where it goes, and of helping in the planning of a democratic future, once President Mugabe has gone.

But already Mr Brown has been told that is not enough: the Archbishop of York – Dr John Sentamu – said military intervention may be needed, and Zimbabwe should be stripped of its European embassies. It should be treated as a pariah state, he said.

And we've seen plenty of people this week who have next to nothing; no money, hardly any food, and little water.

We came here to highlight their suffering, to give a clearer vision of what one man – Robert Mugabe – has done to his own once thriving country.

What happens now is up to the politicians.

And that's the end of our special programming from Zimbabwe's border. And that's tonight's news.[15]

When looking at the above news script through the Eight Key Factors I have identified as being key to a 'good news story', it appears the story and the reports from Zimbabwe comprise most of the eight factors. The story and the presentation are both unique and new with elements presented as exclusive. The story is presented emotionally with key elements such as 'desperation' and 'crying out for help', highlighted for the viewer to relate to. Although geographically distant, the story is culturally and historically connected to the UK viewer, as Zimbabwe was once a British colony (then Southern Rhodesia). Furthermore, the news reports from Zimbabwe were presented as important, informative and educative for the viewer, with morally good values. Above all, the script above attempts to highlight wrongdoings, calling for the viewer and for the authorities to better the world, as the presenter ends the reports: 'What happens now is up to the politicians'.

Today, ten years after, the above script is still interesting on many different counts. Firstly, it is a practical example of how journalists like to present themselves, and an example of what a good news story is, according to the news journalists I have worked among. The script above was referred to by news staff from all levels of the ITV news division as exemplary work. At BBC and at Channel 4 News, news staff also talked about the ITV news from Zimbabwe as 'good' work. The script has also gained international appraisal leading to a nomination in the Current Affairs category of the 2008 Emmy Awards in New York.

Secondly, the script is an example of how journalists perceive their role in society. As the script is presented as good work, it can be seen as an illustration of the role that news journalists perceive themselves to play: making morally right news that educates and informs the viewer while at the same time changing world events to the better. The above script and indeed the entire week of news from Zimbabwe give a good introduction to how news workers like to view their work, as a spotlighting of what they consider bad, in order to motivate authorities and the people to make a change. Particularly, the last few lines from the above script shows how news workers were hoping to make politicians act on the news.

Thirdly, the above script shows how much news work *can* change events and make politicians relate to the topics addressed. The script is not only an illustration of the role that news workers perceive themselves to play, but also an illustration of the power that journalism does in fact have in relation to world events. As the script reveals, politicians, such as the then Prime Minister Gordon Brown, did take note of the special news reports and acted on what ITV News presented. The fact that the news managed to make politicians react to the news in such a short time was often mentioned when staff talked about the importance of the Zimbabwe programmes.

7.5 Conclusions

Though conditions and challenges for news workers today are very different to those a decade or twenty years ago, staff today perceive their key ideals to be as old as the profession itself. With this chapter I illustrated how staff members see their job as journalists as strongly connected to old and 'classic' journalistic values of bettering the world, responsible for putting a spotlight on the wrongdoings in the world.

Previously, the physical similarities within the four newsrooms have been explored. With this chapter, another less tangible level has been introduced: the everyday ideals of each news worker. Though news workers may describe themselves as being very different, and may indeed have different ways of presenting a news story, I have found staff to share fundamentally similar criteria for what a 'good news story' is. In this sense, the news workers I have studied have one and the same constant ideal, just as they perceive themselves as belonging to a shared community of practice across broadcasters. The shared ideal of a good news story is found in the very core of what staff members at all four newscasters perceive as their professional ideal. I have illustrated that this fundamental shared consensus plays a vital part in the everyday choices and selection of stories. Thus, though the products that the broadcasters create are presented differently, the foundations on which they are built are very similar.

Within this chapter, I have explored ways in which news staff have explained one of the newsrooms' most frequently used phrases, '*that*'s a good news story'. In exploring the different definitions, I have identified eight primary factors that staff members see as key to a good news story. As the Eight Key Factors have been identified primarily through interviews, I find them most useful for studying how news workers express their values, rather than an absolute definition. Still, as I have found the values to be shared, explicitly, this could point towards a cross-broadcast and cross-practice community set of shared values. When essential values are shared, as argued by media researcher Kjøller: 'The substance in the news is the same from channel to channel, while they compete in the presentation of it' (Kjøller in Ahrens and Selliken 2007).

In my exploration of the idea of the 'good' journalist, I have illustrated how members of staff define 'good work' in two different ways, either focusing on the best practice, or on work that betters the world. The last of these two definitions is a central motivation for news staff to work in news. Staff discuss the ideal of bettering the world as very 'scout-like', and while they appear driven by an urge to better the world and encourage viewers to make a positive change, I have also identified at least two other motives for why staff enjoy working in news: A feeling of power and the chase for an adrenalin kick. I have characterised these two traits as belonging to the Power Tripper and the News Junkie.

Giving an illustration of what news staff term 'good' work, I have ended the chapter by presenting a script from ITV's News from *Zimbabwe Week*, which in many ways matches both the ideals of 'a good news story' and those of 'good' journalism.

Notes

1 I am indebted to Brian Winston for pointing me towards this quote (quoted in Winston 2003: 1).
2 Interview with DR Head of News, conducted in 1st floor meeting room at DR Byen, 10 January 2008.
3 Adding to the confusion, in a study of the textual use of the term 'Public Service', Mouritsen (2007) has pointed towards at least five different definitions generally used by the public and press alike. As Mouritsen concludes: 'The public service debate shows a striking disagreement about what the term actually means' (2007: 47, my translation from Danish by the author).
4 Five years after this exchange, Dohm became the head of DR, and five years later Haagerup left his job.
5 See Chapter 2.3 for the four questions and their order. I strived to ask all staff the exact same questions, in the exact same order during fieldwork. After these questions were posed, occasionally I found time to ask other questions, but I would always strive to commence an interview with these four.
6 Mentioned in conversation by BBC news journalists and directly in interviews with DR News Editor (19 June 2007), DR News Editor (26 June 2007) and DR Graphic (26 June 2007).
7 Schultz (2007) translates these criteria from the Danish as 'timeliness'.
8 In her study on news values in Danish television, using the theoretical framework of Bourdieu's reflexive sociology, Schultz (2007: 201–04) identifies what she terms 'the sixth news criteria' as 'exclusivity', as she finds the positioning of news stories a vital element to the everyday work of news journalists.

9   In her study of how journalists select news, Gravengaard (2010: 108) similarly points towards the journalist's feeling of being 'turned on' and being engaged by a story as central to a story being selected.

10 The issue of journalists choosing what is perceived as Our culture over the culture of Others is a topic worthy of much debate (see for instance Van Dijk 2009a, 2009b: 200; Said 1981).

11 Interestingly, in her study of DR Nyheder, Schultz (2006) also finds journalists mentioning their mother as an important imagined viewer of their news work.

12 When considering the definitions that I found during interviews with broadcast news staff in 2007–08 in relation to those of Galtung and Ruge (1965), which were decided on after content analysis of Norwegian newspapers in 1965, it should be noted that there are a number of methodological and historical differences between the two approaches, which makes direct comparison problematic.

13 DR Field book 1, p. 19.

14 Among the news workers at DR I met a former soldier who told me that he felt the adrenalin kick to be similar to being in battle. That 'adrenalin kick', he told me, was the main thing he loved about his work.

15 Script copied from ITV News' digital ENPS system. Written by scriptwriter and Programme Editor David Stanley, who has been responsible for writing the presenter lead-ins for ITV News for almost two decades.

Part VI

Exiting the Newsroom

Chapter 8

Conclusion: A Profession Under Pressure

On new struggles to reach old ideals and the future of TV journalism

The findings of this study have two connected themes. Firstly, the study shows how news divisions across the differently financed Public Service Broadcasters work in very similar ways. Secondly, the study shows how staff at all four news divisions share essential values, which they sense as increasingly under pressure. This book has presented journalists as experiencing current changes to news work as problematic for upholding values of journalistic professionalism. As journalists experience a mismatch between new working routines and shared values of professionalism, this book shows how everyday work can be defined as a constant struggle between the ideal and the real. It has been the aim throughout this book to be both descriptive and analytic in discussions of broadcast journalists at work. With this concluding chapter, I summarise key points, connect themes arising from the different chapters and suggest implications.

It has been central to the study to define values, and experiences of work from the journalists' point of view. The method of conducting participant observation has aided this approach in that I have had first-hand experience of the working routines in the field of study. The focus of analysis has been that of professionalism and practice communities. Using Wenger (1998a, 1998b) and Freidson (2005) professions theory has been coupled with the study of ideal typical values with a practice-focus. While professionalism is a much discussed theme in journalism studies (see for instance Deuze 2005; Alridge and Evetts 2003; Singer 2003, 2004; Witschge 2013), the ethnographic approach of this study thus presents a new practice focus for exploring professionalism at work among journalists today.

8.1 Connections Across Newsrooms

I began this study with the assumption that licence-fee funded news staff work in different ways compared to news staff employed at commercial broadcasters. This assumption may have been strengthened by the fact that an institutional bias of difference appears to exist at each news division – and as I have myself been working as a journalist at one of the broadcasters, I too was biased towards differences rather than similarities. Through empirical observations and analyses of interviews, I have shown how staff talk about each news division as being different, always in opposition to the competition. Despite news workers talking about crucial differences in working styles at different broadcasters, notably the licence-fee funded versus the commercial broadcasters, in practice I have found that staff at all four broadcasters work in very similar ways.

Based on observations from within the four different newsrooms, I reveal how newsroom layout and studios look increasingly similar. The study reveals that editors and management from all four news divisions are constantly connected and often visit each other in order to gain inspiration. The new circular newsroom and current news studio layouts are examples of mutual influence and of circulation of managerial practices among leading European broadcasters, particularly those in the core public service territories. While such circulation of spatial layout may also have taken place among newscasters in the past, today management have more ways of communicating, meet more often and visit each other's newsrooms to get inspiration. In this way, newsroom trends can easily be shared, which can help explain the many shared ways of working across broadcasters.

Discussing communities of practice, it has been shown how the different communities within newsrooms view themselves as connected through at least seven different layers of belonging, with the overarching levels of belonging being towards all working in TV news and all working in journalism. As the study illustrates, staff members from one broadcaster perceive a connection between themselves and *all* those working in journalism. The shared values of news journalism constitute the perceived bonds between different staff working in journalism, and these appear to be stronger than the perceived bond between those within the same practice community or those at the same broadcaster. Journalists at the four different newsrooms have been found to share language, key terms being the same across Denmark and the UK. Within all four newsrooms journalists have shared the same definitions of what makes a good news story. And when it comes to the motivation for working in news, staff have all been found driven by some or all of the traits of what I have defined as either the News Junkie, the Power Tripper or the Scout.

8.2 New Struggles to Reach Old Ideals?

The sketch (Fig. 8.1) was given to me during fieldwork by a graphic illustrator at DR TV Avisen. He had drawn and given the sketch to his superior, the Head of News, he told me, in order to illustrate how frustrated he often feels at work. According to the male graphic, the sketch shows him reaching up for the 'good' work, but being held down by the machines required for him to do his job. He entitled the sketch '*I'd like to, but…*' as a way of conveying that he is fully aware of what he would like to do, but is also aware that something outside of himself is preventing him from reaching those goals. The graphic showed me his illustration one day and described it as 'a good picture of how his work often feels'.[1]

The illustration above aptly illustrates the sense of struggle in adhering to professional ideals (cf. Freidson 2001), which I have heard news workers express at all four news divisions all throughout the last ten years of studying newsrooms. Though technology and online media changed much during 2007–17 staff never appeared to stop finding their work challenged by technology. As Channel 4 News Chief Writer, Felicity Spector, tells me in

Fig. 8.1: *Id like to, but…*, anon. graphic, DR newsroom.

December 2016 when I ask what she sees as the biggest challenges in her everyday work: 'making the technology work is still one of the biggest challenges'.

As such, the above illustration visualises a theme that has been ongoing throughout this book. While this particular graphic may have perceived slow and old machines to be the strongest obstacle holding him down from doing 'star-quality' work, other news workers have experienced other external and internal forces holding them down in their everyday work towards meeting the ideals of good work.

Early in 2007, I was present when presenters were told to begin doing blog posts. In 2017, both presenters and reporters are expected to use Twitter, Instagram or Snapchat to engage viewers in the broadcasters stories at all times during the day. Throughout the years 2007–17, most newsroom staff perceived their jobs to be under threat from forces both within and without the news division. Historically, staff at ITV and TV2 have had a competitive relation with the staff at Public Service Broadcasters, BBC and DR. Now, due to the rise in new media platforms and new news content providers, journalists working in traditional media newsrooms find that their jobs are threatened more than ever. At the same time, News Editors have begun to expect journalists to multi-skill in their job and create content on many different media platforms, both during, before and after a news report. During the last ten years multi-skilling has only been more and more encouraged. As well as producing a news item a reporter is now also expecting to produce updates on Twitter, use the newest Facebook features such as 'Going Live' and making a '360-degree video'.

A successful news story is not only one which has many viewers on TV but one that gets retweeted, shared, liked and commented on online. This new measure enforced internally has made particularly the older generation of journalists further fear for their jobs. Just like Freidson (2001) defines professionalism as being characterised by specialised knowledge and skill, journalists talk of multi-skilling as not suiting the traditional ideals, referring to traditional values in their rhetoric against the change in work demands (see Chapter 5.3).

Along with the constant threat to job positions within the news division, at the time of fieldwork staff appeared to be constantly struggling on many other fronts with regards to meeting ideals of good journalism. As described in Chapters 4 and 5, the newly designed newsroom and the new structure of meetings within the newsrooms make for important changes and challenges within the everyday work of news workers today. Viewing the new newsroom as an open stage upon which staff act out the role that they imagine their superiors want them to assume, the newsroom functions as both an agent for unity and an agent for control and surveillance of what staff do at work. While the open structure of the room has given more opportunity for collaboration and communication with colleagues, the new room has also taken away journalists' ability to be, act and work alone in the everyday. When journalists at the same time have an ideal of working in original and unique ways, the shared room can be seen as a challenge to this ideal. Referring to models of professionalism, I have argued that journalists may experience the restructured newsroom as a sign of mismatch between management ideals and journalistic ideals. As journalists perceive themselves as part of a profession, they expect editors and management to trust their work to be of a good quality and trust in professional 'self-control' (Freidson 2001: 34, also Fox 1974: 26–35). This expectation of discretion towards members of a profession is arguably countered by the new newsroom design, which enables ever more observation and control of journalists in the workplace.

The empirical data of this study has pointed towards the fact that this lack of private places within the new newsrooms adds to the news workers' sense of being observed and being always 'on' during the working day. As illustrated, when journalists feel an urge to behave out of the norm, they leave the room and go to spaces outside of the newsroom, such as toilets, the kitchen or a smokers' yard. Thus, in the everyday staff are constantly negotiating behaviour to suit the expectations within the newsroom.

While the idea of 'multi-skilling' among journalists is talked about as a threat to quality journalism, the notion of specialist units are talked about as crucial for delivering good in-depth content. During fieldwork journalists have been found to be grouped in specialism areas such as crime, business or health. These different specialism groups work as closely knit communities that are strengthened by their shared practice work. Drawing on theories of communities of practice (see Wenger 1998a) this study shows how such closely knit communities are important to journalists' identity.

The 'good news story' is a central value within all communities of practice in the newsroom. As the notion of 'the good news story' is often used to negotiate which stories to broadcast, it was crucial to analysis to attempt an identification of what the term means to journalists. While other journalism researchers have listed factors included in the 'good news story' from the point of view of news content, this study uses the journalists' own definitions of 'the good news story' in order to create a list of important factors. The factors identified as important to the good news story consist of eight key elements (see Chapter 7).

Of the eight elements described by staff as important for making a 'good news story', this study presents the last factor, that a story can 'help better the world', as particularly interesting. The journalists studied all appeared to have very high idealistic ideals of journalism's role in bettering society. This perceived role has been explained by staff as very 'scout-like'. While this study points towards journalists as driven by other motives, such as the feeling of powerfulness and the rush of adrenalin associated with working on a big story, observations have shown staff to be primarily driven by the 'scout' ideals of 'bettering the world'. Among the different practice communities at the different news divisions and broadcasters, I have been surprised to find an apparent agreement with the eight identified key factors for making a good news story. Staff members often referred to the eight factors for making a 'good news story' as 'traditional', 'classic' and 'old' values within journalism.

'You are only as good as your next news story!' – this phrase was often repeated both in jest and in all seriousness among news journalists and editors at all four broadcasters. Thus, though a journalist may have made an excellent news story, suiting all factors for a good news story, journalists never considered themselves capable of resting, nor did they ever consider their job to be done. Both in and out of working hours, staff members at the four news divisions were under a 'constant peer review' (see Chapter 6.3). The professional cloak of being a journalist has been described as one that cannot be shrugged off.

8.3 Methodological Considerations

With this study I have used fieldwork within national newsrooms of Denmark and Britain as cases for an analysis of the everyday work of broadcast journalists today. The choice of case and fieldwork methods no doubt impacts on conclusions. Likewise, the fact that the study was conducted by a former journalist may have affected conclusions. Choosing to use the theories from within the study of professions for analysis of empirical findings has both worked to open and to limit my understanding of the field. In the following, I address some of the limitations of the study and suggest ideas for future research.

Limitations of study

The research question, which guided fieldwork analysis, was a very open one (see the Introduction). Posing two such open questions has been both fruitful and limiting for research. The analysis of fieldwork has centred on exploring similarities among newsrooms and news journalists. Looking for similarities during analysis has limited the presentation and discussion of differences between broadcasters. Similarities and shared transorganisational values (Soloski 1989: 218) have become central in analysis of newsrooms, since I found this approach to convey the truest account of what I had observed during fieldwork. However, had I chosen to focus on the organisational and intraorganisational (Soloski 1989) values, the study would have been different. While I have found central shared values at all four newsrooms, it is important to note that the broadcasters display crucial differences in policy, organisation, economic models and historical foundations, which translate into differences within the newsrooms (as described in Chapter 3).

As discussed elsewhere (see Chapter 2), I see the access to and the acceptance by my field of study as created largely by the fact that I have worked as a broadcast journalist myself. I believe that having worked as a journalist gave me a practical insight, an ability to do participant observation and also enabled a certain connection with the field that I would not have had otherwise. Having been a journalist myself may have also attuned my research towards noticing similarities between newsrooms. However, the fact that I have myself been a part of the field may have also led to a few blind spots and sympathies, which non-journalists would not have shared. As an example, researchers who have never been in a newsroom would likely be interested in the language that news workers use. Having attended plenty of editorial meetings before I began fieldwork, I did not make a note of how much news workers swear during editorial meetings. To me, the ironic distancing to world events and frequent swearing was natural and uninteresting. Only late in the process of fieldwork, when I had decided to log word-by-word what was being said during an editorial meeting, did I realise how different the langue used in editorial meetings was from everyday language among non-news workers (see Chapter 6).

It is worth questioning whether the choice of four arguably elite, national public service newsrooms enables generalisations of the state of journalistic work. As Wahl-Jorgensen (2010) has argued, there is a tendency for research of news divisions to 'study up' and to stay in the fixed locality of the newsroom when doing ethnographic research.[2] As journalists today do not necessarily work inside the newsroom and have the ability to collaborate with the news division from outside of the newsroom, I have found it important to follow journalists in their work outside of the newsroom too. However, fieldwork has mostly taken place within the newsrooms. Thus, as is evident in my analysis, I too have come to have a certain 'Newsroom-Centricity' (Wahl-Jorgensen 2010). At the four national news bulletins studied, the newsroom is still a central place of work, as all primary staff members are asked to turn up for the morning meeting and be present at the debrief in the evening after each bulletins. With the broadcasters' own newsroom-centricity in mind, I believe the space of fieldwork to be justified. However, it would be interesting for future studies to spend less time in the newsroom and more outside it, away from management, editors and other factors which may work to hinder the staff's critical reflection on their work.

During the time of study I visited other broadcast newsrooms such as the newsrooms of Channel 4, Al Jazeera, Bloomberg News, Reuters London and print newsrooms such as *The Guardian* and *The Independent* in London and *Jyllands-Posten* in Denmark. At these other newsrooms I have encountered other working practices than those described within this book. Visiting other newsrooms than the four on which this study is based has shown me just how different working structures in print newsrooms and news agency newsrooms are compared to those in national public service broadcast newsrooms. However, while I have seen newsrooms structured differently across organisations, upon talking to journalists from different media organisations I have encountered strikingly similar perspectives and agreements to the ideals of journalistic professionalism that I outline.

During fieldwork I have experienced newsrooms to be restructured and re-organised. The rooms which I found during fieldwork are changing. In the words of Creswell: '[…] places are never complete, finished or bounded but are always becoming – in process. […] Places are constructed by people doing things and in this sense are never "finished" but are constantly being performed' (2004: 37). With this in mind, I believe that though my description and analysis concern the newsrooms of 2007–17, with the most experience-near insights given during fieldwork in 2007–08, it offers an insight with which to understand the newsrooms and newsroom practices of today. Although my case studies are newsroom-centric, limited to a specific time, and to the national newsrooms of BBC, ITV, DR and TV2 I believe it is possible to draw on my conclusions for a debate on the state of newsrooms and news journalists today.

8.4 Primary Contributions to the Research Field

In researching newsrooms and journalists, this study connects with the first wave of newsroom studies that had its heyday in the mid-1970s. However, methodologically the study proceeds from sociological research methods often favoured by this particular wave of newsroom studies, as the methodology has been developed within the framework of cultural anthropology. Aiming to create a situated knowledge based on participant observation among journalists at the above four newsrooms, I hope to have provided new insights into the everyday work of news workers today. Connecting this situated knowledge with theories of the profession has enabled me to analyse the observations of everyday work from a new perspective.

As this study has had an explicit interest in describing news work from the perspective of news workers rather than theories of news workers, it has been crucial that research questions were inspired by empirical findings. The danger of such research is that the empirical findings can single-handedly decide the focus of research. With this in mind, I have aimed to be constantly walking the thin edge between findings *in* the field and theory *of* the field. Rather than one theory being the foundation for my entire study, theories have worked as starting points for empirical research, which in turn led to theories *about* the empirical findings. It has therefore been crucial to have both an a priori research question and an a posteriori research question. Thus, I did not begin my study with an interest in professions, but in the light of empirical findings the professions perspective was found relevant for the analysis.

Will current challenges change TV news journalism?

As I returned to the newsrooms of BBC, ITV, DR and TV2 ten years after my first fieldwork visits, I was curious to ask staff what they saw as the biggest change in everyday at work. No doubt the biggest change felt by news staff comes in the shape of the Internet and the increasing mobile news platforms. By the end of 2017, the journalists I met in TV newsrooms where very aware of the falling TV news bulletin ratings. One evening in October 2017, after having presented the regional evening news, TV2 Anchor Man Jacob Rytz looks up at me and says: 'I feel more and more like a dinosaur sitting in my suit and makeup in this studio. People do not sit down and watch the TV news anymore. They watch it on Facebook. They want it quick, fast and superficial!'.

In 2017 news staff would often lament the declining number of viewers. However, while I saw plenty of digital changes and new innovative ways of using social media in the production and presentation of news, journalists did not talk of their job as being different to before. As a Deputy Programme Editor at ITN told me in December 2016, when I asked if anything had changed over the last ten years: 'Since you came to study the newsroom ten years ago, my job has not changed. Today I just have to do the same but even faster, even quicker than before'. But how exactly is change measured? And how does work practices, habits of a working routine and social structures become changed?

> Social structures are embedded in systems of meaning, value, belief and knowledge; such systems comprise the culture of an organization. To change an organization's structure, therefore, one must attend not only to rules, roles and relationships, but to systems of beliefs, values, and knowledge as well.
>
> (Schlechty 1990: xvi–xvii)

A similar point as the one above could be made in relation to the transorganisational (Soloski 1989: 218) group working within the profession of TV news journalism. Today, the traditional news journalism broadcasters BBC, ITV, DR and TV2 are being challenged both economically and politically from many fronts. As illustrated, TV news workers within the four news divisions perceive themselves to be challenged in their everyday work like never before. While the demands of an editor and management may have changed, the news worker struggles to become what s/he defines as being a 'good journalist'. However, the systems of belief which Schlechty writes of above, i.e. the close bonds among fellow journalists and the shared definition of being a 'good journalist' and making 'good news stories', appear to remain unchanged.

Will the current challenges change TV news journalism? During the last ten years, the four newscasters have changed their way of presenting news in so many ways, all centred around engaging the user more and using social media more. The news divisions must constantly strive to adapt to the wants of the news consumers and they must strive to follow the digital evolution. Staff with social media skills are constantly being prioritised. In all four of the newsrooms there are now reporters employed to publish work solely on social media and news apps. As Media Manager at ITV, Lincoln Hooper, told me in 2016: 'Social media is gradually taking the lion's share of consumers. We are constantly expanding that team and looking for new and innovative ways of attracting new viewers on mobile devices' (5 September 2016). At TV2 in Denmark, a news Programme Editor explains: 'if we did exactly the same today as we did five years ago then I'd be damned if anyone would watch us. No, we have to keep hitting people wherever they are' (interviewed 21 October 2016).

By the time this book is printed, the four newsrooms will no doubt all have changed their ways of presenting the news from how they did it in the Winter of 2017. The TV news programmes will keep on changing. However, I believe the primary change will be in the *presentation* of journalism. By and large the shared ideology of journalism however struggling will remain unchanged within the four news divisions for a period at least. In this sense, the change in journalism can primarily be observed on the surface, while the reasoning for content will be guided by the same shared systems of belief, values and shared knowledge illustrated within this book. The presentation of news may change while journalists will continue to legitimise their work through timeless values. Back in 2007, ITV's deputy editor explained this eloquently when I asked him to tell me what if anything, in the midst of newsroom changes, he thought would stay the same:

LHT: Now everything is changing [...] What stays the same in the new newsroom? Is there something which stays the same?

ITV DEPUTY EDITOR: Stories, storytelling, people. It should always be about the same things, it's about making a connection and making our programmes, making the news essential viewing for people. Making it important, relevant, vital for people to watch. And that should always be the same. Things will change, the amount of graphics that are used, whether the presenter stands up, sits down, new technology, interactivity – but the basic core is making stories that people care about, which affect them, which matter to them. That is the same, and that should always be the same.

(Deputy editor, ITV News, Grays Inn Road, London, interviewed in his office, overlooking the newsroom, 26 October 2007)

Apocalypse or opportunity?

The issue of whether to trust the media has often been raised over the last decade. As Donald Trump became president of the US in 2016/17, the term 'Fake News' was suddenly on the lips of all levels of society – both in jest and in all seriousness. Over the last decade, there has been an increase in critical discussion of the state of journalism both among academics, journalists and users of the news. It has been argued that the journalism profession is 'suffering from osteoporosis' after constant 'refractures' (Broersma 2013: 41–44). As discussed in the Introduction, a number of high profile controversies within the public service broadcast organisations – BBC and DR – have led to a public questioning of the professional values of public service journalism. With this study, it has been illustrated that though journalists struggle with the current challenges they have not lost their professional ideals. These ideals can be seen as traditional broadcast media's strongest selling point. Though the profession is at a critical point, I agree with the ideas put forward by scholars such as Alexander et al. (2016) (see also Schlesinger 2006; McNair 2013) who call for a reconsideration of the notion of a 'crisis' in journalism. As the Reuters Institute *Digital News Report 2017* report states: The future of journalism is not all doom and gloom – though there are increased cuts in traditional media, there are also numerous innovative approaches to journalism funding models and successful new ways (such as messaging apps) for traditional broadcasters to present news.

News journalism today is not the same as it once was. But the changes to journalism as we know it may not necessarily mean that the journalism profession is in a 'state of crisis'. As Schudson has pointed out: '[T]he blends and hybrids of journalistic coverage and commentary' can be seen as 'exciting and energizing, not the heralds of apocalypse' (Schudson 2013: 198). The current Head of News products at Google is one of today's optimists: 'The future of journalism can and will be better than its past', he has said (Richard Gingras in Briggs 2013: 2). While platforms such as Google and Facebook have an interesting market-driven approach to news, I am certain that there are also economic advantages in journalism driven by professional ideals. Indeed, the fact that journalists still strive towards ideals of journalistic professionalism can be seen as a sign of hope for the profession as a whole.

These are times of opportunity for the old media, particularly when journalists hold on to such ideological values as the ideals of professionalism presented within this study. Rather than leaving the ideologies of the profession behind in the race to follow new media demands, it will likely be fruitful to uphold the values of the profession. Arguably, ideals and goals, such as those of 'bettering the world' and providing 'a public service', are not the driving forces of the majority of new media news providers today, and thus the values of professionalism make the traditional broadcasters stand out in an ever fragmented media sphere. The current challenges to traditional media production could be seen as opportunities to strengthen the values of the profession, and as Broersma and Peters have suggested, view 'this public service element of journalism' as 'its definitive mission' (Broersma and Peters 2013: 11). While the advance in technology is creating new opportunities for producing and presenting news, technology is also one of the biggest challenges facing journalism today. As Chief Writer at Channel 4 News, Felicity Spector told me in December 2016: 'Today the information technology is really quick. In a way things are easier. But you can also easier be misled. Today curating of news and journalism is much more needed than ever'. Being curators of news that can be trusted is arguably one of the primary missions of traditional broadcasters today.

While I have seen newsrooms and news practices change over the course of fieldwork, I have not found the core values and ideals of 'good' journalism and the 'good news story' to change. In this way, the professional ideals of journalists can be seen as a strong ideology in line with Bloch's definition: 'One of the characteristic constitutive elements of ideology is the power to remain un-changed when other things are changing' (1989: 134).

The journalists I have studied are primarily driven by professional ideals. Management and editors alike would use this understanding of journalists when introducing new media tools in the newsroom. As Brady has argued: 'In too many newsrooms, these tools are introduced through training that's more technical in nature than journalistic' (2013: xvii). Digital tools and social media may be seen as a great new tool for collecting sources and cases, but at the same time journalists have been found to be sceptical and critical to the point where technology is perceived as contributing to a variety of tensions and potential conflicts within the newsroom (see also Chadha and Wells 2016). My study points towards journalists being interested primarily in making what they define as 'good journalism', not in using digital tools. Upon being introduced to new media tools the journalists may therefore be more interested if focus is on what these tools may do for the journalistic product, rather than what revenue it will bring. Ryfe (2006) has pointed out the following: 'Journalists tend to conflate the newspaper with journalism, and often react with moral indignation when their bosses do not honour their standards of quality. They can also become confused, even by relatively small changes and are often suspicious of their bosses' motives' (Ryfe 2012: 114). I see the suspicion pinpointed by Ryfe as closely linked to the perception among journalists that management does not share their ideals of journalistic professionalism. As this study reveals journalists to view professional ideals as a crucial motivation to work in news, it would no doubt aid management-journalist relations if management were to include and make use of these ideals in future organisational restructures.

Nossek has written of the future of journalism that the most imminent 'threat facing journalism is de-professionalization, which means that everyone can be a journalist and nobody actually is one' (2009: 358). With this study, I have shown how public service journalists define their professional values. Arguably, the biggest threat to traditional media is the loss of these and other values of professionalism. As discussed previously (see the Introduction and Chapter 1), news journalism can be regarded as crucial for democracy and as a key part of shaping an ideological foundation for how the world should be understood (Helland 2001: 231). If the media has a part to play in a democracy then it is of crucial importance to understand and lessen the struggle between working conditions and the ideals of good journalism practice displayed by public service journalists at work today.

The fact that journalists perceive their everyday work as a constant struggle towards reaching often unobtainable ideals may leave them feeling dissatisfied at work. As shown in the epilogue, I found that many of the most successful and idealistic journalists left their jobs within the time of fieldwork. Michael Schudson has characterised organisations such as *The Investigative News Network* as the natural place for journalists to go when they want to work 'without giving up the professional dedication that has sometimes, over the long century of its emergence, made journalism worth our highest regard' (Schudson 2013: 199).[3] While new organisations of journalists are increasing, if the journalists with the highest ideals of journalistic professionalism all leave the traditional media, public service journalism really is in a dire crisis. As shown through this book, those journalists who remain with the traditional broadcast media have not given up the struggle for their professional values. Should the journalists all give up their daily struggle to reach the old ideals of public service journalism this would no doubt affect not only the state of journalism but the state of democracy.

On future research

One of the primary shared values found among the four news divisions was that of being a 'good journalist' and making the 'good news story'. However, I also found other interesting similarities between the news divisions, which I chose not to include in my analysis.

I made a number of observations on gender and race representation within the news divisions, but as the issue of representation was not my primary focus, these observations were largely left out of my study. In journalism research, studies of representation have mainly focused on news content, rather than news production (see for instance Len-Ríos et al. 2005; Gertsema 2009). For research on gender representation in the news, however, I believe, with Van Zoonen (1988), that it is worthwhile to couple news content study with news production study. Studies and campaigns focusing on the issues of gendered broadcast content have had much success in engaging the media business (see Storm and Williams 2012; Cochrane 2012).[4] It would be a fruitful addition to the recent wave of newsroom studies to add to debates of newsroom culture an exploration of which cultures, which genders and which races can be said to play a central part of the news division.

I have been particularly interested in studying national news divisions with a public service remit. For further studies into journalism values and everyday practices, I believe it would be fruitful to study local newsrooms connecting the regions to the national broadcaster and print media newsrooms too. At a time of globalisation and ever expanding news casting, such regional journalism may provide a new bastion for audience engaged journalism. This study has revealed a close connection between management at the four different broadcasters, sharing both ideas for newsroom layout, studio design and news agency feeds. For further studies, it would be interesting to follow these connections further and investigate whether the similarities in working styles are limited to the four news divisions I have studied, or whether they extend further across national boundaries.[5]

Finally, you may ask for whom I wrote this book, journalists or journalism researchers? It is my hope that my study caters to both professions. I do not think it is the job of ethnographic analysis to provide companies (or countries) with ready-made suggestions as to how they could work better. Neither has it been my intention with writing this book that any of the broadcasters included should use it to restructure, reorganise or rearrange their ways of working. However, it is my hope that the study will give news workers and people interested in news a way of understanding how news workers work, by using the research as a window opening for new perspectives on current practices within the world of TV news making today.

Notes

1   As I took an interest in the illustration, the graphic was happy for me to use it.
2   Arguably, classical anthropology has been shaped on the principle that relatively powerful Western academics 'study down' on less powerful often poor and geographical distant groups. Compared to this classical anthropological approach I agree with Wahl-Jorgensen in that 'the cultural distance between researchers and reached in a newsroom ethnography derives from the practice of "studying up" [...]' (Wahl-Jorgensen 2010: 27).
3   There are now more than 70 member organisations of the Investigative News Network making possible collaboration of investigative journalism between what they describe as 'high-quality newsrooms' in the US (see investigativenewsnetwork.org).
4   I have found the work of organisations such as the Commission for Racial Equality, particularly the annual *Race in the Media Award*, to be important to the four news divisions studied. As British TV is still unrepresentative of its ethnic minorities, engaging in such debates is crucial (Creeber 2004). Also in the UK, the 2012 campaign *Expert Women*, led by City University's Director of Broadcasting Liz Howell and broadcast trade magazine *Broadcast*, has engaged both media practitioners and researchers in working towards a 30 per cent quota of female experts in broadcast content. In April 2012, the campaign led to the BBC Academy-funded organisation Fast Train running a master class to tackle the issues raised and train senior production freelancers in casting women experts. In journalism research, Melin's (2008) study of newsroom gender issues in Sweden and Britain has approached the issues of gender dominance in the newsroom from an interesting functionalist perspective.
5   After a presentation of this study at the European Communication Conference, ECREA (Thomsen 2008) a number of European journalism researchers suggested that the trend in newsroom design was much the same across national news divisions in the rest of Europe as in Denmark and the UK.

Epilogue

Ten years later

'My job has not changed in the last ten years. But I am expected to work even faster and produce even more. What you wrote in your Ph.D. is true, but today our challenges have many-doubled', a producer at ITN told me in the autumn of 2016. The initial fieldwork that inspired this book took place already in 2007. A lot has changed since then. But indeed, many of the past conflicts, struggles and new media challenges are still very much present today. As I returned to the newsrooms in 2017, staff appeared to be under even more pressure than back in 2007.

In 2007, the newsrooms studies were still getting to grips with new media, and the idea of doing things such as 'blogging' about a news piece. Some reporters and presenters were not keen on using the Internet for promoting news stories. Anger would rise at the suggestion that a story should be leaked on the broadcaster's online news-site before broadcast of the evening news bulletin, in the name of 'cross promotion'. Today, all journalists are expected to use social media strategically as part of promoting all news items produced. In 2007 and 2008, some news staff told me that they thought online news and social media would be the death of TV news. Today, ten years after staff appear certain that TV news is facing a new kind of existence, still TV staff seem do not seem worried about becoming extinct. As the newly appointed head of TV2 Nyhederne, Jacob Kwon, tells me in autumn 2016: 'TV is still by far the biggest media around when you talk about quality and income. TV news is far from dead or dying'.

Recently, I had a chance encounter that gave me a new realisation about the everyday struggle of working with such shared ideals of professionalism as those of the journalists I have portrayed. The ongoing struggle towards trying to make a difference and better the world, I realised, can for even the most highly positioned staff member feel so impossible that one has to exit the news profession.

I had taken the weekend off to spend time with my family. There we were, sat in an outdoor cafe by a forest mill just outside Aarhus, Denmark, when suddenly I saw a person from the London ITV Newsroom at a nearby table. In 2007 and 2008, when I conducted fieldwork at ITV, this particular news worker was enjoying a prominent position in the newsroom. Promoted from producer to assistant Programme Editor, he was very much a part of the decision-making for the flagship news bulletin of ITV. To me, at the time of my fieldwork he appeared very much an 'ITV-man' and I had no doubt he would be staying at that newsroom indefinitely.

Now in Aarhus, years after my fieldwork at ITV, the man stood up, walked towards me and said hello. It turned out he was in Denmark visiting a friend. I was keen to tell him of my project and to hear what he thought of my findings. But before I could tell him much he explained: 'I don't work in the news any more. I just didn't feel I could make a difference any more. So I felt I had to leave'. Finding out that this seemingly devoted and successful newsman would choose to leave his job was a big surprise to me. During the time I have spent working on this project, a number of journalists have left their jobs with similar explanations of not feeling able to make the difference that they once hoped to make. I had considered this particular employee too dedicated and well-positioned to want to leave news journalism.

The chance encounter made me remember how I too had left the newsroom at times when I had felt that I could not meet expectations within the room. I remembered how I left the newsroom to cry in the toilets during the tsunami in 2005. Just as I had been aware that I should leave the newsroom if I felt like behaving differently from what was expected of me as a staff member, this former ITV journalist had felt that his ideals of journalism had made it impossible to carry on working. To this particular news worker, though highly positioned within the news division, working towards meeting an ideal of doing 'good' journalism and 'making a difference' today had felt an impossible struggle.

Summary

TV Journalism - A Profession Under Pressure

This book takes its reader into the newsrooms of national news broadcasters in order to explore the everyday work of news journalists. The story I present is three-fold. Firstly, I present how different institutions define themselves always in opposition to their competitors. Secondly, I explain how, underneath these differences, there are shared ideals of good practice and a shared community of practice exists among all the news workers studied. Thirdly, this book illustrates how a tension exists between the shared professional ideal of good practice and the realities of the individual TV journalists at work. This tension between the reality of practice and ideals of practice is explored and illustrated, drawing on eighteen months unique access into the four largest national TV newsrooms of Britain and Denmark, with week-long, day-long or brief follow up visits and constant contact throughout a ten-year period.

This study reveals newsrooms and news journalists at differently financed Public Service Broadcasters to work in remarkably similar ways across Britain and Denmark. While staff at the commercial broadcast news divisions see their way of working as 'much better' than how a licence-fee funded news division works, licence-fee funded news staff have expressed a similar fear of becoming similar to the commercially funded broadcast news. However, this study has found shared values across all four Public Service Broadcasters, which guide the way that news workers choose and select which events to cover as stories. These overarching shared values make the main differences between the licence-funded and the commercially funded Public Service Broadcasters primarily one of imagined differences and differences in presenting news.

I have studied the shared ideals of journalists with a focus on professional values. Exploring the shared professional ideals of journalists the study analyses what journalists perceive as doing 'good work' and working towards the 'good story'. When asked, news workers often explain the shared way of working across broadcasters with the fact that they all share the same idea of what is 'good journalism' and what is a 'good news story'. This book explores the idea of shared professional values and concludes that news workers across newsrooms and broadcasters share much the same definitions of what 'good' news stories are and what makes a 'good' journalist – a definition which they daily struggle to reach.

A key factor of the shared ideals is that journalism is done to better the world, educate the people and hold authorities accountable on behalf of the people. The fact that I have found many shared ideals of wanting to better the world and supporting democracy among all the TV news workers contradicts ideas of news making today as being organised around rational, economic, modernist values. However, it is shown how journalists experience the restructure of the newsroom and restructure of news work as driven by a market logic which does not match the professional logic by which journalists are driven in their everyday work.

With a central interest in the everyday work inside the newsrooms, the study emphasises the way news workers talk about their work, the way that I have experienced staff as working, as well as the way their work is structured in time and place. While focus is not on content but on content production, in my exploration of what a 'good news story' is, I introduce examples of content that staff refer to as 'good work'. Thus, my analysis takes into account multiple factors shaping the journalists' identity while at work. The study points towards the importance of including explorations of locations, situations, observations and experiences of everyday practices in studies of journalists at work. This multi-levelled analysis is unusual in current journalism studies. Using ethnographic methods of long periods of participant observation it is the aim of this book to suggest new ways of studying journalists and supplying new insights into the everyday reality of TV news journalists today.

Appendix

Words and phrases used within the news divisions

In compiling this list I am indebted to news workers who have taken time to patiently describe their phrases to me. For the Danish list, I am indebted to a female producer at DR TV Avisen who shared with me a list she had made of words which might be new 'for the uninitiated'. The list (in Danish entitled 'Fagudtryk') had primarily been made for a new presenters who asked for a translation of the many news terms (according to email correspondence, 19 June 2007).

Inside the different newsrooms in Denmark and the UK, I have found a very similar language used, using English terms, acronyms or slang. Throughout this book I have strived to use the same words and phrases as the news workers as I find them crucial 'experience near' concepts (Geertz 1983). Below is a vocabulary of news worker-defined terms that I have found used, firstly across all four newsrooms, and secondly in specific newsrooms and countries. Danish staff may adapt the English words to suit the Danish language by changing the ending of an English term or by using an entire English phrase as one noun.

A) **Technical words and phrases shared across all four newsrooms:**

Attack: When a news item starts without introduction from a presenter.

Cut and Tail: A phrase British television journalists often use for the job of cutting the beginning and the end of a video feed – this most simple of news editing can today be done by news workers at their desk, as all computers (in the newsrooms I visited) are equipped with basic editing tools.

Cut away: A type of camera shot which is talked about as 'essential' for the journalist to have to make a news item. A single shot of a key object in the story, in which the camera literally moves away from the object. Thus a 'Cut-away' is thought to give the viewer a distance from the object, which is helpful to use as an aid for a script which moves away from a certain object or case-study.

Feed: A supply of broadcast programme items. These often arrive to the newsroom over a remote connection such as ISDN, satellite or mobile links vehicle.

Intro: The beginning of the news bulletin.

KGN: Text with names of people and places on screen.

Outside Broadcast OB: Doing 'an OB' refers to the making of a live radio or TV broadcast of an event, via a Satellite Newsgathering vehicle (SNG) to be used in a TV news bulletin.

Outro: The end of the news bulletin.

Prompter: The machine which runs all the text for the newsreader/presenter to read from the studio.

Running order: The order of the entire news bulletin in a schematic form, which is worked on and viewed on a computer. All staff working for the news bulletin can access its Running Order. Some of the staff can add text or film to the running order but only a few, such as the Programme Editor and News Editor can delete material from a running order.

Rushes: Raw footage. When a reporter and cameraman have been out on a shoot they may return to the newsroom with many tapes of rushes, out of which only a small part will be used for the final news piece. The full rushes are rarely shared with anyone except the journalist and cameraman/editor of the piece. However, in September 2011, the BBC, ITN and Sky News were reportedly forced to hand over hundreds of hours of non-broadcast footage of the UK riots in August 2011, after being served with court orders by the police.

SNG: Satellite Newsgathering. Reporters and cameramen drive off in SNG vehicles when they are requested to do Outside Broadcast (OB) at live events, rather than doing a pre-recorded story.

Speak: When a presenter speaks when not shown in vision. Same as a Voice Over (VO).

SYNC: A soundbite with 100% sound from the server.

Ulay: Short for 'underlay'. A news item made up of pre-edited video with no sound, which will be commentated by the news presenter, as he reads up the pre-written text from the autocue.

Voice Over (VO): When the news presenter speaks while pictures (here 'a Ulay') are shown on screen.

B) Other newsrooms phrases or words:

A Dream Team: At DR, this phrase was used about specific teams of reporter and cameraman who would work together. A Dream Team cameraman would collaborate more with the reporter than others and join editorial meetings that other cameramen did not.

A 'Big News Day': In all newsrooms, this term was used to describe a day of a very big event, which will be remembered for years to come.

A Just-Fucking-Do-It-Reporter: At ITV, this description was given to young reporters who can also film.

Nouse: Both at ITV and BBC this somewhat ambiguous but overall very highly valued term was used among English news staff. Being a pun on the word 'news' and 'nose', it is used as a term for someone with a very good sense of news stories.

Rent-a-gob: This term is used by news workers in reference to a person who is often used as an expert and who is known to journalists as talking a lot. May charge the broadcaster for appearing.

References

Abu-Ludghod, L. (1995), 'The objects of soap opera: Egyptian television and the cultural politics of modernity', in D. Miller (ed.), *Worlds Apart*, London: Routledge, pp. 190–210.

Agar, Michael H. (1986), *Speaking of Ethnography*, London: Sage Publications.

Ahrens, M. M. and Selliken, K. K. (2007), 'Fra Træmand til TV-stjerner', *Berlingske Tidende*, 21 January, http://www.business.dk/fra-traemaend-til-TV-stjerner. Accessed 1 July 2011.

Aldridge, M. and Evetts, J. (2003), 'Rethinking the concept of professionalism: The case of journalism', *The British Journal of Sociology*, 54:4, December, pp. 547–64.

Allan, S. (2004), *News Culture – Issues in Cultural and Media Studies*, Berkshire: Open University Press.

Alexander, J. C., Butler-Breese, E. B. and Luengo, M. (eds) (2016), *The Crisis of Journalism*, New York: Cambridge University Press.

Allison, M. (1986), 'A literature review of approaches to the professionalism of journalists', *Journal of Mass Media Ethics*, 1:2, pp. 5–9.

Aitheide, D. L. (1976), *Creating Reality: How TV News Distorts Events*, Beverly Hills and London: Sage Publications.

Alvehus, J. (1999), *Mötets metaforer: En studie av berättelser om möten*, Linköping: Instititionen för datavetenskap, Linköpings universitet.

Anderson, C. W. (2009), 'Breaking journalism down: Work, authority and networking local news, 1997–2009, unpublished doctoral dissertation, New York: Columbia University.

—— (2010), 'Journalistic networks and the diffusion of local news: The brief, happy news life of the Francisville Four', *Political Communication*, 27:3, pp. 289–309.

—— (2011a), 'Blowing up the newsroom: Ethnography in an age of distributed journalism', C. Paterson and D. Domingo (eds), *Making Online News – Vol 2: News Ethnography in the Second Decade of Internet Journalism*, New York: Peter Lang Publishing, pp. 151–60.

—— (2011b), 'Between creative and quantified audiences: Web metrics and changing patterns of newswork in local US newsrooms', *Journalism*, 12, p. 550.

Arlidge, J. (2002), 'Dyke's new mantra for the future BBC: Only connect', *The Observer*, 6 January, http://media.guardian.co.uk/bbc/story/0,7521,628842,00.html. Accessed 21 February 2002.

Arpi, S. (2004), *De Nære Nyheder: Et casestudium af TV2/Nyhedernes journalistik*, Roskilde: Roskilde Universitetsforlag.

Askew, K. (2002), 'Introduction', in R. R. Wilk and K. Askew (eds) (2002), *The Anthropology of Media: A Reader*, Malden and Oxford: Blackwell Publishers Ltd, pp. 1–14.

Askew, K. and Wilk, R. R. (eds) (2002), *The Anthropology of Media – A Reader*, Oxford: Blackwell.

Asmussen, K. and Meilby, M. (1977), *Før Deadline: Dagblads-journalistikkens grundtrin*, Aarhus: Institut for Presseforskning, Danmarks Journalisthøjskole.

Atton, C. (2002), *Alternative Media*, London: Sage.

—— (2009), 'Alternative and citizen journalism', in K. Wahl-Jorgensen and T. Hanitzsch (eds), *The Handbook of Journalism Studies*, New York: Routledge, pp. 265–78.

Atton, C. and Hamilton, J. F. (2008), *Alternative Journalism*, London: Sage.

Bak, A. (2007), 'Nyheder i Øjenhøjde', *Prent*: *Avisen I Undervisningen*, November, Svendborg: Svendborg Tryk.

Bakhtin, M. M. (1981), *The Dialogic Imagination: Four Essays* (ed. by M. Holquist, trans. C. Emerson and M. Holquist), Austin: University of Texas Press.

Bantz, C., McCorkle, S. and Baade, R. C. (1980), 'The news factory', *Communication Research*, 7:1, pp. 45–68.

Barber, B. (1965), 'Some problems in the sociology of the professions', in S. L. Kenneth (ed.), *The Professions in America*, Boston: Houghton Mifflin, pp. 15–34.

Bardoel, J. and Deuze, M. (2001), 'Network journalism: Converging competencies of old and new media professionals', *Australian Journalism Review*, 23:2, pp. 197–03.

Barnhurst, K. G. (2013), 'Trust me, I'm an innovative journalist', in C. Peters and M. Broersma (eds), *Rethinking Journalism: Trust and Participation in a Transformed News Landscape*, London and New York: Routledge, pp. 210–20.

Barth, F. (1969), *Ethnic Groups and Boundaries*, Boston: Little, Brown and Company.

—— (1989), 'The analysis of culture in complex societies', *Ethnos*, 54:3, 120–42.

—— (1993), *Balinese Worlds*, Chicago and London: The University of Chicago Press.

—— (1994), *Manifestasjon og Prosess*, Oslo: Universitetsforlaget, Det Blå Bibliotek.

Bate, S. P. (1997), 'Whatever happened to organizational anthropology? A review of the field of organizational ethnography and anthropological studies', *Human Relations*, 50:9, 1147–75.

Bauman, Z. ([1998] 2001), *Globalisering: De Menneskelige Konsekvenser*, Copenhagen: Hans Reitzel.

BBC (2012), 'The BBC Story: 1920s', BBC, http://www.bbc.co.uk/historyofthebbc/resources/factsheets/1920s.pdf. Accessed 2 March 2012.

BBC Trust (2007), *Public Purpose Remit: Representing the UK, Its Nations, Regions and Communities*, London: BBC Trust, http://www.bbc.co.uk/bbctrust/assets/files/pdf/about/how_we_govern/purpose_remits/nations.pdf. Accessed 24 June 2012.

—— (2011), 'Annual Report and Accounts 2010–2011', Presented to Parliament by the Secretary of State for Culture, Olympics, Media and Sport by command of Her Majesty, London: BBC Trust, www.bbc.co.uk/annualreport. Accessed 26 March 2012.

—— (2012), 'Governance Framework', *BBC Trust online*, http://www.bbc.co.uk/bbctrust/about/how_we_govern/charter_and_agreement/index.shtml. Accessed 26 March 2012.

Bechmann, A. (2007), 'Realizing cross-media', in T. Storsul and D. Stuedahl (eds), *Ambivalence towards Convergence: Digitalization and Media Change*, NORDICOM, pp. 57–72.

—— (2009), 'Crossmedia: Innovationsnetværk for traditionelle medieorganisationer', Ph.D. thesis submitted to the Department of Media and Information Studies. Aarhus: SUN-TRYK.

————— (2011), 'Closer apart? The networks of cross-media news production', in D. Domingo and C. Paterson (eds), *Making Online News 2: Newsroom Ethnographies in the Second Decade of Internet Journalism. Vol. 2.* New York: Peter Lang, pp. 15–29.

————— (2012), 'Towards cross-platform business models: Four patterns of circulation and control', *Information, Communication and Society*, 15:6, pp. 888–908.

Becker, H. S. (1964), 'Problems in the publication of field studies', in A. J. Vidich, J. Bensman and M. R. Stein (eds), *Reflection on Community Studies*, New York: Wiley, pp. 267–84.

Bell, M. (2003), *Through Gates of Fire*, London: Weidenfeld and Nicolson.

Bennett, T. (1982), 'Media, "Reality", Signification', in M. Gurevitch, T. Benett, J. Curran and J. Wollacott (eds) (1996), *Culture, Society and the Media*, London: Methuen, pp. 285–307.

Berghahn Books online (2011), 'Berghahn Series', http://www.berghahnbooks.com/series.php?pg=anthro_media. Accessed 16 October 2017.

Bernstein, C. (1992), 'The idiot culture', *The New Republic*, 8 June, pp. 22–28.

Bird, E. S. (2010a), 'The anthropology of news and journalism, why now?', in E. S. Bird (ed.), *The Anthropology of News & Journalism: Global Perspectives*, Bloomington: Indiana University Press.

————— (ed.) (2010b), *The Anthropology of News and Journalism*, Bloomington: Indiana University Press.

Bjerlöf, M. (1999), *Om lärande i verksamhetsanknutna samtal. En studie av prat och lärande i möten på en arbetsplats*, Stockholm: Arbetslivsinstitutet.

Blankenship, J. C. (2016), 'Losing their "MOJO"?', *Journalism Practice*, 10:8, pp. 1055–71.

Bloch, M. (1989), *Ritual, History and Power: Selected Papers in Anthropology*, London: Athlone.

Blumer, H. (1954), 'What is wrong with social theory?', *American Sociological Review*, 18, pp. 3–10.

Blumler, J. G. (2010), 'Foreword', *Journalism Practice*, 4:3, pp. 243–45.

Boczkowski, P. J. (2004), *Digitizing the News: Innovation in Online Newspapers*, Cambridge: MIT Press.

Bogart, L. (1991), 'The American media system and its commercial culture', *Media Studies Journal*, 5:4, 13–33.

————— (2000), *Commercial Culture: The Media System and the Public Interest*, Oxford: Oxford University Press.

Bonde, J. (1998), 'En kritisk analyse af TV, Dansk efterskrift', *Om TV – og journalistikkens magt* (ed. M. Bourdieu, trans. K. Nicolaisen), Copenhagen: Tiderne Skifter.

Born, G. (2004), *Uncertain Vision: Birt, Dyke and the Reinvention of the BBC*, London: Vintage.

Bourdieu, P. (1986), 'The forms of capital', in J. G. Richardson (ed.), *Handbook for Theory and Research for the Sociology of Education*, New York: Greenwood, pp. 241–58.

————— (1996), *Symbolsk Makt: Artikler I utvalg*, Oslo: Pax Forlag A/S.

Bourdieu, P. and Passeron, J.-C. ([1977] 2000), *Reproduction in Education, Society and Culture*, London: Sage.

Brady, J. (2013), 'Foreword', in M. Briggs (ed.), *Journalism Next: A Practical Guide to Digital Reporting and Publishing*, 2nd ed., Thousand Oakes: Sage, pp. xv–xviii.

Brante, T. (1989), 'Professioners identitet och samhälliga vilkor', in S. Selander (ed.), *Kampen om yrkesutövning, status och kunskap: Professionaliseringens sociala grund*, Lund: Studenterlitteratur, pp. 37–55.

—— (2001), 'Staten og Professionerne', in T. R. Eriksen and A. M. Jørgensen (eds), *Professionsidentitet i Forandring*, Copenhagen: Akademisk Forlag, pp. 16–35.

—— (2010), 'Professional fields and truth regimes: In search of alternative approaches', *Comparative Sociology*, 9, pp. 843–86.

Breed, W. (1955), 'Social control in the newsroom: A functional analysis', *Social Forces*, 33:4, pp. 326–35.

Brevini, B. (2012), 'Southern European Public Service Broadcasters expanding online: A policy study of RAI and RTVE's online activities', M. Burns and N. Brügger (eds), *Histories of Public Service Broadcasters on the Web*, New York: Peter Lang Publishing, pp. 118–34.

Briggs, A. (1995), *The History of Broadcasting in the United Kingdom (Volume 1–5)*, Oxford: Oxford University Press.

Briggs, M. (2013), *Journalism Next: A Practical Guide to Digital Reporting and Publishing*, 2nd ed., Thousand Oaks: Sage.

Broadcast Magazine (2009), 'BDA graphics give ITV News "human element"', *Broadcast Magazine online*, http://www.broadcastnow.co.uk/technology/bda-graphics-give-iTV-news-human-element/5007726.article. Accessed 21 July 2011.

Broersma, M. (2013), 'A refractured Paradigm: Journalism, hoaxes and the challenge of trust', in C. Peters and M. Broersma (eds), *Rethinking Journalism: Trust and Participation in a Transformed News Landscape*, London and New York: Routledge, pp. 28–44.

Broersma, Marcel and Peters, Chris (2013), 'Introduction', in C. Peters and M. Broersma (eds.), *Rethinking Journalism: Trust and Participation in a Transformed News Landscape*, London and New York: Routledge, pp. 1–12.

Brook, Stephen (2007), 'Horrocks: "Strong support" for BBC industrial action', *The Guardian Online*, 27 September, http://www.guardian.co.uk/media/2007/sep/25/bbc.television1. Accessed 2 November 2011.

Greenslade, Roy (2016), 'BBC websites dominate the market in Online News views', *The Guardian Online*, 9 February, https://www.theguardian.com/media/greenslade/2016/feb/09/bbc-websites-dominate-the-market-in-online-news-views. Accessed 10 October 2017.

Brügger, N. (2012), 'The idea of public service in the early history of DR online', in M. Burns and N. Brügger (eds), *Histories of Public Service Broadcasters on the Web*, New York: Peter Lang Publishing, pp. 91–104.

Bruun-Hansen, K. (2014), 'Fyret Nils Lindvig nægter at blive væk fra DR', *Journalisten.dk*, 16 October, http://journalisten.dk/fyret-niels-lindvig-naegter-blive-vaek-fra-dr. Accessed 10 October 2017.

—— (2016), 'Mød de Usynlige Korrespondenter', *Journalisten*, 5 April, http://journalisten.dk/moed-de-usynlige-korrespondenter#.VwTKitotKGo.facebook. Accessed on 9 October 2016.

Buchanan, D., Boddy, D. and McCalman, J. (1988), 'Getting in, getting on, getting out and getting back', in A. Bryman (ed.), *Doing Research in Organizations*, London and New York: Routledge, pp. 53–67.

Burns, T. (1977), *The BBC: Public Institution and Private World*, London: Macmillan.

Campbell, L. M., Gray, N. J., Meletis, Z. A., Abott, J. G. and Silver, J. J. (2010), 'Gatekeepers and keymasters: Dynamic relationships of access in geographical fieldwork', *Geographical Review*, 96: 1, pp. 97–121.

Carey, J. W. (1998), 'Political ritual on television', in T. Liebes, J. Curran and E. Katz (eds), *Media, Ritual, and Identity*, London: Routledge, pp. 42–70.

—— (2007), 'A short history of journalism for journalists', *The Harvard International Journal of Press and Politics*, 12:3, pp. 3–16.

Chadha, K. and Wells, R. (2016), 'Journalistic responses to technological innovation in newsrooms', *Digital Journalism*, 4:88, pp. 1020–35.

Chalaby, J. (1998), *The Invention of Journalism*, New York: St. Martin's Press.

Chapman, J. (2008), 'Broadcast journalism: Yesterday, today and the future', in J. Chapman and M. Kinsey (eds), *Broadcast Journalism: A critical Introduction*, London: Taylor Francis, pp. 7–16.

Chapman, J. and Kinsey, M. (2008), *Broadcast Journalism: A Critical Introduction*, London: Taylor Francis.

Charmaz, K. (1983), 'The grounded theory method: An explication and interpretation', in R. Emmerson (ed.), *Contemporary Field Research*, Prospect Heights: Waveland Press, pp. 109–26.

Charles, A. (2014), *The End of Journalism- Version 2.0: Industry, Technology and Politics*, Oxford: Peter Lang Ltd.

Churnalism.com (2012), 'Frequently Asked Questions', www.churnalism.com/faq/. Accessed 12 January 2012.

Clausen, L. (2001), *Global News Production*, Copenhagen: Copenhagen Business School Press.

Clifford, J. and Marcus, G. E. (1986), *Writing Culture*, Berkeley: University of California Press.

Cochrane, K. (2012), 'Women's representation in media: Who's running the show?', *The Guardian Online*, http://www.guardian.co.uk/news/datablog/2011/dec/06/women-representation-media#data. Accessed 30 April 2012.

Coman, M. (2005), 'Cultural anthropology and mass media – A processual approach', in E. Rothenbuhler and M. Coman (eds), *Media Anthropology*, London: Sage, pp. 46–56.

Conboy, M. (2011), *Journalism in Britain: A Historical Introduction*, London: Sage.

Conlan, T. (2008), 'BBC 10pm news audience is double ITV's', *The Guardian Media Section*, 17 April, http://www.guardian.co.uk/media/2008/apr/17/TVnews.television. Accessed 19 July 2011.

Conlan, T. and Topping, A. (2010), 'Real spend of high-tech BBC newsroom set to be revealed', *The Guardian Online*, 22 February, http://www.guardian.co.uk/media/2010/feb/22/bbc-spend-broadcast-newsroom-revealed. Accessed 21 June 2012.

Cook, T. (1998), *Governing with the News: The News Media as a Political Institution*, Chicago: Chicago University Press.

Cottle, S. (1999), 'From BBC newsroom to BBC newscentre: Changing news technologies and changing journalist practices', *Convergence*, 5, pp. 22–43.

—— (2000), 'New(s) times: Towards a 'second wave' of news ethnography', *Communications*, 25, pp. 19–42.

—— (2001), 'Rethinking news access', *Journalism Studies*, 1:3, pp. 427–48.

—— (2007), 'Ethnography and news production: New(s) developments in the field', *Sociology Compass*, 1:1, pp. 1–16.

Couldry, N. (2005), 'Media rituals: Beyond functionalism', in E. Rothenbuhler and M. Coman (eds), *Media Anthropology*, London: Sage, pp. 59–69.

Couldry, N. and McCarthy, A. (eds) (2005), *MediaSpace: Place, Scale and Culture in Media Age*, London: Routledge.

Creeber, G. (2004), '"Hideously white": British television, glocalization and national identity', *Television New Media*, 5:27, pp. 27–39.

Creswell, T. (2004), *Place: A Short Introduction*, Coventry: Blackwell Publishing.

Crossley-Holland, D. (2004), 'Dominic Crossley-Holland Diary', *Press Gazette*, 27 February, http://www.pressgazette.co.uk/story.asp?storyCode=28608&sectioncode=1. Accessed 26 June 2012.

Crouch, T. (1973), *Boys on the Bus*, New York: Ballantine Books.

Curran, J. and Seaton, J. (1997), *Power without Responsibility: The Press and Broadcasting in Britain*, London: Routledge.

Curran, J. and Gurevitch, M. (1996), *Mass Media and Society*, London: Arnold.

Currie, R. (2011), 'Freedom of Information Request – RFI20110015', 2 February, London: BBC Information, Policy & Compliance Office.

Cushion, S. (2012), *Television Journalism. Journalism Studies: Key Texts*, London: Sage.

Dahl, H. M. (2005), 'Fra en klassisk til en (post?)moderne opfattelse af professioner?', in T. R. Eriksen and A. M. Jørgensen, *Professionsidentitet i Forandring*, Copenhagen: Akademisk Forlag, pp. 36–57.

Dahle, R. (2008), 'Profesjon og kjønn', in A. Molander and L. I. Terum (eds), *Profesjonstudier*, Oslo: Universitetsforlaget, pp. 216–32.

Daily Mail Reporter (2011), 'BBC beats ITV in ratings war (but Royal Wedding audience only just tops an episode of Only Fools And Horses)', *The Daily Mail*, 2 May, http://www.dailymail.co.uk/news/article-1382589/Royal-wedding-ratings-BBC-beats-ITV-audience-just-tops-Only-Fools-And-Horses.html#ixzz1VTW7Eopn. Accessed 12 August 2011.

Das, V. (1995), 'On soap opera. What kind of anthropological object is it?', in D. Miller (ed.), *Worlds Apart*, London: Routledge, pp. 190–210.

Davies, N. (2009), *Flat Earth News: An Award-winning Reporter Exposes Falsehood, Distortion and Propaganda in the Global News*, London: Vintage Books.

Dayan, D. and Katz, E. (1992), *Media Events – The Live Broadcasting of History*, Cambridge: Harvard University Press.

Delaney, C. and Kaspin, D. (2011), *Investigating Culture: An Experiential Introduction to Anthropology*, 2nd ed., West Sussex: John Wiley & Sons.

Denzin, N. K. (1970), *The Research Act in Sociology*, Chicago: Aldine.

——— (1989), *Interpretive Interactionism*, Newbury Park: Sage.

Deuze, M. (2002), 'National news cultures: A comparison of Dutch, German, British, Australian and US journalists', *Journalism Quarterly*, 79:1, pp. 134–49.

——— (2004), 'What is multimedia journalism?', *Journalism Studies*, 5:2, pp. 139–52.

——— (2005), 'What is journalism?: Professional identity and ideology of journalists reconsidered', *Journalism*, 6, p. 442.

——— (2007), *Media Work*, Cambridge: Polity Press.

——— (2008), 'Understanding journalism as newswork: How it changes, and how it remains the same', *Westminster Papers in Communication and Culture*, 5:2, pp. 4–23.

——— (2009) 'Convergence Culture and Media Work', in A. Perren and J. Holt (eds), *Media Industries: History, Method, and Theory*, Malden: Blackwell, pp. 144–56.

────── (2011), 'What is journalism?: Professional identity and ideology of journalists reconsidered', in D. A. Berkowitz (ed.), *Cultural Meanings of News: A Text Reader*, London: Sage, pp. 17–32.

Deuze, M. and Paulussen, S. (2002), 'Online journalism in the low countries: Basic occupational and professional characteristics of online journalists in Flanders and the Netherlands', *European Journal of Communication*, 17, pp. 237–46.

Dickey, S. (1993), *Cinema and the Urban Poor in South India*, Cambridge: Cambridge University Press.

────── (1997), 'Anthropology and its contributions to studies of mass media', *International Science Journal*, 49:153, pp. 413–27.

────── (2001), 'Opposing faces: Film star fan clubs and the construction of class identities in South India', in R. Dwyer and C. Pinney (eds), *Pleasure and the Nation*, Delhi: Oxford University Press, pp. 212–46.

Domingo, D. (2006), 'Inventing online journalism. Development of the Internet as a news medium in four Catalan online newsrooms', Ph.D. thesis, Universitat Autonoma de Barcelona.

────── (2008), 'When immediacy rules: Online journalism models in four Catalan online newsrooms', in C. Patersson and D. Domingo (eds), *Making Online News: The Ethnography of New Media Production*, New York: Peter Lang Publishing Inc, pp. 113–26.

Domingo, D. and Paterson, C. (eds) (2008), Making Online News: The Ethnography of New Media Production, New York: Peter Lang Publishing.

Doyle, G. (2006), 'Financial news journalism: A post-Enron analysis of approaches towards economic and financial news production in the UK', *Journalism*, 7:4, pp. 433–52.

DR Byen (2006), *Ny Strategi for TV Avisen: Skarp og Nærværende. TV Avisen 2007-2009*, November, Copenhagen: DR Byen.

DR P1 (2009), 'Jensen (Jesper Bo talking to host Poul Friis)', *P1 Formiddag*, 31 March.

DR TV Avisen online (2011), 'TV AVISEN- moderne og begavet', *DR.dk*, http://www.dr.dk/DR1/TVAVISEN/2011/0518142723.htm. Accessed 29 March 2012.

Drucker, P. F. (1966), *The Effective Executive*, New York: Harper & Row.

────── (1974), *Management*, New York: Harper & Row.

Drummond, L. (1996), *American Dreamtime: A Cultural Analysis of Popular Movies, and Their Implications for a Science of Humanity*, Lanham: Rowman & Littlefield.

Duhe, S. F., Mortimer, M. and Chow, S. S. (2004), 'Convergence in TV-newsrooms: A nationwide look', *Convergence*, 10:2, pp. 81–104.

Dyrby, M. (2009), 'Respons fra TV2 Nyhederne', presented for the debate section entitled: 'Hvad er (god) Public Service på nyheds- og aktualitetsområdet – nu og i fremtiden?', *Public Service-de ti Bud*, CBS, 28 January.

Ehn, B. and Löfgren, O. ([2001] 2006), *Kultur-analyser*, Århus: Forlaget Klim.

Eide, M. (2001a), 'Journalistisk Makt', in M. Eide (ed.), *Til Dagsorden! Journalistikk, makt og demokrati: Makt- og demokratiutredningen, 1998-2004*, Oslo: Gyldendal Norsk Forlag, pp. 13–59.

────── (ed.) (2001b), *Til Dagsorden! Journalistikk, makt og demokrati: Makt- og demokrati utredningen, 1998–2004*, Oslo: Gyldendal Norsk Forlag.

Elliott, P. (1977), 'Media organizations and occupations: An overview', in J. Curran, M. Gurevitch, T. Bennet and J. Woollacott (eds), *Mass Communication and Society*, London: Arnold, pp. 142–73.

Epstein, E. J. (1973), *News from Nowhere: Television and the News*, New York: Random House.

Erdal, I. J. (2007), 'Researching media convergence and crossmedia news production: Mapping the field', *Nordicom Review*, 28:2, pp. 51–61.

——— (2008), 'Cross-media news journalism: institutional, professional and textual strategies and practices in multi-platform news production', Doctoral thesis submitted for the degree of Ph.D. Faculty of Humanities, University of Oslo, March, http://www.duo.uio.no/publ/mediekomm/2008/85738/85738_erdal.pdf. Accessed 20 October 2011.

Ericson, R., Baranek, P. and Chan, J. (1987), *Visualizing Deviance: A Study of News Organisation*, Milton Keynes: Open University Press.

——— (1991), *Representing Order*, Milton Keynes: Open University Press.

Eriksen, T. R. and Jørgensen, A. M. (eds) (2003), *Professionsidentitet i Forandring*, Copenhagen: Akademisk Forlag.

Ettema, J. and Glasser, L. T. (1998), *Custodians of Conscience: Investigative Journalism and Public Virtue*, New York: Columbia University Press.

Evetts, J. (1999), 'Professions: Changes and continuities', *International Review of Sociology*, 9:1, pp. 75–86.

Fenton, N. (2010), 'Drowning or waving? New media, journalism and democracy', in N. Fenton (ed.), *New Media, Old News: Journalism and Democracy in the Digital Age*, London: Sage, pp. 3–16.

Ferraro, G. ([2006] 2008), *Cultural Anthropology: An Applied Perspective*, 7th ed., Belmont: Thomson Wadsworth.

Fishman, M. (1980), *Manufacturing the News*, Austin: University of Texas Press.

Forde, J. (2013), 'The news triumvirate', *Journalism Studies*, 14:1, pp. 113–29.

Ford, Henry (1922), *My Life and Work*, London: Wyman and Son.

Foucault, M. (1977), *Discipline and Punish* (trans. A. Sheridan), London: Penguin Books.

Fox, A. (1974), *Beyond Contract: Work, Power and Trust Relationships*, London: Faber & Faber.

Franklin, B. (1997), *Newszak and the News Media*, London: Arnold.

——— (2006), *Local Journalism and Local Media: Making the Local the Local News*, London: Routledge.

Freedman, D. (2010), 'The political economy of the "new" news environment', in N. Fenton (ed.), *New Media, Old News: Journalism and Democracy in the Digital Age*, London: Sage, pp. 35–50.

Freidson, E. (1986), *Professional Powers: A Study of the Institutionalization of Knowledge*, Chicago: Chicago University Press.

——— (1999), 'Theory of professionalism: Method and substance', *International Review of Sociology*, 9:1, pp. 117–19.

——— (2001), *Professionalism, the Third Logic: On the Practice of Knowledge*, Chicago: The University of Chicago Press, in association with Blackwell Publishers Ltd.

From, P., Andersson, R. and Reinecke, K. (2016), 'Improving Productivity in the Newsroom?', *Journalism Practice*, 10:8, pp. 1005–18.

Galtung, J. and Ruge, M. H. (1965), 'The structure of foreign news', *Journal of Peace Research*, 2, pp. 64–91.

Gans, H. (1979), *Deciding What's News. A study of CBS Evening News, NBC Nightly News and Time*, New York: Pantheon.

Gardner, H., Csikszentmihalyi, M. and Damon, W. (2001), *Good Work: When Excellence and Ethics Meet*, New York: Basic Books.

Gauntlett, D. and Hill, A. (1999), *TV Living: Television, Culture and Everyday Life*, London: Routledge.

Geertz, C. (1968), 'Thinking as a moral act: Ethical dimensions of anthropological fieldwork in the new states', *Antioch Review*, 28:2, pp. 139–58.

—— (1973), *The Interpretation of Cultures*, New York: Basic Books.

—— (1983), *Local Knowledge: Further Essays in Interpretive Anthropology*, London: Fontana Press.

Gehl, J. (2010), *Byer for Mennesker*, København: Bogværket.

Gellner, D. and Hirsch, E. G. (2001), 'Introduction: Ethnography of organizations and organizations of ethnography', in D. Gellner and E. Hirsch (eds), *Inside Organizations: Anthropologists at Work*, Oxford: Berg.

Gertsema, M. (2009), 'Women and news: Making connections between the global and the local', *Feminist Media Studies*, 9:2, pp. 149–72.

Giddens, A. (1979), 'Central problems in social theory: Action, structure and contradiction', in A. Giddens, *Social Analysis: Action, Structure and Contradictions in Social Analysis (Contemporary Social Theory)*, California: University of California Press.

—— (1990), *The Consequences of Modernity*, Cambridge: Polity Press.

—— (1991), *Modernity and Self-Identity: Self and Society in the Late Modern Age*, Cambridge: Polity Press.

Ginsburg, F. (1991), 'Indigenous media: Faustian contract or global village?', *Cultural Anthropology*, 6:1, pp. 92–112.

Ginsburg, F. D., Abu-Lughod, L. and Larkin, B. (eds) (2002), *Media Worlds: Anthropology on New Terrain*, Berkeley: University of California Press.

Glasser, T. and Marken, L. (2005), 'Can we make journalists better?', in H. de Burgh (ed.), *Making Journalists*, London: Routledge.

Goffman, E. (1967), 'Where the action is', in E. Goffman (ed.), *Interaction Rituals: Essays on Face to Face Behaviour*, Chicago: Aldine Publishing Company.

—— (1974), *Frame Analysis: An Essay on the Organization of Experience*, Cambridge: Harvard University Press.

—— (1983), 'The interaction order', *American Sociological Review*, 48, pp. 1–17.

—— ([1959] 1990), *The Presentation of the Self in Everyday Life*, New York: Doubleday.

Golding, P. and Elliott, P. (1979), *Making the News*, London: Longman.

Goodall H. L., Jr. (2003), 'What is interpretive ethnography? An eclectic's tale', in R. P. Clair (ed.), *Expressions of Ethnography*, Albany: Sunny Press, pp. 55–64.

Goodwin, M. (2016), 'American journalism is collapsing before our eyes', *New York Post*, 21 August, http://nypost.com/2016/08/21/american-journalism-is-collapsing-before-our-eyes/. Accessed 23 August 2016.

Gravengaard, G. (2010), *Journalistik i praksis: Valg og fravalg af nyhedsideer*, Frederiksberg: Forlaget Samfundslitteratur.

Gregor, T. A. and Tuzin, D. (eds) (2001), *Gender in Amazonia and Melanesia: An Exploration of the Comparative Method*, Berkeley: University of California Press.

Gubrium, J. F. and Holstein, J. A. (2001), 'Introduction: Trying times, troubled selves', in J. F. Gubrium and J. A. Holstein (eds), *Institutional Selves: Troubled Identities in a Postmodern World*, Oxford: Oxford University Press, pp. 1–22.

Gudeman, S. and Rivera, A. (1995), 'Del coche a la casa (From car to house)', *American Anthropologist, New Series*, 97:2, pp. 242–50.

Gulløv, E. and Højlund, S. (2006), 'Materialitetens Pædagogiske Kraft: et antropologisk perspektiv på børneinstitutioner', in K. Lanen (ed.), *Arkitektur, krop og læring*, Copenhagen: Hans Reitzel.

Haarder, B. (2011), 'Medierne – et demokratisk problem', *Berlingske*, 19 February, p. 20.

Hahn, E. (1994), 'The Tongan tradition of going to the movies', *Visual Anthropology Review*, 10:1, pp. 103–11.

Hall, S. (1982), 'The rediscovery of ideology: Return of the repressed in media studies', in M. Gurevitch, T. Bennett, J. Curran and J. Woollacott (eds), *Culture, Society, Media*, London: Methuen.

Hall, S. Critcher, C., Jefferson, T., Clarke, J. and Roberts, B. (1978), *Policing the Crisis: Mugging, the State and Law and Order*, Basingstoke: Macmillan Education Ltd.

Halliday, J. (2012), 'ITV news relaunches website', *Media Guardian*, 19 March, http://www.guardian.co.uk/media/2012/mar/19/iTV-news-relaunches-website. Accessed 16 April 2012.

Hallin, D. C. (1992), 'The passing of the "high modernism" of American journalism', *Journal of Communication*, 42:3, pp. 14–25.

Hallin, D. C. and Mancini, P. (2004), *Comparing Media Systems: Three Models of Media and Politics*, Cambridge: The Press Syndicate of the University of Cambridge.

Hammersley, M. and Atkinson, P. (1996), *Feltmetodikk*, Oslo: Ad Notam Gyldendal.

Hannerz, U. (1992), *Cultural Complexity: Studies in the Social Organisation of Meaning*, New York and Chichester and West Sussex: Columbia University Press.

—— (2001), 'Journalists, anthropologists and the cosmopolitan imagination', paper delivered at the *American Anthropological Association Conference*, Washington, DC.

—— (2004), *Foreign News: Exploring the World of Foreign Correspondents*, Chicago: University of Chicago Press.

Hansen, E. E. (2016), 'Dear Mark. I am writing this to inform you that I shall not comply with your requirement to remove this picture', *Aftenposten*, 26 December, p.1.

Hansen, H. P. (1995), 'Feltarbejde som forskningsstrategi', *Humanistisk forskning indenfor Sundhedsvidenskab*, Copenhagen: Akademisk Forlag.

Harcup, Tony (2011), *Journalism: Principles & Practice,* 2nd ed., London: Sage.

Harker, R. (1990), 'Education and cultural capital', in R. Harker, C. Mahar and C. Wilkes (eds), *An Introduction to the Work of Pierre Bourdieu: The Practice of Theory*, London: Macmillan Press.

Harrison, J. (2000), *Terrestial TV News in Britain: The Culture of Production*, Manchester: Manchester University Press.

—— (2001), 'Constructing news values', in G. Creeber (ed.), *The Television Genre Book*, London: BFI publishing.

Hartley, J. M. (2011), 'Radikalisering af Kampzonen: En analyse af netjournalistisk praksis og selvforståelse I spændingsfeltet mellem idealer og publikum', doctoral thesis submitted for the degree of Ph.D., Roskilde University.

—— (2013), 'The online journalist between ideals and audiences', *Journalism Practice*, http://www.tandfonline.com/doi/pdf/10.1080/17512786.2012.755386. Accessed 11 January 2013.

Hastrup, K. (1992), *Det Antropologiske projekt om Forbløffelse*, Copenhagen: Gyldendal.

Hedegaard, F. (ed.) (2006), 'Medier, Trends & Tendenser nr 3', *DR Medie Research*, 27 November, Copenhagen: DR.

Heering, A. (2008), 'Jes Dorph Kongen I Prinsebryllup', *Berlingske Tidende*, Berlingske Business, 26 May, http://m.business.dk/touch/article.pml?guid=2456368. Accessed 21 March 2012.

Heinonen, A. (1999), 'Journalism in the age of the net: Changing society, changing profession', University of Tampere, http://acta.uta.fi/pdf/951-44-5349-2.pdf. Accessed 17 December 2012.

Helland, K. (1995), *Public Service and Commercial News: Contexts of Production, Genre Conventions and Textual Claims in Television*, Report No. 18, Bergen: University of Bergen, Department of Media Studies.

—— (2001), 'TV-Nyhetenes Eksponeringsmakt – fra nyhetskriterier til eksponeringskriterier', in M. Eide (ed.), *Til Dagsorden! Journalistikk, makt og demokrati: Makt- og demokratiutredningen, 1998-2004*, Oslo: Gyldendal Norsk Forlag.

Hemmingway, E. (2004), 'The silent heart of news', *Space and Culture*, 7, p. 409.

—— (2008), *Into the Newsroom: Exploring the Digital Production of Regional Television News*, Abingdon: Routledge.

Herman, E. S. and Chomsky, N. (1988), *Manufacturing Consent: The Political Economy of the Mass Media*, New York: Pantheon.

Hochild, A. ([1983] 2003), *The Managed Heart: Commercialisation of Human Feeling*, Berkeley and London: University of California Press.

Hoff, T. J. and McCaffrey, D. (1996), 'Adapting, resisting, and negotiating: How physicians cope with organizational and economic change', *Work and Occupations*, 23, p. 165.

Holm, H. H., Svith, F. and Kartveit, K. (2008), *Når Nyheder Bliver Til på DR og TV2*, Århus: Forlaget Ajour.

Holton, K. and Holden, M. (2012), 'UK government turns up heat on BBC over sex abuse scandal', *Reuters Online*, 24 October, http://www.reuters.com/article/2012/10/24/us-bbc-savile-idUSBRE89N0T420121024. Accessed 27 November 2012.

Hoonard, W. C. V. den (1997), *Working with sensitizing concepts: Analytical field research*, Thousand Oaks, CA: Sage.

Horrocks, P. (2007), 'Multimedia news', The Editors, blog, 12 November, http://www.bbc.co.uk/blogs/theeditors/2007/11/multimedia_news.html. Accessed 15 June 2011.

House of Lords Hansard (1952), 'Lord Reith Speech on Broadcasting Policy', *HL Deb 22 May 1952 vol 176 cc1289-347*, http://hansard.millbanksystems.com/lords/1952/may/22/broadcastingpolicy#S5LV0176P0_19520522_HOL_12. Accessed 23 March 2012.

Højesteret (2011), 'Jægersoldater til Irak, Instans: Højesteret', *Update.dk*, 8 February, http://www.update.dk/cfje/Lovbasen.nsf/ID/LB05916703. Accessed 13 December 2011.

IFJ (International Federation of Journalists) and ILO (International Labour Organization) (2006), *The Changing Nature of Work: A Global Survey and Case Study of Atypical Work in the Media Industry*, Brussels: International Federation of Journalists.

Infomedia.dk (2011), 'Vores Kildeunivers', *Infomedia.dk*, http://www.infomedia.dk/overvaagning/overvaagning-kilder/. Accessed 17 November 2011.

Information (2012), 'TV avisen flytter til 21:30', *Information.dk*, 19 March, http://www. information.dk/telegram/296417. Accessed 22 March 2012.

Ingold, T. (2007), *Lines: A Brief History*, London and New York: Routledge.

INNOVATION (2007), 'The Daily Telegraph case: Multimedia newsroom integration', presented at the World Newspaper Congress in Cape Town, South Africa, 26 June, http://www.youtube. com/watch?v=2yXT_1pvDv4. Accessed 11 October 2017.

Jameson, F. (1993), 'Postmodernism and Consumer Society', in A. Gray and J. McGuigan (eds), *Studying Culture: An Introductory Reader*, New York and Oxford: Oxford University Press, pp. 206–17.

——— (1988), 'Postmodern and consumer society', in E. A. Kaplan (ed.), *Postmodernism and Its Discontents*, New York: Verso, pp. 13–29.

Janis, I. L. (1972), *Victims of Groupthink*, New York: Houghton Mifflin.

Jensen, L. (2009), 'Efterkritik: Journalistik om Journalistik', in A. B. Lund, I. Willig and M. Blach-Ørsten, *Hvor kommer nyhederne Fra?Den Journalistiske Fødekæde i Danmark før og nu*, Århus: Forlaget Ajour.

Johnson, C. and Turnock, R. (2005), *ITV Cultures: Independent Television over Fifty Years*, London: McGraw-Hill International.

Kabel, L. (2009), *Nyheder i Nutid*, Aarhus: Ajour.

Kalleberg, A. L. (1996), 'Changing contexts of careers: Trends in labor market structures and some of the implications for labour force outcomes', in A. C. Kerckhoff (ed.), *Generating Social Stratification: Toward a New Research Agenda*, Boulder: Westview Press, pp. 343–58.

Kaplan, R. (2006), 'The news about new institutionalism: Journalism's ethic of objectivity and its political origins', *Political Communication*, 23:2, pp. 173–85.

Kawakita, J. (1991), *The Original KJ Method*, rev. ed., Meguro: Kawakita Research Institute.

Kimer, M. (2016), *Krigen indeni: skæbnefortællinger fra revolutionen i Ukraine*, Copenhagen: Politiken.

Kirkbak, J. J. and Bakalus, S. (2011), 'Jes Dorph: Nils Giversen er et gedigent Røvhul', *BT.dk*, 13 December, http://www.bt.dk/danmark/jes-dorph-nils-giversen-er-et-gedigent-roevhul. Accessed 13 December 2011.

Klausen, A. M. (1986), *Med Dagbladet til tabloid. En studie i dilemmaet 'børn og katedral'*, Oslo: Gyldendal Norsk Forlag.

Klinenberg, E. (2005), 'Cultural Production in the Digital Age: An Introduction', *Annals of the American Academy of Political and Social Science*, 597:6, pp. 48–64.

Klinenberg, E. and Fayer, H. (2005), 'Quick read synopsis: Cultural production in a digital age', *The Annals of the American Academy of Political and Social Science*, 597, pp. 223–44.

Kohut, H. and Goldberg, A. and Stepansky, P. E. (1984), *How Does Analysis Cure?*, Chicago and London: University of Chicago Press.

Krause-Kjær, N. (2003), *Den politiske landsby - om Christiansborg, journalisterne og politikerne*, Aarhus: Forlaget Ajour.

Krumsvik, A. H. (2009), 'The online news factory: A multi-lens investigation of the strategy, structure, and process of online news production at CNN and NRK', Ph.D. thesis, Acta Humaniora No 394, Oslo: University of Oslo/Unipub.

Kulturministeriet (2003), *Tilladelse til TV 2/DANMARK A/S til at udøve public service programvirksomhed*, Copenhagen: Kulturministeriet, http://www.bibliotekogmedier.dk/fileadmin/user_upload/dokumenter/medier/radio_og_TV/landsdaekkende_regional/TV_2_danmark/Tilladelse_til_TV_2_DANMARK_A_S_til_at_udoeve_public_service-programvirksomhed.pdf. Accessed 16 April 2012.

—— (2006), *Public Service kontrakt mellem DR og Kulturministeren for perioden 1. januar 2007 til 31. december 2010, J.Nr. 2004-15402-45*, Copenhagen: Kulturministeriet, http://kum.dk/Documents/Kulturpolitik/medier/DR/Publicservicekontraktennyudgave%5B1%5D.pdf. Accessed 20 February 2012.

Kuper, A. (2000), *Culture: The Anthropologists' Account*, London: Harvard University Press.

Kvale, S. (1996), *InterViews: An Introduction to Qualitative Research Interviewing*, Thousand Oaks and London: Sage.

—— (2006), 'Dominance through interviews and dialogues', *Qualitative Inquiry*, 12, p. 480.

Kvale, S. and Brinkman, S. (2009), *InterViews: Learning the Craft of Qualitative Research Interviewing*, 2nd ed., California: Sage Publications Inc.

Lakoff, G. and Johnson, M. (1980), *Metaphors We Live By*, Chicago: University of Chicago Press.

Larson, M. S. (1977), *The Rise of Professionalism: A Sociological Analysis*, Berkeley: University of California Press.

—— (1990), 'In the matter of experts and professionals, or how impossible it is to leave nothing unsaid', in R. Torstendahl and M. Burrage (eds), *Professions in Theory and History*, London: Sage.

Lave, J. and Wenger, E. ([1991] 2001), *Situated Learning: Legitimate Peripheral Participation*, Cambridge: Cambridge University Press.

Lefebvre, H. (1974), *La production de l'espace*, Paris: Anthropos.

Leigh, D. (2007), 'Anthony Sampson Chair inaugural lecture', City University, 1 November. http://www.docstoc.com/docs/74943932/in-this-lecture---Lecture-given-by-David-Leigh_-Anthony-Sampson-. Accessed 16 June 2012.

Len-Ríos, M. E., Rodgers, S., Thorson, E. and Yoon, D. (2005), 'Representation of women in news and photos: Comparing content to perceptions', *Journal of Communication*, 55, pp. 152–68.

Leonard, T. (2001), 'Battle of the bongs as BBC and ITV news go head-to-head at Ten', *The Daily Telegraph*, 23 January, http://www.telegraph.co.uk/news/uknews/1318997/Battle-of-the-bongs-as-BBC-and-ITV-news-go-head-to-head-at-Ten.html. Accessed 17 July 2011.

Lester, M. (1980), 'Generating newsworthiness: The interpretive construction of public events', *American Sociological Review*, 18, pp. 3–12.

Lewis, J. (1991), *The Ideological Octopus: Explorations into the Television Audience*, New York: Routledge.

Lewis, J., Williams, A. and Franklin, B. (2008a), 'A compromised fourth estate? UK news Journalism, public relations and news sources', *Journalism Studies*, 9:1, pp. 1–20.

—— (2008b), 'Four rumours and an explanation', *Journalism Practice, January*, 2:1, pp. 27–45.

Lewis, J., Williams, A. Franklin, B., Thomas, J. and Mosdell, N. (2008), *The Quality and Independence of British Journalism: Tracking the Changes over 20 Years*, Cardiff: Cardiff University, http://www.cardiff.ac.uk/jomec/resources/QualityIndependenceofBritishJournalism.pdf. Accessed 9 January 2013.

Lichtenberg, J. (1991), 'In defense of objectivity', in J. Curran and M. Gurevitch (eds), *Mass Media and Society*, London: Arnold.

Littek, W. and Charles, T. (eds) (1995), *The New Division of Labor: Emerging Forms of Work Organization in International perspective*, Berlin: Walter de Gruyter.

Lofland, J. and Lofland, L. H. (1984), *Analyzing Social Settings*, 2nd ed., Belmont: Wadsworth.

Lund, A. B. (2000), *Først med det sidste - en nyhedsuge i Danmark*, Aarhus: Ajour.

——— (2001), 'Invitation til Mediesociologi', *dansoc*, 12:2, pp. 80–83.

——— (2002), *Den redigerende magt - nyhedsinstitutionens politiske indflydelse*, Aarhus: Aarhus universitets forlag.

Lund, A. B., Nord, L. and Roppen, J. (2009), *Nye Udfordringer for Gamle Medier: Skandinavisk Public Service i det 21, Århundrede*, Gothenborg: Nordicom.

Lund, A. B., Willig, I. and Blach-Ørsten, M. (2009), *Hvor kommer nyhederne fra? – Den journalistiske fødekæde i Danmark før og nu*, Aarhus: Forlaget Ajour.

Lule, J. (1992), 'Journalism and criticism: The Philadelphia inquirer Norplant editorial', *Critical Studies in Mass Communication*, 9, pp. 91–109.

Macdonald, S. (2001), 'Ethnography in the science museum, London', in D. Gellner and E. Hirsch (eds), *Inside Organizations: Anthropologists at Work*, Oxford: Berg pp. 77–96.

Madsen, F. W. (2012), 'TV2: Vi har stadig de bedste Sendetider', *MetroXpress online*, 19 March, http://www.metroxpress.dk/nyheder/TV-2-vi-har-stadig-de-bedstesendetider/KOblcs! dwukx8xkXEqc/. Accessed 22 March 2012.

Marcus, G. (1999), 'The uses of complicity in the changing Mise-en-scene of anthropological fieldwork', in S. Ortner (ed.), *The Fate of 'Culture' Geertz and Beyond*, Berkeley, Los Angeles and London: University of California Press, pp. 85–108.

Marcus, G. E. (1995), 'Ethnography in/of the world-system – The emergence of multi-sited ethnography', *Annual Review of Anthropology*, 24, pp. 95–117.

Marr, A. (2004), *My Trade: A Short History of British Journalism*, Basingstoke and London: Macmillan.

Martin, F. R. (2007), 'Digital dilemmas: The Australian Broadcasting Corporation and interactive multimedia publishing, 1992–2002', Ph.D. theses, Lismore, NSW: Southern Cross University, http://epubs.scu.edu.au/cgi/viewcontent.cgi?article=1069&context=theses. Accessed 16 April 2012.

Martin, N. (2008), 'Revamped news at ten fails to dent BBC', *The Daily Telegraph*, 15 January, http://www.telegraph.co.uk/news/uknews/1575652/ITVs-revamped-News-at-Ten-fails-to-dent-BBC.html. Accessed 21 June 2012.

Mascarenhas-Keyes, S. (2001), 'Inside organizations: Anthropologists at work', in D. N. Gellner and E. Hirsch (eds), *Understanding the Working Environment: Notes Towards a Rapid Organizational Analysis*, Oxford: Berg, pp. 205–32.

Mathiesen, T. (1997), 'The viewer society: Michel Foucault's "Panopticon" revisited', *Theoretical Criminology*, 1:2, pp. 215–34.

McNair, B. (2005), 'What is journalism?', H. de Burgh (ed.), *Making Journalists*, London: Routledge.

——— (2013), 'Trust, truth and objectivity: Sustaining quality journalism in the era of the content-generating user', in C. Peters and M. Broersma (eds), *Rethinking Journalism: Trust and Participation in a Transformed News Landscape*, London and New York: Routledge, pp. 75–88.

McNelly, J. T. (1959), 'Intermediary communications in the international flow of news', *Journalism Quarterly*, 36, pp. 23–26.

McQuail, D. (2000), *McQuail's Mass Communication Theory*, 4th ed., London: Sage Publications Ltd.

Mead, M. (1953), 'National character', in A. L. Kroeber (ed.), *Anthropology Today*, Chicago: University of Chicago Press, pp. 642–67.

Melin, M. (2008), *Gendered Journalism Cultures: Strategies and Tactics in the Fields of Journalism in Britain and Sweden*, Malmö: JMG, University of Gothenburg, http://dspace.mah.se/dspace/bitstream/handle/2043/12450/Inlaga%20final;jsessionid=35319A9C0A02348C7CE7ADF67D101EA2?sequence=2. Accessed 5 May 2012.

Miller, D. (1997), *Capitalism: An Ethnographic Approach*, Oxford: Berg.

Moe, H. and Syvertsen, T. (2009), 'Researching public service broadcasting', in K. Wahl-Jorgensen and T. Hanitzch (eds) (2009), *The Handbook of Journalism Research*, New York: Routledge, pp. 398–412.

Mølgaard, M. (2011), 'DR er gået fra Information til Interaktion', *DR.dk*, http://www.dr.dk/Nyheder/Kultur/2011/09/26/133121.htm. Accessed 23 April 2012.

Monbiot, G. (2017), 'The election's biggest losers? Not the Tories but the media, who missed the story', *The Guardian Online*, 13 June, https://www.theguardian.com/commentisfree/2017/jun/13/election-tories-media-broadcasters-press-jeremy-corbyn. Accessed 11 October 2017.

Mortense, F. (2013), *EU og privatiseringen af TV 2*, Doktordisputats: Aarhus Universitet.

—— (ed.) (2008), *Public Service i Netværkssamfundet*, Frederiksberg C: Forlaget Samfunds litteratur.

Mouritsen, P. (2007), 'Fem opfattelser af fjernsyn og radio i kampen om "i folkets tjeneste"', in M. Carstensen, F. Svith and P. Mouritsen (eds), *DR og TV2 – i folkets tjeneste?*, Aarhus: Ajour.

MS and LR (2011), 'Nyhed: Tilliden Størst til DR og TV2', *Mediawatch online*, 1 March, http://mediawatch.dk/artikel/nyheder-tilliden-stoerst-til-dr-og-TV-2. Accessed 20 June 2011.

Munch-Nielsen, S. (2007), 'Arkitekten som Visuel Instruktør', *ArkFokus TIDSSKRIFT FOR ARKITEKTUR, DESIGN, BY OG LAND*, 3:8, Copenhagen: Arkitektforbundet, http://www.arkitektforbundet.dk/cgi-files/mdmgfx/file-557-129556-8768.pdf. Accessed 31 October 2011.

Murphy, D. (1976), *The Silent Watchdog: The Press in Local Politics*, London: Constable.

Murphy, P. (2011), 'Locating media ethnography', in V. Nightingale (ed.), *The Handbook of Media Audiences*, London: Blackwell Publishing.

Netcraft online (2012), 'Most visited web sites', http://toolbar.netcraft.com/stats/topsites. Accessed 2 April 2012.

Newman, N. (ed.) (2012), *Reuters Institute Digital News Report 2012: Tracking the Future of News*, Oxford: Reuters Institute for the Study of Journalism.

Niblock, S. and Machin, D. (2006), *News Production: Theory and Practice*, Abingdon: Routledge.

Nielsen, R. K. (2012), *Ground Wars: Personalised Communication in Political Campaigns*, New Jersey: Princeton University Press.

Nightingale, V. (1993), 'What's "ethnographic" about ethnographic audience research?', in G. Turner (ed.), *Nation, Culture, Text: Australian Cultural and Media Studies*, London: Routledge pp. 164–78.

Nonaka, I. (1994), 'A dynamic theory of organizational knowledge creation', *Organization Science*, 5:1, pp. 14–37.

Nonaka, I. and von Krogh, G. (2009), 'Tacit knowledge and knowledge conversion: Controversy and advancement in organizational knowledge creation theory', *Organization Science*, 20:3, May–June, pp. 635–52.

Nonaka, I. and Takeuchi, H. (1995), *The Knowledge-Creating Company*, Oxford: Oxford University Press.

Nossek, H. (2009), 'On the future of journalism as a professional practice and the case of journalism in Israel', *Journalism*, 10:3, pp. 358–61.

Nybroe, J. (2011), 'Nyhedernes Nye Nødvendigheder', *Center for Journalistik Online*, 18 January, http://ahaheder.dk/?p=705. Accessed 22 March 2012.

Nygren, G. (2007), 'The changing journalistic work: Changing professional roles and values', presented at conference on 'The Future of Newspapers' Cardiff Centre for Journalism, Media and Cultural Studies, Cardiff University, 12–13 September.

Ofcom (2007), *New News, Future News: The Challenges for Television News after Digital Switchover – A Discussion Document*, London: Ofcom.

Olsson, H. and Poulsen, H. (1995), *Ryd Forsiden? – om nyhedsformidling*, Frederiksberg: Dansklærerforeningen.

Ortner, S. (1984), 'Theory in anthropology since the sixties', *Comparative Studies in Society and History*, 26:1, pp. 126–66.

O'Sullivan, J. and Heinonen, A. (2008), 'Old values, new media: Journalism role perceptions in a changing world', *Journalism Practice*, 2:3, pp. 357–71.

Otto, T. (1997), 'Informed participation and participating informants', *Canberra Anthropology*, 20:1&2, pp. 96–108.

Padovani, C. and Tracey, M. (2003), 'Report on the conditions of public service broadcasting', *Television & New Media*, 4:2, pp. 131–53.

Parsons, T. (1954), 'A sociologist looks at the legal profession', *Essays in Sociological Theory*, rev. ed., Glencoe: The Free Press.

—— (1968), 'Professions', in W. A. Darity Jr, *International Encyclopedia of the Social Sciences*, New York: The MacMillan Company and The Free Press.

Paterson C. (2007), 'International news on the internet: Why more is less', *Ethical space: The International Journal of Communication Ethics*, 4:1, pp. 57–66.

—— (2011), *Making Online News – Vol 2: News Ethnography in the Second Decade of Internet Journalism*, New York: Peter Lang Publishing.

Pavlik, J. (2000), 'The impact of technology on journalism', *Journalism Studies*, 1:2, pp. 229–37.

Paulu, B. (1981), *Television and Radio in the United Kingdom*, Minneapolis: The University of Minnesota Press.

Pedelty, M. (2010), 'Musical news: Popular music in political movements', in E. S. Bird (ed.), *The Anthropology of News & Journalism: Global Perspectives*, Bloomington: Indiana University Press.

Pedersen, L. N. and Rasmussen, P. E. (2010), 'Lydfil bliver i Plummers lommer', *Jyllands Posten*, 23 April, http://spn.dk/mobil_vm/?aid=2047451. Accessed 19 December 2011.

Peterson, M. A. (2003), *Anthropology & Mass Communication: Media and Myth in the New Millennium*, New York and Oxford: Berghahn Books.

—— (2010), 'Getting the news in New Delhi', in E. S. Bird (ed.), *The Anthropology of News & Journalism: Global Perspectives*, Bloomington: Indiana University Press.

Phillips, E. B. (1976), 'Novelty without change', *Journal of Communication*, 26, pp. 87–92.

Pierson, C. (1998), *Conversations with Anthony Giddens: Making Sense of Modernity*, Stanford: Stanford University Press.

Pittelkow, R. (1986), 'TV-Avisen set indefra', in *Forskningsrapport Nr. 7B/86*, Copenhagen: Danmarks Radio.

Polanyi, M. (1964), *Science, Faith and Society*, Chicago: The University of Chicago Press.

Porter, T. (2005), 'Kicking the Pack journalism habit', in T. Porter, *First Draft by Tim Porter: Newspapering, Readership & Relevance in a Digital Age*, April 6, http://www.timporter.com/firstdraft/archives/000433.html. Accessed 5 December 2012.

Postill, J. and Brauchner, B. (2010), *Theorising Media and Practice*, New York: Berghahn Books.

Postill J. and Peterson M. A. (2009), 'What is the point of media anthropology', *Social Anthropology*, 17, pp. 334–37.

Powdermaker, H. (1950), *Hollywood the Dream Factory: An Anthropologist Looks at the Movie-Makers*, Boston: Little, Brown.

Powdermaker, H. (ed.) (1953), 'Mass communications seminar', proceedings of an Interdisciplinary Seminar held under the auspices of the Wenner-Green Foundation for Anthropological Research, Inc., 11–13 May 1951, New York: Wenner-Green Foundation for Anthropological Research.

—— (1962), *Copper Town: Changing Africa. The Human Situation on the Rhodesian Copperbelt*, Westport: Greenwood Press.

Press Gazette (2002), 'BBC in strike action threat over multi-skilling deal', *Press Gazette*, 12 April, http://www.pressgazette.co.uk/story.asp?storyCode=21377&sectioncode=1. Accessed 11 January 2012.

Preston, P. (2009), *Making the News: Journalism and News Cultures in Europe*, Abingdon: Routledge.

—— (2016), 'The people have spoken on Brexit. But did the media tell them the truth?', *The Guardian*, 26 June, https://www.theguardian.com/media/2016/jun/26/people-spoken-brexit-did-media-tell-the-truth-eu-referendum. Accessed 23 August 2016.

Preston, P. and Kerr, A. (2001), 'Digital media, nation-states and local cultures: The case of multimedia "content" production', *Media, Culture and Society*, 23, pp. 109–31.

Puijk, R. (1990), *Virkeligheter I NRK. Programprodksjon i fjernsynets Opplysningsavdeling*, Lillehammer: Dr. Philos. dissertation.

—— (2008), 'Ethnographic media production research in a digital environment', in C. Paterson and D. Domingo, *Making Online News: The Ethnography of New Media Production*, New York: Peter Lang Publishing.

Quandt, T. and Singer, J. B. (2009), 'Convergence and cross-platform content production', in K. Wahl-Jorgensen and T. Hanitzsch (eds), *The Handbook of Journalism Studies*, London: Routledge.

Quinn, B. (2011), 'Royal wedding television audience hit 24m peak in UK', *The Guardian Online*, 30 April, http://www.guardian.co.uk/uk/2011/apr/30/royal-wedding-television-audience. Accessed 12 August 2011.

Quinn, G. and Trench, B. (2002), *Online News Media and Their Audiences*, Heerlen: Mudia, International Institute of Infonomics.

Rao, U. (2010), *News as Culture: Journalistic Practices and the Remaking of Indian Leadership Traditions*, New York: Berghahn Books.

Richards, B. and Ress, G. (2011), 'The management of emotion in British journalism', *Media, Culture & Society*, 33:6, pp. 851–67.

Ringgaard, A. (2014), 'Venstre-drama: Journalisterne viste deres sande ansigt', *Videnskab.dk*, 4 June, http://videnskab.dk/kultur-samfund/venstre-drama-journalisterne-viste-deres-sande-ansigt. Accessed 23 August 2016.

Ritzau, A. (2011), 'Hør klip fra lækage-sagens lydfil', *DR.dk*, 13 December, http://www.dr.dk/Nyheder/Indland/2011/12/13/100708.htm. Accessed 13 December 2011.

—— (2012), 'Vi ser flere nyheder og mere kultur på TV', *Børsen*, 23 March, http://borsen.dk/nyheder/medier/artikel/1/228852/vi_ser_flere_nyheder_og_mere_kultur_paa_TV.html. Accessed 27 March 2012.

Robinson, J. (2004), 'In search of the "news at when"', *The Guardian Online*, 6 June, https://www.theguardian.com/media/2004/jun/06/business.broadcasting. Accessed 25 October 2017.

Rosenberg, H. and Feldman, C. S. (2008), *No Time to Think: The Menace of Media Speed and the 24-hour News Cycle*, New York and London: The Continuum International Publishing Group.

Rossi, A. (2011), *Page One inside the New York Times*, US: Magnolia Pictures.

Rothenbuhler, E. (2008), 'Media anthropology as a field of interdisciplinary contact', in E-seminar 25 on *Media-anthropology-net*, 22 October–5 November, http://www.media-anthropology.net/rothenbuhler_interdiscontact.pdf. Accessed 6 December 2012.

Rothenbuhler, E. and Coman, M. (eds) (2005), *Media Anthropology*, London: Sage.

Rusbridger, A. (2001), 'Politicians, the press and political language', *The Hetherington Memorial Lecture 2001*, http://www.fmj.stir.ac.uk/hetherington/alan-rusbridger.php. Accessed 7 January 2013.

Ryfe, D. M. (2006), 'The nature of news rules', *Political Communication*, 23, pp. 203–14.

—— (2011), 'Broader and deeper: A study of newsroom culture in a time of change', in D. A. Berkowitz (ed.), *Cultural Meanings of News: A Text Reader*, Thousand Oaks: Sage Publishing, Inc.

—— (2012), *Can Journalism Survive? An Inside Look at American Newsrooms*, Cambridge: Polity Press.

—— (2017), *Journalism and the Public*, Cambridge: Polity Press.

Sahlins, M. D. (1985), *Islands of History*, London: Tavistock.

Said, E. W. (1981), *Covering Islam: How the Media and the Experts Determine How We See the Rest of the World*, New York: Pantheon.

Sandler, J. and Thedvall, R. (2017), *Meeting Ethnography: Meetings as Key Technologies of Contemporary Governance*, New York: Routledge.

Sanjek, R. (ed.) (1990), *Fieldnotes*, Ithaca: Cornell University Press.

Scannell, P. (2002), 'History, media, communication', in K. B. Jensen (ed.), *A Handbook of Media and Communication Research: Qualitative and Quantitative Methodologies*, Oxon: Routledge.

Schlechty, P. C. (1990), *Schools for the 21st Century: Leadership Imperatives for Educational Reform*, San Francisco: Jossey-Bass.

Schlesinger, P. (1978), *Putting 'Reality' Together*, London: Methuen.

—— (2006), 'Is there a crisis in British Journalism?', *Media, Culture & Society*, 28, p. 299.

Schudson, M. (1989), 'The sociology of news production', *Media Culture and Society*, 11, pp. 263–82.

—— (1997), 'The sociology of news production', D. A. Berkowitz (ed.), *Social Meanings of News: A Text Reader*, London: Sage Publications.

—— (2013), 'Would journalism please hold still!', in C. Peters and M. Broersma (eds), *Rethinking Journalism: Trust and Participation in a Transformed News Landscape*, London and New York: Routledge.

Schudson, M. and Anderson, C. (2009), 'Objectivity, professionalism, and truth seeking in journalism', in K. Wahl-Jorgensen and T. Hanitzsch (eds), *The Handbook of Journalism Studies*, London: Routledge.

Schultz, I. (2006), *Bag Nyhederne: Værdier, idealer og praksis*, Frederiksberg C: Forlaget Samfundslitteratur.

—— (2007), 'The journalistic gut feeling: Journalistic doxa, news habitus and orthodox news values', *Journalism Practice*, 1:2, pp. 190–207.

Schultz, I. and Thomsen, L. H. (2008), 'The spirit of public service: How public broadcasters in Denmark understand "public service" – and how this understanding has changed significantly from 2003 to 2008', paper presented at The Working Group for Media Production Analysis at the *International Association for Media and Communication Research Conference*, 21–25 July, Stockholm.

Schwartzman, H. B. (1989), *The Meeting: Gatherings in Organizations and Communities*, New York: Plenum Press.

—— (1993), *Ethnography in Organizations*, Newbury Park and London: Sage.

Secretary of State for Culture, Media and Sport by Command of Her Majesty (2006), 'BROADCASTING: An Agreement Between Her Majesty's Secretary of State for Culture, Media and Sport and the British Broadcasting Corporation Presented to Parliament by the Secretary of State for Culture, Media and Sport by Command of Her Majesty', July 2006, Norwich: The Licencing Division HMSO, http://www.bbc.co.uk/bbctrust/assets/files/pdf/about/how_we_govern/agreement.pdf. Accessed 23 February 2011.

Shankman, P. (2001), 'Requiem for a controversy: Whatever happened to Margaret Mead?', *Skeptic*, 9:1, pp. 48–53.

Shoemaker, P. J. (1991), *Gatekeeping*, Newbury Park, California and London: Sage.

Shoemaker, P. J. and Reese, S. (1996), *Mediating the Message: Theories of Influences on Mass Media Content*, New York: Longman.

Shoemaker, P. J. and Vos, T. P. (2009), *Gatekeeping Theory*, New York and London: Routledge.

Sigal, L. V. (1973), *Reporters and Officials. The Organization and Politics of Newsmaking*, Lexington: D. C. Heath & Co.

Silverstone, R. (2007), *Media and Morality: On the Rise of the Mediapolis*, Cambridge and Malden: Polity Press.

SimilarWeb (2017), 'SimilarWeb 2016 Highlights Report – UK', https://www.similarweb.com/corp/similarweb-2016-highlights-report-uk/. Accessed 8 December 2017.

Singer, J. (2003), 'Who are these guys?: The online challenge to the notion of journalistic professionalism', *Journalism*, 4, p. 139.

———— (2004), 'Strange bedfellows? The diffusion of convergence in four news organisations', *Journalism Studies*, 5:1, pp. 3–18.

Siverts, O. B. (1984), *Nyheter i BT? Endrings- og vedlikeholdsprosesser i Vestlandets storavis*, Bergen University: Sosialantropologisk institutt, Magistergradsavhandling.

Skrivunder.net (2014), 'Protest mod DR/P1-ledelsens fyring af "Orientering"s Niels Lindvig', skrivunder.net, 10 October, http://www.skrivunder.net/niels_lindvig. Accessed 11 October 2017.

Snow, J. (2004), *Shooting History: A Personal Journey*, London: Harper Collins Publishers.

Soloski, J. (1989), 'News reporting and professionalism: Some constraints on the reporting of the news', *Media, Culture and Society*, 11:2, pp. 207–28.

Sørensen, S. K. (2008), 'TV2 vandt Bryllupskrigen', *Ekstra Bladet*, 26 May, http://ekstrabladet.dk/flash/filmogTV/TV/article1012078.ece. Accessed 26 June 2012.

Sparre, K. (2009), 'En bryllupsdag med mange facetter', *Update*, 29 May, http://www.update.dk/CFJE/Vidbase.nsf/ID/VB01806161. Accessed 20 March 2012.

Spradley, J. P. (1979), *The Ethnographic Interview*, New York and London: Holt, Rinehart and Winston.

Stacey, R. D. (2007), *Strategic Management and Organisational Dynamics: The Challenge of Complexity to Ways of Thinking about Organisations*, Harlow: Pearson Education Limited.

Stassinos, E. (2009), 'An early case of personality: Ruth Benedict's autobiographical fragment and the case of the biblical "Boaz"', *Histories of Anthropology Annual*, 5, pp. 28–51.

Staugård, H. J. (2011), 'Professionsbegrebet', in M. B. Johansen and S. G. Olesen (eds), *Professionernes Sociologi og Vidensgrundlag*, Aarhus: Via systime, pp. 161–75.

Steensen, S. (2011), 'The featurization of journalism', *Nordicom Review*, 32:2, pp. 49–61.

Stevenson, N. (1995), *Understanding Media Cultures: Social Theory of Mass Communication*, London: Sage.

Storm, H. and Williams, H. (2012), *No Woman's Land: On the Frontlines with Female Reporters*, London: International News Safety Institute.

Svith, F. (2008), 'TV-nyheder mellem stærke billeder og kloge ord', H.-H. Holm, F. Svith and K. Kartveit (eds), *Når Nyheder Bliver til – På DR og TV2. Public Service – Medier og Demokrati*, Aarhus: Forlaget Ajour.

Syvertsen, T. (1993), 'Allmennkringkasting, nyheiter og politisks legitimitet. Ei drøfting av utviklinga i nyheiteravdelinga til BBC', in I. Hagen and K. Helland (eds), *Verda på Skjermen: Om Nyheiter og Fjernsyn*, Oslo: Det Norske Samlaget.

Syvertsen, T. and Moe, H. (2007), 'Media institutions as a research field: Three phases of Norwegian broadcasting research', *Nordicom Review, Jubilee Issue 2007*, pp. 149–67.

Tardes, G. (1903), *The Laws of Imitation*, New York: Henry Holt and Company.

Thomsen, L. H. (2001), 'Inside the British cults', MA thesis, London City University, unpublished.

———— (2007a), 'Indistinct identities', paper presented at the conference *Minding the Gap: Reflections on Media Practice & Theory*, held at the Reuters Institute for the Study of Journalism, University of Oxford, Oxford, 12 May.

———— (2007b), 'Introduction: Theoretical models as mass media practice: Perspectives from the West', in C. Baldwin, L. Thomsen, V. Vemuri and D. Sills-Jones (eds), *Networking Knowledge: Journal of the MeCCSA PGN*, 1:1, Oxford: MeCCSA.

———— (2008), 'Inside the new digital TV newsrooms – From square to circle', paper presented at the panel *Online Media and the Changing Paradigms of Journalism of the Journalism Studies, ECREA*, University of Barcelona, 27 November.

———— (2014a), 'Ethnographic fieldwork: Studying journalists at work', in *SAGE Research Methods Cases*, London: SAGE Publications, Ltd.

———— (forthcoming), 'How Danish journalists connect across broadcasters', in Freedman, E., Goodman, R. and Steyn, E. (eds.) *Critical Perspectives on Journalistic Beliefs*, Oxford: Routledge, n.pag.

Thorsen, E. (2010), 'BBC news online: A brief history of past and present', in N. Brügger (ed.), *Web History*, New York: Peter Lang Publishing.

Thurman, N., Cornia, A. and Kunert, J. (2016), *Journalists in the UK*, Oxford: Reuters Institute for the Study of Journalism.

Tiffen, R. (1989), *News and Power*, Sydney: Allen & Unwin.

TNS Gallup TV-Meter (2016), *Seertal uge 21*, 23–29 May, http://docplayer.dk/21578008-Hvor-meget-tv-ser-danskerne.html. Accesed 11 October 2017.

Tracey, M. (1998), *The Decline and Fall of Public Broadcasting*, New York: Oxford University Press.

Tuchman, G. (1972), 'Objectivity as strategic ritual: An examination of newsmen's notion of objectivity', *The American Journal of Sociology*, 77:4, January, pp. 660–79.

———— (1973), 'Making news by doing work: Routinizing the unexpected', *The American Journal of Sociology*, 79:1, pp. 119–31.

———— (1978), *Making News: A Study in the Social Construction of Reality*, New York: Free Press.

Tumber, H. and Prentoulis, M. (2005), 'Journalism and the making of a profession', in H. de Burgh (ed.), *Making Journalists*, London: Routledge.

Tunstall, J. (1971), *Journalists at Work, Specialist Correspondents: Their News Organizations, Sources and Competitor-colleagues*, London: Constable.

Turner, T. (1991), 'Representing, resisting, rethinking: Historical transformation of Kayapo culture and anthropological consciousness', in G. Stocking Jr (ed.), *The History of Anthropology: Colonial Situations*, Madison: University of Wisconsin Press.

———— (1992), 'Defiant images: The Kayapo appropriation of video', *Anthropology Today*, 8:6, pp. 107–12.

Rasy (2011), 'En Introduktion til TV2 Nyhederne', tv2.dk, 24 February, http://nyhederne-dyn.TV2.dk/article.php/id-37659269:introduktion-til-nyhederne.html. Accessed 21 July 2011.

Tverskov, E. and Tverskov, K. (2010), *Sådan Gør Journalister – en håndbog for alle andre*, Aarhus: Ajour.

Ursell, G. D. M. (2001), 'Dumbing down or shaping up? New technologies, new media, new journalism', *Journalism and New Technologies*, 2:2, pp. 175–96.

Usher, N. (2010), 'Goodbye to the news: How out-of-work journalists assess enduring news values and the new media landscape', *New Media Society*, 12, p. 911.

Vågan, A. and Grimen, H. (2008), 'Profesjoner I maktteoretisk perspektiv', in A. Molanderand and L. I. Terum (eds), *Profesjonstudier*, Oslo: Universitetsforlaget, pp. 411–28.

van der Krogt, T. (2007), 'Towards a new professional autonomy in the public sector: A pledge for re-professionalization on a collective level', paper presented at the EGPA Annual Conference, Madrid, Spain, 19–21 September.

Van Dijk, T. A. (2009a), *Society in Discourse: How Context Controls Text and Talk*, Cambridge: Cambridge University Press.

—— (2009b), 'News, discourse and ideology', in K. Wahl-Jorgensen and T. Hanitzch (eds), *The Handbook of Journalism Research*, New York: Routledge, pp. 191–204.

Van Ginneken, J. (1997), *Understanding Global News: A Critical Introduction*, London: Sage.

Van Maanen, J. (2001), 'Afterword: Natives "R" us: Some notes on the ethnography of organizations', in D. N. Gellner and E. Hirsch (eds), *Inside Organizations: Anthropologists at Work*, Oxford: Berg, pp. 233–61.

Van Zoonen, L. (1988), 'Rethinking women and the news', *European Journal of Communication*, 3, p. 35.

Viegas, S. de M. (2009), 'Can anthropologists make valid generalizations? Feelings of belonging in the Brazilian Atlantic Forest', *Social Analysis: Berghahn Journals*, 53:2, pp. 147–62.

Volkmer, I. and Firdaus, A. (2013), 'Between networks and "hierarchies of credibility": Navigating journalistic practice in a sea of user-generated content', in C. Peters and M. Broersma (eds), *Rethinking Journalism: Trust and Participation in a Transformed News Landscape*, London and New York: Routledge, pp. 101–13.

Wadel, C. (1991), *Feltarbeid i egen kultur*, Flekkefjord: Seek A/S.

Wahl-Jorgensen, K. (2007), *Journalists and the Public: Newsroom Culture, Letters to the Editor, and Democracy*, New Jersey: Hampton Press, Inc.

—— (2010), 'News production, ethnography and power: On the challenges of newsroom-centricity', in E. S. Bird (ed.), *The Anthropology of News & Journalism: Global Perspectives*, Bloomington: Indiana University Press, pp. 21–34.

Wallis, R. and Baran, S. (1990), *The Known World of Broadcast News: International News and the Electronic Media*. London: Routledge.

Ward, S. J. A. (2004), *The Invention of Journalism Ethics: The Path to Objectivity and Beyond*, Montreal and Kingston: McGill-Queen's University Press.

Warren, C. A. B, Barnes-Brus, T., Burgess, H., Wiebold-Lippisch, L., Hackney, J., Harkness, G., Keneddy, V., Dingwall, R., Rosenblatt, P., Ryen, A. and Shuy, R. (2003), 'After the interview', *Qualitative Sociology*, 26:1, spring, pp. 93–110.

Weaver, D. H (ed.) (1998), *The Global Journalist: News People around the World*, New Jersey: Hampton Press.

Weaver, D. H. (2005), 'Who are journalists?', in H. De Burgh (ed.), *Making Journalists*, London: Routledge, pp. 44–57.

Wenger, E. (1998a), *Communities of Practice: Learning, Meaning and Identity*, Cambridge: Cambridge University Press.

———— (1998b), 'Communities of practice learning as a social system', *Systems Thinker*, June, http://www.co-i-l.com/coil/knowledge-garden/cop/lss.shtml. Accessed 20 October 2011.

Westling, G. (2002), 'Balancing innovation and control: The role of face-to-face meetings in complex product development projects', doctoral thesis, Stockholm: Stockholm School of Economics.

Whelan, N. (2008), 'Will specialist journalism survive in our multi-skilling age?', *The Guardian Online*, 16 June, http://www.guardian.co.uk/media/organgrinder/2008/jun/16/post68. Accessed 3 February 2012.

White, D. M. (1950), 'The "Gate Keeper": A case study in the selection of news', *Journalism Quarterly*, 27, pp. 383–96.

Winston, B. (2003), 'Appendix 64: Memorandum submitted by Professor Brian Winston, University of Lincoln', *Culture, Media and Sport – Written Evidence*, printed online by the House of Commons, 21 May 2007.

———— (2007), 'If it bleeds it leads', key note speech at *Minding the Gap: Reflections on Media Theory and Practice*, symposium for Postgraduates and Early Career Researchers held at The Reuters Institute, Oxford University, 12 May.

Willis, P. (2000), *The Ethnographic Imagination*, Cambridge: Polity Press.

Witschge, T. (2013), 'Transforming journalistic practice: A profession caught between change and tradition', in C. Peters and M. Broersma (eds), *Rethinking Journalism: Trust and Participation in a Transformed News Landscape*, London and New York: Routledge, pp. 160–72.

Witschge, T. and Nygren, G. (2009), 'Journalism: A profession under pressure?', *Journal of Media Business Studies*, 6:1, pp. 37–59.

Wolcott, H. F. (1990), *Writing Up Qualitative Research*, London: Sage.

———— (1995), 'Making a study "more ethnographic"', in J. Van Maanen (ed.), *Representation in Ethnography*, Thousand Oaks: Sage, pp. 79–111.

Wolf, E., R. (1966), 'Kinship, friendship, and patron-client relations in complex societies', in M. Banton (ed.), *The Social Anthropology of Complex Societies*, Association of Social Anthropologists Monograph, London: Routledge, pp. 1–22.

Wolfenstein, M. (1953), 'Movie analysis in the study of culture', in M. Margaret and R. Metraux (eds), *The Study of Culture at a Distance*, Chicago: University of Chicago Press, pp. 267–80.

YouGov (2010), 'YouGov survey results: Sample size: 1854 GB adults fieldwork: 18th–19th August 2010', *YouGov.com Archives*, http://today.yougov.co.uk/sites/today.yougov.co.uk/files/YG-Archives-Pol-PublicTrust-190810.pdf. Accessed 21 July 2011.

Zelizer, B. (1993), 'Has communication explained Journalism?', *Journal of Communication*, 43, pp. 80–88.

———— (2004), *Taking Journalism Seriously: News and the Academy*, Thousand Oaks, CA: Sage.

———— (2017), *What Journalism Could Be*, Cambridge: Polity Press

Zuckerman, M. (1970), *Peaceable Kingdoms: New England Towns in the Eighteenth Century*, New York: Alfred A. Knopf Inc.

Index